EDUCATIONAL ADMINISTRATION AS A SOCIAL PROCESS
Theory, research, practice

Jacob W. Getzels
University of Chicago

James M. Lipham
University of Wisconsin

Roald F. Campbell
University of Chicago

HARPER & ROW, PUBLISHERS

New York, Evanston, and London

LB
2806
.G4

EDUCATIONAL ADMINISTRATION AS A SOCIAL PROCESS
Theory, research, practice
Copyright © 1968 by Jacob W. Getzels, James M. Lipham, and Roald F. Campbell

Printed in the United States of America. All rights reserved. No part of this book may be used or reproduced in any manner whatsoever without written permission except in the case of brief quotations embodied in critical articles and reviews. For information address Harper & Row, Publishers, Incorporated, 49 East 33rd Street, New York, N.Y. 10016.

Library of Congress catalog card number: 68-19144

Contents

Editor's Introduction xiii

Preface xv

Acknowledgments xix

[1]
The Interaction of Administrative Theory, Research, and Practice   1

The Study and Practice of Administration: Traits, Techniques, Theories   1

On the Continuity Between Theory, Research, and Practice: An Illustrative Case   9

The Practical Concomitants of Avoiding Theory and the Objections to the Use of Theory in Practice   16

[2]
The Development of Administrative Theory   23

The Managerial Point of View   23

The Human Relations Point of View   30

The Social Science Point of View   39

[3]
A Framework for the Study of Administrative Behavior: The Dimensions   52

The Basic Unit for Administrative Analysis: The Social System   53

Analytic Dimensions of the Social System   56

THE NORMATIVE (NOMOTHETIC) DIMENSION   56

THE PERSONAL (IDIOGRAPHIC) DIMENSION   65

Summary   77

[4]
A Framework for the Study of Administrative Behavior: The General Model   79

The Articulation of Role and Personality   79

v

The Dynamics of Role-Personality Interaction   83
ROLE-SETS   84
SELECTIVE PERCEPTION   86

Biological and Cultural Dimensions   89
THE BIOLOGICAL DIMENSION   90
THE CULTURAL DIMENSION   92

A Model for Studying Behavior in a Social System   102

Summary   105

[5]
Conceptual and Empirical Derivations   108
Sources of Conflict: Fulcra for Administrative Intervention   108
CONFLICT BETWEEN CULTURAL VALUES AND INSTITUTIONAL EXPECTATIONS   110
CONFLICT BETWEEN ROLE EXPECTATIONS AND PERSONALITY DISPOSITIONS   112
CONFLICT BETWEEN ROLES AND WITHIN ROLES   113
CONFLICT DERIVING FROM PERSONALITY DISORDERS   115
CONFLICT IN THE PERCEPTION OF ROLE EXPECTATIONS   116

Mechanisms of Integration   119
ROLE ADAPTATION AND SELF-ACTUALIZATION   119
SOCIALIZATION OF PERSONALITY AND PERSONALIZATION OF ROLE   123

Criteria of Organizational Behavior   126
EFFECTIVENESS AND EFFICIENCY   127
SATISFACTION AND MORALE   129

On the Nature of Subordinate-Superordinate Relationships and Leadership-Followership Styles   133
SUPERORDINATE-SUBORDINATE RELATIONSHIPS   133
LEADERSHIP-FOLLOWERSHIP STYLES   145

On the Dynamics of Change in Social Systems   150

Summary   155

[6]
Cultural Differences and Institutional Expectations   157
Expectations for the Schools: Composite Expectations and Subcultural Expectations   157
COMPOSITE EDUCATIONAL EXPECTATIONS   159
OCCUPATIONAL STATUS, EDUCATIONAL LEVEL, AND EDUCATIONAL EXPECTATIONS   161
SOCIAL CLASS STATUS AND EDUCATIONAL EXPECTATIONS   164
DIFFERENCES IN EDUCATIONAL EXPECTATIONS BY GEOGRAPHIC REGION, AGE, RELIGION, AND RACIAL COMPOSITION   168

Expectations for the Schools: Differences Between Educators and Noneducators   172
DIFFERENCES IN EXPECTATIONS   172
DIFFERENCES IN THE PERCEPTION OF THE HIGH SCHOOL GRADUATE   173

Toward Further Inquiry   178

Summary   180

[7]
Institutional Expectations   182

Conflict Between Roles   183
ROLE CONFLICT AND SCHOOL BOARD MEMBERSHIP   184
ROLE CONFLICT AND THE SUPERINTENDENCY   195
ROLE CONFLICT AND THE TEACHER   198

Conflict Between Reference Groups   202
THE SUPERINTENDENT AND HIS REFERENCE GROUPS   202

Conflict Within a Reference Group   209

Toward Further Inquiry   211

Summary   216

[8]
Institutional Role and Individual Personality   218

The Study of Role-Personality Relations: The Personality-Assessment Method   220
ADMINISTRATIVE ROLE-PERSONALITY RELATIONS AND PROMOTABILITY IN A BUSINESS ORGANIZATION   220
ADMINISTRATIVE ROLE-PERSONALITY RELATIONS AND EFFECTIVENESS IN A SCHOOL SYSTEM   228

The Study of Role-Personality Relations: The Role-Definition Method   236
TEACHER ROLE-PERSONALITY RELATIONS   237

Toward Further Inquiry   244

Summary   248

[9]
Individual Personality   250

The Relation Between Teacher Personality, Subject Matter Taught, and Teacher-Administrator Interaction   250
TEACHER PERSONALITY AND SUBJECT MATTER TAUGHT   251
TEACHER PERSONALITY AND TEACHER-ADMINISTRATOR INTERACTION   254

The Relation Between Personality and Role Conflict in the Teaching Situation   258
PERSONALITY AND ROLE CONFLICT IN A MILITARY TEACHING SITUATION   259

PERSONALITY AND ROLE CONFLICT IN A PUBLIC SCHOOL
   SITUATION   266

Personality and Reaction to Supervision   270
ON THE CURVILINEARITY OF THE RELATIONSHIP BETWEEN STRESS
   AND PERFORMANCE   270
THE EXPERIMENT   273
IMPLICATIONS OF THE STUDY OF ROLE STRESS, PERSONALITY, AND
   BEHAVIOR: DIFFERENTIAL SUPERVISION AND GROUPING   280

Toward Further Inquiry   282

Summary   284

[10]
Value Orientations and Selective Perception   286

Individual Value Orientations in the School System   287
PUPIL, TEACHER, AND PRINCIPAL VALUES   287

Value Orientations and Relations in Role-Sets   292
PUPIL-TEACHER RELATIONS   292
TEACHER-PRINCIPAL RELATIONS   293
CITIZEN-SUPERINTENDENT RELATIONS   294

Perception of Roles   297
TYPES OF PERCEPTUAL ERROR   298
EFFECT OF AGREEMENT OR DISAGREEMENT IN ROLE
   PERCEPTION   303

Self-Role Perceptions   306
SELF-ROLE PERCEPTIONS OF TEACHERS   307

On the Process of Perception   310

Toward Further Inquiry   315

Summary   317

[11]
Staff Relationships   318

Entrance into Teaching   318
ROLE COMPATIBILITY   318
PERSONALITY COMPATIBILITY   320

Employment and Assignment   321
JOINT EXPLORATION   321
SITUATIONAL LIMITS AND DIVERSITY   323

Supervision and Work Conditions   325
SELECTIVE INTERPERSONAL PERCEPTION   326
CLARIFICATION OF ROLE EXPECTATIONS   327
MAXIMIZING PERSONAL SATISFACTION   330

Evaluation of Staff Performance   332
BUILDING AGREEMENT ON PURPOSE   332
RECOGNIZING DIFFERENTIAL ROLES   334

RECOGNIZING DIFFERENTIAL STYLES   335
JUDGING EFFECTIVENESS   336

Reassignment and Dismissal   337
ASSESSING ROLE-PERSONALITY RELATIONS   338
PERSONALIZING THE ROLE   338
REASSIGNING ROLES   340
DISMISSAL   342

The Administrator in a Transactional Role   344
REINFORCING ORGANIZATIONAL EXPECTATIONS   344
EMPATHIZING WITH ORGANIZATION MEMBERS   345
SELF-UNDERSTANDING AND SELF-CONTROL   346

Summary   347

[12]
Board Relationships   348

The Nature of Controlling Boards   348
INTERSTITIAL POSITION OF THE BOARD   348
THE BOARD AND ROLE CONFLICT   349

Selection of Board Members   352
ELECTION OR APPOINTMENT   352
SOCIOECONOMIC STATUS OF BOARD MEMBERS   355

Motivations of Board Members   356
SELF-ROLE CONFLICT   356
ROLE CONFLICT   358

Selecting the Chief Executive   359
ROLE CONFUSION   360
ROLE USURPATION   361
PERCEPTUAL DIFFERENCES   363

Relationships of Board and Executive   364
AGREEING ON PURPOSES   364
RECOGNIZING PERSONAL DISPOSITIONS   365
CLARIFYING ROLES   367
REDUCING PERCEPTUAL DIFFERENCES   368

Negotiating with Teachers' Organizations   370
SOCIAL CONDITIONS   370
ORGANIZATIONAL CHARACTERISTICS   371
ROLE OF THE ADMINISTRATOR   374

Summary   375

[13]
Community Relationships   376

The Organization and the Community   376
SOURCES OF COMMUNITY CONTROL   377
THE COMMUNITY AS A PLURALISTIC CULTURE   378
EXTENSION OF THE SCHOOL COMMUNITY   378

Community Issues and Cultural Values   381
QUALITY EDUCATION   381
CULTURAL DEPRIVATION   384
SCHOOL INTEGRATION   385
RELIGION AND THE SCHOOL   387
FINANCIAL SUPPORT   388

Cultural Values and Institutional Expectations   390

Implications for the Administrator   393

Summary   395

[14]
Some Retrospective and Prospective Considerations   397
Organizational Statics and Dynamics   398

Administrative Behavior and Individuality   400

Strategies of Inquiry   403

Applicability of the Model to Administrative Dilemmas   407

Summary   410

Index   413

List of figures

3-1. The normative dimension   65
3-2. The personal dimension   77
4-1. The normative and personal dimensions of social behavior   80
4-2. Varying proportions of role and personality components in social behavior   82
4-3. The relationship of the organismic and personalistic dimensions of behavior   92
4-4. The relationship of the cultural and institutional dimensions of behavior   102
4-5. General model of the major dimensions of behavior in a social system   105
4-6. Operational model of the major dimensions of social behavior   106
5-1. Personalization and socialization forces on normative and personal axes of behavior   123
5-2. Relationships between role and personality proportions of behavior in a social system, and the use of postinduction and preinduction mechanisms of individual-institutional integration   126
5-3. Relation of role expectations and need-dispositions to effectiveness, efficiency, and satisfaction   128
5-4. The dimensions of morale   131
5-5. Three leadership-followership styles   146
5-6. Relationships before change in values   153
5-7. Relationships after change in values   153
5-8. Relationships after change in values and expectations   155
5-9. Relationships after change in values, expectations, and dispositions   155
6-1. Profile of the real and ideal image of the high school graduate by educators   176
6-2. Profile of the real and ideal image of the high school graduate by noneducators   177
9-1. Curvilinear relationship of drive level to effective performance on complex tasks   272

xi

Editor's introduction

As a student and practitioner of educational administration for many years, this editor has experienced at firsthand many of the developments traced in the historical section of this book. The major shifts have been from what the authors call the traits of administrators to techniques of administering through human relations to the present concern with theories of administration founded in the social or behavioral sciences. Within this last and current emphasis, various formulations have drawn differentially from sociology, psychology, anthropology, economics, and political science. But there can be no question of the central place of interdisciplinary social-psychological conceptions and research in these formulations. The present book is founded in these social-psychological conceptions and research. Indeed, alternate titles of this volume might well have been "Behavioral Foundations of School Administration" or "Social-Psychological Foundations of Educational Administration."

The work deals with a theoretical view, a social process model of administration, and brings together in the single volume published and unpublished research deriving from this model. There is no doubt that this model has been a fruitful stimulus for training and empirical investigation in educational administration. Yet the authors are aware of the need to consider the continuity between what they term the science of administration and the art of administering—hence, the descriptive subtitle: Theory, Research, Practice. They are also aware of the inevitable discontinuities between the study of administration and its practice. They urge that what they have presented—a theoretical framework, related research, and implications for practice—be dealt with as tentative formulations subject to continued test through thought, investigation, and action.

It is with pride and pleasure that I commend this book to a wide audience who will find profit in the ideas and in the breadth and depth of scholarship. This audience includes not only students of administration, present and potential administrators both in education and in other fields, and the controlling boards and professional staffs of educational institutions, but all who are involved in that most crucial of social systems in our society—our schools.

JOHN GUY FOWLKES

Preface

There are occasions when men and their environments come into particularly productive relationships. Such an occasion prevailed at the Midwest Administration Center of the University of Chicago in the 1950s. Francis S. Chase, the director, collected faculty and students and set them free to explore the possible interaction of behavioral science theory, research, and practice in educational administration. Among the theoretical formulations developed was a social process model of organizational behavior—a model that came shortly to serve as the framework for scores of studies in administration at Chicago and elsewhere, and through the years has been extended and applied in many unanticipated directions.

This book is founded in this work, and places the study of educational administration in the context of behavioral science theory. Our primary aim is to examine the applicability of such theory, and more specifically of a particular theoretical model, to research and practice in educational administration. Accordingly, we begin by considering the nature of the theoretical approach, making clear that although we favor a particular point of view, it is only one among many, each with its own strengths and weaknesses. We proceed to an historical account of other approaches to administration, and describe in detail the social process model in its original and extended forms. We then report selected empirical investigations deriving from the model, and finally we indicate a number of possible applications of the model and the research for administrative practice, particularly in staff, board, and community relations. Our intent throughout is not to purvey ready-made conclusions to problems but to explore ways of thinking about the problems.

We are aware that theory building in behavioral science is still at an elementary stage, that current research is subject to subsequent improved design and execution, and that understanding growing out of theory and research is at best only suggestive for practice. It may be argued that an attempt to synthesize theory, research, and practice in administration is as yet premature. But it may also be argued that beginnings must be ventured, even in the face of known risks, if only to provide explicit comparisons with other approaches, and to offer points of departure and guides to ensuing efforts leading to higher levels of understanding.

We are aware too that all theoretical models have limitations; all abstractions deal with restricted aspects of the phenomena they seek to codify just as all maps deal with restricted aspects of the terrain they seek to describe. The social process model is no exception. It is a formulation concerned primarily with the social-psychological aspects of human behavior, and is therefore more immediately relevant to the internal dynamics of an organization than to, say, its economic and political ramifications. Additional formulations, some of which may be economic and political, are required. Whatever the formulation, two things seem clear: the centrality of the social-psychological aspects of administration cannot be overlooked; and no single effort to deal with the multitudinous aspects of administration can pre-empt the field. No one view—whether theoretical or phenomenological—encompasses all it seeks to clarify. Residual elements to be explained inevitably remain.

The social process model then must not be taken for more than it intends to be. But it should not be taken for less. One of the uses of theory is what may be called its prophetic function: it points to dimensions for inquiry beyond its immediate concerns. A conceptual framework serves not only to codify the observations made in the specific categories it provides but to call attention to categories of events that have been omitted and observations that still need to be made. It thus helps to order what is already known and leads us to inquire into what is yet to be known. A second aim of this volume, then, is to encourage theoretical and empirical investigation in educational administration. It is for this reason that in addition to describing work that has already been done, the book devotes substantial sections to work that needs to be done.

We wish to express our gratitude to the many people—both those mentioned and unmentioned in the text—who contributed to this work. We are particularly grateful to Egon Guba, who participated in the development of the original model, and for some sections can almost be considered a fourth author. He has been most generous in permitting us to utilize, we trust appropriately, his very great contribution. An immeasurable debt is due to Francis Chase, who, as we have already noted, encouraged widespread interest in theory and research at the Midwest Administration Center. We are profoundly indebted to the former students of the Center—now themselves distinguished administrators and teachers of administrators—who have so generously permitted us to cite widely from their work. Although much of what we report was done at the University of Chicago, students and faculty at other universities also utilized the model, adapted it to their purposes, and contributed to the concepts and research dealt with in this book. They, too, granted us permission to cite from their work, and we are grateful to them.

Our hope is that this document will prove useful to those who study and those who practice administration. In several sections of the book we suggest directions for further research, and we are confident additional issues for inquiry will occur to the reader. In other sections we try to look at specific practical problems from the view of theory; perhaps these illustrations may help the administrator with similar problems. But more important than any single issue or solution is the demonstration of possible general continuities between theory, research, and practice—between, if we may put it this way, the science of administration and the art of administering. On the one hand, practical problems give impetus to theory and research, fostering a science of administration; on the other, a science of administration—theory and research—while in no sense constituting a set of recipes, may offer the administrator conceptual and empirical illumination as he practices his art of administering.

J. W. G.
J. M. L.
R. F. C.

Chicago, Illinois
Madison, Wisconsin

Acknowledgments

We wish to express our deep appreciation to those who have permitted us to utilize their published and unpublished work. We are particularly thankful to those whose original investigations comprise much of the research content of the volume. But for the following, this book would hardly have been possible: Max G. Abbott, John H. M. Andrews, Alan F. Brown, Merton V. Campbell, Lawrence W. Downey, Elmer F. Ferneau, Samuel Goldman, Stephen P. Hencley, R. Jean Hills, Albert H. Malo, Donald J. McCarty, Roderick F. McPhee, Robert P. Moser, Donald C. Moyer, Richard Prince, Roger C. Seager, Allen T. Slagle, and Robert E. Sweitzer.

The general indebtedness to Egon G. Guba has already been noted. We wish here to acknowledge specifically his permission to utilize widely articles written in collaboration with J. W. Getzels, and the permission of the publishers of these articles: the American Sociological Association and the *Sociology of Education*, Duke University Press and the *Journal of Personality*, and the University of Chicago Press and the *School Review*. We gratefully acknowledge our debt to Professor Arthur P. Coladarci for material from *The Use of Theory in Educational Administration*, written in collaboration with J. W. Getzels, and to Professor William R. Odell, editor, and to the School of Education, Stanford University, the publishers. Similarly, we record our indebtedness to Herbert A. Thelen for permission to cite extensively from "The Classroom as a Unique Social System," written in collaboration with J. W. Getzels. Addison-Wesley Press, Allyn and Bacon, the *Educational Administration Quarterly*, the Midwest Administration Center and the *Administrator's Notebook*, the National Society for the Study of Education and the University of Chicago Press permitted us to use material by one or more of us published by them earlier.

We are grateful also for permission from the authors and publishers to abstract or quote from the following: W. W. Charters, Jr., "The Social Background of Teaching," in N. L. Gage, editor, *Handbook of Research on Teaching*, American

Educational Research Association and Rand-McNally Company; Neal Gross, "Some Contributions of Sociology to the Field of Education," *Harvard Educational Review*; Robert K. Merton, *Social Theory and Social Structure*, Macmillan Company; Charles Morris, *Varieties of Human Value,* University of Chicago Press; Talcott Parsons, Robert F. Bales, and Edward A. Shils, *Working Papers in the Theory of Action*, Macmillan Company; and Talcott Parsons and Edward A. Shils, *Toward a General Theory of Action*, Harvard University Press. A special note of appreciation is due to Professor Dwight W. Allen, who permitted us to use material from his paper, "Modelling Dynamic Social Structure."

It is of course impossible to be aware of or to acknowledge specifically even in the many textual references the sources of all ideas. Many individuals will recognize in the book something they have said or written. This is especially true of our graduate students at the University of Chicago and the University of Wisconsin, to whom we are further indebted for perceptive criticism of the manuscript during its several revisions.

Educational Administration As a Social Process

1

The interaction of administrative theory, research, and practice

The study and practice of administration are beset with controversy. There are opposed conceptions of administrative behavior and, accordingly, of the most fruitful ways for selecting and preparing administrators. There are unsettled issues regarding the relations among theories of administration, research in administration, and the practice of administration. There are those who argue that knowledge of organizational and administrative theory and research is a burden rather than a help to the practicing administrator, and those who assert that the practice of administration must be founded on theoretical understanding and research, however imperfect these may be, or it will be founded on myth, emotion, and unquestioned recipe.

In this introductory chapter we explore a number of opposing points of view in the study and practice of administration; we examine the possible relations among administrative theory, research, and practice generally; and we formulate a position, at least as a working hypothesis, with respect to the interaction of theory, research, and practice in educational administration specifically. We are not implying that this is the only possible point of view. Rather, by stating our position in explicit terms at the outset, we intend to provide a baseline for immediate discussion. What is more important, we offer a point of departure for other formulations and for alternate positions, to be held, we hope, like our own, as hypotheses—but explicitly stated hypotheses—for further inquiry.

The study and practice of administration: traits, techniques, theories

There are at least three possible positions regarding the study and practice of administration. The first, which may be called the *trait* point of view, holds that administration is best conceived of as an uncodified art. Thus the successful administrator is the one who has a large number of traits required for the practice of this art. The administrator is an administrator by predisposition, just as the artist is an artist by predisposition. The successful artist *has* artistic ability, the successful leader *has* leadership ability, the successful administrator *has* administrative ability. Neither the development of the successful administrator and what he does nor the development of the artist and what he does can be codified. As one university president, himself an eminent administrator, argues, "The successful administrator has skills which (despite the striving of academic departments which teach administration) have not been reduced to order and codified in textbooks. . . . Administration . . . is an uncodified art. Therefore, the only sure way to learn administration is to administer."[1]

From this point of view, trying to study administration systematically and to produce administrators through specialized training is futile. The improvement of administration is not a problem of science or of education but of breeding, or at least of selection.

Advocates of this "born ability" or trait position cite known cases of excellent administration by business and military leaders who were unspoiled by specialized education and sometimes had hardly any education at all. They just seemed to have the required "leadership ability" or "administrative traits." To be sure, one may find such cases. On the other hand, there are few generals and admirals who have not been through West Point or Annapolis, and large enterprises regularly recruit personnel from schools of business administration. Many of the largest and presumably best-managed organizations maintain expensive executive training programs. In short, we may cite as many cases for one side as for the other, and the issues will not be settled by *ad hominem* argument and debate.

Nor does it seem fruitful to resurrect the ancient "heroes are born—heroes are made" controversy of occupational choice and proficiency. The natural-leadership-ability position generates more heat than light, the issues inevitably deteriorating into a "case that I know." Stogdill examined 124 studies on the relationship between so-called leadership traits and leadership behavior, concluding, "A person does not become a leader by virtue of the possession of some combination of traits, but the pattern of personal characteristics of the leader must have some relevant relationship to the characteristics, activities, and goals of the followers. Thus, leadership must be conceived in terms of the

---

[1] Eric Ashby, "The Administrator: Bottleneck or Pump," *Daedalus*, 91 (Spring, 1962), 266–276.

interaction of variables which are in constant flux and change."[2] Similarly, Myers analyzed more than 200 studies of leadership and felt that the "personal characteristics of leaders differ according to the situation," and "leaders tend to remain leaders only in situations where the situation is similar."[3] Gibb, in a comprehensive summary of the literature, states unequivocally that the "numerous studies of leaders have failed to find any consistent pattern of traits which characterize leaders."[4] The study of traits alone will not explain leadership or administrative behavior, and the shibboleth that "leaders and administrators are born, not made" as a governing principle is untenable.

This is not to imply that successful administrators in given situations do not display personal characteristics that set them apart from unsuccessful administrators in the same situations. Indeed, in due course we will present empirical evidence showing that certain personal characteristics *are* necessary for successful administration in certain situations. But to say that particular qualities, skills, and types of personality are *necessary* for successful administrative behavior in some situations is not the same as saying that they are the same for *all* situations, or even *sufficient* by themselves in the given situation. Actually, few thoughtful administrators or students of administration hold seriously to either extreme of the trait position, and the major contention is between a second and a third point of view.

The second point of view is that administration is best conceived of as a *technology*, a matter of applying appropriate techniques to the solution of relevant practical problems. It is in effect a kind of engineering—human engineering. Either the engineer wants to maintain the optimum operation of a given state of affairs or he starts with one state of affairs and wants to achieve another. In any case, he must know the steps to be followed, or, to use a geographic analogy, he must know the appropriate *itinerary* of getting from one place to another. The administrator is similarly concerned with the solution of practical problems, with reaching specific goals, with attaining certain ends. He too must know and apply rules, principles, and

---

[2] R. M. Stogdill, "Personal Factors Associated with Leadership, a Study of the Literature," *Journal of Psychology*, 25 (1948), 64.

[3] R. B. Myers, "The Development and Implications of a Conception of Leadership for Leadership Education," Doctoral dissertation, University of Florida, 1954, p. 107.

[4] C. A. Gibb, "Leadership," in Gardner Lindzey, ed., *Handbook of Social Psychology*, vol. 2, Cambridge, Mass., Addison-Wesley, 1954, p. 889.

techniques; he also must follow an appropriate itinerary of getting from where he is to where he wants to be.

Exactly what, then, should the successful administrator know and do? It is maintained that for each practical problem facing the administrator there are certain techniques applicable to its solution. If he knows the techniques and follows the steps prescribed, he will solve the problem. Here, for example, are some typical problems and the techniques for handling them as given in a widely used treatise representing this point of view.

The practical problem is: How can an administrator gain the confidence of his subordinates? The solution is given in fifteen rules. The confidence of subordinates can be gained if the administrator "(1) Is helpful and anxious to share the other person's problems. (2) Has a sense of humor and is cheerful. (3) Is friendly and tries to put others at ease. (4) Shows an interest in others."[5] And so on to rule 15, which turns out to be that an administrator can gain his subordinates' confidence if he "Is reliable."[6]

Or again, and more specifically: How can the principal of a school improve his conferences with teachers? There are, once more, fifteen rules—nine "Dos" and six "Don'ts." Among the Dos are "(1) Remember that a principal must be interested in growth on the part of the teacher.... (2) Allow plenty of time for the conference.... (3) Attempt to put the teacher at ease; it is the principal's responsibility to create the desired climate in the conference. (4) Be objective in the discussion.... (5) Accentuate the positive."[7] The Don'ts are "(1) Don't be a know-it-all.... (2) Don't threaten.... (3) Don't disparage or make unfavorable comparisons between the work of one teacher and another. (4) Don't ride pet hobby horses.... (5) Don't hurry.... (6) Don't summon the teacher to the office for the conference. It is probably better for the conference to take place in the teacher's room when the children are not present, but if the conference must take place in the office, it should be at a mutually agreed upon time."[8]

This prescriptive approach is not limited to narrow day-to-day problems but is applied also to issues of major policy. For

---

[5] Byron W. Hansford, *Guidebook for School Principals*, New York, Ronald Press, 1961, p. 25.
[6] *Ibid.*
[7] *Ibid.*, p. 167.
[8] *Ibid.*, pp. 167–168.

example, another and more comprehensive treatise on administration lists five techniques for "planning improvement in the educational program": "(1) A broad perspective should be maintained at all times.... (2) Proposals for improvement should be based on systematic studies of problems, needs, and possibilities.... (3) Needed studies should be planned and conducted cooperatively.... (4) Competent resource people should be located and utilized in carrying out the study.... (5) The findings and conclusions should be given careful and bona fide consideration by the superintendent and board with due attention for implications for the total program."[9]

From this point of view, the improvement of administration depends on the discovery and communication of more effective techniques and prescriptions—the production of more expedient administrative itineraries, as it were. The successful administrator is one who knows and applies the techniques and prescriptions—who follows the itineraries.

The third position is that the focus of both scholarly and practical effort in administration must be not so much on techniques and prescriptions as on conceptualizations and theories—not on simple directions to be followed but on complex relationships to be understood. If we may continue our geographic analogy (which is of course not to be taken too literally), the emphasis is to be on *maps*, not itineraries.[10] Advocates of this position argue that ultimately administration will be improved less by empiricism than by conceptualization—less by collecting empirical solutions to operational problems than by understanding administrative and organizational processes in more fundamental and necessarily more abstract terms.

Placed against the technique-centered point of view, this concept-centered position seems far removed from reality and from the daily problems of the administrator. The dominant issues seem recondite, the significant problems "only theoretic" or, as an editorial in the *Nation's Schools* put it some time ago, "up on Cloud 17."[11] Theory may be "all right" for academic analysis and perhaps even for research, but it is irrelevant if not

---
[9] Edgar L. Morphet, Roe L. Johns, and Theodore L. Reller, *Educational Organization and Administration*, Englewood Cliffs, N.J., Prentice-Hall, 1967, p. 363.
[10] For certain analogies between the use of maps and of theories, see Stephen Toulmin, *The Philosophy of Science*, London, William Brendon and Son, Ltd., 1953, especially pp. 105–139.
[11] "The Administrator's Clinic," *The Nation's Schools*, 64 (July, 1959), 6.

actually confusing for the working administrator. He needs *practical* methods for solving *practical* problems.

But a closer look reveals that the so-called practical or technical approach solves few of the *really* practical problems pressing upon the administrator. No one would disagree violently with any of the techniques prescribed in the illustrations we cited. But of what real use is it to say that to gain a subordinate's confidence the administrator should be helpful, cheerful, friendly, and reliable? In what way are these specifically *administrative* principles? And of what value is it to enunciate that an administrator can improve his conferences if he is "interested" in the people with whom he is conferring, allows "plenty of time for the conference," attempts to put the other person "at ease," is "objective in the discussion," and "accentuates the positive"? What interpersonal relationship would *not* be the better for this kind of behavior?

Or, how really practical in the sense of *operationally useful* are the prescriptions for "planning improvement in the educational program" listed a few paragraphs back? Under what circumstances should a broad perspective *not* be maintained? When should proposals for improvement *not* be based on the relevant problem? When should resource people *not* be competent? When should findings and conclusions *not* be considered with attention to the total program?

To be sure, there is nothing wrong with these principles. But they are of such general order and applicability that they are no more than the commonplaces of desirable behavior under *any* circumstances: Be reliable, be cheerful, be friendly, plan well, and so on. They are no more specific to administrative behavior than is the statement of the Boy Scout oath or the maxim that "an ounce of prevention is worth a pound of cure."

Moreover, there are so many prescriptions—often, as we shall show, quite contradictory ones—that the administrator may be at a loss to decide which one to use? With only itineraries and no map, how does he choose which itinerary to follow? And what if the specific technique he has been given does not work? Does he just try another—*any* other? Suppose the itinerary he starts with becomes impracticable—a change in routes is mandatory—and he does not have a map. Does he ask someone? Whom?

To cite one example for many, how does the administrator go about implementing the prescription "Competent resource people should be located and utilized"? On what basis does he choose the competent resource person? If he has a problem in guidance and counseling, does he choose Menninger and the psychoanalysts or Rogers and the client-centered therapists? For a problem in learning, how does he choose among, say, Harlow, Skinner, and Spence, all of whom are clearly competent but differ dramatically in their conception of learning? When the person is chosen, the theory is chosen. The technique-centered point of view, far from doing away with the theoretical issue, merely passes it on.

The point is that maps and theories are unavoidable and indispensable for administrator and investigator alike. Both must have valid observations for the solution of their problems. Both must begin by collecting the facts. But, as Morris Raphael Cohen has said, "Begin by collecting the facts? Aye, but what facts?"[12] Pure empiricism will not do. Observations and measurements, no matter how precise, do not of themselves lead to stable, practical knowledge except through the application of some directing concepts, however tentative, that serve as guides to *what* to observe and measure and *how* to interpret what has been observed and measured. As Larrabee points out:

The advice to "get the facts" is not a blanket injunction to expose oneself to anything in the way of experience that may come along. It leads one to the query: "But what facts?" Certainly if facts and theories are to be fitted together in such a way as to yield reliable knowledge, "just any old facts" will not do, nor will "any old theory" do either. Relevant facts do not label themselves as relevant. That is an element which must be added by the knower. Unless he is a mere random collector of odds and ends, the seeker of knowledge cannot go through life merely looking *at* things; he must be looking *for* something; and that means active inquiry with some directing factor in control.[13]

Neal E. Miller puts the issue bluntly:

Pure empiricism is a delusion. A theory-like process is inevitably involved in drawing boundaries around certain parts of the flux of experience to define observable events and in the selection of the events that are observed. Since multitudinous events could be observed and an enormous number of relationships could be determined among all of these events, gathering all the facts with no bias

---

[12] Morris R. Cohen, *Reason and Nature*, 2nd ed., New York, Free Press, 1953, p. 76.
[13] H. A. Larrabee, *Reliable Knowledge*, Boston, Houghton Mifflin, 1945, p. 167.

from theory is utterly impossible. Scientists are forced to make a drastic selection, either unconsciously on the basis of perceptual habits and the folklore and linguistic categories of the culture, or consciously on the basis of explicitly formulated theory.[14]

Perhaps this is the sense, as Coladarci and Getzels suggest, in which to interpret Huxley's famous admonition that "those who refuse to go beyond fact rarely get as far as fact."[15]

Theory, then, has a number of vital functions in the study and practice of administration, as indeed in any area where observations must be collected and interpreted to solve problems.[16] One function is *taxonomic*. A theory or a conceptual schema provides the framework for collecting data. Since, in any case, a selection from all possible observations will be made, it is better made on conscious or explicit grounds than on unconscious or implicit grounds. Another function is *explanatory*. A fruitful theory not only states the classes of events to be observed but suggests possible antecedent-consequent and other dynamic relationships among the events. In this sense, theory acts not only to describe and to order phenomena but to explain and ultimately to predict.

A third function of theory is *heuristic*—it points to problems calling for solution. Because it contains dynamic elements, theory leads from hypotheses to new observations and from observations to new hypotheses. As parts of a theory are tested—by practice or by research—new and significant issues for application or investigation present themselves. Ultimately, this may be the most important function of theory for the administrator, for among the critical problems facing him as well as the researcher is the question of how to identify and define the underlying problems rather than merely the symptoms. As Corey has shown, problems are often identified so impressionistically and casually that only their superficial or irrelevant aspects are handled and the essential issues are neglected.[17] Thomas puts

---

[14] N. E. Miller, "Liberalization of Basic S-R Concepts: Extensions to Conflict Behavior, Motivation, and Social Learning," in S. Koch, ed., *Psychology: A Study of Science*, New York, McGraw-Hill, 1959, vol. 2, p. 200.

[15] For a fuller statement of the argument, see A. P. Coladarci and J. W. Getzels, *The Use of Theory in Educational Administration*, Stanford, Calif., Stanford University School of Education, 1955.

[16] See E. G. Guba and J. W. Getzels, "Personality and Teacher Effectiveness: A Problem in Theoretical Research," *Journal of Educational Psychology*, 46 (April, 1955), 330–343.

[17] Stephen M. Corey, "Scientific Enquiry and the Practising Teacher," *Canadian Education*, 9, no. 4 (1954), 31–42.

the argument as follows: "Without the guidance of a theory, the analysis and discrimination which is necessary to convert an indeterminate situation into a formulated problem is severely handicapped, or worse yet, foregone."[18]

All this is by way of saying that theory is not an objective in itself. It is a tool—a map—providing indispensable guidance for practice and research alike. In effect, both practice and research become the testing of hypotheses, and theory provides a check on what might otherwise be only hit-or-miss activities. It offers the administrator a basis for defining underlying problems, it suggests hypotheses for action, and it supplies a framework for constant, systematic self-criticism and improvement. Dewey puts the matter as follows:

> Facts which are ... interrelated form a system, a science. The practitioner who knows the system ... is evidently in possession of a powerful instrument for observing and interpreting what goes on before him. This intellectual tool affects his attitudes and modes of response in what he does. Because the range of understandings is deepened and widened he can take into account remote consequences which were originally hidden from view and hence were ignored in his actions. Greater continuity is introduced; he does not isolate situations and deal with them in separation as he was compelled to do when ignorant of connecting principles. At the same time, his practical dealings become more flexible. Seeing more relations he sees more possibilities, more opportunities. He is emancipated from the need of following tradition and special precedents. His ability to judge being enriched, he has a wider range of alternatives to select from in dealing with individual situations.[19]

On the continuity between theory, research, and practice: an illustrative case

Lest we fall into the familiar trap of dealing only with exhortations and unsupported abstractions, we shall take a specific problem and examine the relationship between the relevant theory, the research, and the administrative practice. The illustration deals with a series of decisions involving school buildings and was chosen because such decisions are perhaps as concrete

---

[18] Lawrence G. Thomas, "Mental Tests As Instruments of Science," *Psychological Monographs*, 54, no. 3 (whole no. 245), (1942), 13.

[19] John Dewey, *Sources of a Science of Education*, New York, Liveright, 1929, pp. 20–21.

and unambiguous in terms of administrative action as any we could find.[20]

At the turn of the century the behavior and learning theorists conceived of the human being or would-be learner as an "empty organism" responding to stimuli more or less automatically and randomly. In learning, a specific response was held to be connected to a specific stimulus when it was rewarded. Both the stimulus (S) and the response (R) were largely under the control of the experimenter or the teacher. All he had to do in order to connect a particular R to a particular S was to reward the R when the organism made the desired R in the presence of the given S.

This was the so-called Connectionist period both in the learning laboratory and in the classroom—which is of course in many ways also a learning laboratory. Experimenters were connecting animal salivating responses to auditory stimuli, and teachers were connecting human verbal responses to visual stimuli. In learning arithmetic, for example, the student was required to respond to a flash card until he gave the answer the teacher wanted, at which point the teacher said, "Right," or "Check," or "Gold star." It was assumed that the correct answer had in this way been "stamped in" or connected with the stimulus.

This description is admittedly an oversimplification and to some extent a caricature, as it must be in so brief a sketch. But the essential point remains: The prevailing conception was that of a more or less empty organism learning to connect discrete stimuli and responses, both of which were under the control of the experimenter or teacher.

Learning was *teacher-centered*, and it was no accident that the prevailing school architecture and furniture were also teacher-centered: Typically, the teacher was placed at the front of the classroom—sometimes indeed on a platform or dais—and the pupils were seated in chairs fastened to the floor facing forward so that they could not turn away from the source of their instruction. Given the theoretical context, what administrative decision regarding the appropriate learning environment could be more eminently "sensible" and "practical"?

---

[20] Adapted from J. W. Getzels, "Theory and Practice in Educational Administration: An Old Question Revisited," in Roald F. Campbell and James M. Lipham, eds., *Administrative Theory as a Guide to Action*, Chicago, Midwest Administration Center, University of Chicago, 1960, pp. 37–58.

11
The interaction of administrative theory, research, and practice

How did we get from this practical rectangular classroom, with the teacher's desk or dais in front and the pupils' chairs securely fastened to the floor, to the more recent, and apparently equally practical but diametrically opposed, octagonal classroom with carrels for individual study and no teacher's desk (to say nothing of the dais) and the pupils' movable chairs pushed all over the place? Surely this transformation did not occur without administrative decision. And surely it was not just that someone happened to have a "bright idea" that children in movable chairs are easier to discipline, or learn more readily, than children in stationary chairs. The transformation may be understood at least in part within the context of the change taking place in theories of behavior and learning.

It became increasingly clear that the Connectionist concepts of learning and of the learner just did not account for all the observed behavior. Other, or at least additional, concepts were needed. The individual did not seem to experience aspects of his environment as discrete stimuli. Instead, apparently discrete stimuli were often seen as "belonging together." For example, three discrete dots placed in a certain relation to each other were perceived as one triangle, two open brackets facing each other were often perceived as one rectangle, and so on. Experimenters began dealing with "closure" and figures and grounds, and teachers began exploring "insight" and relations and integrations. Connectionist theory was being leavened by Gestalt and cognitive theory. Even the great exponent of Connectionism, Thorndike, was compelled to add the "law of belongingness" to his preceding associationist "laws of learning."

But this was not all. Prevailing personality theory was postulating that the learner was not passive in the face of the environment. He did not merely "receive" a stimulus; he "did" something to it. He accepted and rejected from among available stimuli, and sometimes he even distorted ("misperceived") a stimulus to conform to his need for a particular unavailable stimulus. He made conscious and unconscious choices as a function of his drives, values, attitudes, and other internal forces. If two sets of equally well-known words, the one pleasant and the other unpleasant, were given for learning, the pleasant set was more likely to be learned than the unpleasant set. If two individuals, one a Republican and the other a Democrat, were required to learn material favorable and unfavorable to the two parties, the Democrat tended to recall the favorable and forget the unfavorable data about the Democrats, and the Republican would do just the reverse. The model of the learner as an empty organism was transformed into a model of the learner as a dynamic organism. Learning was thought of as not only a connective or even cognitive process but an emotional and affective one as well. From this point of view, the learner was at the very center of the learning process. Experimenters became increasingly concerned with the relationship between personality and learning, and teachers with the learner's needs, conflicts, and adjustment to the school situation. Learning became *child-centered*.

It was no accident then—surely no administrative whim—that decisions about what was practical school architecture or what was practical classroom furniture underwent something of a revolution during this period. The teacher-centered classroom became the child-centered classroom. The teacher's dais had disappeared before this, but even his desk—the symbol of authority and control—was shifted from the center of the room to the side, or moved out of the room altogether. The pupil's chair was torn from the floor for him to move as *he* needed to move it. The old rigid chair, which had formerly seemed so sensible, became quaint if not primitive. A chair that could be moved at the will of the child now became eminently reasonable and practical, at least in part—and this is the point of our argument—as a function of the prevailing theories of learning and of the learner.

If the initial period to which we referred was teacher-centered, and the second child-centered, the final period to which we should like to refer briefly may be called *group-centered*. Human behavior was conceptualized as a social process, each person in a group serving as the stimulus to every other person in the group. The prevailing theory was *interpersonal* theory. In the laboratory, research focused on such issues as "social perception" and "small group processes." In the classroom, the teacher became concerned with "sociometric relationships" and "group dynamics." Certain concomitant changes could again be observed in the decisions about what was practical school architecture. If learning is a matter of group interaction and interpersonal processes, then a circular or an octagonal classroom where everyone could conveniently face everyone else, or at least a circular or octagonal conference table (which can serve the same purpose), is certainly the most sensible learning environment. School desks were built in such way that they could be put together to form a multisided conference table, and some schools were constructed with circular or octagonal classrooms.

This is as far as we need go with our illustration of the symbiotic relationship, however subtle and indirect, among theory, research, and practice. We ought perhaps to add, if it is not self-evident, that the periods were by no means as sharply demarcated as writing about them schematically tends to suggest. They shaded into one another and overlapped, the significant phenomenon at any given time being one of relative emphasis rather than the all-or-none presence or absence of a particular point of view. Nevertheless, to take two extreme instances, it is certain that the image of the child was substantially different before and after the advent of psychoanalytic theory, and the image of the classroom was substantially different before and after the advent of group dynamics theory. And of course we are not arguing that the transformations in theory were the only or, for that matter, even the most immediate factors in the changes in practice of our illustration. We would maintain, however, that they were relevant and significant factors. Decisions regarding the educational environment were directly or indirectly influenced by them. The educational administrator who was aware of the context within which the decisions were being made, and who had an explicit framework (instead of a bagful of prescriptions and precedents) within which to work, was in a more strategic position not only to understand what was going on but also to decide for himself rather than follow the crowd, ask someone, or just do nothing at all.

It is in these terms that we may see the subtle and neverending relationship between theory and practice, between research and theory, between practice and research. The relationship may not be direct and immediate, and the issues of the one may not be translatable without intervention into the issues of the other. Although at any given time the interaction may be tenuous—there is an inevitable "culture lag" between technology and theory—ultimately the one acts as a guide and check to the other. Nor, as Toulmin points out, is it possible always to specify whether the observation or the theory, the practice or the concept, came first.[21] Nonetheless, the problems and findings of the physician are not unrelated to what the physiologist or the bio-

---
[21] Toulmin, *op. cit.*, p. 122.

chemist does. What the metallurgist and physicist, and nowadays even the "pure" astronomer, do is not unrelated (at least in time) to what the engineer does. Even social science, that most recent and controversial of the disciplines, has found its way into the determinations of one of the most crucial national policy decisions of our era, that on school segregation. The Supreme Court cited social-psychological theory and research in support of its decision.[22] When the administrator argues that he is being guided in his decisions by practical "common sense" and not by any "theoretical assumptions," he is confessing that he cannot make the assumptions within which he is working explicit and that he is not willing to examine them objectively. As James Bryant Conant points out, so-called common-sense ideas no less than scientific concepts are based on certain assumptions, albeit usually implicit rather than explicit. Conant writes:

> Literally every step we take in life is determined by a series of interlocking concepts and conceptual schemes. Every goal we formulate for our actions, every decision we make, be it trivial or momentous, involves assumptions about the universe and about human beings. To my mind, any attempt to draw a sharp line between common-sense ideas and scientific concepts is not only impossible but unwise.[23]

John Dewey, in considering the same relationship, states:

> In all this, there is no difference in kind between the methods of science and those of the plain man. The difference is the greater control by science of the statement of the problem, and of the selection and use of relevant material, both sensible and conceptual. The two are related to each other just as the hit-or-miss, trial-and-error inventions of uncivilized man stand to the deliberate and consecutively persistent efforts of a modern inventor to produce a certain complicated device for doing a comprehensive piece of work. Neither the plain man nor the scientific inquirer is aware, as he engages in his reflective activity, of any transition from one sphere of existence to another. He knows no two fixed worlds—reality on one side and mere subjective ideas on the other; he is aware of no gulf to cross. He assumes uninterrupted, free, and fluid passage from ordinary experience to abstract thinking, from thought to fact, from things to

---

[22] *United States Reports*, Cases Adjudged in the Supreme Court at October Term, 1953, Washington, D.C., U.S. Government Printing Office, vol. 347, (1954), pp. 483–496.
[23] James B. Conant, *Modern Science and Modern Man*, New York, Columbia University Press, 1952, p. 80.

theories and back again. Observation passes into development of hypothesis; deductive methods pass into use in description of the particular; inference passes into action, all with no sense of difficulty save those found in the particular task in question. The fundamental assumption is *continuity*.

This does not mean that fact is confused with idea, or observed datum with voluntary hypothesis, theory with doing, any more than a traveler confuses land and water when he journeys from one to the other. It simply means that each is placed and used with reference to service rendered the other, and with reference to the future use of the other.[24]

In so stressing the *continuities* between theory and practice, we have not dwelt sufficiently on the self-evident discontinuities between them. There is of course a difference between the work of the theorist and that of the administrator, as Charters points out.[25] The common-sense assumptions by which the administrator guides his decisions must range far, supplying ways of coming to terms with the tremendous diversity of events with which he must deal. The theorist typically encompasses only a narrow segment of the world the administrator inhabits. He most often handles a single aspect of reality "holding other things equal," even when he knows that they are not really equal, as witness the economist's convenient abstraction, "economic man."

The administrator gains scope at the expense of rigor; the theorist usually gains rigor at the expense of scope. The theorist's most immediate world is a world of concepts, abstractions, generalizations. His commerce with the administrator's world is necessarily restricted, and to the administrator often shortsighted. His theories give rise to predictions about small pieces of reality, taken out of context of the multitude of ongoing situations in which it is embedded and which the administrator cannot disregard. When he tests his predictions, he limits his attention to those small pieces of reality, ignoring the kaleidoscope of other processes occurring around him.

The administrator must deal with the complex here and now. He is part of a concrete situation with its own history and its own cast of idiosyncratic characters. For him economic man is indeed only an abstraction. When the administrator predicts, as

---

[24] John Dewey, *Essays in Experimental Logic*, Chicago, University of Chicago Press, 1916, p. 86.
[25] Roald F. Campbell, W. W. Charters, Jr. and William L. Gragg, "Improving Administrative Theory and Practice," in R. F. Campbell and J. M. Lipham, eds., *op. cit.*, pp. 171–189.

he must, he predicts about real people in a real situation in which other things are never equal.

Charters states that he has "purposely overdrawn the differences between the world of the scientist and the administrator"[26] in order to make a point of the discontinuities rather than the continuities between theory and practice. Even so, and despite the discontinuities, which have been purposely overdrawn, whether the issue is approached by way of the subtle and usually ignored continuities between theory and practice or by way of the self-evident and frequently emphasized discontinuities between them, the answer to the essential question (that is, whether the study and practice of administration are more likely to be forwarded by greater attention to techniques or to theory) remains the same. As Charters writes:

> The concepts and theories of social science afford the man of practical affairs alternative ways of viewing the world around him. Each set of concepts serves him, in effect, as a pair of spectacles, bringing into focus a few selected aspects of his world which he would not have singled out for attention otherwise. . . .
> The words or concepts we use, after all, are our tools for coming to terms with the infinitely complex world in which we must act. They tell us what to notice and what to ignore. In my opinion, the proper function of mid-century social science is to give the man of practical affairs a diversity of concepts to apply, a variety of viewpoints from which to see his problems. If concepts are tools, his tool-kit should be full. In this way he achieves a flexibility of vision. Social science, then, says to the administrator confronting his specific concrete situation, "Look at it this way. Maybe you will see something which has escaped you. Maybe things will make sense. No? . . . Well, try looking at it from this angle, or from this perspective."[27]

The practical concomitants of avoiding theory and the objections to the use of theory in practice

There are a number of unfortunate and persistent habits which preclude a maximally intelligent consideration of the theoretical, and even sustained attention to it, by the administrator.[28] The relation between these habits and the avoidance of theory is

---
[26] *Ibid.*, p. 177.
[27] *Ibid.*, pp. 179–180.
[28] Coladarci and Getzels, *op. cit.*, p. 10. Much of this section is based on pp. 10–14 of this monograph.

circular and, if not severed, self-extensive. We are afraid because something is unknown; it remains unknown because we are afraid of it. On the one hand, we do not know theory and therefore fear it; on the other, we fear theory and therefore avoid it.

Coladarci and Getzels refer to several of these untoward concomitants of avoiding the theoretical. The first is *Factualism*. B. O. Smith has observed that the attempts to make education as "scientific" as possible have been directed merely to making it as "factual" as possible.[29] Thus both research and practice have been pushed more and more into empiricism without the support of theoretical and explanatory concepts. As a result, studies in administration are often a matter of collecting interesting and even precise but disconnected and irrelevant pieces of information. We have already tried to make clear that such data or "facts" do not themselves carry directions for their application. It may be added here that the "factualistic" administrator must rid himself of this persuasion before he can conceptualize at profitable levels.

A second concomitant of avoiding theory is the *unwarranted respect for the authority of experts, principles, and techniques*. Witness, for example, the distressing frequency with which educational research incorporates as a validating criterion, that is, as the ultimate arbiter, "the opinion of experts in the field." Or consider the extent to which principles and techniques of administration are defended by the assertion that they have been recommended by someone—preferably someone with an honorific and high-sounding title. The point is not that experts do not deserve their titles, or even that they might not be used judiciously as consultants. But we must avoid substituting unquestioning reliance on the authoritative statements of experts for the critical inquiry engendered by hypothetical statements of theory. Similarly with the so-called principles of practice, which are invoked as if they were incontrovertibly valid. These principles were often derived from such basic subjects as physiology, psychology, political science, and economics. The subjects themselves have undergone considerable transformation in substance as a function of transformation in theory. But the principles have often remained unchanged. It must not be forgotten that principles are not axioms; they are tentative formulations needing constant testing and verification.

---

[29] B. O. Smith, "Science of Education," in W. S. Monroe, ed., *Encyclopedia of Educational Research*, New York, Macmillan, 1950, pp. 1145–1152.

A third concomitant of the absence of explicit theorizing is *lack of an adequate professional language*. Effective attention to theory requires the development of rigorously defined concepts and a language adequate for communicating with precision. Without theory, any old terms and any old notions are bandied about as if they had been explicitly defined. For this reason the language of education is sometimes accused of being "pedagese," or "gobbledygook." It is not the presence of a specialized terminology in a discipline, as witness economics or political science, that makes for gobbledygook but its absence. Consider, for example, the term "need." In psychology, it has a specific—we are not saying correct—meaning referring to an explicitly defined concept in Murray's theory of personality.[30] One may disagree with the theory or with the usefulness of the concept, but no one would accuse the language of being gobbledygook. In education, the same term, as used in "meeting the needs of children," is left undefined and seems to have as many meanings as there are people who use it, or *no* meaning. What *does* "meeting the needs of children" mean? Does it refer to Murray's needs, as technically defined? To the needs of children as what they "lack"? What they "want"? What they "require" whether they want it or not? The term as used in education is justly accused of being gobbledygook. Consider too the terms "democratic leadership," "effective administration," "teacher morale." Just what do they mean? They need clear definition. But they cannot be clearly defined without reference to the conceptual formulation from which they derive their meaning. The administrator who employs them without the appropriate conceptual reference is not thinking systematically. Nor is he really communicating. While he assumes he is saying one thing, his listeners may believe—and often do believe—he is saying *something else or nothing at all*.

A final pernicious concomitant of the absence of theory is *emotional identification with personal views*. When the dialogue of competing theories is avoided, one is in danger of becoming emotionally and blindly wedded to his own professional ideas. This precludes the possibility of looking upon one's own formulations as tentative, demanding criticism, and needing testing. Those who eschew the theoretical tend to hold their beliefs not as hypotheses but as cherished possessions and are unable to

---

[30] H. A. Murray, *Explorations in Personality*, New York, Oxford University Press, 1938.

participate in the open-ended evaluation and reformulation of the assumptions underlying their decisions and professional actions. As Gordon Allport puts it, "Our [strongest] censure should be reserved for those who close all doors but one. The surest way to lose truth is to pretend that one already wholly possesses it."[31]

If there are, as we argued, certain unfortunate concomitants of avoiding theory in practice, there are also a number of objections to the application of theory. Clearly, the use of theory, despite the advantages that have been proposed, is not without problems and dangers of its own. Coladarci and Getzels[32] consider five of the more frequently mentioned objections: (1) Theory is too difficult. (2) Theory restricts the administrator's freedom of judgment. (3) Since so many theories exist and they are so short-lived, there is little point to giving them serious thought. (4) The imposition of a theoretical structure may prohibit the unbiased observation of phenomena. (5) There is the danger of becoming irrevocably identified with a single theory.

The first objection, that theory is too difficult, may be dismissed out of hand as unbecoming modesty and an underestimation of ability. Theory in administration is no more difficult than theory in other areas. The expressed or felt fear is a consequence of administrative education; assuredly theorizing is difficult for the person whose professional education has made it seem so. This attitude is a reflection not on the usefulness of theory but on the nature of the educational programs for administrators.

The objection that scientific theory may lead to "push-button decision-making" and restrict the administrator's freedom of judgment may also be dismissed as untenable. The use of theories, or, to return to our earlier analogy, of maps is not the same as the present use of prescriptions and itineraries. It is the application of a prescription, like the following of an itinerary, that limits inventiveness and removes the "art" from the practice of administration. The understanding provided by relevant theories, on the other hand, like the alternate routes exhibited by a map, allows the administrator the greatest freedom of judgment and opportunity to apply inventiveness and ingenuity in his job.

---
[31] Gordon W. Allport, *Becoming*, New Haven, Yale University Press, 1955, p. 17.
[32] Coladarci and Getzels, *op. cit.*, pp. 10–14.

The objection that there is little point in giving theories serious consideration because of their multiplicity and the fact that they are so short lived seems to us equally untenable. As Neal E. Miller writes: "The value of a theory is not measured by the length of its life. A theory can be wrong and still lead to progress."[33] Smyth provides excellent examples from the history of physics of theories that changed rapidly—that is, to use Miller's term, were "wrong"—but were enormously useful.[34] The various theories—and there were many—had exceedingly short life spans. No sooner was a theory explicitly formulated than new observations *prompted by it* led to its revision, and a new theory was formulated *on the basis of the experience with the old one*. But no one would seriously assert that the old theory was a waste of time. In this sense explicit theory—even wrong theory—is better than implicit theory or the belief in no theory ("just the facts").

The fourth and fifth objections—that the imposition of a theoretical structure may bias the observation of phenomena, and that there is danger of becoming emotionally identified with a given theory—are more serious. As MacLeod shows, theoretical assumptions may in fact prejudice our observations.[35] An organism-centered theory of behavior, for example, tends to seek the sources of human action in forces emerging from the organism, to the exclusion, or at least de-emphasis, of other possibilities; a genetic theory tends to seek the sources for the same action in forces that operated in previous times, again to the exclusion or de-emphasis of other possibilities; a sociological theory tends to seek the sources in the structure of society, also excluding or de-emphasizing other sources; and so on. In administrative theory, as we shall see, similar difficulties prevail: One theory tends to focus on the personality of the administrator, another on the interpersonal relations between administrator and administered, another on the administrative unit as a social system. And as has been pointed out, originators and proponents of given conceptions may become so emotionally identified with their particular view that when events do not conform to their formu-

---

[33] Neal E. Miller, "Comments on Theoretical Models: Illustrated by the Development of a Theory of Conflict Behavior," *Journal of Personality*, 20 (1951), 88.

[34] H. D. Smyth, "From X-Rays to Nuclear Fission," *American Scientist*, 35 (1947), 485–501.

[35] R. B. MacLeod, "The Phenomenological Approach to Social Psychology," *Psychological Review*, 54 (1947), 193–210.

lation, instead of altering their theories, they try to account for the phenomena within the formulations they have invented.[36]

These objections are well taken and, indeed, serious. But there are certain safeguards built into the theory process itself and certain precautions the user of theory can take. The assumptions, concepts, and methods of the various theories are out in the open, as, say, those underlying the pronouncements of experts and soothsayers are not. They can be examined for possible biasing and limiting effects. It is possible to look at the world of events before deciding which theoretical formulation is relevant. For example, we know what to expect from psychoanalytic and from sociological theory, and if the distorting effects of each are unavoidable, they are recognizable and can be taken into account. A fruitful theory has in it the seeds of its own revision and even rejection. There is a difference between authoritarian closed-end statements and the hypothetical open-end statements of theory that invite testing and further inquiry. A dialogue—even a competition—takes place between theories, and ultimately the arbiter is the world of events. A formulation, however attractive, that distorts the world of events will be superseded, as the rise and fall of theories in all disciplines will attest, as surely as a map that misrepresents the terrain is superseded.

None of this means that there are no pitfalls in the use of theory in administration, as elsewhere. Indeed, the pitfalls may be somewhat greater, since the field is newer. But MacLeod states, even while pointing to the pitfalls, "No science can proceed without systematic assumptions."[37] As Coladarci and Getzels observe:

> The educator who behaves on a hit-or-miss basis, one whose professional arsenal consists merely of pat techniques for specific situations, is operating in intellectual low gear and is denied self-initiated, self-critical inquiry and innovation that are possible with the wider frame-of-reference available to the theory-conscious or thoughtful practitioner.... A clarified and well-thought-out theory, no matter how provisional, is a frame-of-reference that creates some order out of what otherwise might appear to be a disorganized situation that invites something of the order of trial-and-error behavior.[38]

---

[36] Garford Gordon, "Better Theories Needed in Research," *Phi Delta Kappan* (March, 1953), p. 219.
[37] MacLeod, *op. cit.*, p. 197.
[38] Coladarci and Getzels, *op. cit.*, pp. 7–8.

Dewey put the issue as follows:

> Theory is in the end . . . the most practical of all things, because the widening of the range of attention beyond nearby purpose and desire eventually results in the creation of farther and wider-reaching purposes, and enables us to make use of a much wider and deeper range of conditions and means than were expressed in the observation of primitive practical purposes.[39]

In the ensuing chapters of this volume we shall present (1) a brief account of the development of theories, concepts, and points of view in administration, from Taylorism at the turn of the century to the more recent contributions from the social sciences; (2) a description in detail of one theoretical framework (or conceptual model) that seems to us especially relevant to the study and practice of administration—with the understanding of course that there are others; (3) a report of a number of research studies undertaken in the terms of this framework; (4) an examination of the implications of the framework for practice; and (5) a reevaluation of the point of view taken in this chapter in the light of our experience with the framework in training, research, and practice.

In presuming to put forward one framework we are not arguing that it is the only possible framework, or that it is in some ultimate sense the best one. We would suggest, however, that this framework has proved useful in stimulating and guiding one line of inquiry into the structure and process of administration, and in making clear certain significant issues and decisions faced by administrators in their day-to-day practice. We have already said that fruitful theory has in it the seeds of its own elaboration and revision. We hope that on the basis of critical examination by students of administration, as well as on the basis of additional experience with it in research and practice, the present formulation will continue to be elaborated and revised as it already has been since it was first set forth.

---

[39] Dewey, *Sources of a Science of Education*, p. 17.

2

The development of administrative theory

The primary purpose of this volume is to present a framework for the systematic study of administration, to report a number of research studies undertaken in the terms of the framework, and to examine the implications of the framework for practice. But first we should like to insert a chapter—really a note—on the historical development of work in this area. It will help us on the one hand to avoid the ever recurrent danger of "provincialism in time" and on the other to hold present knowledge, no matter how dearly acquired and forcefully argued, as inevitably "problematic."

We may identify three major points of view in the study of administration: (1) a managerial emphasis, (2) a human relations emphasis, (3) a social science emphasis.

The managerial point of view

One view of administration—and perhaps the earliest systematic view—was that administration was intended to maximize the output of workers in an organization by applying the principles of *scientific management*. The most noted representative of this view was Frederick W. Taylor. At the turn of the century, Taylor gave as his goal the rational analysis of administrative procedures for exploiting human and material resources in order to attain the objectives of an organization most expeditiously. Excellence in management, he thought, resided in "knowing exactly what you want men to do, and then seeing that they do it in the best and cheapest way."[1] To be sure, Taylor recognized that "no system or scheme of management should be considered which does not in the long run give satisfaction to both employer and employee."[2] But having said this, he took as the cornerstone of his system the assumption that "what the workmen want from their employers beyond anything else is high wages, and what

---
[1] Frederick W. Taylor, *Shop Management*, New York, Harper & Row, 1911, p. 21.
[2] *Ibid.*

employers want from their workmen most of all is a low labor cost of manufacture."[3] Taylor's underlying attitude toward the worker (or any subordinate) may be apprehended from his following remarks:

> It is the writer's judgment . . . that for their own good it is as important that workmen should not be very much overpaid, as it is that they should not be underpaid. If overpaid, many will work irregularly and tend to become more or less shiftless, extravagant, and dissipated. It does not do for most men to get rich too fast. The writer's observation, however, would lead him to the conclusion that most men tend to become more instead of less thrifty when they receive the proper increase for an extra hard day's work. . . . They live rather better, begin to save money, become more sober, and work more steadily. And this certainly forms one of the strongest reasons for advocating this type of management.[4]

The type of management Taylor advocated is described in his *Principles of Scientific Management*, and may be summarized in these steps:

1. *Time-study principle*. All productive effort should be measured by accurate time study and a standard time established for all work done in the shop.
2. *Piece-rate principle*. Wages should be proportional to output and their rates based on the standards determined by time study. As a corollary, a worker should be given the highest grade of work of which he is capable.
3. *Separation-of-planning-from-performance principle*. Management should take over from the workers the responsibility for planning the work and making the performance physically possible. Planning should be based on time studies and other data related to production, which are scientifically determined and systematically classified; it should be facilitated by standardization of tools, implements, and methods.
4. *Scientific-methods-of-work principle*. Management should take over from the workers the responsibility for their methods of work, determine scientifically the best methods, and train workers accordingly.
5. *Managerial-control principle*. Managers should be trained and taught to apply scientific principles of management and control (such as management by exception and comparison with valid standards).

---
[3] *Ibid.*, p. 22.
[4] *Ibid.*, p. 27.

6. *Functional-management principle.* The strict application of military principles should be reconsidered and the industrial organization should be so designed that it best serves the purpose of improving the coordination of activities among the various specialists.[5]

Taylor and others were enormously influential in establishing these principles in such powerful organizations as Midland Steel, Bethlehem Steel, Santa Fe Railway, and Acme Wire Company, among others. Labor, however, fought the idea of scientific management which in its opinion conceived of men as if they were machines for exploitation. In 1912 the movement came under investigation by the Social Committee of the House of Representatives, and Congress attached a rider to the military appropriations bill specifically prohibiting the use of any of the funds for time and motion studies.

From today's perspective it seems clear that Taylor took a narrow view of administrative behavior and organizational relationships. He ignored the motivational, interpersonal, and emotional factors involved in mobilizing human effort for common purposes. But he did demonstrate that many jobs could be done more efficiently. And more important, however obsolete the specific principles of Taylorism, the scientific management movement remains a monument to the idea that administration can be studied systematically.

Another early contributor to the systematic study of administration was the Frenchman Henri Fayol, who in 1916 published the influential treatise *Administration Industriale and Générale.*[6] Although at first, attempts were made to represent his approach as antithetical to Taylor's, in 1925, at the Second International Congress of Administrative Science in Brussels, Fayol attested that such an interpretation was erroneous. Both he and Taylor, it was held, applied the same scientific methods, the latter focusing on the operative level at the bottom of the administrative hierarchy, the former on the managerial level at the top of the hierarchy.

The main points of Fayol's system were the now famous *elements* of planning, organizing, commanding, coordinating, and controlling. He wrote the following words.

[5] Raymond Villers, *Dynamic Management in Industry*, Englewood Cliffs, N.J., Prentice-Hall, 1960, p. 29.
[6] Henri Fayol, *General and Industrial Management*, trans. Constance Storrs, London, Sir Isaac Pitman and Sons, 1949.

Therefore I have adopted the following definition: To manage is to forecast and plan, to organize, to command, to co-ordinate, and to control. To foresee and provide means examining the future and drawing up the plan of action. To organize means building up the dual structure, material and human, of the undertaking. To command means maintaining activity among the personnel. To co-ordinate means binding together, unifying and harmonizing all activity and effort. To control means seeing that everything occurs in conformity with established rule and expressed command.[7]

Although Fayol remarks that from this point of view management is "neither an exclusive privilege nor a particular responsibility of the head or senior members of business; it is an activity spread, like all other activities, between head and members of the body corporate,"[8] his emphasis was clear. There were the controllers and the controlled, and everything must be made to occur "in conformity with established rule and expressed command." The outcome of Fayol's system, like that of Taylor's, was a set of administrative principles or, as Fayol called them, "precepts." For example:

The manager who has to command should—
1. Have a thorough knowledge of his personnel.
2. Eliminate the incompetent.
3. Be well versed in the agreements binding the business and its employees.
4. Set a good example.
5. Conduct periodic audits of the organization and use summarized charts to further this.
6. Bring together his chief assistants by means of conferences, at which unity of direction and focusing of effort are provided for.
7. Not become engrossed in detail.
8. Aim at making unity, energy, initiative, and loyalty prevail among the personnel.[9]

Fayol's elements and precepts were derived mainly from experience with industrial enterprises. Soon others were applying the same or similar formulations to the public realm. Chief among them was Luther Gulick, who suggested how the office of the President of the United States might be organized in these terms. He raised the question "What is the work of the chief

---
[7] *Ibid.*, pp. 5–6.
[8] *Ibid.*, p. 6.
[9] *Ibid.*, pp. 97–98.

executive?" His answer was, "POSDCoRB," each letter representing an activity essential to the proper functioning of the office. Gulick describes the activities as follows, the debt to Fayol being specifically acknowledged:

> Planning, that is working out in broad outline the things that need to be done and the methods for doing them to accomplish the purpose set for the enterprise;
> Organizing, that is the establishment of the formal structure of authority through which work subdivisions are arranged, defined and coordinated for the defined objective;
> Staffing, that is the whole personnel function of bringing in and training the staff and maintaining favorable conditions of work;
> Directing, that is the continuous task of making decisions and embodying them in specific and general orders and instructions and serving as the leader of the enterprise;
> Coordinating, that is the all important duty of interrelating the various parts of the work;
> Reporting, that is keeping those to whom the executive is responsible informed as to what is going on, which thus includes keeping himself and his subordinates informed through records, research and inspection;
> Budgeting, with all that goes with budgeting in the form of fiscal planning, accounting and control.[10]

Although Gulick was here speaking of the office of the President of the United States, he contended that the same analysis is applicable to the activities of any chief executive, including, it may be supposed, the school executive.

The principles of scientific management, and later the work of Fayol and Gulick, were in fact applied by a number of early students of school administration to the educational enterprise. For example, in 1913 Bobbitt wrote a lengthy paper for the National Society for the Study of Education significantly entitled "Some General Principles of Management Applied to the Problems of City-School Systems."[11] He began by stating explicitly:

> At a time when so much discussion is being given to the possibilities of "scientific management" in the world of material production, it seems desirable that the principles of this more effective form

---

[10] Luther Gulick and L. Urwick, eds., *Papers on the Science of Administration*, New York, Institute of Public Administration, Columbia University, 1937, p. 13.
[11] F. Bobbitt, in *The Supervision of City Schools*, Twelfth Yearbook of the National Society for the Study of Education, Part I, Chicago, University of Chicago Press, 1913.

of management may be examined in order to ascertain the possibility of applying them to the problems of educational management and supervision.[12]

He then went on to say, paralleling quite closely the principles we have just been describing:

> In any organization, the directive and supervisory members must clearly define the ends toward which the organization strives. They must coordinate the labors of all so as to attain those ends. They must find the best methods of work, and they must enforce the use of these methods on the part of the workers. They must determine the qualifications necessary for the workers and see that each rises to the standard qualifications, if it is possible; and when impossible, see that he is separated from the organization. This requires direct or indirect responsibility for the preliminary training of the workers before service, and for keeping them up to standard qualifications during service. Directors and supervisors must keep the workers supplied with detailed instructions as to the work to be done, the standards to be reached, the methods to be employed, and the material and appliances to be used. They must supply the workers with the necessary materials and appliances. They must place incentives before the worker in order to stimulate desirable effort. Whatever the nature or purpose of the organization, if it is an effective one, these are always the directive and supervisory tasks.[13]

In education, we would be well advised to do as industry does: apply scientific procedures for setting the desired standards of school production, the specific methods of production, the qualifications of the producers (that is, of the teachers), and the training of the producers, and provide them with "detailed instructions as to the work to be done, the standards to be reached, the methods to be employed, and the appliances to be used."[14] The task of the teacher will then be only to produce the standard results by applying the standard methods and materials.

Education, argued Bobbitt, had been backward in the recognition and exploitation of these principles. Indeed, from the scientific management point of view, "educational labor" was on so low a level that many preliminary steps would have to be taken before educational methods could be raised to the more "refined forms of empiricism; or yet, to the still higher plane of

---

[12] *Ibid.*, p. 7.
[13] *Ibid.*, pp. 7–8.
[14] *Ibid.*, p. 89.

scientific control."[15] But the way was clear, and the requisite scientific principles were at hand.

The early textbooks in educational administration—those by Cubberley, Strayer, and Reeder, among others—may not have followed Taylor as faithfully as had Bobbitt, but their approach, if not their language, was often similar. Cubberley, for example, in his enormously influential *Public School Administration*,[16] held that there are three phases in the work of every superintendent of schools, no matter how large or small the system. The superintendent must be the *organizer*, the *executive*, and the *supervisor* of what is done in the school. As organizer, he must plan the educational policy to be followed, even though "the details of this policy he may find it wise to keep to himself."[17] As executive, he must "come to exercise rather large powers."[18] As supervisor, his "broader professional knowledge and his larger insight into educational needs must . . . find expression in the daily work of teachers and pupils. . . . "[19]

What kind of person must the superintendent be in order to accomplish this threefold function? "The man who would be superintendent of schools—the educational leader of a city— must be clean, both in person and mind; he must be temperate, both in speech and act; he must be honest and square, and able to look men straight in the eye; and he must be possessed of a high sense of personal honor."[20] But he must also be "more than a teacher of teachers, and more than merely the executive officer of the board of education. He must be a man of affairs, possessed of good common and business sense, and good at getting work out of other people, but keeping himself as free as possible from routine service so as to have time to observe, to study, to think, to plan, to advise, to guide, and to lead."[21]

What must the superintendent know how to do? In a series of chapters analyzing the tasks of the superintendent, Cubberley provided instructions on how the superintendent should train teachers, report to the board, deal with book salesmen, maintain the school plant, and so on. A sampling of the chapter titles pro-

---

[15] *Ibid.*, p. 9.
[16] Ellwood P. Cubberley, *Public School Administration*, Boston, Houghton Mifflin, 1916.
[17] *Ibid.*, p. 145.
[18] *Ibid.*, p. 149.
[19] *Ibid.*, pp. 155–156.
[20] *Ibid.*, p. 137.
[21] *Ibid.*, p. 143.

vides an idea of the things the good school administrator should know and do: Selection and Tenure of Teachers; Training and Supervision; Pay and Promotion; Courses of Study; Testing Results; Health Supervision; Attendance; Business and Clerical; School Properties; and Costs, Funds, and Accounts.

To cite but one more instance, Reeder,[22] in a widely used textbook, similarly indicated that the superintendent must be good at getting work out of people. He devoted prescriptive chapters to selecting teachers, computing the school budget, dealing with the janitor, procuring supplies, measuring pupil abilities and achievement, constructing curricula, and keeping school accounts.

We are not undertaking here a full history and analysis of the development of administration as a field of study.[23] But we have said enough to suggest three major effects of the early technical point of view:

1. With respect to the study of administration, it encouraged the fragmentation of the administrative function into the smallest component units of activity, that is, the separate tasks.
2. With respect to training in administration, it encouraged instruction in principles and prescriptions of standard tasks that need to be done and standard techniques for doing them.
3. And perhaps fundamentally, with respect to the administrative process itself, it tended to focus on the organizational requirements and institutional elements of administration to the neglect of the interpersonal and human elements.

It was inevitable that there be a reaction—perhaps an overreaction—against this one-sided view. The early reaction found an able protagonist in Mary Parker Follett.

The human relations point of view

In a series of extraordinary books and papers, beginning at the turn of the century and continuing for more than 25 years,

---
[22] Ward G. Reeder, *The Fundamentals of Public School Administration*, New York, Macmillan, 1931.
[23] A thorough analysis of this period in administration may be found in R. E. Callahan, *Education and the Cult of Efficiency*, Chicago, University of Chicago Press, 1962.

Mary Parker Follett contended that the central problem of any enterprise, be it local or national government, business organization or school system, is the building and maintaining of dynamic yet harmonious human relations. The argument of her volume *Creative Experience*, which in many ways represents her basic outlook, has been accurately characterized as follows:

> Its thesis is the reciprocal character—the interpenetration—of all psychological phenomena, from the simplest to the most complex: Human relationships—the warp and woof of society and of industry—are at their best when difference is solved through conference and cooperation, when the parties at interest (1) evoke each other's latent ideas based on the facts of the situations, (2) come to see each other's viewpoints and to understand each other better, and (3) integrate those viewpoints and become united in the pursuit of their common goal.[24]

More specifically, with respect to administration, in a paper entitled "Business as an Integrative Unity," she says:

> It seems to me that the first test of business administration, of industrial organization, should be whether you have a business with all its parts so co-ordinated, so moving together in their closely knit and adjusting activities, so linking, interlocking, interrelating, that they make a working *unit*—that is, not a congeries of separate pieces, but what I have called a functional whole or integrative unity.[25]

The argument, then, is not about the worth of job-analytic methods as such, but that job-analytic methods should be applied by experts, managers, and workers *together*. It should be recognized that almost everyone has *some* managing ability. Analyzing the job of every workman so that he could understand what opportunities he had for managing (if only in the form of awards for suggestions) would have both a direct and an indirect positive influence on production. The direct influence would come from the workman's ability consciously to improve his efficiency. The indirect and perhaps greater influence would come from the "increase in the workman's self-respect and pride in his work, which is so necessary for the best results."[26] Or again, with respect to prevailing methods of hiring and firing at the whim

---

[24] Henry C. Metcalf and L. Urwick, *Dynamic Administration: The Collected Papers of Mary Parker Follett*, New York, Harper & Row, 1940, p. 14.
[25] *Ibid.*, p. 71.
[26] *Ibid.*, p. 86.

of management, the objection from the integrative point of view is not that such methods are unfair to the workman. It is not a matter of sentiment or altruism. Rather, a change in methods would benefit not only the workman but the business as a whole. For—and this is the basic premise—"when you have made your employees feel that they are in some sense partners in the business, they do not improve the quality of their work, save waste in time and material, because of the Golden Rule, but because their interests are the same as yours."[27]

Follett made *coordination* the underlying strategy of effective organization. She saw coordination as involving four fundamental principles:

1. *Coordination by direct contact of the responsible people concerned.* That is, control should be effected horizontally through cross-relations between departments instead of up and down in line through the chief executive.

2. *Coordination in the early stages.* That is, the direct contact must begin *while* policy is being formed, not *after* the policy has been laid down, when all that remains is compliance.

3. *Coordination as the reciprocal relation of all the factors in a situation.* This is the central principle, and Follett says about it: "... you cannot envisage the process accurately by thinking of *A* as adjusting himself to *B* and to *C* and to *D*. *A* adjusts himself to *B* and *also* to a *B* influenced by *C* and to a *B* influenced by *D* and to a *B* influenced by *A* himself. Again he adjusts himself to *C* and *also* to a *C* influenced by *B* and to a *C* influenced by *D* and to a *C* influenced by *A* himself—and so on and so on."[28]

4. *Coordination as a continuing process.* Follett writes in a notable discourse on the relation between collective planning and individual freedom:

Now continuous machinery for working out the principles of relation, whether it be in a factory or nation or internationally, is of the very essence of freedom. For it tends toward freedom when the rest of the world is following certain principles; we are bound when someone's actions toward us may be of one kind to-day and another tomorrow. The latter is the relation of slave and master, but the slave relation exists in many other places, not only when a nation uses its

[27] *Ibid.*, p. 82.
[28] *Ibid.*, p. 299.

greater power arbitrarily, or an employer his, but it may exist between two people. *Collectively* to discover and follow certain principles of action makes for *individual* freedom. Continuous machinery for this purpose is an essential factor in the only kind of control we can contemplate....

Ignorance always binds. Knowledge always frees. Collective research must be the basis of all planning. The knowledge thereby obtained will help much toward the release and the freeing without which business prosperity cannot be secured.[29]

Mary Parker Follett was the first great exponent of the human relations point of view in administration. The systematic empirical data in support of it were provided by Elton Mayo and his colleagues—notably F. J. Roethlisberger and William J. Dickson. From 1923 to 1932 they performed the now famous series of experiments at the Hawthorne plant of the Western Electric Company, culminating in the volume *Management and the Worker.*[30]

It had long been assumed in industrial administration that wages and physical working conditions were the chief factors in employee motivation and productivity. The objective of the first experiments at Hawthorne, from 1923 to 1926, was quite simple: to test the effect of one of the physical conditions—illumination—on working productivity. The finding was straightforward —and surprising: Illumination was not significantly related to productivity. It seemed clear to the experimenters that this and perhaps others of their previous basic assumptions about productivity needed reconsideration and empirical investigation. Perhaps, indeed, hitherto neglected factors such as individual attitudes and group relationships might be involved. As Roethlisberger and Dickson say, "Although the results from these experiments on illumination fell short of the expectations of the company in the sense that they failed to answer the specific question of the relation between illumination and efficiency, nevertheless they provided a great stimulus for more research in the field of human relations."[31]

The experimenters therefore instituted a series of inquiries to explore the problem more thoroughly. They selected six girl

---
[29] *Ibid.*, pp. 304–305.
[30] F. J. Roethlisberger and William J. Dickson, *Management and the Worker*, Cambridge, Mass., Harvard University Press, 1939.
[31] *Ibid.*, p. 18.

operatives for careful study as to what factors might be related to their work patterns. The findings were again straightforward —and again surprising. Whatever factors were changed—rest period, length of day, methods of payment—even when change meant only returning to the original condition, productivity increased. Moreover, the girls were more satisfied with their job, and their attendance showed greater regularity. Perhaps most striking was the observation that in attempting to "control" the experiment, the experimenters had to treat the subjects differently from the way they were treated in the shop—for example, they were put together in a separate room, they received personal attention, they had a particular type of supervision, and so on— and it was this special treatment more than the given experimental variable that seemed to make the difference in productivity.

As Roethlisberger and Dickson put it, "in human situations not only was it practically impossible to keep all other factors constant, but trying to do so in itself introduced the biggest change of all. . . . In the process of setting the conditions for the test, they [the experimenters] had altered completely the social situation of the operators and their customary attitudes and interpersonal relations."[32] The crucial result of the first studies, confirmed and reconfirmed by all ensuing studies, was to demonstrate the importance of employee attitudes and preoccupations. All attempts to eliminate such considerations were unsuccessful. The experimenters stated their central finding as follows:

> It became clear to the investigators that the limits of human collaboration are determined far more by the informal than the formal organization of the plant. Collaboration is not wholly a matter of logical organization. It presupposes social codes, conventions, traditions, and routine or customary ways of responding to situations. Without such basic codes or conventions, effective work relations are not possible.[33]

Roethlisberger and Dickson concluded their book with this blanket statement:

> If the . . . investigators were asked to generalize their experience for personnel administration, they would have no hesitancy in saying

---
[32] *Ibid.*, p. 183.
[33] *Ibid.*, p. 568.

this. Adequate personnel administration in any particular industrial plant should fulfill two conditions: (1) Management should introduce in its organization an explicit skill of diagnosing human relations. (2) By means of this skill management should commit itself to the *continuous* process of studying human situations—both individual and group—and should run its human affairs in terms of what it is continually learning about its own organization.[34]

Mayo, analyzing the findings in 1933,[35] suggested that the most significant change in the total situation of the experimental group bore only a casual relation to the piecemeal experimental changes. The truly important change was a modification in "mental attitude." He called attention to the following critical, if experimentally unintended, conditions. Before every change in program the group was consulted. Its comments were listened to and discussed. The members were allowed to overrule a managerial suggestion. The group developed a sense of participation in the critical determinations and became something of a social unity. In consequence, a new industrial milieu was established for these workers—"a milieu," as Mayo says, "in which their own self-determination and their social well-being ranked first and the work was incidental."[36] How different all this is from the usual milieu of the shop, with its rigid logic of production demanding only blind conformity to the job-analyzed tasks of the workers!

Mayo concluded:

Human collaboration in work, in primitive and developed societies, has always depended for its perpetuation upon the evolution of a non-logical social code which regulates the relations between persons and their attitudes to one another. Insistence upon a merely economic logic of production—especially if the logic is frequently changed—interferes with the development of such a code and consequently gives rise in the group to a sense of human defeat. This human defeat results in the formation of a social code at a lower level and in opposition to the economic logic. One of its symptoms is "restriction." In its devious road to this enlightenment, the research division had learned something of the personal exasperation caused by a continual experience of incomprehension and futility. It had

---

[34] *Ibid.*, p. 604.
[35] Elton Mayo, *The Human Problems of an Industrial Civilization*, New York, Macmillan, 1933.
[36] *Ibid.*, p. 73.

also learned how serious a consequence such experience carries for industry and for the individual.[37]

The work of Mayo and his associates has had considerable critical examination.[38] Some students find two major biases in the experiments. It is held that Mayo may have had a managerial bias, since he was employed by business to help solve business problems. He is also seen as having an a-theoretical and clinical bias, a criticism that does not seem to us well taken. Regardless of the criticisms, one must recognize that through long and meticulous observation Mayo and his associates collected a large body of data making clear that what goes on inside the workman and between workmen is more significant for production than what goes on outside, even in the most rigorously job-analyzed work situations.

The human relations movement in administration was influenced, perhaps even more than by the Hawthorne studies, by an experiment not in the field of administration at all—an experiment with children. This was an inquiry into the psychological dynamics of democratic, authoritarian, and laissez-faire leadership with 11-year-olds. The investigators were Kurt Lewin, Ronald Lippitt, and Ralph K. White, the year was 1938, and the setting was the Iowa Child Welfare Station at the University of Iowa.[39]

The central experiment was rather simple. It involved groups of 11-year-old children, five children in each group, meeting after school under an adult leader and carrying on an interesting activity (carpentry, soap carving, painting). The one factor that was deliberately and systematically varied was the type of leadership; all other factors were held as constant as possible. Trained observers took continuous notes on the behavior of the children. Would there be systematic differences in their behavior as a function of the different types of leadership?

The three types of leadership were defined as follows.

---
[37] *Ibid.*, pp. 120–121.
[38] See, for example, Delbert C. Miller and William H. Form, *Industrial Sociology*, New York, Harper & Row, 1951, pp. 78–83.
[39] There were actually two complementary experiments; the initial reports were published in the *Journal of Social Psychology*, 10 (1939), 271–299, and in the *University of Iowa Studies in Child Welfare*, 16, no. 3 (1940), 43–195. The discussion here draws upon the book by Ralph K. White and Ronald O. Lippitt, *Autocracy and Democracy: An Experimental Inquiry*, New York, Harper & Row, 1960.

The development of administrative theory

Autocratic (or Authoritarian)	Democratic	Laissez-faire
1. All determination of policy by the leader.	1. All policies a matter of group discussion and decision, encouraged and assisted by the leader.	1. Complete freedom for group or individual decision, with a minimum of leader participation.
2. Techniques and activity steps dictated by the authority, one at a time, so that future steps are always uncertain to a large degree.	2. Activity perspective gained during discussion period. General steps to group goal sketched, and where technical advice is needed, the leader suggests two or more alternative procedures from which choice can be made.	2. Various materials supplied by the leader, who makes it clear that he will supply information when asked. He takes no other part in work discussion.
3. The leader usually dictates the particular work task and work companion of each member.	3. The members are free to work with whomever they choose, and the division of tasks is left up to the group.	3. Complete non-participation of the leader in determining tasks and companions.
4. The leader tends to be "personal" in his praise and criticism of the work of each member, but remains aloof from active group participation except when demonstrating.	4. The leader is "objective" or "fact-minded" in his praise and criticism and tries to be a regular group member in spirit without doing too much of the work.	4. Infrequent spontaneous comments on member activities unless questioned, and no attempt to appraise or regulate the course of events.[40]

The salient results were as follows:

1. Laissez faire was not the same as democracy. There was less work done in it, and poorer work. More discontent was manifest during the meetings, and in interviews preference was expressed for the democratic leader.
2. Democracy can be efficient. The quantity of work done in autocracy was somewhat greater, but work motivation was stronger in democracy as shown when work was continued

---
[40] White and Lippitt, *op. cit.*, pp. 26-27.

after the leader left the room. Originality was greater in democracy.
3. Autocracy can create much hostility and aggression, including aggression against scapegoats.
4. Autocracy can create discontent that does not appear on the surface. Some boys dropped out during autocratic club periods in which overt rebellion did not occur. More discontent was expressed in autocracy than in democracy, even when the general reaction was submissive. Nineteen out of twenty boys preferred their democratic leader.
5. There was more dependence and less individuality in autocracy. Individual differences in task performance tended to diminish.
6. There was more group-mindedness and also more friendliness in democracy. Spontaneous subgroups were larger, and there was a tendency to share group property more readily.

We venture to say that, despite the unlikely source of the findings, no other psychological experiment so rapidly and completely captured the imagination of both students and practitioners of administration, perhaps especially of educational administration. The terms "democratic," "authoritarian," and "laissez faire" became everyday words, "democratic" leadership being, of course, "good" and "authoritarian" leadership "bad." "Group dynamics," which in a sense was launched by this experiment, took firm root in both the language and practice of administration.

There was an outpouring of treatises and books with a human relations and often more specifically group dynamics point of view. We cite only a sample of the titles that come to mind: *Practical Applications of Democratic Leadership, Human Relations in Educational Organization, Democracy in School Administration, Human Relations in School Administration, The World of Work: Industrial Society and Human Relations*, and *Improving Human Relations in School Administration*. Typically, the last-named volume cites the aforementioned experiment and points to the "discovery that under domination the quality of work deteriorated greatly when the autocratic leader was not present, while the quality of work in democratic climates continued at approximately the same levels." The author concludes, "Apparently, in terms of the environment in which individuals work, it is better to let groups make their own choices, whether leadership is present or not, than it is to try to control the lives of others."[41]

The following general principles of school administration are presented:

1. Democracy is primarily concerned with human relations; therefore a most important consideration is the principal's dealings with teachers individually and collectively.
2. Simple problems of human relations almost always have wider frames of reference.
3. The single-school faculty is the most natural and efficient unit of democratic action.
4. The principal is in the most advantageous position to offer leadership to the faculty in its attempts to provide itself with democratic experiences.
5. The faculty is a complex social group which requires expert handling to achieve its own best desires.
6. The primary responsibility of the principal is that of facilitation of the interactions of the faculty group so that they may result in maximum benefit to the teachers.
7. All individuals affected by any decision should have a share in determining its character and form.[42]

All this is a far cry indeed from Taylor's separation-of-planning-from-performance principle and his scientific-methods-of-work principle: that "management should take over from the workers the responsibility for their methods of work, determine scientifically the best methods, and train the workers accordingly."[43] It is an equally far cry, more specifically with respect to educational administration, from Bobbitt's dictum that directors and supervisors must keep school personnel supplied with "detailed instructions as to the work to be done, the standards to be reached, the methods to be employed, and the appliances to be used."[44]

The social science point of view

We need hardly point out that the chronology of the development we have been tracing was by no means as schematic as our out-

---
[41] Wilbur A. Yauch, *Improving Human Relations in School Administration*, New York, Harper & Row, 1949, p. 40.
[42] *Ibid.*, pp. 11–16.
[43] Villers, *op. cit.*, p. 29.
[44] Bobbitt, *op. cit.*, p. 89.

line. The human relations point of view did not *follow* the managerial point of view in the sense that the one stopped when the other began. There were of course overlappings. But in general Taylor's influence on administrative thought preceded Follett's and Mayo's.

In 1938 came the statement of a significantly different approach from the others, albeit not totally divorced from them. Chester Barnard first formulated it in a series of lectures for the Lowell Institute in Boston and later elaborated it in that remarkable treatise *The Functions of the Executive*.[45] Here the clear and explicit need for a general *theory* of administrative relationships was set forth and the placing of such theory in the context of the *social science* of behavior advocated.

At the time of his writing, Barnard estimated, there were no less than 5 million executives, 100,000 of them in major executive positions. The technical aspects of their work had been well covered in literature and instruction. But, as Barnard put it, concerning "the instrumentality with which they work—the organization—and the techniques appropriate to it, there is little." Indeed, "more important is the lack of an accepted conceptual scheme with which to exchange their thought."[46]

Barnard's book, then, is divided into two parts. The first provides a conceptual scheme in the form of a theory of cooperation and organization; the second is a study of the function and of the methods of operation of executives in formal organizations. The first part is based on the sciences concerning the conditions of social behavior; the second on Barnard's personal experience and observation from thirty years as an executive. The purpose of the book is not so much to provide principles for immediate application as to formulate a systematic position for the study and understanding of the relevant phenomena, which will result in improved practice.

The details of the rich and complex argument cannot be adequately summarized in this brief historical sketch. Nor is a detailed summary necessary for the point we are making. We have already indicated Barnard's central theme: the need for a systematic conceptual scheme of administrative behavior within a social science framework.

Nonetheless, we wish to suggest the nature of Barnard's

---

[45] Chester I. Barnard, *The Functions of the Executive*, Cambridge, Mass., Harvard University Press, 1964 (originally published in 1938).
[46] *Ibid.*, p. 289.

substantive attack on the problem. Barnard argues that the executive, whether military, religious, manufacturing, or academic, always works *within* the organization, which is "a system of consciously co-ordinated activities or forces of two or more persons."[47] He proceeds to make a significant distinction between the concepts of *effectiveness* and *efficiency*. The former refers to the accomplishment of the cooperative purpose, which is essentially nonpersonal in character. The latter refers to the satisfaction of individual motives, which is personal in character. The persistence of cooperation in an organization, Barnard contends, depends on exactly these two conditions: its effectiveness and its efficiency.[48]

He summarizes his basic formulation regarding organizations as follows:

Organization, simple or complex, is always *an impersonal system of coordinated human efforts*; always there is purpose as the coordinating and unifying principle; always there is the indispensable ability to communicate, always the necessity for personal willingness, and for effectiveness and efficiency in maintaining the integrity of purpose and the continuity of contributions.[49]

Although Barnard dealt mainly with the structure and function of the *formal* organization, he also pointed out that each formal organization contains *informal* organizations. How an organization works cannot be understood solely from its organizational chart, its charter, its rules and regulations, or even from watching its personnel. " 'Learning the organizational ropes' in most organizations is chiefly learning who's who, what's what, why's why of its informal society."[50]

Informal organizations characteristically occur and continue "without any specific conscious *joint* purpose."[51] But, although common or joint purposes are excluded, "common or joint results of important character nevertheless come from such organizations."[52] Whatever their origins, the informal contacts, interactions, and groupings change not only the experience, knowledge, attitudes, and emotions of the individuals affected but also their functioning in the formal organization.

---
[47] *Ibid.*, p. 72.
[48] *Ibid.*, p. 60.
[49] *Ibid.*, pp. 94–95.
[50] *Ibid.*, p. 121.
[51] *Ibid.*, p. 114.
[52] *Ibid.*, p. 115.

In short, informal organizations are inevitably related to formal organizations everywhere. Indeed, "the attitudes, institutions, customs, of informal society affect and are partly expressed through formal organization. They are interdependent aspects of the same phenomena—a society is structured by formal organizations, formal organizations are vitalized and conditioned by informal organization."[53] The informal organization has three necessary functions within the formal organization: (1) communication; (2) the preservation of the feeling of personal integrity, self-respect, and independence of choice; and (3) the maintenance of group cohesion through regulating the willingness to serve and the stability of objective authority. The formal and the informal aspects of organization cannot exist without one another, and if the one fails the other disintegrates.[54]

Barnard's analysis of the relationship between effectiveness and efficiency, formal and informal organization, cooperative achievement and personal satisfaction, provides a heuristic framework for studying and understanding the most crucial aspects of administrative behavior. If the formulation did not entirely solve all the problems it raised (and which subsequent formulations have solved them?), it succeeded in putting the technical view of administration as represented by Taylor and Fayol and the human relations view as represented by Follett and Mayo into appropriate perspective. Barnard stands as the anchoring point for subsequent work in this area.

What about more recent views? As we approach our own period it becomes increasingly difficult to judge what current work will in time take its place with that of Taylor and Fayol, Gulick and Urwick, and Mayo and Barnard (and perhaps more indirectly with that of Lewin and the group dynamicists) as having had a perceptible impact on the study and practice of administration. One thing is certain: there has been much speculative and lately even some empirical work in the field, most of it within what we have called the theoretical social science point of view. Not that there is any consensus, let alone unanimity, regarding the particular concepts likely to prove most fruitful! The work of Argyris, Bakke, Bass, Blau, Gouldner, Griffiths, Gross, Halpin, Homans, Katz, March, Presthus, Selznick, and Simon, to mention only a few of those who have published full-length books during the past decade, illustrates the richness and

---
[53] *Ibid.*, p. 120.
[54] *Ibid.*, p. 122.

variety of the effort and would deserve detailed examination were our aim here an exhaustive historical analysis.

For present purposes, however, it will suffice to say a little more about two current formulations that seem to us to have drawn the greatest attention. This is not the same, we hasten to add, as saying they will necessarily prove of greater ultimate worth than the others.

The influential and, we may perhaps already safely say, classic treatise *Administrative Behavior*, by Herbert A. Simon, was first published in 1945.[55] It carried the subtitle "A Study of Decision-Making Processes in Administrative Organization." As Simon himself was later to point out, the title and subtitle, if not the entire work, had a prophetic quality, for they incorporated what were to become the most fashionable terms in social science—"behavior," "decision-making," and "organization." In 1957 the book was reissued in a second edition, carrying a foreword by Chester Barnard. This was entirely appropriate, for Simon's work is well within the position, if not the specific conceptual scheme, advocated in *The Functions of the Executive*.

Simon began by stating flatly that the accepted principles of administration are "little more than ambiguous and mutually contradictory proverbs."[56] A different approach was needed—one that would establish a consistent and useful administrative theory. Such an approach was to be found in shifting the emphasis from the principles of administration to a study of the *conditions* under which competing principles are applicable.

More specifically, Simon argued that before a science could develop principles it must possess concepts. Before a law of gravitation could be formulated, it was necessary to have the notions of acceleration and weight. The first task of administrative theory must be to develop a set of concepts that will permit the description, in terms relevant to the theory, of administrative situations. To be scientifically useful, these concepts must be operational—that is, their meanings must correspond to empirically observable phenomena. What then is a scientifically relevant description of an organization? "It is a description that, so far as possible, designates for each person in the organization what decisions that person makes, and the influences to which he is subject in making each of these decisions."[57] Further, "It is

---
[55] Herbert A. Simon, *Administrative Behavior*, New York, Macmillan, 1945.
[56] *Ibid.*, p. 240.
[57] *Ibid.*, p. 37.

the central thesis of this study that an understanding of the underlying conditions for the applicability of administrative principles is to be obtained from an analysis of the administrative process in terms of decisions."[58]

Administration must be concerned with the construction and operation of an organization in order to accomplish its work "efficiently." A fundamental aim of "good" administration is to increase the *rationality* of organizational decisions. That is, among several alternatives involving the same expenditure the one should be chosen that leads to the greatest accomplishment of administrative ends; and among several alternatives leading to the same accomplishment the one should be chosen that involves the least expenditure. The principle of "efficiency" is characteristic of any activity that attempts rationally to maximize the attainment of certain ends with the use of scarce means. In this sense, the principle is as much a part of administrative theory as it is of economic theory, and "the 'administrative man' takes his place alongside the classical 'economic man.'"[59]

Actually in this context the principle of efficiency should be considered a definition rather than a principle. As Simon points out, it defines "good" or "correct" administrative behavior. It does not tell *how* rationality in organizational decisions is to be maximized. It merely states that this maximization is the aim of administrative activity, and that administrative theory must describe under what conditions the maximization takes place.

Now, if there were no limits to human rationality there would clearly be no need for administrative theory: Everyone would automatically make the correct decision and thus maximize the organizational output. But since this is obviously not the case in practice, Simon poses the question "What are the factors that determine the level of efficiency which is achieved by an administrative organization?" His approach to the answer is:

> Perhaps the simplest method of approach is to consider the single member of the administrative organization, and ask what the limits are to the quantity and quality of his output. These limits include (a) limits on his ability to *perform*, and (b) limits on his ability to *make correct decisions*. To the extent that these limits are removed, the administrative organization approaches its goal of high

---
[58] *Ibid.*, p. 240.
[59] *Ibid.*, p. 39.

efficiency. Two persons, given the same skills, the same objectives and values, the same knowledge and information, can rationally decide only upon the same course of actions.[60]

In effect:

> The individual can be rational in terms of the organization's goals only to the extent that he is *able* to pursue a particular course of action, he has a correct conception of the *goal* of the action, and he is correctly *informed* about the conditions surrounding his action.... Administrative theory must be concerned with the limits of rationality, and the manner in which organization affects these limits for the person making a decision.[61]

Simon asserts that the most fruitful approach to understanding and improving administrative behavior is through this "decisional" framework.

Bakke, Argyris, and their colleagues at the Labor and Management Center at Yale University also argue for the primacy of theory in administrative behavior. As Bakke says, "Every leader of organized activity whether he be a manager of a business, an official of a union, an executive of government, the pastor of a church, a commander of a military force, a president of a university, or a father or mother of a family, bases his decisions and actions on an organizational theory."[62] But the formulation they propose is quite different from that of Simon, and there is hardly any mention of decision-making as a central concept. Argyris gives the reason:

> Since the basic topic of change is not discussed, one will not find a discussion regarding the decision-making process within an organizational context. However, even if change were discussed, an examination of the literature reveals a meager amount of research on decision-making. There is little known as to how a decision is first created and how it travels through the organization in order to have its intended effect.[63]

The assumption underlying the Bakke-Argyris framework is that there is a fundamental and inevitable incongruity between

---
[60] *Ibid.*
[61] *Ibid.*, p. 241.
[62] E. Wight Bakke, *Organization and the Individual*, New Haven, Labor and Management Center, Yale University, 1952, p. 1.
[63] Chris Argyris, *Personality and Organization*, New York, Harper & Row, 1957, p. xiii.

the needs of mature personality and the requirements of formal organization. The mature personality tends to develop from the state of passivity as an infant to increasing activity as an adult, from dependence to relative independence, from receiving aspects of the culture to controlling aspects of the culture, from the ability to behave in only a few ways to the ability to behave in different ways, from occupying a subordinate position as a child in the family to occupying an equal or superordinate position as an adult in the family and in other situations.[64] But formal organizations place the mature personality in an environment which permits him little control over his world, usually calls for passivity rather than initiative, often forces him to occupy a subordinate position, makes him feel dependent upon other agents (bosses, foremen), allows minimum personality flexibility, and emphasizes only one ability or a few abilities (and those often of a minor sort).[65] And of course, as Argyris points out, "If the analysis is correct, this inevitable incongruency increases as (1) the employees are of increasing maturity, (2) as the formal structure (based on the above principles) is made more clear-cut and logically tight for maximum formal organizational effectiveness, (3) as one goes down the line of command, and (4) as the jobs become more and more mechanized (i.e., take on assembly line characteristics)."[66]

The "essential processes" constituting what Bakke calls the "dynamic core" of an organization are:

1. Workflow process—activities which directly produce whatever product or service the organization is set up to produce.
2. Authority process—activities which direct the operations and the people doing them.
3. Reward and penalty process—activities which motivate people and persuade or compel them to act in ways which are beneficial to the organization and its members.
4. Perpetuation process—activities which keep the organization supplied with the quantity and quality of people, materials, ideas, and nurture it needs.
5. Communication process—activities which acquaint people with the information they need to have.

---

[64] Cf. E. W. Bakke and C. Argyris, *Organizational Structure and Dynamics: A Framework for Theory*, New Haven, Labor and Management Center, Yale University, 1954, p. 15, and Argyris, *op. cit.*, p. 66.
[65] Cf. Bakke and Argyris, *op. cit.*, pp. 21–22, and Argyris, *op. cit.*, p. 66.
[66] Argyris, *op. cit.*, p. 66.

6. Evaluation process—activities which establish criteria for and define levels of importance for people, materials, ideas, and other activities, and which rate them and allocate them to these levels.
7. Identification process—activities which establish criteria for and define, express, and symbolize the organization as a whole, establish its uniqueness and identity as an organization, and which maintain its wholeness.[67]

When an individual and an organization come together, the organization will attempt to impress its pattern upon the individual, and the individual will attempt to impress his pattern upon the organization. The first process may be called the *socializing process*; the second, the *personalizing process*. A fundamental proposition derived from the framework is that many of the problems of administration are caused by the friction between the two processes or, to put it in Argyris' terms, "by the basic incongruence between the nature of relatively mature individuals and healthy formal organizations,"[68] each seeking to obtain optimum self-actualization.

From this point of view, then, how are good administration and effective leadership achieved? They are achieved essentially through the "fusion process." As Argyris says:

... if the organization's goals are to be achieved, and knowing that both will always strive for self-actualization, it follows that effective leadership behavior is "fusing" the individual and the organization in such a way that both simultaneously obtain *optimum* self-actualization. The process of the individual using the organization to fulfill his needs and simultaneously the organization "using" the individuals to achieve its demands has been called by Bakke the *fusion process*.[69]

No description of the period would be complete without mention of Talcott Parsons and his attempts to construct a *general* theory of social action.[70] Although he has not written

---

[67] E. W. Bakke, *The Fusion Process*, New Haven, Labor and Management Center, Yale University, 1955, pp. 11–12.
[68] Argyris, *op. cit.*, p. 211.
[69] *Ibid.*, p. 13.
[70] See, for example, Talcott Parsons, *The Structure of Social Action*, New York, McGraw-Hill, 1937; Talcott Parsons and Edward A. Shils, eds., *Toward a General Theory of Action*, Cambridge, Mass., Harvard University Press, 1951; and Talcott Parsons, *The Social System*, New York, Free Press, 1951.

extensively on administration,[71] he has greatly influenced, directly or indirectly, many who have. As early as 1938, explicit reference to his work was made by Barnard in *The Functions of the Executive*, and no social theorist is cited more frequently in a book-length empirical study of school superintendents written twenty years later.[72]

We shall not attempt a summary of the general theory here, for any exegesis in the brief space at our disposal is bound to be inadequate. The argument is highly abstract, and the rhetoric is often abstruse. We shall be content merely to give the flavor of various aspects of Parsons' thinking by citing a number of his assumptions and concepts.

1. Social action is *goal-directed*, and simple stimulus-response theories are inadequate to account for the facts of such action.
2. As a symbol-using animal, man is able to *generalize* from experience and to stabilize patterns of behavior through time.
3. These patterns may be analyzed most fruitfully in terms of *systems*.
4. Social action itself may be seen as a system representing a *"compromise"* in the interactions of the cultural, organic, personal, and social subsystems.
5. Perfect *integration* within an action system is not found in the empirical world, as motivated actors contend with the exigencies of survival in a particular environment.[73]
6. Although perfect integration is probably unattainable, no system of action can survive unless the component subsystems are mutually *consistent* within some degree of tolerance.

---

[71] There are three specific papers, although there is relevant material throughout: "Suggestions for a Sociological Approach to the Theory of Organizations—I," *Administrative Science Quarterly* (June, 1956), pp. 63–85; "A Sociological Approach to the Theory of Organizations—II," *Administrative Science Quarterly* (September, 1956), pp. 225–239; "Some Ingredients of a General Theory of Formal Organization," by Talcott Parsons, in Andrew W. Halpin, ed., *Administrative Theory in Education*, Chicago, Midwest Administration Center, University of Chicago, 1958, pp. 40–72.

[72] Neal C. Gross, Ward S. Mason, and Alexander W. McEachern, *Explorations in Role Analysis*, New York, Wiley, 1958.

[73] Robin M. Williams, Jr., "The Sociological Theory of Talcott Parsons," in Max Black, ed., *The Social Theories of Talcott Parsons: A Critical Examination*, Englewood Cliffs, N.J., Prentice-Hall, 1961, p. 93.

7. In view of the strain toward *inconsistency* among the interconnecting systems, there is need for *coordination* within an action system so that there may be "continual action in concert."
8. The need for close coordination is most clearly seen in an *organization*, which may be defined as a "system of cooperative relationships" capable of "continual action in concert" and having "primacy of orientation to the attainment of a specific goal."[74]
9. It is not sufficient for members of action systems to share cognitive and cathectic standards; they must also share *value* standards.
10. Among the value problems faced as *"dilemmas of choice"* in all action systems are:
    a. *Affectivity—affective neutrality.* That is, to get immediate gratification or to exercise self-restraint in the light of longer-term considerations.
    b. *Self-orientation—collective orientation.* That is, to serve self-interest or to serve the interest of a group to which one belongs.
    c. *Universalism—particularism.* That is, to treat objects and persons in accordance with a general norm covering all objects or persons in that class or to treat them in accordance with their standing in some particular relationship to oneself.
    d. *Ascription—achievement.* That is, to treat an object or a person in the light of "what it is" or to treat it in the light of "what it does" or may be expected to do.
    e. *Diffuseness—specificity.* That is, to respond to many aspects of an object or person or to respond to a selection of those aspects.[75]

We have perhaps said enough to give some idea of Parsonian thinking, if not of the actual theory in its intricate ramifications. It remains only to add that if Parsons is notable for the influence he has cast, he is even more notable for the controversy he has occasioned. There are those who believe that his is the preeminent social theory of our time. Others assert that not only is what he is saying trite but it is also harmful to the future

---

[74] Cf. Chandler Morse, "The Functional Imperatives," in Black, ed., *op. cit.*, p. 111.
[75] Cf. Max Black, "Some Questions About Parsons' Theories," in Black, ed., *op. cit.*, pp. 285–286.

development of social science. Thus, a very able and eminent sociologist raises the point publicly and in all earnestness:

> Sociology today has many burdens and not the least of these is a persistent and somewhat humiliating question: Are the theoretical excursions of Talcott Parsons worth taking seriously? The issue is not so much intellectual disagreement over contrasting views of man and society. It is rather a case of the Emperor's clothes. Is his complexly textured raiment really there? Or is it all (or largely) an illusion, a conjuration, a bad and costly joke?[76]

In contrast, ten of the senior faculty in sociology, psychology, economics, philosophy, and political science at Cornell University apparently believed Parsonian thought of sufficient significance to devote two years' discussion to it, culminating in a volume of essays entitled *The Social Theory of Talcott Parsons*.[77] And, although he recognizes that it may be premature to give a treatise like *The Social System* its ultimate place, Robert K. Merton is able to say, "But on the evidence, both of research stemming from Parsons' formulations and of critical theoretical review, it is plain that this represents a decisive step toward a methodical statement of current sociological theory."[78]

This is not the place to attempt any judgment between those for whom Parsonian theory is a "decisive step" and those for whom it is only a "costly joke." In any case, there is no doubt of its impact, for good or for ill, on past and increasingly on current work in the social sciences, including of course organizational behavior. Whether the work would have advanced farther and faster without the influence of Parsons, as the rabid "anti's" contend, is an unanswerable question. Perhaps the most rational present position amidst the impassioned arguments is provided by Robin Williams' summary statement to his paper "The Sociological Theory of Talcott Parsons":

> My conclusion is that the full returns are yet to be seen and that a definitive judgment on the overall merits of Parsonian sociology cannot now be made. Even while saying this, I recognize that two further fairly significant appraisals are possible even at this time: (1) that the system has demonstrated a high degree of provocative

---

[76] Philip Selznick, "The Social Theories of Talcott Parsons," *American Sociological Review*, 26, no. 5 (1961), 932.
[77] Black, ed., *op. cit.*
[78] Robert K. Merton, *Social Theory and Social Structure*, rev. ed., New York, Free Press, 1957, p. 83.

value in stimulating other workers to examine data in the light of this conceptual scheme, and that important results have thereby been obtained; (2) that the empirical usefulness of the scheme, thus far, has been in the application of limited *parts* of it to the interpretation of data, to the development of hypotheses, and to the descriptive ordering of information about particular institutions and societies.[79]

As will be seen, the framework presented in this volume has also been influenced by *parts* of Parsons' formulations where these parts seemed fruitful, without thereby necessarily accepting the entire structure of the *general* theory.

---
[79] Williams, *op. cit.*, p. 99.

3

A framework for the study of administrative behavior: the dimensions

We may begin with a general conception, if not a definition, of administration. Not that we believe this conception to be unexceptionable. But at least the explicit statement of a point of view, even a tentative one, will provide a formulation for inquiry, to be agreed with or departed from in definite and meaningful terms.

We conceive of administration as a social process and of its context as a social system. It may be examined from three points of view: structurally, functionally, and operationally.

Structurally, administration is seen as the hierarchy of superordinate-subordinate relationships within a social system.[1] To use the terms "superordinate" and "subordinate" thus bluntly and at the outset in this day and age, when the concept of authority has become confused with the concept of authoritarianism, is to invite objection at once. In due course we shall show that the person in the superordinate position is not always dominant and the one in the subordinate position is not inevitably submissive. Nonetheless, in the structure of an organization there are related higher and lower, as well as parallel, positions having greater and lesser vantages for asserting influence vis-à-vis each other and in the affairs of the system as a whole.

Functionally, this hierarchy of relationships is the locus for allocating and integrating roles and facilities in order to achieve the goals of the system. It is here that the assignment of statuses, the provision of facilities, the organization of procedures, the regulation of activity, and the evaluation of performance take place. Of course, these functions are the responsibility of the superordinate member of the hierarchy. But each function becomes effective only insofar as it "takes" with the subordinate member. The superordinate may decide, but his decision is empty if the subordinate does not implement.

Operationally, the administrative process takes effect in

---

[1] See J. W. Getzels, "A Psycho-Sociological Framework for the Study of Educational Administration," *Harvard Educational Review*, 22 (Fall 1952), 235–246.

situations involving person-to-person interaction. In a sense the given structural superordinate-subordinate relationship is enacted in two separate and dynamic personal situations, one embedded in the other. One member perceives and organizes the relationship in terms of *his* needs, skills, goals, and past experiences; the other member perceives and organizes in terms of *his* needs, skills, goals, and past experiences. The two situations are connected through the existential structures, objects, and symbols which have to some extent—but most often *only to some extent*—a counterpart in both situations. No matter how minutely the administrative structure of an organization is defined, in practice the individuals involved in the structure do not thereby necessarily see eye to eye with each other. Even in the military, there is a certain amount of slippage between the structural arrangements of the table of organization and the operating relationships of the flesh-and-blood people.

The basic unit for administrative analysis: the social system

The fact that administration always functions within a network of interpersonal or, more broadly, social relationships makes the nature of this network a crucial factor in the administrative process. Thus the study of administration must be put within the most general context of interpersonal or social behavior—that is, the given social system.[2]

As used here, the term "social system" is of course conceptual rather than descriptive. It must not be confused with "society" or "state," or be thought of as somehow applicable only to *large* aggregates of human interaction. At the most general and abstract level a social system has been defined by Linton as follows:

> Perhaps the nature of a social system can best be understood if we compare it to a geometric figure, a bit of "nothing intricately

---

[2] Portions of the following are drawn from: *ibid.*; J. W. Getzels and E. G. Guba, "Social Behavior and the Administrative Process," *School Review*, 65 (1957), 423–441; J. W. Getzels, "Administration as a Social Process," in Andrew W. Halpin, ed., *Administrative Theory in Education*, Chicago, Midwest Administration Center, University of Chicago, 1958, pp. 150–165; J. W. Getzels and H. A. Thelen, "The Classroom as a Unique Social System," in N. B. Henry, ed., *The Dynamics of Instructional Groups*, Fifty-ninth Yearbook of the National Society for the Study of Education, Chicago, University of Chicago Press, 1960, pp. 53–82.

drawn nowhere." Actually, there is nothing else within the range of common experience which would be so closely comparable. A geometric figure consists of a series of spatial relationships which are delineated by points. These points are established by the relationships and can be defined only in terms of the relationships. They have no independent existence. Each of the patterns which together compose a social system is made up of hypothetical attitudes and forms of behavior, the sum total of these constituting a social relationship.[3]

Numerous and varying dimensions have been adduced to describe social systems in detail. Surely the "hypothetical attitudes and forms of behavior" mentioned by Linton are not the only ones. But although the question of which specific dimensions are most fruitful remains an open issue, the usefulness of the social-systems approach is generally recognized, and the concept has been widely applied. Carr's usage, for example, is quite different from Linton's, but the essential value of the systems concept as a focus for theoretical analysis and empirical investigation of networks of human interaction is unchanged. Carr writes:

Each of us lives in some local social system.
The word *system* comes from the Greek, *synistanai*, meaning "to place together." As Webster puts it, a system is "an assemblage of objects united by some form of regular interaction or interdependence, an organic or organized whole." So by local social system we refer to an "assemblage" or *aggregation of individuals and institutional organizations located in an identifiable geographical locality and functioning in various degrees of interdependence as a permanent organized unit of the social order.*[4]

The three characteristics of social systems to be noted in this formulation are the interdependence of the parts, their organization into some sort of whole, and the intrinsic presence of both individuals and institutions. Parsons, using a somewhat different set of dimensions, also emphasizes the usefulness of seeing human behavior in the context of social-systems theory. He too points to a social system as comprising a more or less restricted and organized network of interactions including both organizationally or culturally structured and individually defined elements. He summarizes his conception of a social system as follows.

---
[3] Ralph Linton, *The Study of Man*, New York, Appleton-Century-Crofts, 1936, p. 256.
[4] L. J. Carr, *Analytical Sociology*, New York, Harper & Row, 1955, p. 167.

Reduced to the simplest possible terms, then, a social system consists in a plurality of individual actors interacting with each other in a situation which has at least a physical or environmental aspect, actors who are motivated in terms of a tendency to the "optimization of gratification" and whose relation to their situations, including each other, is defined and mediated in terms of a system of culturally structured and shared symbols.[5]

Most often the concept of a social system has been applied to large aggregates of human relationships. For example, distinctions have been made in magnitude and complexity of the social system in the neighborhood, the local community, the metropolitan center, the metropolitan region, and so on up to the level of society at large.[6] But as Homans among others has demonstrated, the usefulness of the social-systems concept is not restricted by either the large or the small size of the interaction under consideration. He states:

The activities, interactions, and sentiments of the group members, together with the mutual relations of these elements with one another during the time the group is active, constitute what we shall call the *social system*. . . . Everything that is not part of the social system is part of the environment in which the system exists. Note that, as the definition of the group is relative, so must be that of the group's environment. If the group we are interested in is the Bank Wiring Observation Room, then the rest of the Hawthorne Plant is part of its environment, but if the Hawthorne Plant itself should be the group in question, then the environment would become everything outside this new system.[7]

In the analysis of administrative behavior, the concept of social system is applicable regardless of the level or magnitude of the system under consideration. For one purpose a given community may be taken as the social system, with the school, business enterprise, hospital, legislative body, and church as subsystems. For another purpose the school, the business, the hospital, the legislature, and the church may be regarded as social systems in their own right. For yet another purpose a classroom, business department, hospital ward, legislative committee, or church auxiliary may be considered a social system.

---

[5] Talcott Parsons, *The Social System*, New York, Free Press, 1951, pp. 5–6.
[6] Carr, *loc. cit.*
[7] G. C. Homans, *The Human Group*, New York, Harcourt, Brace & World, 1950, p. 87.

Analytic dimensions of the social system

For general analytic purposes, and more especially for the analysis of administrative processes, we may conceive of the social system as involving two classes of phenomena which are at once conceptually independent and phenomenally interactive: (1) the institutions, with certain roles and expectations, that will fulfill the goals of the system; and (2) the individuals, with certain personalities and dispositions, inhabiting the system, whose observed interactions comprise what we call social behavior. We shall assert that this behavior may be understood as a function of these major elements: institution, role, and expectation, which together constitute the nomothetic or *normative* dimension of activity in a social system; and individual, personality, and need-disposition, which together constitute the idiographic or *personal* dimension of activity in a social system.

In a sense, one dimension may be thought of as the "sociological" level of analysis; the other, as the "psychological" level of analysis. To understand the nature of observed behavior—and to be able to predict and control it—we must understand the character and interaction of these elements.

THE NORMATIVE (NOMOTHETIC) DIMENSION

The component conceptual elements of the normative dimension of a social system are institution, role, and expectation, each term serving as the analytic unit for the term next preceding it. We shall consider each concept in turn.

Institution. The term "institution" has had a variety of definitions. As early as 1929, Hertzler found over 25 different concepts included in various meanings given the term and attempted to weave these statements into a single formulation. He wrote:

> Thus institutions are (1) "ways in which a people behave or act," "apparatus of social life," "modes or organs," "forms of order," "systems of action"; (2) "well-adapted" for fulfilling socially necessary or desirable ends ("deliberately approved ends"), or for carrying on "some particular function" in the community as a whole or some special part of it; (3) taking the form of "usages (or complexes thereof) governing certain social relations of men," or "organized forms of social activity" or "systems of relationship," "groupings," "sets of activities"; or, if social psychologically expressed, taking the

form of "definite and established phases of the public mind" or "states of mind"; (4) made "relatively permanent and formal," "recognized and established," "sanctioned," "systematized," "prized, defended, perpetuated, and if need be, enforced"; (5) "by the authority of communities," or "by some common will," or "by groups," or "by society"; and (6) concretely expressed in "social habits," "overt activities," and "similar and reciprocal habits of individual behavior."[8]

All social systems, it is sufficient to point out for present purposes, have certain imperative functions that come in time to be accomplished in relatively routinized patterns. The functions—in communities, for example, the functions of governing, educating, policing, and so on—may be said to have become "institutionalized," and the agencies established to carry them out for the social system as a whole may be called institutions.

Institutions generally have at least five basic properties:

1. *Institutions are purposive.* Institutions come into being or are established to carry out certain goals. Thus, in the community as a social system, the home, the school, the chamber of commerce, the social welfare department, and so on are institutions for the maintenance and furtherance of the social system as a whole. Similarly, in the school as a social system within the community, the board of education, the faculty, the office of student counseling, the building and grounds department, the secretarial pool, and so on are institutions for the maintenance and furtherance of that social system as a whole. The purposes of the institution may be evaluated against the needs and goals of the social system, and the institutional practices may, in turn, be evaluated against the purposes of the institution. It is in this sense, for example, that one may think of certain institutional practices and indeed even total institutions as functional or dysfunctional to the social system. To cite but one instance for many, the cavalry just before World War II seems to have ceased to be functional. Probably all social systems retain some institutions that are as vestigial to the current functioning of the system as, say, the dermiform appendix is to the human body.

2. *Institutions are peopled.* If institutions are to carry out their functions, human agents are required. We are of course concerned here with people in their institutional and not personalistic sense. The selective criterion on which they are differentiated from their fellows is not what they are like or not like

---

[8] J. O. Hertzler, *Social Institutions*, New York, McGraw-Hill, 1929, p. 7.

idiosyncratically (a matter to which we shall turn in due course) but what they are supposed to do or not to do institutionally. To avoid confusion, we may adopt the term "actor" instead of "person" at this level of analysis. The selective nature of people in institutions has been described as follows:

> Like any social organization, an institutional organization is carried on by people who haven't come into organized relationships merely by chance.... Every social organization ... is a system of exclusion as well as inclusion. It keeps out as well as takes in—and to get in you have to conform to the institutional pattern: to set up a family, you marry; to join a business organization, you "buy in" or get hired in; to get into Congress as a member, you must be duly appointed or elected. Even to get into college you have to present the necessary "credits." There are all sorts of selective processes by which organizations pick and choose. The result in any specific case is always a selected personnel.[9]

3. *Institutions are structural.* To carry out a specific purpose requires some sort of organization, and organization implies component parts, with rules about how the parts should be interrelated. If the goals of the institution are known, the tasks to achieve them may be specified and organized into relevant *roles*. Each role is assigned certain responsibilities and concomitant resources, including authority, for implementing the tasks. Usually the table of organization or blueprint of roles and role relationships is set up *before* any real incumbents are selected for the roles; it is set up in terms of actors, in the sense previously defined. The actors, it is hoped, will perform their institutional functions by behaving in accordance with their roles. The issue of whether the real person does or does not fit the role in terms of the structure and goals of the institution poses one of the critical dilemmas of administration.

4. *Institutions are normative.* The fact that tasks for achieving the institutional goals are organized into prescribed roles implies that the roles serve as norms for the behavior of the role incumbents. Each actor must behave in more or less *expected* ways if he is to retain his legitimate place in the institution. Simon describes this normative aspect of institutions as follows: "It is a fundamental characteristic of social institutions that their stability and even their existence depend on expecta-

---
[9] Carr, *op. cit.*, p. 82.

tions of this sort. In so far as behavior of another person can be accurately predicted, it forms a portion of the objective environment, identical in its nature with the nonhuman portions of that environment."[10] Applying these considerations to the field of administration, as Simon did, we note that the administrative organization involves purposive behavior on the part of the participants, and that such behavior is guided by the reciprocal expectations—that is, the complementary rights and responsibilities—of the role incumbents as defined by institutional norms.

5. *Institutions are sanction-bearing.* The existence of norms is of no consequence unless there is adherence to them. Accordingly, institutions must have at their disposal appropriate positive and negative sanctions for insuring compliance, at least within broad limits, to the norms. On the negative side are expression of disapproval, withdrawal of cooperation, and direct infliction of punishment. On the positive side are praise, rewards, and the granting of special perquisites for conformity and institutional achievement. More than this, as Parsons points out, insofar as influence on the action of others becomes an institutionalized expectation of a role, we have the roots of *authority*. That is, one role incumbent has the right to impose "coercive" sanctions on another who fails to act as the former has an institutionalized right to expect him to act. In a strict sense, every member of a social system has some authority. Even the lowliest feels justified in resisting—at least passively—"unreasonable" demands upon him. In effect, he says, "If you do this, I won't do thus and so" (something expected). This surely looks like coercive sanction. In common usage, however, the term "authority" is restricted to the superordinate members of the administrative hierarchy. We speak, for example, of managerial authority over workers but not of workers' authority over their managers, just as we speak of parental authority over children and not of children's authority over their parents.[11]

Role. The most important analytic unit of the institution is the role. Like "institution," the term "role" has received a multitude of definitions. Indeed, one review of the literature claims to

---

[10] Herbert A. Simon, *Administrative Behavior*, New York, Macmillan, 1945, p. 252.
[11] Talcott Parsons, *Essays in Sociological Theory*, rev. ed., New York, Free Press, 1954, pp. 392–393.

have found the term used in more than a dozen different ways.[12]

In general, there seem to be three distinct categories of usage: (1) In relation to personality development, one may speak of the child's learning certain roles or aspects of roles. Thus, the process of socialization has been viewed as the successive identification with appropriate age, sex, and other relevant roles. (2) In relation to society as a whole, role has been regarded as synonymous with patterns of observed behavior. Thus, Kingsley Davis writes in *Human Society*, "How an individual actually performs in a given position, as distinct from how he is supposed to perform, we call his role."[13] Sarbin similarly states that role is simply what a person does—"a patterned sequence of learned *actions* or deeds performed by a person in an interaction situation."[14] (3) In relation to specific groups or institutions in a social system, roles may be thought of as the structural or normative elements defining the behavior expected of role incumbents or actors, that is, their mutual rights and obligations. In this sense, it is what is supposed to be done in order to carry out the purposes of the system rather than what is actually done that defines the institutional role. As Parsons and Shils say, "The role is that organized sector of an actor's orientation which constitutes and defines his participation in an interactive process. It involves a set of complementary expectations concerning his own actions and those of others with whom he interacts."[15] Even if some particular judges were dishonest, or even if *all* judges in a particular community were dishonest, the role of judge as a structural and normative point of orientation within the legal institution would not thereby be altered to include behaving dishonestly ("injudiciously"). Indeed, one way the judges' dishonesty would be measured is by the discrepancy between the observed behavior and the expected behavior, that is, between the performance and the role.

It is the third definition of role that seems to us most useful for the analysis of administrative behavior. Thus conceived, role has a number of notable characteristics.

---

[12] L. J. Neiman and J. W. Hughes, "The Problem of the Concept of Roles— A Re-Survey of the Literature," *Social Forces*, 30 (December, 1951), 141–149.
[13] Kingsley Davis, *Human Society*, New York, Macmillan, 1949, p. 90.
[14] T. R. Sarbin, "Role Theory," in Gardner Lindzey, ed., *Handbook of Social Psychology*, Reading, Mass., Addison-Wesley, 1954, vol. I, p. 225.
[15] Talcott Parsons and Edward A. Shils, eds., *Toward a General Theory of Action*, Cambridge, Mass., Harvard University Press, 1951, p. 23.

1. *Roles represent positions, offices,* or *statuses within an institution.* Linton has described this aspect of role most clearly:

> A status, as distinct from the individual who may occupy it, is simply a collection of rights and duties....
>
> A *role* represents the dynamic aspect of a status. The individual is socially assigned to a status and occupies it with relation to other statuses. When he puts the rights and duties which constitute the status into effect, he is performing a role. Role and status are quite inseparable, and the distinction between them is of only academic interest. There are no roles without statuses or statuses without roles.[16]

The relation between status and role has been much debated, but we would agree with Linton that it is of only academic interest. More important is the idea that a role exists only within a particular social system, represents a particular position within that system, and implies a pattern of more or less obligatory behavior on the part of the role incumbent in relation to other role incumbents in the system. Persons who act within the framework of that social system thus find their activities at least broadly organized by the role structure of the system.

2. *Roles are defined in terms of role expectations.* A role has certain normative rights and duties, which we may call role expectations. When the role incumbent puts these rights and duties into effect, he is said to be performing in his role. The expectations define what the actor, whoever he may be, should or should not do under various circumstances while occupying the particular role in the social system.

In this sense Sarbin is exactly right when he says, "A position in a social structure is equivalent to an organized system of role expectations."[17] On the one hand, the person in a given social system acts in a particular way by virtue of the role he occupies; on the other, he legitimately expects the other persons in the system to act in particular ways by virtue of the roles they occupy. These expectations are not directly seen but, as Sarbin makes clear, must be inferred from phenomenological report or from the analysis of other kinds of data. At the most general level, there are two kinds of expectations: rights and duties. In a way, the rights of one role incumbent in a system are the duty

---

[16] Linton, *op. cit.*, pp. 113–114.
[17] Sarbin, *op. cit.*, p. 226.

of another; the duties of the other are the right of the one. A child has a right to protection by his mother, and the mother has a duty to provide protection for her child.[18]

3. *Role expectations are institutional givens.* Role expectations are ordinarily formulated before the actors who will serve as the role incumbents are known. They are usually the "givens" in the institution, not "made to order" for specific individuals. Although the expectations may be misperceived or even serve as points of departure for any particular role incumbent, their crucial significance as blueprints of what *should* be done is not thereby nullified. In rigidly established and formal organizations —say, in a religious order—the group interaction is obviously guided along predetermined lines and is related at least initially more to the defined role than to the individual per se. In less rigidly established and less formal organizations—say, in a university—an attempt is made from the beginning not only to "fit the man to the job" but to "fit the job to the man." Generally speaking, however, as Krech and Crutchfield point out, "When a man takes a new job or joins a fraternity or enters a military unit, his relations to his superiors, inferiors, and associates are, to a very considerable extent, predetermined for him."[19]

4. *Roles are more or less flexible.* The behaviors associated with a role may be thought of as lying along a continuum from "required" to "prohibited." Certain expectations are held to be crucial to the role. The appropriate behaviors are mandatory; other behaviors are forbidden. Between the extremes lie other activities, some of which would perhaps be encouraged and others discouraged, but all of which would be considered permissible, at least in the ordinary case. Their exact nature is a function of the particular incumbent. Parsons and Shils have described the flexibility of roles as follows:

> An important feature of a large proportion of social roles is that the actions which make them up are not minutely prescribed and that a certain range of variability is regarded as legitimate. Sanctions are not invoked against deviance within certain limits. This range of freedom makes it possible for actors with different personalities to fulfill within considerable limits the expectations associated with roughly the same roles without undue strain.[20]

---
[18] *Ibid.*
[19] D. Krech and R. S. Crutchfield, *Theory and Problems of Social Psychology*, New York, McGraw-Hill, 1948, p. 372.
[20] Parsons and Shils, *op. cit.*, p. 24.

5. *Roles are complementary.* Roles are interdependent in that each role derives its meaning from other related roles in the institution. In a sense, a role is a prescription not only for the role incumbent but also for those in other roles within the organization, so that, as we have already observed, the rights of one role may be the obligations of a second interlocking role. Indeed, the expectations for the first role may to some extent form the sanctions for the expectations for the second. For example, the role of sergeant and the role of private in the army cannot really be defined or implemented except in relation to each other. Similarly, parent-child, patient-doctor, foreman-worker, teacher-pupil roles cannot readily be understood apart from each other. This quality of complementariness fuses two or more roles into a coherent, interactive unit and makes it possible for us to conceive of an institution or a social system as having a characteristic structure.

6. *Roles vary in scope.* The range of expectations involved in a given role relationship may be defined with reference to two types of interaction: functionally diffuse and functionally specific. These types of interaction describe the number and quality of rights and obligations legitimately included as matters for allocation and interaction among the role incumbents.[21] In functionally diffuse interaction the role incumbents are intimately bound in such a way that the rights and obligations of the participants are taken for granted and are in a sense limitless. In functionally specific interaction the rights and obligations are restricted to those elements in the relationship that are defined by the technical competence and the institutional status of the participants. There are exact boundaries beyond which the role incumbents may not venture without getting out of the sphere of the legitimate expectations binding the roles into a functional unit within the institution. In the functionally diffuse relationship it is necessary to prove that a particular expectation is *not* within the province of the relationship; in the functionally specific relationship it is necessary to prove that a particular expectation *is* within the province of the relationship.

Most administrative relationships, at least as defined by the institutional givens to which we have already referred, are set up in functionally specific terms. The legitimate relationships between boss and secretary, officer and enlisted man, foreman

---
[21] *Ibid.*, pp. 57–58.

and worker are defined by the expectations characteristic of their institutional roles. But this is the administrative dilemma: The functionally specific relationships tend to drift into functionally diffuse relationships. The boss may come to demand special favors of the secretary, and the secretary of the boss; the officer may command certain personal services from the enlisted man, and the enlisted man to anticipate extra privileges from the officer; the foreman may casually send the office boy around the corner for his lunch, and the office boy may be helpless to refuse but bitterly resentful because such errands are not part of his job. In short, despite the institutional requirement of functional specificity, because of personal involvements the administrative relationship sometimes develops unavoidable patterns of functional diffusion. Although this circumstance is by no means an inevitable evil, and may in fact even become a virtue, it does pose problems for the administrator.

Expectation. We have already observed that the components of the normative dimension of a social system are institution, role, and expectation, each concept serving as the analytic unit for the concept immediately preceding it. A social system may be described by the component institutions, the institutions by the component roles, the roles by the component expectations. Since the nature of expectations has already been described in some detail in the preceding discussion of roles, we need only summarize the most general definition here. In the present framework, expectations are those rights and duties, privileges and obligations—in a word, those prescriptions—that delineate what a person should and should not do under various circumstances as the incumbent of a particular role in a social system. When the role incumbent acts in accordance with these expectations, he is said to be performing his role in the social system.

This level of analysis points to only one determinant—the normative—of behavior in a social system, and there is obvious slippage between the normative and the phenomenal. But to say that it deals with only one determinant and to recognize the slippage in no way derogates the power of the level of analysis. Indeed, for certain types of understanding, prediction, and control of activity this is exactly the right level of abstraction. If we know the institutions, roles, and expectations in a given system, we can make some rather accurate conjectures about the nature of the behavior in that system without reference to any of the actual people involved.

For example, when visiting a military base, we generally know what the hierarchical structure, or "pecking order" will be —who will make what decisions for whom and why—regardless of the age, sex, social class, personality type, or needs of the particular individuals in the situation. Further, we can even say something about what are ordinarily rather personal matters, such as the clothing that will be worn, who will get off the sidewalk for whom, where various persons will reside—and again usually without reference to age, sex, social class, personality type, or individual need. We can predict with reasonable accuracy who will get the big house on the hill, even if he has no children, and who will get the little house down in the ditch, even if he has a dozen children. We would be mightily surprised if the enlisted man got the place on the hill, and the general the house in the ditch. That is, we would be surprised if in that system the personal need, even with the ability to pay, took precedence over the institutional role.

This type of analysis is perhaps more immediately applicable to a rigid organization than to a more flexible one, although we do not intend to imply that the military organization is inevitably rigid and the civilian organization invariably flexible. But, at least for the purpose of further exploration, the study of behavior in a social system in terms of the concepts of institution, role, and expectation can contribute to our understanding of the administrative processes in the system, whether it be military, industrial, or educational, if not everywhere with the same power and precision. This dimension is represented schematically in Figure 3–1.

Social System → Institution → Role →
Expectation → Institutional Goal Behavior

FIGURE 3–1. *The normative dimension.*

THE PERSONAL (IDIOGRAPHIC) DIMENSION

To this point, role incumbents have been conceived as only actors (or, as may be said, robots programmed by institutional expectations) devoid of personalistic or other individualizing characteristics, as if all incumbents were exactly alike and implemented a given role in exactly the same way. But social systems are inhabited by living people with hates and loves, fears and aspirations. Roles are filled by flesh-and-blood individuals, no two of whom are quite alike. Each individual stamps the role he occupies with the unique style of his own pattern of expressive behavior. Social action is a function not only of public mandate but of private necessity, and mandate and necessity may not coincide. Not all administrators administer, not all teachers teach, not all students study—at least not in the same way. Even in the case of the relatively inflexible roles of officer and enlisted man, no two officers and no two enlisted men fulfill their roles in precisely the same way. Sometimes they fulfill them in very different ways, and on occasion they choose not to fulfill them at all.

To understand the specific behavior and social interaction of *particular* role incumbents, it is not enough to know the nature of the roles and expectations—although, to be sure, their behavior cannot be understood apart from these. We must also know the nature of the individuals inhabiting the roles and their modes of perceiving and reacting to the expectations. That is, in addition to the normative or nomothetic aspects of social behavior, we must consider the personal or idiographic aspects. We must, in short, attempt to integrate the individual or psychological level of analysis with the institutional or sociological level of analysis.

Now, just as we were able to break down the institutional dimension into the component elements of role and expectation, so we may break down the individual dimension into the component elements of personality and need-disposition.

Personality. Despite its common usage, the term "personality," like "institution" and "role," has had a variety of meanings. Personality remains an inordinately elusive concept. Indeed, some years ago Gordon Allport reported finding some fifty different definitions of it, and he confessed that he might have missed a few.[22] In general, however, the more widely applied definitions in psychology and perhaps in the behavioral sciences may be classified in three main categories: (1) personality as the totality of what can be observed about an individual, including his habitual behavior; (2) personality as the external-stimulus value of one individual for another individual or group; and (3) personality as the internal motivational system of an individual that determines his unique reactions to the environment.[23]

---

[22] Gordon W. Allport, *Personality*, New York, Holt, Rinehart and Winston, 1937, p. 50.
[23] J. W. Getzels, "Methods Used to Study Personality," *Journal of the National Association of Deans of Women, 16* (1953), 154–158.

1. *Personality as the Totality of Behavior.* Typical of this conception of personality is the one by John B. Watson, who defines personality as the individual's "reaction mass" as a whole.[24] From this point of view, personality is the sum total of one's habitual behavior. In this category may also come such formulations of personality as the totality of a person's roles and as "everything a person is or does." An instance of the latter definition is given by Menninger: "As we shall use it, [personality] means the individual as a whole, his height and weight and loves and hates and blood pressure and reflexes; his smiles and hopes and bowed legs and enlarged tonsils. It means all that anyone is and all that he is trying to become."[25] This conception of personality does not seem to us very fruitful, at least not for our purposes, and we agree with Allport, who reacted to this class of definitions as follows:

> Such omnibus definitions render absolutely no service to science. They are glib and reckless, and at best define merely by *enumeration*. They omit the most outstanding phenomenon of all mental life, namely, the presence of *orderly arrangement*. The mere cataloguing of ingredients defines personality no better than the alphabet defines lyric poetry.[26]

2. *Personality as Social Stimulus Value.* Typical of this conception of personality is the definition by Mark May: "Personality is the social stimulus value of an individual. It is the responses made by others to the individual as a stimulus that defines his personality."[27] There are numerous specifications for this basic position. In one, for example, personality is considered to be those "habits or actions which successfully influence other people"; in another, the sum total of the effect made by an individual upon society.[28] These views of personality are open to serious objection on at least two grounds. For one thing, they invite the perilous distinction between "more" and "less" personality, and with it the practice of talking about someone's "having lots of personality" or "having no personality" on the basis of his

---

[24] John B. Watson, *Psychology from the Standpoint of a Behaviorist*, Philadelphia and London, Lippincott, 1919, p. 420.
[25] Karl Menninger, *The Human Mind*, New York, Knopf, 1930, p. 21.
[26] Allport, *op. cit.*, p. 44.
[27] Mark A. May, "The Foundations of Personality," in P. S. Achilles, ed., *Psychology at Work*, New York, Whittlesey House, McGraw-Hill, 1932, p. 83.
[28] H. C. Link, *The Return to Religion*, New York, Macmillan, 1936, p. 89.

degree of social effectiveness. In this sense, as Allport points out, a movie queen seen by millions of people "would have incomparably 'more' personality than the complex and tortured poet dwelling in attic obscurity."[29] For another thing, the value of a stimulus is not determined by the nature of the stimulus alone, but by the character of the respondent as well. Quite often it is determined more by the latter than by the former. The social stimulus value of Lenin is not the same for an American as for a Russian; the social stimulus value of a Negro is not the same for a Southerner as for a Northerner; the social stimulus value of your mother is not the same for you as for your neighbor. In short, the social stimulus value of individual A for individual B and for individual C may be more a function of the personalities of individual B and individual C than of the personality of individual A, that is, the personality in question. What in A is fair for B may be foul for C. This is not to say that social impact is not an important feature of what we want to know about people—witness our interest in the ratings made by others when we are evaluating someone. But reputation is not personality. The social stimulus aspects of an individual as such cannot be made the core of a serviceable conception of personality. Again, it may perhaps be safer to add, at least not for the type of analysis we are attempting.

3. *Personality as Motivational System*. Typical of this conception of personality is the classic definition by Allport: "Personality is the dynamic organization within the individual of those psychophysical systems that determine his unique adjustments to his environment."[30] This is essentially the conception we shall adopt, but with one significant modification, or really specification. The term "psychophysical systems" does not seem to have any exact referent, Allport himself regarding them rather ambiguously as "habits, specific and general attitudes, sentiments, and dispositions of other orders."[31] We shall instead use Parsons and Shils' term, "need-dispositions," by which we shall mean both the affective needs to seek out certain types of experiences and activities and the cognitive dispositions, and we may add capacities to structure the experience and activities in certain ways. Our definition of personality, then, is as follows:

---
[29] Allport, *op. cit.*, p. 41.
[30] *Ibid.*, p. 48.
[31] *Ibid.*

Personality is the dynamic organization within the individual of those need-dispositions and capacities that determine his unique interaction with the environment.

The key terms in this definition may be further defined:

a. *Dynamic organization.* As Allport puts it, "To escape from the sterile enumerations of the omnibus definitions it is necessary to stress active organization.... Yet this organization must be regarded as constantly evolving and changing, as motivational and self-regulating; hence the qualification 'dynamic.' "[32]

b. *Need-dispositions.* We have already indicated the double function of this term in suggesting both the affective sets and cognitive styles that impel the individual to behave in certain ways and not in others. In Parsons and Shils' terms, "The conjoined word *need-disposition* itself has a double connotation; on the one hand, it refers to a tendency to fulfill some requirement of the organism, a tendency to accomplish some end state; on the other hand, it refers to a disposition to do something with an object designed to accomplish this end state."[33]

c. *Determine.* Personality is not synonymous with behavior, any more than role is; nor is it merely the impression the behavior makes on others. It is instead a conception of what "lies *behind* specific acts and *within* the individual."[34] The systems constituting personality are "determining tendencies" impelling the individual toward particular expressive and cognitive activities.

d. *Unique.* We have pointed out that every human act is in somewise unique. No two people can do exactly the same thing in exactly the same way. Even the most restrictively defined role makes some provision for individual differences. In this sense the term "unique" is redundant in the present formulation. It becomes important, however, as we shall see, in the empirical study of systematic variations among individuals in relation to others and to their particular roles in a given social system.

e. *Interaction.* We consider personality not merely "adjustive," as may be inferred (erroneously, we believe) from Allport's definition, but *interactive.* That is, personality is capable not only of responding when prodded by stimuli from the environment

---

[32] *Ibid.*
[33] Parsons and Shils, *op. cit.*, p. 115.
[34] Allport, *op. cit.*, p. 48.

but of initiating interaction with the environment on its own account. The view of personality as a homeostatic mechanism moving only to adjust to stimuli does not cover all the observations about human beings. Exploratory and innovative acts may indeed be seen as adjustive in the face of certain noxious stimuli. But they are not that alone. The scientist, for example, who poses the question, "What would happen if . . . ?"; the artist who asks of himself, "What would it look like if . . . ?"; and the administrator who says, "Why not try this . . . ?" are not merely adjusting to stimuli impinging upon them from the environment but seem instead to be seeking—no, creating—stimuli within the environment with which to interact. It is in this sense that personality must be seen as interacting with or, perhaps even better, acting upon the environment as well as adjusting (and maladjusting) to it.[35]

f. *Environment.* It is of course obvious that by environment we mean not only the surrounding geographical setting, the objects and individuals in the setting, and the culturally structured and shared symbols but also the available roles and statuses, the rights and duties—in a word, the expectations—which, as Simon rightly suggests, form a portion of the objective environment equivalent to the nonhuman portion.

Need-Disposition. Central to the foregoing dynamic definition of personality are the analytic elements that have been referred to as need-dispositions. Just as role may be defined by the component expectations, so personality may be defined by the component need-dispositions. The following generalizations describe need-dispositions.

1. *Need-dispositions are conceived as forces within the individual.* Every human being has a characteristic style of life. Not only is he a creature of his biological drives or animal necessities, but he strives to fulfill wants having no apparent relationship to the maintenance of merely physiological well-being. He seeks to know and to discover, to create and to master, to achieve and to affiliate, to dominate and to comply, beyond what is needed to remain alive. An artist perseveres despite rebuffs; an anchorite forswears all earthly pleasures; a test pilot risks life and limb. Each is expressing himself in some particular

---
[35] *Ibid.*, p. 50.

way, reflecting what is said to be at least in part his personality.[36]

If we study the actions of an infant, we observe that initially almost its entire behavior is given over to the gratification of primary drives. But in due course there is a change: It reaches out for certain objects and displays certain types of behavior which cannot by any stretch of the imagination be seen as fulfilling only some immediately recognized biological requirement. The infant is becoming a child and is gaining a pattern of characteristic tendencies and modes of behavior—a personal identity.

The forces underlying these distinctive modes of behavior have been conceptualized in numerous ways. Among the more familiar concepts are *preference, interest, attitude, drive, need*, and *need-disposition*. These concepts overlap, and in some ways the use of one as against another is a semantic issue. Nonetheless, an attempt to differentiate among them, especially with respect to need-disposition, may lead to a better understanding of the conception of personality utilized here.

Let us first distinguish between a preference and an interest as related to need-disposition. One may have a preference for an object without having any interest in it. He may, for example, prefer broccoli to asparagus but not have any interest in either. He would not expend even a tiny effort to acquire or learn more about the one than the other. The difference between a preference and an interest is that a preference is relatively passive whereas an interest is dynamic. Preference implies a readiness to *receive* one object rather than another; it does not induce the *seeking out* of the object. In this sense, a need-disposition is more akin to an interest than a preference.

Again, to use interest as the point of departure, neither an interest nor a need-disposition is merely a *positive attitude*. One may have a positive attitude toward the Eskimos without having any particular interest in them. In contrast, one may have a decidedly negative attitude toward the Soviets but be keenly interested in them. An attitude implies a readiness to react in a particular direction with respect to a given object. We do not

---

[36] Portions of this section are drawn from J. W. Getzels, "The Nature of Reading Interests: Psychological Aspects," in H. M. Robinson, ed., *Developing Permanent Interest in Reading*, Proceedings of the Annual Conference on Reading Held at the University of Chicago, 1956, *Supplementary Educational Monographs*, Chicago, University of Chicago Press, 1956, vol. XVIII, pp. 5–9.

ordinarily speak of being driven by an attitude; we are necessarily driven by our interests. In this sense also, a need-disposition is more akin to an interest than an attitude, for it too is a force not only waiting to be "triggered" by an external stimulus but being itself a "trigger" to action.

One more distinction may be useful before we turn specifically to the nature of needs and need-dispositions as forces. There is a difference between a drive and an interest. A drive has its source in a particular physiological disequilibrium, and the individual seeks conditions that will reduce the drive or supply the lack. An interest has its source in experience and challenges us to exert ourselves even though there is no necessity in any biological sense. Technically, a drive is a function largely of instinctual or biological processes; an interest, largely of learned or acquired processes.

It is here that interest and need or need-disposition are most sharply differentiated. An interest may be defined as a characteristic tendency, organized through experience, which impels an individual to seek out particular objects, activities, understandings, and skills for attention or acquisition. A need, as Murray points out, may have its source in viscerogenic as well as experiential processes, not only impelling the individual to attend to or acquire some *particular* object, but underlying a *whole range* of behavior, both real and fantasied.[37] In its essentials this definition of need as a force seeking appeasement through fantasy or manifest behavior is also what we mean by need-disposition. But as it stands, the formulation seems to us deficient in a salient respect. It is too deeply embedded in a drive-reduction framework, with consequent overemphasis on the immediate gratification aspects of human motivation and underemphasis on the longer-term directional aspects of human motivation. For these reasons the concept of need-disposition, which is of course a derivative of the need construct, also stressing the ultimate motivating force of personality but with the double connotation of directionality as well as gratification, seems to us preferable.

2. *Need-dispositions are goal-oriented.* Need-dispositions refer to tendencies to achieve some end state. As Kluckhohn and Murray say, "Conforming with Lewin and many others, we may use the term 'need' or 'need-disposition' to refer to the roughly measurable 'force' in the personality which is coordinating activ-

[37] Henry A. Murray *et al., Explorations in Personality,* New York, Oxford University Press, 1938, pp. 123–124.

ities in the direction of a roughly definable goal; and we may use the term 'aim' to refer to this need's *specific* goal (to be achieved perhaps in association with a *specific* object in a *specific* place at a *specific* time)." For example, a man may be motivated by a general *need* for dominance (power, authority, leadership, a decision-making role, an administrative position, and so on), but his *aim* at a particular time may be to persuade residents of Bordeaux to elect him mayor of that city.[38] This is precisely our meaning when we say that both the immediate gratifications and long-term directionality of behavior are related to the individual's need-disposition. In the instance cited, the long-term directionality of the individual's behavior is given by the need-disposition for dominance, and the immediate gratification of being elected mayor may be understood as a function of this enduring aspect of his personality.

3. *Need-dispositions are determinants of cognitive and perceptual as well as of other forms of behavior.* Need-dispositions influence not only the goals an individual will try to attain in a particular environment but also the way he will perceive and cognize the environment itself. A person with a high need for dominance tends to structure the environment in terms of its opportunities for ascendance; a person with a high need for affiliation, in terms of its opportunities for sociability; and a person with a high need for cognizance, in terms of its opportunity for understanding. For the first, a university is primarily a place where it is possible to rise in the hierarchy; for the second, a place to seek friendships; for the third, a place to pursue studies.

Consider in this connection two early and now classic laboratory experiments on the effect of need-dispositions on perception and cognition. McClelland and Liberman[39] investigated the influence of need for achievement on the perception of need-related words. They found that subjects with high "n Achievement" recognized positive achievement words such as "success" and "strive" faster than subjects with low "n Achievement." In effect, there was selective perception as a function of need-

---

[38] H. A. Murray and C. Kluckhohn, "Outline of a Conception of Personality," in C. Kluckhohn, H. A. Murray, and D. M. Schneider, eds., *Personality in Nature, Society, and Culture*, 2nd ed., New York, Knopf, 1953, p. 15.

[39] Reported in D. C. McClelland, "Measuring Motivation in Phantasy: The Achievement Motive," in H. Guetzkow, ed., *Groups, Leadership, and Men*, Pittsburgh, Penn., Carnegie Press, 1951, pp. 191–205.

dispositions. Atkinson[40] studied the influence of "n Achievement" as a personality characteristic on the memory for completed and incompleted tasks. He found that for subjects high in this need the number of incompleted tasks recalled regularly *increased*, whereas for subjects moderate in this need the number of incompleted tasks recalled *decreased*. Again there was selective cognition—in this case reflected in the memory process—as a function of need-disposition.

The influence of need-dispositions on perception and cognition is of the greatest moment in understanding role behavior. It suggests that a person not only will seek a particular role in accordance with his personality but when assigned to *any* role will tend consciously or unconsciously to perceive, cognize, and order it at least partially in accordance with his need-dispositions. When the expectations of the role and the need-dispositions of the individual are congruent, there is no discrepancy between what the person wants and what the role requires. Those in complementary roles see eye to eye regarding their mutual rights and obligations, with consequent clarity in communication and unity in purpose. When the expectations and need-dispositions are incongruent, there *is* discrepancy between what the individual wants and what the role requires. Those in complementary roles do not see eye to eye regarding their mutual rights and obligations, with consequent failure in communication and loss in unity of purpose.

4. *Need-dispositions vary in specificity.* Just as roles and the component expectations may vary in functional specificity or diffusion, so may need-dispositions vary in the specificity or generality of objects through which they find expression. The relationship between a need-disposition and an object (or role) may be described in terms of two alternatives. In one case the significance of the object for the individual depends on its membership in a general class, so that any object conforming to this class is equally appropriate for engagement by the particular need-disposition. That is, the need can find satisfaction through a range of objects, situations, or roles. Parsons and Shils refer to this as the "universalistic alternative."[41] In the other case, the significance of the object rests on its standing in a particular relationship to the given need-disposition. The need-disposition can find satisfaction only through a particular object, situation,

---

[40] Reported in McClelland, *ibid*.
[41] Parsons and Shils, *op. cit.*, p. 117.

or role, and no other objects, situations, or roles will serve. Parsons and Shils refer to this as the "particularistic alternative."[42]

Murray and Kluckhohn have also commented on the specificity and generality of needs in relation to objects. They state:

> A need is a general disposition which commonly becomes associated (through "focalization," or "canalization," as Murphy would say) with a number of specific entities (e.g., a certain doll, or dog, or person, or group, or town, or theory, or work of art, or religion, etc.), and (through "generalization") with a number of *kinds* of (*semi-specific*) entities (e.g., French wines, or horses, or women, or music, or novels, or philosophies, etc.).
>
> These focalizations (specificities and semi-specificities) rarely exhaust the possibilities of need-activity. Unless the structure of the disposition has become rigid and fixated, it is always capable of becoming attached to a new object—new kind of food, new place, new acquaintance, new organization, new kind of art, new ideology. . . .[43]

This characteristic of need-dispositions has important consequences for behavior in social systems. Insofar as a need-disposition is general, it can find expression in a variety of situations, and the same person can move with ease into numerous roles. If, as we observed, a role is ordinarily flexible enough to permit effective performance by a variety of personalities, so personality is ordinarily flexible enough to function satisfactorily in a variety of roles. But the individual may give the variety of roles the singular style of his own personality. For example, whatever Churchill did (whether as statesman, soldier, or journalist) had his particular mark. This does not necessarily hinder and indeed it may enhance the role performance.

5. *Need-dispositions are patterned.* A final characteristic of need-dispositions is that they are patterned or interrelated. The needs are organized hierarchically (as well as patterned horizontally) to give personality a structure not explicable by the mere listing of the separate need attributes. A parallel may be drawn between the organization of expectations from greater to lesser immediacy in a given role and the organization of need-dispositions from greater to lesser immediacy in a given person-

---
[42] *Ibid.*
[43] Murray and Kluckhohn, *op. cit.*, pp. 19–20.

ality. Maslow describes this essential of personality rather nicely. He points out that the relation among needs is not that they exist randomly like a great many sticks lying around side by side, but that they lie like a nest of boxes, one box containing three others, each of these three containing ten others, each of these ten containing fifty others, and so on.[44] Just as the disturbance of one box changes in some wise the arrangement of the others, so the activation of one need affects in some wise the expression of the other needs. As Maslow says:

> ... the chief principle of organization in human motivational life is the arrangement of needs in a hierarchy of less or greater priority or potency. The chief dynamic principle animating this organization is the emergence of less potent needs upon gratification of the more potent ones. The physiological needs, when unsatisfied, dominate the organism, pressing all capacities into their service and organizing these capacities so that they may be most efficient in this service. Relative gratification submerges them and allows the next higher set of needs in the hierarchy to emerge, dominate, and organize the personality, so that instead of being, e.g., hunger obsessed, it now becomes safety obsessed. The principle is the same for the other sets of needs in the hierarchy, i.e., love, esteem, and self-actualization.[45]

Without in any way assenting to the specific hierarchy implied by Maslow, we do feel that need-dispositions are patterned vertically as well as horizontally. The satisfaction of one need has an effect on the activation of other needs. The significance of this interaction for understanding the flux of behavior in a social system is that the relationship between the individual and the institution—between the personality and the role—is not *static* but *dynamic*. Once having placed a person in an apparently suitable role (or for that matter even if the person has chosen the role himself), the administrator cannot just leave the matter there. The gratification of the need on which the initial "fit" was made may call out other needs that must be taken into account.

It is easy to sympathize with the employer who was heard to remark bitterly about an employee he had befriended, "When I took him in off the street starving, he thought the job was just great and he would remain forever, but now that he's had a couple of meals, he thinks what he's doing is not good enough for

---

[44] A. H. Maslow, *Motivation and Personality*, New York, Harper & Row, 1954, p. 70.
[45] *Ibid.*, p. 107.

him. He wants something interesting!" One must, however, also understand that the very gratification of the prior need may have activated other needs. That this causes some difficulties in organizational stability is self-evident. But it may also provide an impetus for greater achievement, for the satisfaction of needs at one level in the hierarchy, such as the need for *food* or *safety*, may activate needs at another level, such as those for *mastery* and *innovation*.

In focusing on need-dispositions as the central concept of personality we have in no way intended to derogate the significance of the other individualizing attributes of a person—his drives, attitudes, interests, perceptual styles, and cognitive abilities. A considerable amount of the actual empirical work in administration has in fact been done most profitably in exactly these other terms. And of course, as has already been revealed in the case of an individual's perceptions and his needs, and as can be shown for a number of the other attributes as well, these attributes are not dissociated from the person and his motivations. In any event, we are not suggesting that the formulation of personality in need-dispositional terms is the only possible formulation. It patently is not. We are suggesting that the concepts provided by the formulation have proved of heuristic value in similar contexts and are clearly relevant in the present context. This dimension is represented schematically in Figure 3–2.

Social System → Individual → Personality →
Need-Disposition → Individual Goal Behavior

FIGURE 3–2. *The personal dimension.*

Summary

For general analytic purposes, and especially for the analysis of administrative processes, we can conceive of administration as functioning within a social system framework. A social system involves two classes of phenomena that are at once conceptually independent and phenomenally interactive. One class constitutes the normative (or nomothetic) dimension of behavior, the other the personal (or idiographic) dimension of behavior.

Useful conceptual elements for the analysis of the normative dimension are institution, role, and expectation, each serving as the analytic element for the one immediately preceding it.

The administrative unit under consideration, whether it be a large industrial organization or a small group within the organization, an entire school or a single class within the school, can be thought of as a social system with characteristic institutions, roles, and expectations. The given administrative unit as a social system is related to the larger (or smaller) unit as a social system, which in turn is related to the next larger (or smaller) unit, and so on. Ideally, the goal behavior of one social system is "geared into" that of the related social systems. Within the single system, goal behavior is achieved through the integration of institutions, the definition of roles, and the setting of expectations for the performance of relevant tasks. In behaving according to the role expectations for him, the administrator "administers"; in behaving according to the role expectations for him, the worker "works."

Parallel conceptual elements for the analysis of the personal dimension are individual, personality, and need-disposition, each again serving as the analytic element for the one immediately preceding it. In the normative dimension, role incumbents were conceived as only "actors" or "robots programmed by institutional expectations," as it were, devoid of personalistic or other individualizing characteristics—as if all incumbents were exactly alike and implemented a given role in exactly the same way. But social systems are inhabited by living people with hates and loves, fears and aspirations, and roles are filled by flesh-and-blood individuals, no two of whom are quite the same. Each stamps the particular role he occupies with the unique style of his own characteristic pattern of expressive behavior. Not all administrators "administer," not all workers "work," not all teachers "teach," not all students "study"—at least not in the same way.

Here then are two components of behavior in a social system, the one conceived as arising in institutional goals and fulfilling role expectations, the other as arising in individual goals and fulfilling personality dispositions. The components may, of course, be at least in some degree congruent or incongruent. How do these dimensions of behavior—the normative and the personal—come together to produce the observed act? It is to this question that we turn in the following chapter.

4

A framework for the study of administrative behavior: the general model

Consider an example from the military. The roles are sergeant and private. Presumably *all* sergeants and *all* privates are required to conform exactly to the expectations for these roles as laid down in the Standard Operating Procedures. Yet no two sergeants and no two privates have precisely the same personality dispositions. In practice each individual will perform his role in a somewhat characteristic manner. Thus we may make an essential distinction in the performance of the same role by two sergeants, one of whom has a high need-disposition for "deference" and the other a high need-disposition for "ascendance." And we may make a similar distinction in the performance of their same role by two privates, one with a high need-disposition for deference and the other for ascendance. Moreover, there will be characteristic differences in the sergeant-private, sergeant-sergeant, and private-private interactions as well. Distinctions of a similar order must be understood in the role fulfillment and personal interaction among administrators and workers generally—where indeed the latitude for differences in role behavior as a function of personality is greater than in the military situation, which is in many ways a limiting case.

In short, as we have remarked before, to understand the performance and relations of specific role incumbents in a specific social system we must take into account both the role expectations and the need-dispositions. Needs and expectations may both be thought of as *substrata for behavior*, the one referable to personalistic sets and propensities, the other to role demands and privileges.

The articulation of role and personality

The preceding chapter defined in some detail the component aspects of (1) the normative dimension of behavior and (2) the personal dimension of behavior. Here we shall attempt to articulate the two, since, to reemphasize the point, observed behavior in a social system is always a function of the interaction between these dimensions. A given social act, that is, is an outcome of an inextricable combination of role and personality factors.[1] Getzels and Guba have represented the relationship pictorially, as indicated in Figure 4-1.

```
                 Normative (Nomothetic) Dimension
              Institution ────────► Role ────────► Expectation
Social       ▲   ⇅                  ⇅                    ⇅    ▲ Social
System       ▼                                                ▼ Behavior
              Individual ────────► Personality ──► Need-Disposition
                  Personal (Idiographic) Dimension
```

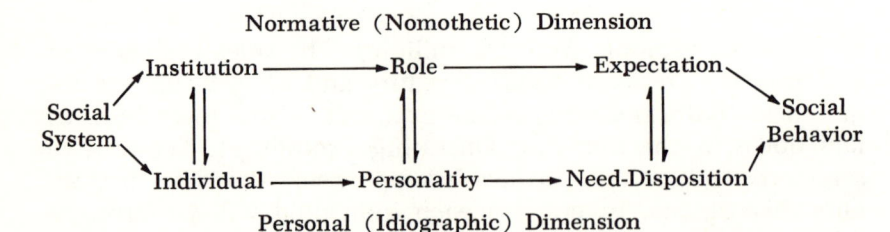

FIGURE 4-1. *The normative and personal dimensions of social behavior (Adapted from J. W. Getzels and E. G. Guba, "Social Behavior and the Administrative Process,"* School Review, 65 [1957], 429.)

The normative axis is shown at the top of the diagram. It consists of institution, role, and role expectation, each term being the analytic unit for the term preceding it. Thus, the social system is defined by its institutions, each institution by its constituent roles, and each role by the expectations attaching to it. Similarly, the personal axis, shown at the lower portion of the diagram, consists of individual, personality, and need-disposition, each term again serving as the analytic unit for the term preceding it.

A given act is conceived as deriving simultaneously from the normative and the personal dimensions, and performance in a social system as a function of the interaction between role and personality. That is to say, a social act may be understood as resulting from the individual's attempts to cope with an environment composed of patterns of expectations for his behavior in ways consistent with his own pattern of needs and dispositions. Thus we may write, by way of a shorthand notation, the general equation $B = f(R \times P)$, where B is observed behavior, R is a given institutional role defined by the expectations attaching to it, and P is the personality of the particular role incumbent defined by his need-dispositions.[2]

---

[1] J. W. Getzels and E. G. Guba, "Social Behavior and the Administrative Process," *School Review*, 65 (1957), 423-441.
[2] *Ibid.*, p. 429.

There is a crucial difference between this formulation and the famous equation, to which this one is indebted, given by Lewin:[3] $B = f(P \times E)$, where P is personality and E is environment—a difference that highlights the specific character of the framework we are describing. In Lewin's formula P and E are not independent, since one defines the other, environment being defined by the perception of the person. In the present formulation R and P are independent, because P is defined by internal processes within the role incumbent and R is defined by external standards set by others. In Lewin's formula E represents a personal life space which cannot be specified apart from the personality of the particular perceiver. In our formula R, which is of course E defined in terms of role expectations, must be specified apart from the personality of the particular perceiver. The role expectations are the givens (like the physical arrangements, for example) in the situation prior to any idiosyncratic role perceptions or role behaviors of the actual role incumbents.

To be sure, the expectations may be misperceived or may serve only as points of departure for the actual role incumbent—an issue to which we shall return in Chapter 10. But the crucial significance of the expectations as "blueprints" for what should be done is not thereby nullified. We could not recognize the misperceptions or misbehavior if there were not the prior givens. As has already been remarked, the fact that people assume judges take graft, or for that matter the fact that many judges do indeed take graft, or even if *all* judges in a particular community *took* graft, does not alter the expectation for the role of judge that he will not take graft. We would still continue to make the distinction between the expectation of honesty for the role and the disposition for dishonesty on the part of the role incumbent.

The proportion of role and personality factors at least potentially determining behavior will of course vary with the specific system, the specific role, and the specific personality involved. The general nature of the interaction is represented graphically in Figure 4-2. The interplay of factors entering into a given segment of behavior may be regarded as a proportion between normative and idiosyncratic variables represented by a line cutting through the role and personality possibilities represented by the rectangle. At the left (line A), the proportion of the act dictated by considerations of role expectations is relatively

---

[3] K. Lewin, *A Dynamic Theory of Personality*, New York, McGraw-Hill, 1935, chap. 3.

large, whereas the proportion of the act dictated by considerations of personality is relatively small. At the right (line C), the proportions are reversed, and considerations of personality become greater than considerations of role expectations. In these terms, generally speaking, the structure of behavior in a military organization would tend toward the left, in an artists' colony toward the right. On the one hand, the situation of an army private requires compliance almost entirely to role demands (line A); on the other, the situation of a free-lance artist permits a much wider opportunity for the expression of personality disposition (line C).

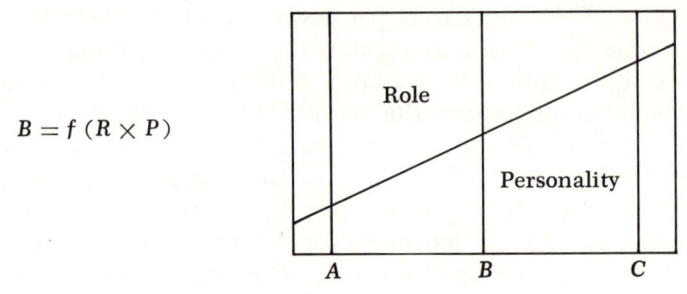

$$B = f(R \times P)$$

FIGURE 4–2. *Varying proportions of role and personality components in social behavior.* (Adapted from J. W. Getzels and E. G. Guba, "Social Behavior and the Administrative Process," School Review, 65 [1957], 430.)

Whether in the military organization or the artists' colony, or in any other social system, administration always deals with the proportions of the role and personality components of behavior. How much must be explicitly prescribed (and proscribed)? How much must be left to individual discretion (and indiscretion)?

In the military, to use the same example, much is prescribed (and proscribed); in the artists' colony much is left to individual discretion (and indiscretion). In educational organizations it could be hypothesized that the proportion of role and personality considerations might be balanced somewhere between the two (line B). But clearly, different educational systems are characterized by different proportions—Summerhill is probably quite different in this respect from Culver, and the typical theological seminary from, say, Reed or Bennington. It would in fact be interesting to do a systematic study of the consequences of one or the other for the functioning of the social system as a whole. Is there one pattern that is somehow "best"?

The foregoing, as we shall see in the sections on research and practice, by no means exhausts the possibilities for raising research and applied issues and clarifying observed administrative phenomena relative to role and personality. The point to be made here is that behavior, insofar as it is social—that is, within a particular social system—is a function of *both* role and personality, although the proportion of each may vary with the particular situation and the particular act. When role is maximized, behavior still retains some personal aspects because no role is ever so closely defined as to eliminate all individual latitude. When personality is maximized, social behavior still cannot be free from some role prescription. Indeed, the individual who divorces himself from such prescription is said to be autistic; he ceases to communicate with his group and may no longer be considered part of the given social system.

The dynamics of role-personality interaction

The preceding analysis focused on the structural elements of the social system with independently defined role expectations and independently defined personality dispositions. But the major problem of behavior in a social system involves this central issue: What are the dynamics of the interaction between the externally defined role expectations and the internally given need-dispositions? Or, to put the matter more concretely, the dual question may be asked: (1) How is it that in some organizations the role expectations seem generally understood and acquiesced in by all, so that role incumbents become aware of their rights and obligations and behave with respect to them with a minimum of strain, and in other organizations this is not the case? and (2) How is it that no matter what the organizational situation, some complementary role incumbents understand and agree at once on their mutual rights and obligations whereas others take a long time in reaching such agreement and quite frequently do not come to terms either with their roles or with each other?

Two relevant concepts may be brought to bear on these issues. One is the concept of *role-set* from sociological theory, as discussed by Merton.[4] The other is the concept of *selective per-*

---

[4] Robert K. Merton, *Social Theory and Social Structure*, rev. ed., New York, Free Press, 1957, pp. 368–384.

ception from psychological theory. The one tends to view the problem from the normative axis of behavior, the other from the personal axis of behavior.

ROLE-SETS

An important distinction may be made between multiple roles and role-set. The term "multiple roles" refers to the complex of roles and concomitant *independent* expectations associated with the various positions in which an individual finds himself—the same individual as teacher, father, deacon, and so on. Role-set refers to the pattern of role relationships and concomitant *complementary* expectations which an individual has by virtue of occupying a single position—the position of teacher necessarily entails role relationships with pupils, colleagues, administrators, and so on. Individuals are subject to pressures arising both from the conflictual expectations of their multiple roles and from their role-set in the given organization. We shall leave the problem of multiple roles for later and focus here only on the interactions among the individuals in a role-set.

That role-sets are almost inevitably liable to internal strain hardly needs documentation. Consider only the crosscurrents of expectations in the role-set of a teacher. There are expectations involving not only immediately related reference groups like pupils, colleagues, and administrators, but also parents, board members, and sometimes taxpayers, pressure groups, and almost anyone who wants to assert influence or who has an ax to grind. To minimize the potential conflict for the role incumbent, the expectations of the various reference groups must be articulated into a more or less specific and stable pattern of rights and obligations.[5]

Merton suggests a number of organizational mechanisms for articulation within a given role-set:

1. There are differential involvements among the individuals in the role relationships, so that certain expectations are not maintained by everyone in the role-set with *equal* intensity. For example, the parents may be more directly engaged in appraising the teacher's behavior than are the members of a taxpayers' group who have no children. The expectations of the parents and of the pressure group may be at odds, but the expectations of the

---

[5] M. G. Abbott, "Intervening Variables in Organizational Behavior," *Educational Administration Quarterly*, 1 (Winter, 1965), 1–14.

one are central to the teacher and of the other are only peripheral. This eases the problem for the teacher of defining his own role and coming to terms with the disparate expectations.

2. Although a role-set is likely to have more powerful and less powerful members, no one group can impose its expectations at will upon any other group or role incumbent—say, the teacher. Individuals subject to conflicting expectations in a role-set can effect *coalitions of power* which neutralize one another, giving the role incumbent relative freedom from conflicting pressures and permitting him to proceed as he wishes.

3. The individual does not engage in a continuous interaction with all other individuals in the role-set. Thus there is the possibility for role behavior which is at odds with the expectations of some of the reference groups to take place without strain. Taxpayers and even parents, for example, cannot barge into a classroom any old time. It is important to note that the *privacy* referred to here is a fact of the institutional structure and not the idiosyncratic disposition of some individuals to conceal parts of their role behavior from certain members of the role-set, which is another matter.

4. It is possible for the individual to make observable to others the conflicting demands and expectations and the disparities between his own wishes and the pressures upon him. As long as members of the role-set are unaware that their demands are contradictory, each member may press his own case from sheer "pluralistic ignorance." But when the conflict is made manifest, the pressure upon the given role incumbent may be relieved, and he may proceed as he is disposed to.

5. There is social support by other role incumbents in similar situations with similar difficulties in coping with an unintegrated role-set. Contradictions in the role-set are recognized not as unique to any one individual or any one situation, and the individual subject to these conflicts need not, therefore, meet them as a wholly personal problem to be handled in a wholly private fashion. As Merton points out, occupational and professional associations constitute one social response to the problem of coping with conflicting personal and organizational demands.[6]

In sum, from the institutional point of view, these are the conditions for maximizing integration and minimizing strain between the individual and his role and among the individuals

---
[6] Merton, *op. cit.*, pp. 371–379.

comprising a role-set: provision for differential involvement by the various role incumbents in the various institutional tasks; the possibility of neutralizing power under certain circumstances; the opportunity for periodic privacy from other individuals in the role-set; channels for making known conflicts in rights and obligations; and social support by others in similar roles and in similar situations. Under these conditions the integration of the individual in the social system is greater and the strain among the individuals less than when these conditions do not prevail.

Such institutional conditions are not, of course, the ultimate panacea. They are necessary, but not necessarily sufficient. The needs and dispositions of the individual role incumbents must also be considered, and this brings us to the psychological concept of *selective perception*.

SELECTIVE PERCEPTION

We may conceive of the prescribed normative relationship between any two complementary role incumbents in a role-set—the means and ends of the interaction between them as set forth in, say, a table of organization—as being enacted in two private situations, one embedded in the other. On the one hand, there is the prescribed relationship as perceived idiosyncratically and organized privately by one role incumbent in terms of his own needs, dispositions, and projections; on the other hand, there is the same prescribed relationship as perceived idiosyncratically and organized privately by the other role incumbent in terms of *his* needs, dispositions, and projections. That is, each individual structures the presumably common objective situation selectively.[7]

In this sense, if we may return to our example of the two sergeants, one with a high need for deference and the other with a high need for ascendance, and the two privates, one with a high need for deference and the other with a high need for ascendance, the objective situation of the prescribed roles and role relationships will be viewed by them *differentially*. The individuals with high need for deference, despite the difference in roles, may see the army situation and their position as a happy occasion for submitting to authority. The individuals with high need for ascendance, despite the difference in *their* roles, may

---

[7] J. W. Getzels, "A Psycho-Sociological Framework for the Study of Educational Administration," *Harvard Educational Review*, 22 (Fall, 1952), 235–246.

see the army situation and their position as a potential opportunity for rising in the hierarchy. The *internal* situations—what Lewin called the "life space"—of the individuals are related through those aspects of the existential public objects, symbols, values, and expectations which have to some extent a counterpart in the perceptions of both persons.

Indeed, when we say that two complementary role incumbents (such as a principal and a teacher, or a foreman and a worker, or for that matter two teachers, two principals, two foremen, or any two members of a role-set) understand each other, we mean that their perceptions and private organization of the mutual expectations overlap and are relatively congruent. When we say that they do not understand each other, we mean that their perceptions and private organization of the prescribed complementary expectations do not overlap and are incongruent.

The institutional integrative mechanisms to which we referred may increase the overlap and congruence of the two private situations—they cannot insure sameness. Further, since role behavior and, more specifically here, administrative activity function within interpersonal relationships, there is inevitably the problem of the personal or affective qualities in the selective perceptions of this relationship. Among the relevant issues here are the general institutional requirements for *universalistic* interpersonal relationships and the concrete individual tendencies toward *particularistic* interpersonal relationships.[8]

An interpersonal relationship is said to be particularistic when the nature of the interaction between the participants is determined by what they mean to each other personally rather than by the positions they hold or the roles they perform within the institution. Emotional rather than functional ties define the mutual rights and obligations. In the universalistic relationship matters are reversed. Emotional considerations are secondary to functional ones. Rights and obligations are determined on the basis of impersonal rather than personal factors. In the particularistic relationship the important question is *who* is involved. In the universalistic relationship the important question is *what* is involved.

Consider the ordinary money relationships between brother and brother, and between banker and client. In the banker-client relationship a request for money evokes the question "What is

---

[8] Talcott Parsons and Edward A. Shils, *Toward a General Theory of Action*, Cambridge, Mass., Harvard University Press, 1951, pp. 81–82.

the risk and what will it profit me?" Whether the one making the request is desperately in need of money is generally as irrelevant as whether the one receiving the request has more money than he will ever use. If, however, the parties to the transaction are brothers, the important questions are entirely different. They relate to how urgently one needs the money and whether the other has it to give. Factors of gain and risk fade into insignificance. Indeed, the same banker who will in the first case pride himself on hardheadedness will in the second case say that after all "blood is thicker than money." The banker-client relationship is predominantly universalistic; the brother-brother relationship, usually particularistic.

The administrative relationship in education, as in other "bureaucratic" institutions, is based on segmental functional rather than total emotional ties—at least according to the table of organization. The rights and obligations of the participants in the interaction are defined by official, not by affective, considerations, and factors of role competence are more important than factors of personal friendship. Decision-making and communication *nominally*—that is, according to the table of organization—take place in a formal hierarchy of offices independently of the personalities of the incumbents of the offices. The relationship is predicated on universalistic rather than particularistic standards.

In practice, however, the administrative act is carried on between flesh-and-blood individuals. Although the relationships may on paper or even initially be based on normative functional rather than idiographic personal grounds, the administrative interaction is in the final analysis between real people—real sergeants and real privates, real superintendents and real teachers—who have particular patterns of inner needs, *selective perceptions*, and preferred modes of social interaction. Ingroups and outgroups cutting across the formal role relationships develop; the distinction between *what* is involved and *who* is involved becomes difficult to maintain. The rights and obligations of both administrator and administered become at least in part a matter of particularistic rather than universalistic considerations. To cite a simple instance: In terms of universalistic criteria it becomes advisable to shift a number of teachers from one unit to another. But if the teachers have during the years of association with the principal become "friends" or "not friends," and the shift entails some personal hardship, the decision whether to shift this teacher or that teacher may be made consciously or unconsciously on the basis of other than purely institutional requirements.

We are not of course arguing that transformations from universalism to particularism are either ultimately "good" or "bad," "functional" or "dysfunctional" for the social system as a whole. The fact is that as a consequence of these transformations, if for no other reason (and as we have seen, there are a good many other reasons), the personal dimension gains importance as a significant variable in the administrative process. It therefore becomes necessary for the administrator to understand the dynamics of the role-personality interaction in his situation from the perspective of *both* the individual and the institutional axes of behavior.

Biological and cultural dimensions

Like all theoretical formulations, the present framework is an abstraction and, as such, an oversimplification of "reality." There is selective perception here too, as it were. Some determinants of social behavior and consequently of the administrative process have been brought into the foreground, others put into the background. A framework of social behavior that includes all possible factors from all possible points of view is quite inconceivable. Sociological analysis necessarily omits some psychological analysis, and psychological analysis some sociological analysis. Both neglect anthropological and biological factors which are clearly determinants of at least some aspects of the observed behavior under consideration. And even if we included, as in fact we shall, these four dimensions—the sociological, the psychological, the biological, and the anthropological—in a single framework, we would still be omitting such other recognizably pertinent sets of variables as the *political* and the *economic*. And we would still face the question of which specific concepts from each domain should be incorporated in the one scheme. In short, choices *must* be made in systematic analysis; indeed, even discursive phenomenological description entails choices of what to look at and what to report. If someone claims that he has looked at everything equally, the chances are that he has seen nothing clearly.

The salient issues, then, are *relevance* and *usefulness*, not comprehensiveness, although obviously that is significant. By focusing on the sociological dimension with the central concept of role and the psychological dimension with the central concept of personality, we have explicitly made a choice that these are crucially, albeit not exclusively, relevant and useful. There are other related and important dimensions for the understanding of social behavior, and it is to two of these, the *biological* and *cultural*, which in fact we have already mentioned, that we should like to turn now. We shall deal with the biological dimension quite briefly, since from the present point of view it is indirectly related to the systematic analysis of the administrative process. The cultural dimension, being more *directly* related to the analysis of the administrative process, will be discussed in greater detail.

THE BIOLOGICAL DIMENSION

Just as we may think of the individual in psychological-personalistic terms, so we may think of him in biological-constitutional terms. His personality is embedded, so to speak, in a biological organism with certain constitutional potentialities and abilities.[9]

Thus the individual may be seen as functioning at interdependent biological levels of behavior. As E. W. Bakke has noted, "The individual has parts" which can be classified as follows:

1. *Biological equipment* with its inherent capacities, providing the substantial biological instruments and the most basic source of energy for activity of all sorts.
2. *Impulses to activation* possessed by components of and organized aggregates of the biological equipment. These impulses are considered to activate the biological equipment toward the maintenance and expression of its inherent and developed capacities, and toward adaptation with objects in its environment (internal and external to the body). Such impulses bring components of the biological equipment into contact and experience with other components and with objects external to them. In the course of this *experience* they develop and acquire abilities.
3. *Abilities* of a physiological, psychological, and social sort, which may be classified as follows:
   a. Sensing and awareness abilities
   b. Doing abilities (for instance to maintain, mobilize, engage, utilize, persist, and produce)

---

[9] J. W. Getzels and H. A. Thelen, "The Classroom as a Unique Social System," in N. B. Henry, ed., *The Dynamics of Instructional Groups*, Fifty-ninth Yearbook of the National Society for the Study of Education, Chicago, University of Chicago Press, 1960, pp. 53–82.

A framework for the study of administrative behavior: the general model

    c. Feeling abilities
    d. Orienting abilities (for instance to differentiate, understand, relate, evaluate, select, resolve)
    e. Goal and objective defining abilities.
4. *Predispositions* are activity readinesses of a physiological, psychological, and social sort. Included in these are such items as reflexes, habits, attitudes, prejudices, convictions, sentiments, intentions.[10]

Our point in citing Bakke at length is not to acquiesce wholly in his particular set of "parts" but to provide an example of biological factors that have been specifically included in at least one formulation of organizational behavior. Our own emphasis is more akin to that of Parsons and Shils' attempt to relate the biological factors to the personality determinants in a social system. They write:

When we go beyond the description of an orientation and seek to explain what has occurred, the actor is not only a point of reference, but also definitely a system of action which we call personality. Even at this level, however, the internal, physiological process of the organism, although highly relevant to the concrete phenomena of action, is only relevant insofar as it affects the system of orientations. The physiological process will enter the picture as the source of the viscerogenic drive or energy of action and in various ways as part of the object system, as a system of qualities and of capacities for performance.[11]

From this point of view, it is on the one hand fatuous to insist on what is self-evident: the human being is a biological organism, and all his behavior must somehow be related to organic processes. But on the other hand, biological processes are not in themselves of central relevance in the analysis of social behavior and administrative interactions. The functioning of the liver or the strength of grip, although highly relevant to clinical analysis, is ordinarily irrelevant in social analysis. Either becomes relevant only insofar as it affects the personality dimension, and then it may of course be of preeminent importance. In this sense we must bear in mind that underlying individual behavior as represented by the psychological dimension is a biological dimension, although the one is not reducible to the

---

[10] E. W. Bakke and C. Argyris, *Organizational Structure and Dynamics*, New Haven, Labor and Management Center, Yale University, 1954, pp. 13–14.
[11] Parsons and Shils, *op. cit.*, pp. 62–63.

other. The *individual* behavior referred to here as distinct from *social* behavior would ensue in the hypothetical case where there was no normative or institutional context for performance. A schematic representation of the relationship between the biological dimension and what we have called the idiographic dimension of behavior is presented in Figure 4–3.

```
Individual ──────▶ Personality ──────▶ Need-Dispositions
    ↕                   ↕                       ↕           ╲
                                                             ▶ Individual
                                                               Behavior
Organism ─────────▶ Constitution ─────────▶ Potentialities  ╱
```

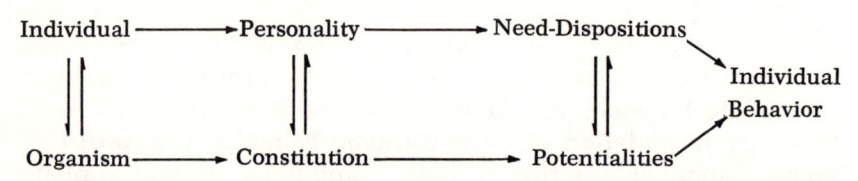

FIGURE 4–3. *The relationship of the organismic and personalistic dimensions of behavior. (Adapted from J. W. Getzels and H. A. Thelen, "The Classroom as a Unique Social System," in N. B. Henry, ed.,* The Dynamics of Instructional Groups, *Fifty-ninth Yearbook of the National Society for the Study of Education, Chicago, University of Chicago Press, 1960, p. 72.)*

THE CULTURAL DIMENSION

The expectations for behavior in a given institution not only derive from the requirements of the social system of which the institution is a part but also are related to the values of the culture which is the context for the particular social system. The expectations in the school, for example, are related to the values of the community. Automobile driving is not usually an important aspect of the curriculum in a community that places a high value on admission to Ivy League colleges; Latin is not likely to remain part of the curriculum in a community that has a high regard for vocational preparation. Most often the relation between the expectations of the school and the values of the community are implicit, but on occasion they become very explicit, as witness the activity of citizens' committees for the examination of textbooks, or the following contract a teacher was required to sign:

I promise to take a vital interest in all phases of Sunday-school work, donating of my time, service, and money without stint for the uplift and benefit of the community. I promise to abstain from all dancing, immodest dressing, and other conduct unbecoming a teacher and a lady. I promise not to go out with any young men except insofar as it may be necessary to stimulate Sunday-school work. . . . I promise to remember that I owe a duty to the townspeople who are paying me my wages, that I owe respect to the school board and the superintendent that hired me, and that I shall consider myself at all times the willing servant of the school board and the townspeople and that I shall cooperate with them to the limit of my ability in any movement aimed at the betterment of the town, the pupils, or the schools.[12]

Clearly this is an ancient and extreme instance, significant more as historical document than as the portrait of any existing situation. Nonetheless, the reason it is an astonishing document is because of its explication of the relation between the expectations of the role and the values of the community which *could* exist rather than for the exceptionality of the principle of the relation between the two. Lieberman makes a parallel observation regarding the current *political* condition of teachers:

At the present time, public education presents a paradox: the work of teachers is dominated by political considerations but the teachers themselves are political nonentities. The need is to transform teachers into political animals so that their work can be based on professional instead of political considerations. Without political power, teachers will never be able to protect the integrity of their work.[13]

One may or may not agree with the specific recommendation, but the point remains: To understand behavior in a social system—in the example, a school system—it is necessary to understand its articulation with the culture in which it is embedded.

Now, just as the component elements of a social system may be analyzed by application of the sociological concepts role and expectation, so the relevant component elements of the culture may be analyzed by application of the anthropological concepts of ethos and value. By ethos we mean merely a distinguishing pattern of values in a culture, quite as by role we meant a distinguishing pattern of expectations in an institution. The essential analytic concept here is *value*.

The term "value," like "role" or "personality," has been defined in various ways and used in various contexts. Among the pioneer efforts putting the concept into operation was that of

---

[12] H. K. Beale, *Are American Teachers Free?* New York, Scribner, 1936, pp. 395-396.
[13] Myron Lieberman, *The Future of Public Education*, Chicago, University of Chicago Press, 1960, p. 285.

Allport and Vernon, who based their *Study of Values* on Spranger's six ideal value types: theoretical, economic, aesthetic, social, political, and religious.[14] Following the Allport-Vernon study, Glaeser and Maller investigated what they called interest values, using four value types found by Thurstone: theoretic, aesthetic, social, and economic.[15] In another study, Ferguson reduced the concept to two dimensions: what might be called religionism and humanitarianism.[16] Woodruff, in his "Study of Choices," defined value as "any object, idea, condition, or activity consciously or unconsciously believed by an individual to have an effect on his well-being or self-realization, either directly to himself or indirectly through those with whom he is concerned, and regardless of the extent to which the individual is aware of such values."[17] He identified the following values: wealth, social position, political power, social service, home life, comfort, religion, security, personal attractiveness, excitement, friends, and intellectual activity.

At a more general and abstract level, Parsons and Shils suggest that one component of any culture is a set of evaluative criteria consisting of standards for solving cognitive problems, standards for solving cathectic or appreciative problems, and "moral" standards for the over-all integration of the various units of the system. The moral standards (the basic values) "set the limits of the permissible costs of an expressive gratification or an instrumental achievement—by referring to the consequences of such action for the other parts of the system and for the system as a whole."[18] They provide a classification of types of standards in the form of *pattern variables* of value orientations involving relationships among such criteria as universalism, particularism, achievement, and ascription.

In a notable philosophic analysis and empirical cross-cultural study, Charles Morris defined values as preferred ways to live and identified 13 such ways:[19]

---

[14] Gordon W. Allport and P. E. Vernon, *Study of Values*, Boston, Houghton Mifflin, 1931.
[15] E. M. Glaeser and J. B. Maller, "The Measurement of Interest Values," *Character and Personality*, 9 (September, 1940), 71.
[16] L. W. Ferguson, "Primary Social Attitudes," *Journal of Psychology*, 8 (1939), 217–223.
[17] A. D. Woodruff, *A Study of Directive Factors in Individual Behavior*, Doctoral dissertation, University of Chicago, 1941, pp. 24–25.
[18] Parsons and Shils, *op. cit.*, p. 166.
[19] Charles Morris, *Varieties of Human Value*, Chicago, University of Chicago Press, 1956, pp. 15–18.

A framework for the study of administrative behavior: the general model

1. In this "design for living" the individual actively participates in his community, not to change it primarily, but to appreciate and preserve the best that man has attained.
2. Here the individual for the most part "goes it alone," stressing privacy, self-sufficiency, knowledge of self.
3. In this way of life, understanding helpfulness and sympathetic concern for other persons are central.
4. Life is something to be sensuously enjoyed, to let oneself go being more important than to do—or even to do good.
5. The individual should merge with a social group and join with others in the realization of common goals.
6. What a man does is more salient than what he feels or on what he speculates, the realistic solution of specific problems being the goal.
7. Life should contain something from all ways of living, and there should be enjoyment, action, and contemplation in about equal amounts.
8. Enjoyment of the simple and easily obtainable pleasures—savory foods, comfortable surroundings, talking with friends—should be the keynote of life.
9. Receptivity, when the self has ceased to make demands and becomes open to wisdom from without, should be the way of life.
10. The good life comes from self-control, understanding one's place in the world, and the guidance of action through reason.
11. The contemplative life is the good life. Here the individual finds the rich internal world of ideas, feelings, and sympathy for others that make him human.
12. The key to the good life lies in the physical zest of overcoming, dominating, and conquering tangible obstacles.
13. A person should let himself be used by others in their growth and in the fulfillment of great objective purposes, and be humble, constant, faithful, and uninsistent.

Even a brief summary of the findings in the United States, Canada, India, Japan, China, and Norway, (all participants in the study) would take us too far afield and would really not be to the point here. Two highly relevant observations may, however, be made. First, there were significant differences in values among the several cultures as represented in the preferences expressed by samples of college students. For example, the way of life ranked highest by the American sample—way of life 7—was ranked lowest by the Chinese sample. Second, and more important from the present point of view, intricate but direct relationships were found between the values and institutional structure and behavior. Morris concluded: "... differentiation of values related to the performance of certain roles in the social system, and differentiations of value related to the press of an immediate problem upon the group."[20] That is, there is an interaction between the values of a culture taken most broadly and the expectations of institutional roles in the component social systems. The role expectations must be understood not only in relation to each other but also in relation to the cultural values.

For purposes of the present analysis, we shall define value, with Kluckhohn, as "a conception, explicit or implicit, distinctive of an individual or characteristic of a group, of the desirable which influences the selection from available modes, means, and ends of action."[21]

Looked at from this perspective, the American scene appears in many ways to be an enigma.[22] As Kaspar Naegele pointed out, "At one time our values appear obvious and clearcut; at another they are elusive and complicated by many cleavages."[23] One oscillates between the conviction that there is a common value orientation and a common type of America, and the doubt as to what indeed is held in common by the Western farmer and the Eastern businessman, the member of the National Association for the Advancement of Colored People in Illinois and the supporters of the White Citizens Council in Mississippi, the subscriber to *Fortune* and the steady reader of *True Romance*. Where do the values overlap? Where do they diverge?

In order to clarify the issues here, we must distinguish between two types of American value: *sacred* and *secular*. The sacred values are part of the American "creed" and constitute our basic and undivorceable beliefs. It is these that are referred

---

[20] *Ibid.*, p. 93.
[21] C. Kluckhohn *et al.*, "Values and Value-Orientations in the Theory of Action," as quoted in Parsons and Shils, *op. cit.*, p. 395.
[22] Portions of the following are drawn from J. W. Getzels, "Changing Values Challenge the Schools," *School Review*, 65 (1957), 92–102.
[23] A number of the formulations in this section were drawn from an unpublished memorandum on selected studies of American values by the late Professor Kaspar Naegele of the University of British Columbia. We are indebted to him.

to when schools are urged to teach the characteristic American values, "the things for which our forefathers laid down their lives": *democracy*, or the belief that the experience of the many is more inclusive than the experience of the few, that what people want is what they need, and that the people are the best judges of their needs; *individualism*, or the belief that "the individual is the fountain source of energy, initiative, and responsibility in society and has a right to self-expression"; *equality*, or the belief that all men should have the same opportunity to develop their talents, their rewards to be by achievement, not by ascription; *human perfectibility*, or the belief in the progressive movement of the person and his society toward the ideal of democracy, individualism, and equality. It is to these values, despite the periodic stresses and strains to which they are liable, that we appeal when we wish to legitimize significant social or national action.

But in a sense we stand in relation to these sacred values as we do to the Ten Commandments or the Golden Rule: At the moment when we may be departing from them most directly we maintain that we are supporting them most firmly. And just as it is impossible to understand our Judeo-Christian culture merely by reading the precepts of the Bible, so it is impossible to understand our operating American culture by knowing only the creed and the sacred values. In addition to these there is a core of working or down-to-earth beliefs which constitute our *secular* values. In effect, to overstate the case, we pay homage to the sacred values on Sundays, state occasions, and curricular declarations, but in our day-to-day activities we most often behave in terms of the secular values.

Traditionally—and the time element must be emphasized, for the secular values are prone to greater alteration than the sacred values—the following have been among the major secular values:[24]

1. *The work-success ethic.* Values of achievement take precedence over values of being. Anyone can get to the top if he tries hard enough, and everyone has an obligation to try hard enough to get to the top. To be sure, as Naegele points out, forbearance, charity, and compassion also have a value, but, he

---
[24] This analysis is based in part on G. D. Spindler, "Education in a Transforming American Culture," *Harvard Educational Review,* 25 (Summer, 1955), 145–156.

adds, success can excuse one for having intermittently broken the Golden Rule.[25]

2. *Future-time orientation.* The future, not the past or even the present, is important. We must be—and note the vernacular—"forward looking" and "on the go," for what is to come is bigger and better than what is now. Time, therefore, becomes a value and is equated with money—again note the vernacular, "time is money." The present is undervalued for the sake of the future, and immediate needs are denied satisfaction for greater satisfactions to come.

3. *Independence, or the autonomous self.* The self is inviolable and as such of greater ultimate significance than the group. The independence of the self must be guarded from authority and from bureaucratic interference. Self-determination, self-activity, self-perfection are the criteria of personal worth.

4. *Puritan morality or, more broadly, moral commitment.* Respectability, thrift, self-denial, and hard work—these are the marks of common decency. Personal virtue is measured by the seriousness of the ethical commitment. To be sure, there is the holiday, the time to have "fun" and "be sociable." But, as Naegele remarked, this is kept out of the values of everyday living.[26] Indeed, for many individuals even now, vacation must be rationalized as the replenishment of energy—a good investment, as it were—for the serious and therefore significant things of life. Sociability for the sake of sociability is held to be akin to sloth, and sloth is a sin second only to idolatry.

The sacred values have remained relatively stable. This is not to say that they have not been under stress and strain or that they may not be periodically reinterpreted. But in the end democracy, equality, individualism, and human perfectibility as values remain sacred. They are celebrated as *ideals* today as they were 150 years ago. The traditional operating or secular values, however,—the work-success ethic, future-time orientation, personal independence, and Puritan morality—have undergone, are undergoing, and presumably will continue to undergo crucial transformation as a function of change in technology and shift in social structure.

---

[25] See footnote 23.
[26] See footnote 23.

The diversities and cleavages in the American scene have been remarked upon often enough. There are *regional* differences. When we go from Maine to Southern California or from New York to Arkansas, we are moving not only from one place to another, but also, in large measure, from one way of life to another. There have always been *rural-urban* differences. Although these are diminishing because of the mass-communication media and industrialization, we have in their stead newly sprung differences between the urban, the suburban, and the so-called exurban cultures. For some observers *social stratification* is the major source of diversity. They would argue that any understanding of our values must take into account the critical differences between lower-class, middle-class, and upper-class membership.

Without in any way minimizing the preceding well-known sources of cleavage in our value system, it may be observed that the most significant source of cleavage at certain times resides in the rapid and crucial transformation that the dominant secular values themselves undergo. From a sociological point of view, Riesman has called our attention to this in his trenchant distinction between our former *inner-directed* values and the prevailing *other-directed* values.[27] From a psychological point of view, Wheelis emphasized this transformation at the personal level in his equally trenchant observation of the replacement of our former *institutional* values by the current *instrumental* values.[28] And Spindler, from an anthropological perspective, remarked upon this transformation as a shift from *traditional* to *emergent* values.[29] Whatever the standpoint, the following changes in the dominant secular values seem to be involved:

1. *From the work-success ethic to an ethic of sociability.* Instead of the work-success ethic, there is an overriding value of sociability and frictionless interpersonal relations. The shift may perhaps be put most sharply as the hard-working, self-determined Horatio Alger hero giving way to the young man in the gray flannel suit as a national model.

2. *From future-time orientation to present-time orientation.* Instead of future-time orientation with consequent self-denial

---

[27] David Riesman *et al., The Lonely Crowd*, New Haven, Yale University Press, 1950.
[28] A. Wheelis, *The Quest for Identity*, New York, Norton, 1958.
[29] Spindler, *op. cit.*

and delayed gratification, there is a hedonistic present-time orientation. The national slogan "a penny saved, a penny earned" gives way to the more modern "no down payment necessary."

3. *From personal independence to group conformity.* Instead of independence and the autonomous self, there is compliance and conformity to the group. As Riesman has put it, we replace our inner gyroscope with a built-in radar that alerts us to the feelings of others.[30] The goal of behavior becomes not personal rectitude but group consensus, not originality but adjustment.

4. *From moral commitment to moral relativism.* Finally, instead of Puritan morality, or at least moral commitment, there are relativistic moral attitudes without strong personal commitments. Absolutes in right and wrong are questionable, and morality becomes a statistical rather than an ethical concept: Morality is whatever the group thinks is moral.

These values, and the conflicts among them, form the context for the expectations for behavior and are held in various degrees by different persons in society and in specific institutions. As Spindler points out with respect to educational organizations, for example, the younger teachers are more likely to be emergent in their values than the older teachers, the superintendents and principals more emergent than the parents and public they serve, the parents and public more emergent than the school board members they elect.[31] So we have, impinging upon each other, in the community and in the school—as well as in other public and private institutions—a context of both stable and shifting, if not altogether conflicting, assumptions about life and value to which institutional behavior is necessarily related. To use Lynd's list, there are the following *dilemmas of value*, as we may call them, within which the functioning of the social system and the component institutions and organizations must be viewed:

1. Individualism, or "survival of the fittest," is the secret of American greatness, and restrictions on individual freedom are un-American and kill initiative. *But*: No man should live for himself alone; for people ought to stand together and work for common causes.

---

[30] Riesman, *op. cit.*, p. 26.
[31] Spindler, *op. cit.*, 151.

2. Religion and the "finer things of life" are our ultimate values and the things all of us are really working for. *But*: A man owes it to himself and to his family to make as much money as he can.
3. Poverty is deplorable and should be abolished. *But*: There never has been enough to go around, and the Bible tells us that "the poor you have always with you."
4. Everyone should try to be successful. *But*: The kind of a person you are is more important than how successful you are.
5. Education is a fine thing. *But*: It is the practical man who gets things done.[32]

The value dilemmas are obviously not as stark in practice as they look on paper, or the entire system would fly apart. Nor are we suggesting that the particular values or transformations in values are necessarily of the order described by Riesman, Wheelis, and Spindler. Others argue that their type of analysis is open to serious question,[33] and we shall deal with some relevant empirical findings in the section on research studies. Moreover, there is no doubt that yesterday's "emergent" values can become today's "traditional" values, which in turn will give rise to another set of emergent values tomorrow. Indeed, Spindler's original findings with respect to certain "transformed values" involving artists and intellectuals have themselves undergone transformation.[34] Although only 20 percent of his subjects' reactions to artists were positive in 1952, 60 percent were positive by 1958; and although only 35 percent of the reactions to intellectuals were positive in 1952, 75 percent were positive by 1958. The most dramatic change seems to have come in 1957, the year of Sputnik, perhaps, as McFee suggests, on account of our entry into the space age and the fear of catastrophe. In 1957, 25 percent of the reactions to intellectuals were positive; in 1958, 75 percent of the reactions were positive.[35] The investigator does not assume that these data were free from certain unavoidable biases in his sample and method, and we are not vouching for the precision of the findings by citing them here. The ques-

---

[32] R. S. Lynd, *Knowledge for What?* Princeton, N.J., Princeton University Press, 1946, pp. 60–62.
[33] S. M. Lipset and L. Lowenthal, *Culture and Social Character*, New York, Free Press, 1961.
[34] June King McFee, *Preparation for Art*, San Francisco, Wadsworth, 1961, pp. 114–117.
[35] *Ibid.*

tion of the exact nature of current value orientations is an empirical problem, which hopefully can be answered with confidence through further investigation.

What we are maintaining here is that *conceptually* the general cultural values—Morris's "ways of life"[36]—and the specific institutional expectations of a given social system must be regarded as somehow articulated. From this point of view the objectives, curricula, methods, and administrative policies and procedures within the educational institution as a particular instance must be understood in the context of the culture and the component values to which they are inevitably related. Thus, interacting with the sociological dimension is the anthropological dimension, although, as in the case of the biological and psychological dimensions, the one is not immediately reducible to the other. The relationship is represented schematically in Figure 4–4.

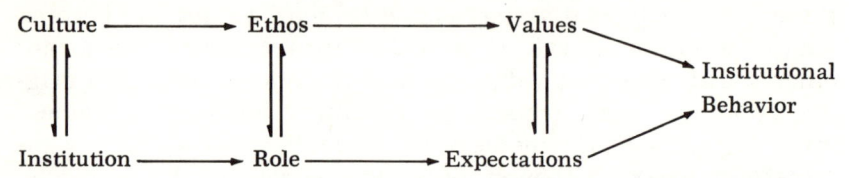

```
Culture ─────────► Ethos ─────────► Values ╲
  ↕↕                 ↕↕               ↕↕     ╲► Institutional
                                              ╱  Behavior
Institution ──────► Role ─────────► Expectations
```

FIGURE 4–4. *The relationship of the cultural and institutional dimensions of behavior.* (Adapted from J. W. Getzels and H. A. Thelen, "The Classroom as a Unique Social System," in N. B. Henry, ed., The Dynamics of Instructional Groups, *Fifty-ninth Yearbook of the National Society for the Study of Education,* Chicago, University of Chicago Press, 1960, p. 72.)

A model for studying behavior in a social system

The salient factors for the study and understanding of behavior in a social system, then, are organismic, personalistic, institutional, and cultural. But, as we have insisted all along and wish to reiterate, even this formidable array of biological, psychological, sociological, and anthropological dimensions is not all-inclusive. A number of potentially significant variables have been omitted. Perhaps most obviously we have failed to say anything about the self-evident circumstance that behavior functions not only in a particular social context but also in a particular physical and economic environment. Surely geographic location, natural

---

[36] Morris, *op. cit.*

resources, and actual available wealth make a difference in the nature of behavior in a social system, and more specifically in the educational system.

We need hardly point in this respect to the ready example of the school where the economic resources of the community have a profound effect on the expenditures for education and, consequently, on the relevant behavior and administrative issues.[37] Especially significant, however, from the point of view of the present framework is the fact that, although the richest school district even in a single county may be as much as thirty times more able to support an educational program than the poorest district, there is *not* a one-to-one correspondence between the economic ability to pay and the social demand for quality education. The aspirations—in present terms, the *values*—of the several school districts must still be taken into account if the level of education the community is *willing to afford* as against what it *can afford* is to be understood. Nonetheless, the environment, especially the economic environment, does of course enter into the functioning of a social system, and it, along with the political environment, must be added at least as a background variable.

Before completing our consideration of the dimensions that have to be included in the study and understanding of behavior in a social system, we must add one comment on the relation between the cultural dimension and the individual dimension, which we have left implicit as almost too self-evident for elaboration. Not only is personality related to its biological substratum, which we have already considered, but it is also *fundamentally and integrally related to the values of the culture in which the organism grows up.*[38] The human organism is not born with a ready-made set of culturally adaptive attitudes and reactions any more than it is born with a culturally adaptive language or set of religious beliefs. Instead the human being must learn to put the question to himself, "May I yield to the impulse within me, or shall I, by doing so, imperil the highest values of my society?" The child must learn on the one hand to suppress or to modify certain of his biological drives and potentialities and on the other hand to acquire certain culturally

---
[37] H. T. James, J. A. Thomas, and H. J. Dyck, *Wealth, Expenditure, and Decision-Making for Education*, Cooperative Research Project No. 1241, Washington, D.C., U.S. Office of Education, 1963.
[38] Getzels and Thelen, *op. cit.*

adaptive attitudes, values, and beliefs. The process of *socialization* is designed to help the child do just this.

A full discussion of the mechanisms by which the child incorporates the values of his culture and makes them as much his own as are his biological drives and impulses is beyond the scope of the present discussion. But one fundamental mechanism should be mentioned: *identification*.[39] As the child struggles at one level to integrate and maintain a stable self-image of who he is and where he fits, and at another level to integrate and maintain a point of contact with those about him, he is led to view himself as at one with another person. At first the parents are the objects of identification. Later he may add older siblings, favorite neighbors, community heroes, school personnel, and other important figures in the various social systems in which he comes to play a part. In making these identifications, he not only assumes the outward manners and expressive behavior of his "significant others" but also attempts to incorporate their values and attitudes.

When the individual finds himself in a period of rapidly changing values, the various significant figures in the different institutions provide inconsistent and contradictory objects for identification. In such situations, identification, if it "takes" at all, results in conflict and anxiety. One obtains no answer to the inevitable inquiry, *"Which* values?" To incorporate one set of values means to reject another: To incorporate the parent's values may mean to reject the teacher's values, to incorporate the teacher's values may mean to reject the community hero's values, to accept the community hero's values may mean to reject the religious leader's values, to accept the religious leader's values may mean to reject the boss's values, and so on.

As a result, the individual faces an extraordinarily difficult problem in adaptation. The solution may be either inflexible incorporation of one set of values or renunciation of all required values. In the one case we have *overidentification* and consequent restriction and inflexibility; in the other we have *underidentification* and consequent disobedience and rebellion. We shall have occasion to return to these issues when we consider the sources of strain in social systems and in administrative behavior. The point we want to make here is that mediating

---

[39] D. R. Miller and M. L. Hutt, "Value Interiorization and Personality Development," *Journal of Social Issues*, 5, no. 4 (1949), 2–30. See also E. H. Erikson, *Childhood and Society*, New York, Norton, 1950.

A framework for the study of administrative behavior: the general model

between the biological dimension and the personality dimension is the cultural dimension; *just as role expectations are related to a context of value, so are personality dispositions related to a context of value.*

If all the dimensions dealt with so far were put into a single, and we are afraid rather unwieldy, pictorial representation, the consequent general model of interrelationships might look like Figure 4–5.

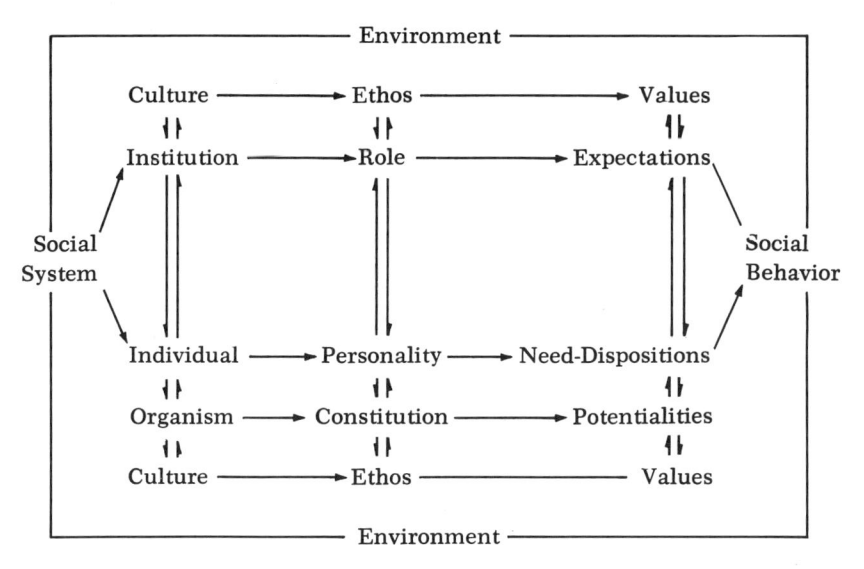

```
┌─────────────────── Environment ───────────────────┐
│         Culture ──────▶ Ethos ──────▶ Values      │
│            ↕↕            ↕↕             ↕↕        │
│         Institution ──▶ Role  ──────▶ Expectations│
│         ↗    ‖‖          ‖‖             ‖‖   ╲    │
│ Social /     ‖‖          ‖‖             ‖‖    ╲ Social
│ System       ‖‖          ‖‖             ‖‖      Behavior
│         ╲    ‖‖          ‖‖             ‖‖    ↗   │
│         Individual ──▶ Personality ──▶ Need-Dispositions
│            ↕↕            ↕↕             ↕↕        │
│         Organism ────▶ Constitution ─▶ Potentialities
│            ↕↕            ↕↕             ↕↕        │
│         Culture ──────▶ Ethos ──────── Values     │
└─────────────────── Environment ───────────────────┘
```

FIGURE 4–5. *General model of the major dimensions of behavior in a social system.*

Summary

In Chapter 3 we argued that for general analytic purposes, and especially for the analysis of administrative processes, administration might be thought of as functioning within a social-system framework. We conceived of a social system as involving two classes of phenomena, one normative, the other individual. In this chapter, behavior in a social system has been seen as a function of the interaction of these two classes of factors, a given social act being the outcome of an inextricable combination of role and personality relations. Thus we were able to write, in a shorthand notation, the general equation $B = f(R \times P)$, where

B is observed behavior, R is a given institutional role defined by the expectations attaching to it, and P is the personality of the individual in the role defined by his needs and dispositions.

The proportion of role and personality factors determining behavior will vary with the specific system, the specific role, and the specific personality involved. In a military organization the proportion of behavior dictated by considerations of *role* is likely to be large relative to that dictated by considerations of personality; in an artists' colony the proportion of behavior dictated by *personality* is likely to be large relative to that dictated by role. But whether in the military or the artists' colony, or in any other social system, administration always deals with the interplay and proportion of role and personality components of behavior.

In addition to these primary determinants of social behavior, a number of other relevant but more or less subsidiary factors must be considered—the biological, the environmental, the cultural, to mention only three—the central one being the cultural dimension with its component *values*. Both the institutional expectations and the individual dispositions have, at least to some extent, their source in and are related to the culture in which the system operates. Although the *general* model includes the five dimensions, which must be borne in mind when considering any element of social behavior, the basic *operational* model in the present analysis of administrative processes in the educational context is composed of these three salient factors: the interaction of *role* and *personality* in the context of *value*. The relations among these are represented graphically in Figure 4–6.

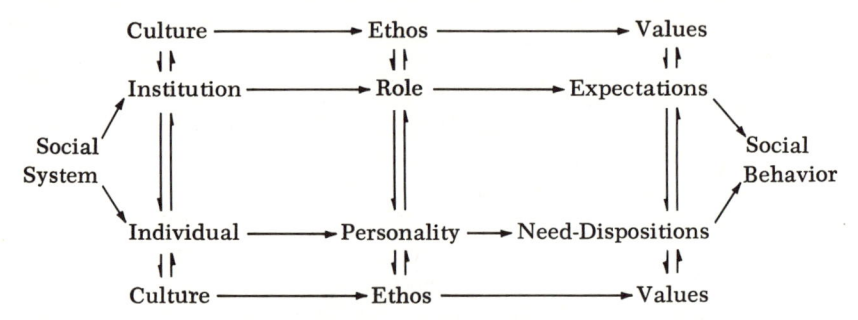

FIGURE 4–6. *Operational model of major dimensions of social behavior.* (From J. W. Getzels, "Conflict and Role Behavior in the Educational Setting," in W. W. Charters, Jr., and N. L. Gage, eds., Readings in the Social Psychology of Education, Boston, Allyn and Bacon, 1963, p. 312.)

It must be understood that any theoretical formulation is a selective abstraction from reality and as such an oversimplification. As Hebb has put it:

> To deal with behavior at present, one must oversimplify. The risk, on the one hand, is forgetting that one has oversimplified the problem; one may forget or even deny those inconvenient facts that one's theory does not subsume. On the other hand is the risk of accepting the weak-kneed discouragement of the vitalist, of being content to show that existing theories are imperfect without seeking to improve them. We can take for granted that any theory of behavior at present must be inadequate and incomplete . . . .[40]

In this sense the present formulation is also an oversimplification. A number of potentially significant variables have necessarily been omitted. But it is wiser in our opinion to know that one has explicitly omitted certain elements in an analysis than to believe foolishly that he has dealt or can deal equally with all the elements, which in fact it is impossible to do at the current stage of conceptual and methodological development. The hope of course is, as Hebb suggests, that from the consideration of these admittedly incomplete formulations may come more inclusive and satisfactory formulations.

In the next chapter we shall consider, in the single set of conceptual and terminological relationships provided by the present framework, some basic issues in administration which have hitherto been treated in separate concepts and varied terms—for example, the problems of conflict, of satisfaction, efficiency, effectiveness, and morale, of leadership style, and of organizational change.

---

[40] D. O. Hebb, *The Organization of Behavior*, New York, Wiley, 1949, p. xiii.

5

Conceptual and empirical derivations

There is little point in general models if they do not give rise to specific conceptual derivations and empirical applications which illuminate, in however modest a degree, significant day-to-day practices or raise fruitful issues for systematic investigation. We have presented a model of social behavior, and we argued that the process of administration deals essentially with social behavior in a hierarchical setting. We shall now turn to a consideration of specific derivations and applications from the model relevant to salient issues in the study and practice of administration. Among the issues are (1) the sources of conflict in a social system; (2) the problem of adaptation and adjustment; (3) the meaning of effectiveness, efficiency, satisfaction, and morale in the administrative setting; (4) the nature of authority and leadership-followership styles; and (5) the problem of organizational change. It will be noted that these issues come from a number of different theorists—for example, the concepts of effectiveness and efficiency are from Barnard, and the nature of leadership styles is from Lewin (see Chapter 4). We need hardly point out that there are conceptual and methodological advantages in power and parsimony in being able to deal with these hitherto disjunctive issues in a single set of terms and relationships, although certain disadvantages must be borne in mind as well.

Sources of conflict: fulcra for administrative intervention

Conflict may be defined most simply here as the mutual interference of parts, actions, and reactions in a social system. To focus thus on the problem of conflict or discontinuity in the school as a social system is not to say that *this* system is inevitably *more* prone to the "mutual interference of parts" than are other systems, nor in fact to imply that conflict may not have its uses. Our point is only that within the present framework we may identify certain systematic sources and types of conflict.

Consider some instances in education and the community.[1] Although the teacher is expected to be a good citizen, he is barred from many of the roles which are the marks of good citizenship. Outspoken participation in a political party, for example, to say nothing of a socially controversial movement, may be prohibited. Partisanship in local politics can be a cause for dismissal.[2] Further, although the teacher is expected to be a mature person, that is, one who can be trusted to act sensibly in accordance with his needs and dispositions, his personal behavior is often circumscribed by rules and regulations laid down for him by others, who incidentally need not, and in fact do not, themselves abide by the same rules. To take what may be an extreme instance, one teacher reports, "I don't lead a natural life. I wouldn't dare smoke or drink. When I go to public meetings where the parents and guests smoke, I have to say no. If the parents can smoke, why can't I?"[3]

Even in school matters proper, presumably the sphere of his own particular competence, the educator is liable to crosspressures. For example, the School Executive Studies found that 20 percent of the superintendents reported facing incompatible demands from their religious and educational affiliations.[4] The members of their churches wanted them to act one way, other people in the community another way. As one Catholic superintendent—and he speaks for other denominations as well—put it:

Sometimes the situation gets pretty touchy. I want to keep my good relations with the Church. Don't forget—most of my school committee members and the local politicians belong to my church. Take this example: One of the Catholic groups wanted to let the kids out early from school. They were having some special meetings, and they wanted the kids to be there. I knew that wouldn't be right. It wasn't fair to the other kids. So what did I do? I refused to give an official O.K. to the request, but at the same time I simply winked at it (letting them out early). I would have offended them if I'd stopped the kids from going, and I just couldn't afford to do that. It really left me bothered.[5]

---

[1] J. W. Getzels, "Conflict and Role Behavior in the Educational Setting," in W. W. Charters and N. L. Gage, eds., *Readings in the Social Psychology of Education*, Boston, Allyn and Bacon, 1963, pp. 309–318.
[2] W. B. Brookover, *A Sociology of Education*, New York, American Book, 1955, pp. 230–262.
[3] *Ibid.*, p. 245.
[4] Neal C. Gross, "Some Contributions of Sociology to the Field of Education," *Harvard Educational Review*, 29 (Fall, 1959), 275–287.
[5] *Ibid.*, p. 284.

In the instances cited, what was at issue was one form or another of conflict—conflict between one role and another role, conflict between the person's needs and the expectations held for him by others, conflict among the several people holding expectations for the same role, and so on. These conflicts are a matter of vital concern not only to the people who are involved and "bothered" but to the administrator who must somehow cope with such apparent dislocations in the social system. The following relevant questions may be raised: What are the various *types* of conflict, for clearly not all conflicts are of the same kind? What are the *sources* of conflict? What are the *consequences* of conflict?

In the terms of the present framework we may identify for illustrative purposes five major types and sources of conflict, although these by no means exhaust the possibilities.[6]

CONFLICT BETWEEN CULTURAL VALUES AND INSTITUTIONAL EXPECTATIONS

A readily apparent type of conflict is that between the expectations of a specific organization or institution and the values of the general culture or subculture. Consider in this respect the position of the Ku Klux Klan in the North and the position of the Council on Racial Equality in the South. The strains between the expectations of the institution and the values of the culture are quite specific and need not be dwelt on. Consider then, from the same point of view, the more general and implicit issues involved in the relation between a school or a factory and the general culture or subculture, assuming only the substantive data regarding the present state of values to be as Riesman, Wheelis, and Spindler, among others, have described them (see Chapter 4).

If the individual is to be productive and innovative, the

---

[6] Portions of the following are drawn from: J. W. Getzels, *op. cit.*, pp. 309–318; J. W. Getzels and E. G. Guba, "Social Behavior and the Administrative Process," *School Review*, 55 (1957), 423–441; J. W. Getzels, "Administration as a Social Process," in Andrew W. Halpin, ed., *Administrative Theory in Education*, Chicago, Midwest Administration Center, University of Chicago, 1958, pp. 150–165; J. W. Getzels and H. A. Thelen, "The Classroom as a Unique Social System," in N. B. Henry, ed., *The Dynamics of Instructional Groups*, Fifty-ninth Yearbook of the National Society for the Study of Education, Chicago, University of Chicago Press, 1960, pp. 53–82.

institutional expectations must support personal independence and autonomy. But our dominant values are said to reward conformity and cheerful compliance to the status quo. If the able person in school or in the factory is to realize his endowment and potentialities, the institutional expectations must be for hard work and the sacrifice of present ease for future achievement. But our values tend to prize sociability and present-time criteria of worth. If the creative individual is to express his exceptional talents, the institutional expectations must make possible firm commitment to one's own standards and one's own beliefs. But again our emerging values are quite opposed; they tend instead to hold in esteem relativistic attitudes without strong personal commitment.

We are obviously not arguing the validity of the substantive data we have used for assumptive purposes, although there is considerable confirmatory evidence. Rather we are illustrating one potential source of conflict—conflict between institutional expectations and cultural values, where one is "traditional" and another "emergent." Insofar as the expectations of the school and the values of the community must necessarily be related, the administrative consequences of extreme conflict between institution and culture are bound to be serious: The school will be charged with not serving the community, bond issues will be defeated, textbooks will be burned, and so on.

There is an additional complication. We have been dealing with the issue at the simplest level—as if there were *one* culture. There may in fact be a *dominant* culture, but there are numerous component subcultures: regional, rural-urban, social-class, to mention only three. The institutional expectations that are attuned to one of the subcultures may not be to another. The same curriculum is not equally related to the values of the middle class and the lower class. Indeed, many of the problems of the school in the lower-class community are a function of exactly this type of conflict: The expectations of the school are unrelated to the values of the subculture. Explicitly or implicitly, the prized activities of the school are based on a middle-class *achievement ethic* with consequent high valuation on symbolic commitment to future success. In contrast, the lower-class child has experienced only a *subsistence ethic* with consequent high valuation on concrete commitment to present gratification. What can the school's appeal to symbolic success mean to a child who has grown up where success could be measured only by subsistence?[7]

CONFLICT BETWEEN ROLE EXPECTATIONS AND PERSONALITY DISPOSITIONS

Discrepancies between patterns of expectations attaching to a role and patterns of need-dispositions characteristic of the incumbents of the role result in conflict. Typical of this kind of conflict are the army private with a high need for ascendance, the assembly-line worker with a high need for self-expression, the administrator with a high need for abasement, the authoritarian teacher in a permissive school, and so on. In all these cases there is mutual interference between the normative expectations and the personal dispositions. The individual must choose whether he will fulfill his particular needs or the institutional requirements. If he chooses to fulfill the requirements, he is in a sense shortchanging himself and is liable to inadequate personal adjustment. His efficiency is diminished, and he is frustrated and dissatisfied. If he chooses to fulfill his needs, he is shortchanging his role and is liable to inadequate role performance. His effectiveness is diminished, and he is criticized and punished.

We shall deal with the considerable empirical work in this area in due course. Here we cite only a sample study of the consequences of what might be called these self-role conflicts—a study that is mentioned not because the results were in any sense surprising but because they demonstrated with precision the anticipated effect. The investigator examined the effect on the teacher's "satisfaction as a teacher" of varying degrees of discrepancy between what the teacher was disposed to do in the classroom and what she was expected to do by her principal. The greater the conflict between the two, the greater the consequent dissatisfaction.[8]

There are certain mechanisms in the social system to keep this type of conflict and its effects at a minimum. No role is ever so closely defined that it requires only one kind of personality for satisfactory performance; selection procedures assure a better

---

[7] See J. W. Getzels, "Pre-School Education," *White House Conference on Education*, prepared for the Subcommittee on Education of the Committee on Labor and Public Welfare, United States Senate, Washington, D.C., U.S. Government Printing Office, 1965, pp. 116–125.

[8] Merton V. Campbell, "Self-Role Conflict Among Teachers and Its Relationship to Satisfaction, Effectiveness, and Confidence in Leadership," Doctoral dissertation, University of Chicago, 1958.

than chance matching of role and personality; avenues are available for redistribution of personnel in cases of mismatching; in-service and other training and retraining programs exist; and so on. Nonetheless, as we shall see in the section on research studies, a good many mismatchings remain, with serious consequences for the social system and crucial decisions for the administrator.

CONFLICT BETWEEN ROLES AND WITHIN ROLES

A variety of conflicts occur when a role incumbent has to conform simultaneously to a number of expectations which are mutually exclusive, contradictory, or inconsistent so that the performance of one set of duties makes performance of another set impossible, or at least difficult. These role conflicts are evidence of dislocations in the normative dimension of the social system and may arise in a number of ways: (1) disagreement within an alter or reference group defining a given role; (2) disagreement among several groups, each defining expectations for the same role; (3) contradiction between the expectations of two or more roles which an individual is occupying at the same time.

Disagreement Within a Group Defining a Given Role. Consider the principal who is expected by some teachers to visit them regularly to "give constructive help" and by other teachers to "trust them as professional personnel" not to demean them by supervision. Or consider the pupil whom some teachers expect to emphasize the mechanics of writing (substance being useful only for the practice of correct form) and other teachers expect to emphasize the substance (form being considered merely a vehicle for content). At a more fundamental level, the entire purpose of education, and therefore of the various roles in the school, may be defined differently by different educators even within the same school system.

In a study to be dealt with in greater detail in Chapter 10, the investigator asked the question, "Are there differences in the basic beliefs and values among educators of different age groups?" He found that both teachers and principals differed in value patterns, depending on their age: The younger the teacher or principal, the more emergent his values ("the most important thing in school is to learn to get along with people"), and the older the teacher or principal, the more traditional his values ("the most important thing in school is to gain knowledge useful in the future"). It is clear that the role expectations of these groups will differ by age, and insofar as there are these differences, the role-sets are liable to strain and conflict. As the investigator concluded, "... value differences between teachers and principals do affect the teacher's rating of the principal's effectiveness. The effects of these value differences will be manifest in the interpersonal relationships carried on in the school."[9]

Disagreement Among Several Groups, Each Defining Expectations for the Same Role. We may illustrate this type of conflict by an instance from the university setting. The university faculty member may be expected by his department head to emphasize teaching, committee work, and service to students, but by his academic dean to emphasize research, scholarship, and visibility in the profession. Although the two sets of expectations for the same role are not necessarily opposed in any ultimate sense, it is clear that the time and energy devoted to implementing one set takes away time and energy from implementing the other. To this extent they are in conflict. Surely anyone who has ever seen a young instructor attempt to deal with these dual expectations—or who has tried to do it himself—will know what is meant.

Or consider the following data from a study of the definition of the superintendent's role by two groups of "role definers": a group of superintendents and a group of school board members.[10] With respect, for example, to the expectation that the superintendent "defend his teachers from attack when they try to present the pros and cons of various controversial social and political issues," 70 percent of the superintendents gave "absolutely must" responses and 29 percent of the board members gave such responses. With respect to the expectation that the superintendent "help teachers get higher salaries," 46 percent of the superintendents gave "absolutely must" responses and 8 percent of the board members gave such responses. And so on. Does the superintendent conform to the expectations of his professional colleagues or to those of his board members?

Contradiction Between the Expectations of Two or More Roles Which an Individual Is Occupying at the Same Time.

---

[9] Richard Prince, "Individual Values and Administrative Effectiveness," *Administrator's Notebook,* 6 (December, 1957), 3.

[10] Neal C. Gross, Ward S. Mason, and Alexander W. McEachern, *Explorations in Role Analysis: Studies of the School Superintendent Role,* New York, Wiley, 1958.

Multitudinous dilemmas arise from the circumstance that role incumbents in one institution are inevitably also role incumbents in other institutions which may have opposing expectations. A traveling salesman is perhaps also a husband and father; a teacher, a wife and mother; a superintendent of schools, a member of a church (with, as we have seen, calls upon him that are contradictory to his responsibilities in the school); a pupil, a member of a gang; and so on. Conformity to one set of expectations may entail nonconformity to the other set of expectations.

Consider the dilemma of the adolescent attempting simultaneously to be an outstanding student and a popular member of the gang. One investigator found that only 5.3 percent of 3,830 high school students felt that their "friends would envy and look up to them" for being appointed assistant in the biology laboratory because of their good work; 50 percent felt that their friends "would kid them about it, but envy them."[11] In effect, there seemed to be expectations or norms with respect to being one of the gang that precluded being an outstanding student. The investigator generalized from his study as follows:

> The result of these norms produces in students a conflict of motivation; put very simply, to be one of the fellows and not work too hard in school, or to work hard in school and ignore the group. Different teenagers resolve the conflict in different ways. Whichever way it is resolved, it sets an artificial dilemma. On the one hand are sociable average students (who could do better); on the other hand are a few academically-oriented, highly competitive isolates. A boy or girl can be oriented to academic achievement *or* to being popular, but it is hard to be both.[12]

CONFLICT DERIVING FROM PERSONALITY DISORDERS

The preceding types of conflict derive from certain dislocations between the institutional and individual dimensions, and from within the institutional dimension itself. There is also a type of conflict that occurs as a function of certain dislocations in the form of opposing needs and dispositions within the personality of the role incumbent. The effect of such personal instability or maladjustment is to keep the individual at odds with the institution either because he cannot maintain a stable relationship to a given role—misperceives the expectations placed upon him—

---

[11] J. S. Coleman, "Academic Achievement and the Structure of Competition," *Harvard Educational Review*, 29 (1959), 330–351.
[12] *Ibid.*, p. 345.

or because he feels excessive strain in a situation where others under the same circumstances do not.

Existential objects and events have minimal representation in his private world, and there is little correspondence between his private world and the worlds of the other role incumbents with whom he must interact. In a sense, no matter what the situation, the role is detached from its institutional setting and function and used by the individual to work out his needs and dispositions, however inappropriate these may be to the goals of the social system as a whole. It is exactly this type of conflict that selection procedures and psychiatric screening of potential role incumbents attempt to circumvent when they reject individuals who are in some degree psychopathic.

A relevant study may be cited here. The investigators hypothesized that individual differences in *felt conflict* within a given social system—in this case the faculty of an Air Force school, where presumably the objective situation was the same for all—would be a function of personality disorder. Accordingly, the officer-instructors scoring in the highest quarter in felt conflict were compared on a number of personality variables with the officer-instructors scoring in the lowest quarter in felt conflict. Those scoring highest in conflict were found on the Guilford-Martin Inventory to have greater "feelings of inferiority," to be more "nervous," "introverted," "depressive," and cyclical in temperament; on the California E-F Scale to be more "rigid" and "stereotyped"; and on the Rosenzweig Picture-Frustration Study to be more "extrapunitive," and "defensive."[13]

CONFLICT IN THE PERCEPTION OF ROLE EXPECTATIONS

Disagreement among complementary role incumbents—say, between superordinates and subordinates in the administrative setting—as to their mutual rights and obligations is not of course a result solely or even primarily of personality disorder. Differences in personality underlie differences in perception, and there is *selective perception* of expectations as there is of other objects and events in the environment. The administrative relationship, like any complementary role relationship, always functions at two levels of interaction. One level derives from the particular

---

[13] J. W. Getzels and E. G. Guba, "Role, Role Conflict, and Effectiveness: An Empirical Study," *American Sociological Review*, 19 (April, 1954), 164–175; "Role Conflict and Personality," *Journal of Personality*, 24 (September, 1955), 74–85.

offices or statuses in the social system and is determined by the nature of the roles involved in the interaction. The other level derives from the particular people in the roles and is determined by the personalities involved in the interaction. The publicly prescribed role relationship is thus enacted in two separate private situations. The character of the complementary role relationship in action—and in this sense the administrative process —will depend on the overlap (that is, on the relative conflict or similarity) of the definitions of the same expectations in the two situations.

In a study of the perception of expectations for the superintendent's role by superintendents and by various reference groups—teachers, school board members, businessmen, and so on—three patterns of conflict illustrative of the present formulation were identified.[14] (1) The superintendent perceived the expectations of a reference group accurately but did not concur in its views. (2) The superintendent believed there was no difference in his view of the expectations and the views of the reference group when in reality significant differences did exist. (3) The superintendent believed there was a difference in his view of the expectations and the views of the reference group when in reality significant differences did not exist.

An item from the pilot study may serve as an illustration: "I expect the superintendent to choose his friends from people who are important in social, civic, and business affairs." Three types of response on a five-point scale from "strongly agree" (scale score 1) to "strongly disagree" (scale score 5) were obtained. One response was the superintendent's expression of his own expectations; a second was the superintendent's estimate of the expectations of each reference group; a third was the actual expectation given by the reference group. Although the superintendent scored 2.0 when he expressed his own expectations, and he estimated 3.0 for the school board reference group and 3.5 for the businessman reference group, the school board actually scored 3.5 and the businessman group actually scored 2.4.

Whatever the kind of conflict, it seems clear that the proper functioning of certain role relationships in the educational setting, as elsewhere, depends on the degree of overlap in the per-

---

[14] S. P. Hencley, "A Typology of Conflict Between School Superintendents and Their Reference Groups," Doctoral dissertation, University of Chicago, 1960.

ception of expectations by the several complementary role incumbents in the given interaction. Stated in extreme terms, the basic hypothesis of the several relevant research studies was: When the perceptions of expectations overlap, the participants in the relationship feel satisfied with the work achieved; when the perceptions of expectations do not overlap, the participants feel dissatisfied.

Ferneau studied the interaction of administrators and consultants in the school setting.[15] He constructed a problem-situation instrument through which varying expectations for the consultant role could be expressed. The instrument was given to 180 administrators who were known to have had the services of educational consultants and to 46 consultants who were known to have provided the consultative service to these administrators. Each administrator and each consultant was also asked to evaluate the outcome of the consultation. It was then possible to compare the overlap in the perception of the expectations for the consultant role held by the consultant and by the consultee, and to analyze the effect of congruence or discrepancy in expectations on the evaluation of the actual interaction.

The results can be summarized most simply as follows: When the administrator and the consultant agreed on the expectations, they tended to rate the actual consultation favorably; when they disagreed, unfavorably. And apparently the favorable or unfavorable evaluation was in a measure independent either of the particular expectations or of the manifest outcome—a consultation tended to be rated favorably provided the participants' perception of the expectations, whatever their character, overlapped.

To recapitulate, attention has often been called to the occurrence of strain and conflict in a social system. We have pointed to a number of types and sources of conflict in social systems generally and in the educational setting particularly. We placed the relevant issues and phenomena within a single framework and illustrated a number of the pertinent role behaviors and types of conflict by reference to specific empirical studies and examples. Nowhere have we intended to imply that conflict is inevitably an evil. On the contrary, certain types of conflict give rise to productive transformations and inventions. The conflicts

---

[15] E. Ferneau, "Role-Expectations in Consultations," Doctoral dissertation, University of Chicago, 1954.

may be seen as symptomatic of the need for integrative alterations and reorganizations in the system. Sensitivity to the sources of conflict gives the researcher significant issues for investigation and provides the administrator with the means for diagnosing dislocations in the system and with clues to where he can intervene and improve it.

Mechanisms of integration

The relevance of the general model for administrative research and practice becomes apparent when it is seen that the administrative process inevitably deals with the fulfillment of both normative (or institutional) role expectations and idiographic (or personal) need-dispositions while the goals of a particular social system are being achieved. The unique task of administration, at least with respect to staff relations, is to integrate the expectations of the institution and the dispositions of the individuals in a way that is at once organizationally fruitful and individually satisfying.

ROLE ADAPTATION AND SELF-ACTUALIZATION

When an individual performs in accordance with role expectations, from the point of view of the role-set he is *adapting to the role*. When an individual performs in accordance with his needs, from the point of view of his personality he is *actualizing himself*. Ideally, the social system should permit both role adaptation and self-actualization, so that the one act fulfills not only the institutional demands but the personalistic dispositions with a minimum of strain. The relationship between the individual and the institution is then *integrated*.

This would obviously be the case if institutional expectations and personal needs were absolutely congruent, for the individual would always will what was mandatory—each person in the role-set would want for every other person in the role-set what each wanted for himself, and he would then do unto others as he would want them to do unto him. Role adaptation and self-actualization would be maximized, and there would be maximum integration.

But this is a limiting case—an ideal formulation—like the statement that a body in motion will remain in motion, if the physical analogy is not taken too seriously. In practice, if we may carry the analogy one step further, there are unavoidable frictions and conflicts. Absolute congruence between expectations and needs, and among expectations in a role-set and among needs in a personality, is not found in reality. Consequently there is inevitably a greater or lesser amount of conflict for the individual and strain in the institution.

Merton describes the situation from a structural point of view:

> It would seem that the basic source of disturbance in the role-set is the structural circumstance that any one occupying a particular status has role-partners who are differently located in the social structure. As a result, these others have, in some measure, values and moral expectations differing from those held by the occupant of the status in question. The fact, for example, that the members of a school board are often in social and economic strata quite different from that of the public school teacher will mean that, in certain respects, their values and expectations differ from those of the teacher. The individual teacher may thus be readily subject to conflicting role-expectations among his professional colleagues and among the influential members of the school board and, at times, derivatively, of the superintendent of schools. What is an educational frill for the one may be judged as an essential of education by the other. These disparate and inconsistent evaluations complicate the task of coming to terms with them all. What holds conspicuously for the status of the teacher holds, in varying degree, for the occupants of other statuses who are structurally related, in their role-set, to others who themselves occupy diverse statuses.[16]

As we have seen, Merton suggests a number of mechanisms for minimizing these strains. There is, for example, provision for differential involvement by the various role incumbents in the various institutional tasks so that certain potential conflicts never become overt issues. There is the possibility of equalizing power through coalitions, thus neutralizing certain crosspressures. There is the opportunity for periodic privacy from other members of the role-set. There are channels for making known conflicts and contradictions in rights and obligations. There is support by others in similar roles and in similar distressing sit-

---

[16] Robert K. Merton, *Social Theory and Social Structure*, rev. ed., New York, Free Press, 1957, pp. 370–371.

uations through the formation of professional and other associations.

But these structural mechanisms do not entirely do away with the strains. As Merton says:

> ... even when these mechanisms are at work, they may not, in particular instances, prove sufficient to reduce the conflict of expectations among those comprising the role-set below the level required for the role-system to operate with substantial efficiency. This residual conflict within the role-set may be enough to interfere materially with the effective performance of roles by the occupant of the status in question....
>
> We do not yet know some of the requirements for maximum articulation of the relations between the occupant of a status and members of his role-set, on the one hand, and for maximum articulation of the values and expectations among those comprising the role-set, on the other. But as we have seen, even those requirements which can now be identified are not readily satisfied, without fault, in social systems. To the extent that they are not, social systems are forced to limp along with that measure of ineffectiveness and inefficiency which is often tolerated because the realistic prospect of decided improvement seems so remote as sometimes not to be visible at all.[17]

In essence, despite the ameliorative structural mechanisms, the crucial conflicts may remain, and the individual faces the dilemma of integrating the role expectations and his need-dispositions in the social system. Three modes of behavior are open to him: (1) He may choose role adaptation. In the face of conflict between role expectations and need-dispositions, he conforms to the expectations, detaching fulfillment of his needs from the institutional setting in question. (2) He may choose self-actualization. In the face of conflict between role expectations and need-dispositions he expresses the dispositions, rejecting the institutional expectations as personally irrelevant and meaningless. (3) He may choose some compromise between the two.

In practice, the first two do not appear in pure form, and it is the third alternative that is found most frequently. Even so, the compromise is always between some greater and lesser degree of adaptation or self-actualization, and a consideration

---

[17] Ibid., p. 380.

of these will point to the issues involved in the integration of an individual and an institution.

The person who emphasizes adaptation seeks criteria for behavior *outside* himself. His attitude is that to get along one does what one should. He attempts to fit into things as they already are and steers a course by the expectations of those above, below, and to the side, not forgetting to keep an eye to the rear. He makes his way in the system through conformity rather than through trying to be creative. The consequence for the institution is the consensuality and uniformity, with only bland commitment—if commitment it is—of the "organization man" or "insider." The consequences for the person are loss of spontaneity and failure in personal authenticity. The individual is induced to play roles rather than be himself, agreeing when his impulse is to disagree, smiling when his impulse is to laugh (or cry). He rejects the aspects of his personality that are inconsistent with his role, permitting his behavior to be defined by others. He does not so much act as react. At extremes, he becomes withdrawn and fearful of decisions and actions altogether. He becomes the "disorganized organization man."

The person who emphasizes self-actualization seeks criteria for behavior *within* himself. He sees the system primarily as a means for fulfilling his needs, rather than himself as a means for attaining the system's goals. He therefore feels free to disregard role expectations when they are contrary to his need-dispositions. However, since his obligations *to* the system are the rights of others *from* the system, the result is manifest failure in the balance of rights and obligations in the role-set. Sanctions may legitimately be invoked and, from the point of view of fair play in the role-set, must be applied. They may take the form of punishment, personal ostracism, or isolation from the role-set. The consequence for the institution is the provoking, sometimes institutionally dangerous, nearly always disruptive intrusion of the "organization maverick" or "outsider." The consequences for the person are loss of belongingness and failure in social integration. The individual underidentifies with the cultural values, rejects institutional responsibility, and becomes the "alienated man." If the extreme of role adaptation leads to separation of the person from authentic selfhood, the extreme of indulging one's needs without regard to the effect upon others leads to alienation from humanity. In a sense, the two are but different sides of the same coin: The result of both is deprivation for the social system and impoverishment of the personality.

SOCIALIZATION OF PERSONALITY AND
PERSONALIZATION OF ROLE

Administration must cope with the indicated organizational conflicts and the potential dysfunctional modes of reaction to them by the individuals in the system. From this point of view, a fundamental task of administration is to reduce the discrepancy between what we have designated as the normative and personal axes of behavior so that individual-institutional integration can be maximized. Two forces may be brought to bear on this problem: *socialization* of the personality and *personalization* of the role in question.[18]

Personalization of role operates on the structure of expectations in the normative axis of behavior by so altering it as to bring it into greater congruence with the needs of a particular role incumbent or incumbents. Socialization of personality operates on the structure of need-dispositions in the individual axis of behavior by so altering it as to bring it into greater congruence with the expectations of a particular role or roles. Both processes, in their different ways, tend to maximize individual-institutional integration.

```
              Personalization
                    ↓
            Role Expectations ╲
                                ╲
                 ↕↕              ──→ Social Behavior
                                ╱
            Need-Dispositions ╱
                    ↑
              Socialization
```

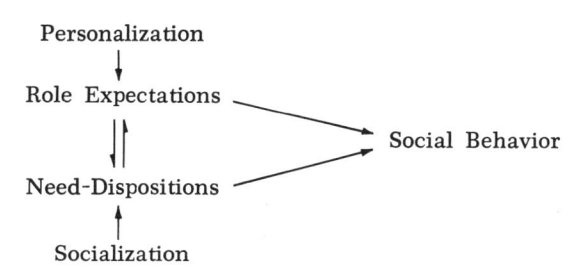

FIGURE 5–1. *Personalization and socialization forces on normative and personal axes of behavior.*

The processes are illustrated in Figure 5–1, which is a reproduction in part of the basic model presented in Figure 4–1. Personalization is shown as a force acting upon role expectations, whereas socialization is shown as a force acting upon need-

[18] E. Wight Bakke, *Organization and the Individual*, New Haven, Labor and Management Center, Yale University, 1952.

dispositions, each tending to push the normative and idiographic axes toward congruence.

Of the two methods theoretically available for improving congruence, at first glance it would seem hardly possible to do a great deal with personalization of roles. It is assumed that the institutional organization will permit little tampering with roles which have presumably been formulated to achieve the goals of the system. Yet role expectations can be successfully altered to conform to the needs of role incumbents. For example, immediately after World War II, many colleges changed their expectations with respect to credentials for admission, courses of study, residence requirements, and parietal rules in accordance with the needs of the returning veterans, who were older and more experienced than the usual student. They found the veterans extraordinarily able and cooperative students and look back upon the period as one of outstanding educational achievement. The colleges that did not take such measures, but held on to the role of the student as previously defined, found the veteran group rather hard to deal with—"grown men who could not adapt to the adolescent status of student," as the administrator of one of the institutions that failed to change its expectations put it. He did not see that there was no need for his institution to maintain the expectations for the role of student in adolescent terms; it could also be defined in adult terms, and the student could be treated as an adult—if adult he indeed was.

Typically, however, the organization must deal with the problem of acquiring individuals to fit the roles that already exist or, failing this, to use training and supervision as a way of making the available individuals fit the roles that have to be implemented. In the latter case, the situation is not too dissimilar from the process described in Chapter 4: the socialization of the person through training and induction procedures so that he acquires the values and skills needed to secure a productive place in the culture.

More specifically, with respect to socialization as a force in maximizing the integration of personnel in a social system, there appear to be several alternatives at the command of the administrator. One is to depend on preinduction socialization; another is to depend on postinduction socialization; a third is of course to utilize some combination of the two.

In the preinduction alternative, an attempt is made to obtain already appropriately socialized personalities through *selection* procedures. Thus the system admits individuals whose needs and abilities are consonant with the expectations for the role and bars from entry individuals whose needs and abilities are not consonant with those expectations. Organizations act just this way when they evaluate the dispositions and skills of a prospective role incumbent both from within and without the system, whether the role be that of student, salesman, weight lifter, professor, or executive vice-president. In the postinduction alternative an attempt is made to obtain any available individuals, assuring only a number of basic requirements, such as appropriate age or sex and organic well-being, and socialize them into the system through *training and supervisory* procedures. The army during draft mobilization is a case in point, although any organization needing great numbers of personnel to fill many roles follows this pattern at least to some extent. Most often a combination of the two alternatives is used, the degree of each depending on the nature of the available pool of manpower and on the level of technical skills and institutional commitment required for the various roles.

Each process has its uses. An organization needing highly skilled professionals must exercise the preinduction socialization alternative; it cannot readily apply postinduction socialization to satisfy its requirements. An organization needing only meagerly skilled nonprofessionals does not ordinarily utilize preinduction socialization but can rely on postinduction socialization to satisfy its requirements. Each process has dangers. Selection procedures are not so precise as invariably to insure successful individual-institutional integration. And the intent or at least the result of the training may not be socialization in any real sense but only inculcation of an automatic pattern of behavior and enforced compliance to the pattern through strict supervision; in this case there is only adaptation without actualization, and consequent failure in the sought-for individual-institutional integration.

In any event, in accordance with these alternatives, a heavy administrative investment may be made in selection procedures and a saving effected in training and supervisory efforts. Or, conversely, a heavy investment may be made in training and supervisory procedures and a saving effected in selection efforts. The choice of one or the other as predominant integrative policy usually depends on the factors already indicated. It is also strongly related, however, to the general administrative emphasis on the institutional or individual axes of behavior, selection procedures stressing the individual axis, supervision procedures the institutional axis. In general, insofar as behavior in a social system is a combination of role and personality in some proportion, the greater the proportion of role elements, the more will the system rely on postinduction socialization and supervision; the greater the proportion of personality elements, the more will the system rely on preinduction socialization and selection.

The relationships are illustrated graphically in Figure 5–2, which is a reproduction in part of the basic model presented in Figure 4–2.

Postinduction		Preinduction
Socialization		Socialization
and		and
Supervision	Personality	Selection

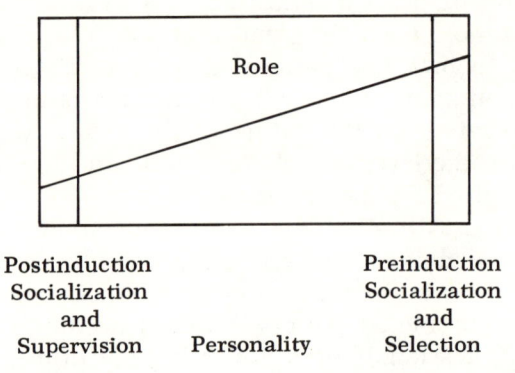

FIGURE 5–2. *Relationships between role and personality proportions of behavior in a social system, and the use of postinduction and preinduction mechanisms of individual-institutional integration.*

Criteria of organizational behavior

A primary concern in the administration of any social system is the development and maintenance of effectiveness, efficiency, satisfaction, and morale. The problems involved here have been confused for want of an appropriate framework for observing the indicated phenomena independently and for understanding the relationships among them within the same conceptual scheme.[19] The use interchangeably of the terms "effectiveness," "efficiency," "satisfaction," and "morale"—for example, in the quotation from

---

[19] Portions of the following are drawn from Getzels and Guba, "Social Behavior and the Administrative Process," pp. 423–441.

Merton "effectiveness" and "efficiency" are synonyms—has tended to obscure the significant issues and the fruitful distinctions implied by these several concepts. The model we are using makes possible a number of clear-cut and heuristic distinctions among the terms so that a given role incumbent may, for instance, be seen as effective without being efficient or efficient without being effective.

EFFECTIVENESS AND EFFICIENCY

Implicitly or explicitly, no conceptual distinction about organizational behavior is made more frequently than that between institutional (or group) goals and individual (or personal) goals. Moreover, no criteria of evaluation of behavior in an organization have been applied more often than effectiveness and efficiency. Egregious confusion results when the distinction between institutional and individual goals is not borne in mind and when the meanings of effectiveness and efficiency are not differentiated.

In his classic *The Functions of the Executive*, Chester Barnard makes the point incisively:

> ... The persistence of cooperation depends upon two conditions: (a) its effectiveness; and (b) its efficiency. Effectiveness relates to the accomplishment of the cooperative purpose, which is social and non-personal in character. Efficiency relates to the satisfaction of individual motives, and is personal in character.[20]

The optimum operation of the organization as a whole depends on these two factors: effectiveness and efficiency. Using a somewhat different terminology, but referring essentially to the same phenomena, Bakke and Argyris say:

> The first problem in all organizational life is how to take an aggregate of varied individual people, with varied capacities and predispositions and get them involved in cooperative activity which adds up to success for the organization and satisfaction for the individuals concerned. In short, the problem is to integrate the individual participants with the organization.
>
> Our first job is to get clearly in mind the essential characteristics of the "things" we are trying to integrate. These things are basically (a) the organization, and (b) the individual.[21]

---

[20] Chester I. Barnard, *The Functions of the Executive*, Cambridge, Mass., Harvard University Press, 1964, p. 60.
[21] E. W. Bakke and C. Argyris, *Organizational Structure and Dynamics*, New Haven, Labor and Management Center, Yale University, 1954, p. 4.

In these terms, Barnard's concept of effectiveness refers to the degree of success for the organization, and his concept of efficiency refers to the degree of satisfaction for the individual.

The Ohio research group has a similar dichotomy in their view of leadership behavior. They postulate two fundamental dimensions, initiating structure and consideration, defined as follows:

> 1. Initiating Structure refers to the leader's behavior in delineating the relationship between himself and members of the work group, and in endeavoring to establish well-defined patterns of organization, channels of communication, and methods of procedure.
> 2. Consideration refers to behavior indicative of friendship, mutual trust, respect, and warmth in the relationship between the leader and the members of his staff.[22]

Superior leadership behavior is associated with above-average performance in both dimensions. Note again the similarity of this dichotomy to effectiveness, which deals with impersonal goals, and to efficiency, which deals with personal goals.

```
Role ─────────────→ Expectations ╲ Effectiveness
                         ↕                        ╲
                    Satisfaction                   ↘ Behavior
                         ↕                        ↗
Personality ──────→ Need-Dispositions ╱ Efficiency
```

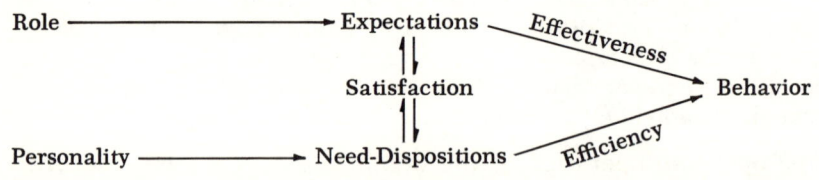

FIGURE 5–3. *Relation of role expectations and need-dispositions to effectiveness, efficiency, and satisfaction. (Adapted from J. W. Getzels and E. G. Guba, "Social Behavior and the Administrative Process,"* School Review, 65 [1957], 433.)

We now return to our general model and recall the basic formulation of social behavior in the administrative setting as a function of role expectations and personality dispositions. The significant distinctions and interactions among effectiveness, efficiency, and satisfaction may be viewed in terms of the relationships among these primary elements of the model. The relationships are shown in Figure 5–3.

The criterion for effectiveness has usually been the observed behavior of the individual being rated, or so it is thought. How-

---

[22] Andrew W. Halpin, *The Leadership Behavior of School Superintendents*, Chicago, Midwest Administration Center, University of Chicago, reprinted 1959, p. 4.

ever, the standard may not be the behavior itself but the observed behavior *relative* to some criterion against which it is evaluated. In effectiveness, this criterion, explicitly or implicitly, is made up of the expectations held for the behavior. Effectiveness is then a measure of the concordance of the role behavior and the role expectations. Two crucial consequences follow: (1) The same behavior may be held effective at one time and ineffective at another time by the same person, depending on the expectations he applies to the behavior. (2) The same behavior may be held effective and ineffective simultaneously because different persons or groups apply different expectations to the behavior. In either case, judgments of effectiveness and ineffectiveness are impossible to interpret unless both the expectations being applied and the behavior being observed are known. In the terms of our model, effectiveness is a function of the congruence of behavior and expectations.

Just as effectiveness depends on the relationship between expectations and behavior, so efficiency depends on the relationship between needs and behavior. To the extent that needs and expectations are not congruent, behavior may conform to the one or the other, or, what is more likely, in some measure to both. When behavior conforms to the needs dimension, it appears "natural," even pleasurable—the individual is doing what he wants to be doing—and is forthcoming with a minimum of strain or expenditure of psychic energy. In this sense the behavior may be said to be efficient. When the behavior conforms to the expectations dimension, and there is a conflict between the expectations and the needs, behavior is "unnatural," even painful—the individual is *not* doing what he wants to be doing—and is forthcoming with a maximum of strain and expenditure of psychic energy. In this sense it is inefficient. In the terms of the model, we may say efficiency is a function of the congruence between behavior and need-dispositions.

SATISFACTION AND MORALE

The term "satisfaction" as used here is more or less synonymous with "contentment." It should not be taken to include such additional concepts as agreement with institutional objectives or the feeling that the institutional environment is up to the individual's standards of technical or professional adequacy. In the sense of contentment, satisfaction results from the absence of role-personality conflicts—the individual is not required to do anything he does not want to do. In the limiting case, if he does not want to do anything, and he is not required to do anything, he may still be satisfied. Criteria of effectiveness and efficiency are irrelevant. In the present terms, satisfaction may be said to be a function of the congruence between individual needs and institutional expectations.

The administrator is of course faced with the dilemma of behaving so as to produce simultaneously the maximum of both effectiveness and efficiency. This is possible only if the institutional expectations and the individual needs coincide, and such an ideal situation is never quite realized. Needs and expectations rarely if ever coincide. Even if they coincided for one role incumbent, they would not for another whose personality differed in any respect. Thus, when needs and expectations are not congruent, satisfaction is automatically less than maximum.

But it does not necessarily follow that *both* effectiveness and efficiency will also automatically be lowered. Since the individual has a choice of behavior to conform either to his needs or to the expectations, either maximum effectiveness or maximum efficiency may be retained, at the expense of the other. Thus, for less than perfect congruence between needs and expectations, effectiveness and efficiency may take any value for a given level of satisfaction. Here is at least one explanation for the not infrequently observed anomaly of periodic high production in an organization in the face of great dissatisfaction. For one reason or another, the individuals choose to conform to expectations rather than to their needs, and thereby retain high effectiveness, although at great internal cost to themselves. Maximum effectiveness with minimal satisfaction can be maintained for only relatively short periods—in bursts of feverish activity, as it were—since it is at exorbitant cost in psychic energy with consequent intolerable frustration. In these terms, effectiveness without satisfaction is ultimately inefficient.

Although the morale of organizations is much talked about, there have been few attempts to define the concept in any systematic way. Morale is generally taken to refer to a feeling-tone of belongingness in a group and identification with the goals of the group. In the present formulation, it is seen as the pattern of affect underlying effectiveness, efficiency, and satisfaction. This viewpoint takes into account the two elements most often included in the literature on morale, namely, belongingness and identification, and suggests a third element, rationality, which, although often overlooked, is as vital as the other two.

The nature of morale from this standpoint may be comprehended by reference to Figure 5-4, which presents the familiar relationship between role expectations and need-dispositions and, an additional factor, the goals of the system. We again postulate a role incumbent bringing to the system his individual pattern of needs, and subject to the expectations of his role. The goals of the system may or may not be at one with the goals of the individual, and the overlap among the expectations, needs, and goals may be more or less congruent or incongruent.

```
Role
Expectations
    ↑  B
       e         Rationality
       l       ─────────────→
       o
       n
       g
       i                            Goals of the System
       n                           ←
       g
       n       ─────────────→
       e         Identification
       s
    ↓  s
Need-
Dispositions
```

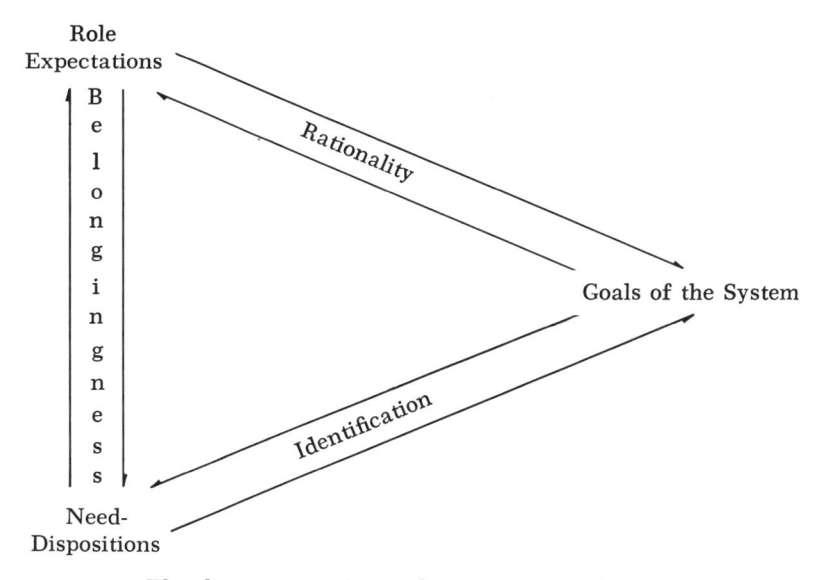

FIGURE 5-4. *The dimensions of morale. (Adapted from J. W. Getzels and E. G. Guba, "Social Behavior and the Administrative Process,"* School Review, 65 [1957], 436.)

When the needs of the individual and the goals of the system are congruent, there is a feeling of *identification* with the system. When the needs of the individual and the expectations of the role-set are congruent, there is a feeling of satisfaction and *belongingness* in the system. When the expectations of the roles and the goals of the system are congruent, there is a feeling of *rationality* regarding the system. A word of elaboration with respect to each of these variables is in order.

The variable *belongingness* refers to the feeling on the part of the role incumbent that he will be able to achieve satisfaction in the role-set, since the institutional expectations appear to him to be in accord with his personal needs. Work in the system is therefore doubly attractive, for in meeting the expectations of the role, the individual also sees himself as actualizing his needs. In effect, the persons in the role-set are related not only through institutional imperatives but also through personalistic dispositions, and in this sense it is "all for one, and one for all." When belongingness is high, everyone in the system is ready to "pull together."

The variable *rationality* represents the extent to which the expectations of a role are felt to be logically appropriate to the achievement of the professed goals of the system. Even if the individuals in the system feel a strong relationship between their needs and the expectations—that is, there is high belongingness—morale may still be low if they believe that what they are expected to do is incongruent with what the system as a whole was set up to do. There is little point in expending effort if what is supposed to be done is not regarded as relevant to the goals to be achieved. Here is the great difference between being "in the know" and being "in the dark" about what is going on. The function of communication in a system—having everyone appreciate the reason for the expected behavior even when he cannot have a say in the nature of the behavior—is just this: It provides a basis for increasing rationality, and hence morale.

The variable *identification* refers to the degree to which the goals of the system are integrated with the needs and values of the individuals in the system. When identification is high, the goals of the system are part of the motivational structure of the individuals, who are therefore ego-involved in what they do. The goals of the system are *their* goals. Two points regarding the relation between rationality and identification must be noted. On the one hand, it is possible to be committed to the goals and yet believe that the role expectations are ill suited to achieving them. In this case there is identification without rationality, and morale is low, since the expenditure of effort in role performance is not seen as contributing to the achievement of the goals. On the other hand, it is possible to believe that the role expectations are well suited to achieving the goals but not to be identified with them. In this case there is rationality without identification, and morale is again low, since the expenditure of effort in role performance is not seen as contributing to any personally relevant goals. There is, thus, no reason to do more than conform in a mechanical way to what is expected. Ego-involvement in role performance in a system—wanting to do more than merely get by—requires identification with the goals of the system.

In the terms of this formulation, then, morale may be understood as a function of three variables: belongingness, rationality, and identification. Morale cannot be high if one of these factors is at a minimum. It can, however, reach acceptable levels if all three elements are maintained to some degree. In this sense, the task of the administrator seeking to develop high morale is to establish reasonable levels of congruence among the expectations of roles, the needs of the role incumbents, and the goals of the system. Concomitants will be satisfaction, effectiveness, and efficiency.

On the nature of subordinate-superordinate relationships and leadership-followership styles

We have observed that administration deals essentially with the conduct of social behavior in a hierarchical setting. Structurally, we have conceived of administration as a series of subordinate-superordinate role relationships within a social system. Functionally, this hierarchy is the locus for allocating and integrating roles, personnel, and facilities to achieve the goals of the system. We may think of the basic interpersonal administrative relationship as a dyad, one member, the superordinate, being the initiator of administrative action and the other, the subordinate, being the recipient of the action. *But it must be emphasized again that the terms "superordinate" and "subordinate," "initiator" and "recipient" are only relative. The subordinate can be the initiator of the action to which the superordinate must respond, and the superordinate can be the recipient of action which the subordinate may initiate.*[23]

SUPERORDINATE-SUBORDINATE RELATIONSHIPS

Administrative relationships may be studied in terms of four crucial variables: (1) the *authority* variable, that is, the source

---

[23] Portions of this and what follows are drawn from J. W. Getzels, "A Psycho-Sociological Framework for the Study of Educational Administration," *Harvard Educational Review*, 22 (Fall, 1952), 235-246.

and nature of the superordination and the subordination, (2) the *scope* variable, that is, the range of expectations, dispositions, and facilities covered in the relationship; (3) the *affectivity* variable, that is, the quality of the "personal" interaction; and (4) the *sanctions* variable, that is, the kinds of rewards and punishments at issue in the relationship.[24]

The Authority Variable. Following Max Weber, we may identify three legitimate types of authority: *traditional, charismatic,* and *rational*. The fact that none of these is likely to be operating in completely pure form in actuality does not prohibit their use as "ideal types" or limiting categories. Indeed, their very nonpurity permits them to serve as relatively unambiguous concepts for ordering empirical observations and for systematic analysis.

Traditional authority is based on the established belief in the sanctity of the traditions under which the one in authority exercises his power. Obedience is owed to him because he occupies a traditionally sanctified position. The monarch is an example. Charismatic authority is based on devotion to the exemplary character and superior general wisdom of an individual. Obedience is owed to him because of personal trust in him and the normative patterns ordained by him. The prophet is an example.

Clearly the business or educational administrator does not claim his right to authority on either traditional or charismatic grounds. His dominance is not based on a superior sanctified status or on the manifestation of superior general wisdom or high moral character. It is based rather on superior knowledge and technical competence in a particular element in the division of labor. The administrator's claim to obedience—or perhaps better here, to cooperation—ideally finds its root in the third source of legitimate authority: rationality. He has the technical training and the competence to allocate and integrate the roles, personnel, and facilities required for attaining the goals of the system.

The requirement of rationality is especially stringent in the educational setting—more so than in, say, the business enterprise, which has other bases for administrative authority. Ownership of the means of production or being the boss's son may

---

[24] The debt of the formulations in this section to the work of Max Weber and of Talcott Parsons, especially to the latter's "The Professions and Social Structure," in *Essays in Sociological Theory*, rev. ed., New York, Free Press, 1954, pp. 34–50, will be evident.

serve as a source of authority. True, reliance on these rather than on objective evidence of technical competence—that is, rationality—may lower morale. The means of eliciting cooperation (or, more exactly in this context, obedience) may become a matter of unilateral coercion rather than reciprocal rationality. For example, the owner of the instruments of production may threaten to close up shop altogether and take his business elsewhere. Nevertheless, except in the extreme instance, it is generally not fatal to the business enterprise if the administrative relationship does depart substantially from pure rationality.

In education, such departure from rationality may be catastrophic. If the educational administrator's claim to obedience, or cooperation, is not grounded in rational considerations of competence, then it can be grounded in little else. The educational administrator is peculiarly without resources for eliciting secondary motivations. He does not have other ready, even if less legitimate, bases for authority. He does not, for example, own the means of production, and it makes no difference if he is the boss's son. If the rational relationship breaks down, his use of arbitrary methods is notably restricted. He cannot threaten to move his shop elsewhere. He cannot easily fire or demote. He often cannot even increase or decrease remuneration. Many teachers have tenure, and there is frequently a fixed salary scale. Any special indirect pressure he may bring to bear, such as onerous chores for some teachers and favoritism to others, is usually reflected in lowered general morale and a concomitant loss in institutional effectiveness. In short, insofar as the educational administrator tries to establish dominance by appealing to nonlegitimate forms of power, he is bound to fail.

Another critical point is that *both* members of the major administrative relationship in education hold professional status. Neither the administrator nor the administered may readily relinquish his professional prerogative to recognition as an expert in his own field without serious loss of face and prestige. An essential feature of the rational administrative relationship is its *reciprocity*. The members of the dyad make functional claims on each other. This reciprocity, important in any case, is reinforced by the fact that both members of the dyad in education, being professionals, are in effect experts in their respective fields.

Within the same general context, but in the set of terms and relationships we have been utilizing, authority may be seen as *vested* or *entrusted*, depending on the source of power. Authority is vested when power resides in the institution—the normative dimension—and obedience is *owed* to the superordinate by the subordinate by virtue of the role each occupies. Perhaps the best example of this type of authority is found in the military. The channels through which power is exercised are clearly and formally defined, and every role incumbent is expected to submit to superior authority as well as to wield the authority attaching to his own role with conviction and dispatch. Authority is entrusted when power resides in the individuals occupying the roles—in the personal dimension—and obedience is *granted* to the superordinate by the subordinate (quite as it is sometimes "delegated" to the subordinate by the superordinate) because of some specific competence he is seen to possess. A university faculty presents a good example of this type of authority. Superordinates are viewed as colleagues or peers rather than superiors. The chairman is *elected*, and although his professors have tenure, the chairman as chairman does *not*. His function is to lead rather than to command, to persuade rather than to compel. The channels of authority are often informal and even somewhat ambiguous. Vested authority resides in and emphasizes the normative or role axis of behavior; entrusted authority resides in and emphasizes the idiographic or personalistic axis of behavior.

The Scope Variable. The scope of expectations, dispositions, and facilities that may legitimately be involved in the administrative relationship is defined with reference to two types of interaction: *functionally diffuse* and *functionally specific*. In the functionally diffuse type of interaction the members of the dyad are intimately bound to each other in such a way that their mutual obligations are taken for granted and are in a sense limitless. In the functionally specific type the obligations are restricted to those elements in the relationship that are defined by the technical competence and the institutional status of the role incumbents. Neither member of the dyad may venture beyond certain exact boundaries without getting out of the sphere of competence on which the authority conceded to him by the other member rests. In the functionally diffuse relationship it is necessary to prove that an expectation or facility *is not* within the province of the relationship; in the functionally specific relationship it must be proved that the expectation or facility *is* within the province of the relationship.

Obviously, from the analysis of the authority variable, the administrative relationship in education cannot be functionally diffuse. It must be functionally specific. The area of administrative authority is limited to a particular technically defined sphere, and what is not specifically conceded to the administrator because of his special competence remains the private affair of the administered.

The requirement of functional specificity is not peculiar to education but is at the very foundation of all administration based on rational authority. Only in matters touching on civic enterprise, for example, does the staff or the man in the street concede to the city manager special competence and grant him authority. In matters touching on spiritual beliefs he is not only denied authority but in the extreme case may be despised as a heathen. The health commissioner is by definition an expert in matters of public health and in a sense the keeper of our hygienic practices, at least as these affect others. He is not an authority on morals, and neither his official subordinates nor the public that yields to him in matters of sanitation will grant him more than the right to a private opinion where matters of conscience are concerned. At the base of all these relationships is the assumption of functional specificity. In this respect the pure case may be defined as one in which the administrative interaction engages only the single relevant role occupied by the participants in the relationship within the structure of the particular system.

Functional specificity is critical in the educational setting. In few areas of administration is the relationship between the subordinate and the superordinate so fraught with multiple pressures as in the educational enterprise. In addition to the shifting institutional needs, personal involvements, and professional differences, there are the inescapable social, political, religious, and economic crosscurrents of the community. Recall the teacher who is not permitted to smoke even when the parents do, the superintendent who must consider the wishes of the church, the principal who may not participate in public controversy. In spite of the ideal requirement of functional specificity the administrative interaction in education is in practice inevitably exposed to the danger of developing patterns of functional diffusion, and the administrator may be seen as "butting into things that are none of his business."

Within the terms and conceptual relationships we have been using, from the point of view of the individual axis of behavior and entrusted authority, which would reserve for the individual the greatest autonomy of action, the scope of the administrative relationship must be limited primarily to matters of technical competence and institutional status. It calls for an interaction between subordinate and superordinate which is functionally specific. From the point of view of the institutional axis of behavior and vested authority, which would reserve for the institution the greatest control of action, the scope of the relationship may be seen as limitless, extending to any area of behavior, however personal to the individual. It calls for an interaction that is functionally diffuse.

When the relationship is specific, in any conflict between the superordinate and the subordinate as to their mutual rights and obligations, the burden of proof lies with the superordinate to show that the disputed expectation or behavior is specifically included among the subordinate's obligations. When the relationship is diffuse, in the same conflict, the burden of proof lies with the subordinate to show that the disputed expectation or behavior is specifically excluded from his obligations. It should be noted that the issue here is not the *number* of expectations involved. Obviously a complex role might contain a great many expectations without being diffuse. The crucial element in diffuseness is the inclusion in the role definition of a number of expectations that are relatively removed from the fulfillment of institutional goals. For example, in the school setting, a teacher is sometimes required to live in the community where he works or to belong to a particular church but not to a particular political party, and so on; in the business setting, a junior executive is sometimes required to have only certain kinds of interests, drive only certain kinds of automobiles, and maintain a particular style of personal behavior. In a democratic state the chief executive may rule only over matters of politics; and matters of religion, morals, and the arts, for example, are seen as outside his official purview. The relationship between government executive and citizenry is functionally specific. In an authoritarian state the chief executive rules not only over matters of politics but over matters of religion, morals, and artistic taste also. His relationship to the citizenry is functionally diffuse.

The Affectivity Variable. Since we have conceived of the administrative act as being carried on within an interpersonal relationship, the crucial problem of the distinctive nature of the "personal" or "affective" qualities of this relationship arises. It is of course easy to prescribe that the relationship be friendly, that it be mutually satisfactory, that it conform to standards of good personal relations—or some other desiderata of human behavior usually applied in this context. But what conceivable interaction between individuals is not the better for being friendly, mutually satisfactory, or in conformity with standards of good personal relations? Formulations pointing to the *distinctive* character of the personal relationship—apart from general goodness or badness—are needed. The concepts of *universalism* and *particularism*, already introduced in relation to emotional factors in the perception of roles, are useful here too.

It will be recalled that an interpersonal relationship is particularistic when the interaction between the participants is determined by what they mean to each other personally, not by the offices they occupy within the institution. Emotional rather than functional ties define their mutual rights and obligations. In the universalistic relationship matters are reversed. Emotional considerations are secondary to functional ones. Rights and obligations are determined on the basis of impersonal rather than personal factors.

There is little doubt that the efficiency of an individual may increase independently of other incentives as a result of the affective aspects of the administrative relationship. The important factor here is not so much the over-all structure of the institution but the nature of the face-to-face relations in the immediate role-set or group of which the individual is a member. Although the blueprint of an organization may be drawn up entirely in terms of universalistic relationships, as indeed it almost always must be, the actual administrative interactions inevitably tend toward particularism. The foreman often takes on the role of patriarch or big brother to his "boys," and when the worker talks of a "good boss I'd do almost anything for," he does not mean the abstraction "management" but the superordinate with whom he is in day-to-day contact, and whom he not infrequently describes in such terms as "being like a father to me."[25]

Similar patterns develop even in the presumably impersonal military organization. Evidence from the last war makes it clear that the motivation of the individual soldier depended more on personal relationships within the face-to-face unit than on any broad ideological or impersonal consideration. Within the same regimental structure, one platoon could have high morale and

---

[25] F. J. Roethlisberger and William J. Dickson, *Management and the Worker*, Cambridge, Mass., Harvard University Press, 1939, p. 333.

another low morale, depending on the affective relationships in the small group. Although on paper no institution is conceived on more universalistic standards than the army, in practice the actual administration is carried on in relationships that tend, especially at the lower levels, to take on all the particularistic qualities of primary groups. In fact, despite the generally severe disciplinary control of the German army, company-grade officers were not only trained to be considerate to the men in their unit but encouraged to use fatherly modes of address to them—*Kinder* (children).[26]

Two standards of affectivity seem to operate in large-scale organizations. On the one hand, top-level administration is usually divorced from direct contact with the vast majority of its personnel, and administrative policies for the achievement of institutional goals are formulated in terms of universalistic criteria. On the other, these policies are implemented at lower levels in primary groups where the relations between administered and administrator are inevitably to some extent particularistic. Consider the difference between the "top brass" who impersonally order that a certain objective must be reached in the face of enemy fire, "no matter who goes," and the company or platoon leader who must choose from among "his men" and give them the order for the task. Or consider the difference between "management" in the head office, ordering that all branches must cut personnel by 10 percent, and the individual branch manager who must choose the individuals to be fired. We would hold it as axiomatic that universalism varies inversely and particularism directly with the distance between statuses and the frequency of the face-to-face contacts between the administrator and the administered.

This circumstance creates a special problem in the educational setting, at least in institutions of usual size. The superintendent is top management, as it were, but he is also in face-to-face proximity with those whom he "manages." Each administrative act becomes a matter of both universalistic and particularistic considerations, with the result that the crucial issue is likely to be confused by the multiplicity of standards consciously or unconsciously applied to it. In the instance we cited in a preceding section, when it becomes necessary to shift teachers from one location to another, does the superintendent

---

[26] E. A. Shils and M. Janowitz, "Cohesion and Disintegration in the Wehrmacht in World War II," *Public Opinion Quarterly*, 12 (1948), 297.

use purely universalistic or particularistic criteria in saying who is to move? What is the effect of the choice of criteria on his later relations to the teachers involved? In this connection also, remember again that since both members of the administrative dyad in education hold (or at least aspire to hold) professional status, the interaction cannot be like that between officer and enlisted man, foreman and factory hand. In short, the affectivity dimension in educational administration is as complex as it is important. Conclusions from industry and the military cannot be taken over without careful scrutiny of the circumstances of the educational setting.

In the context of the terms and relationships of the general framework we are utilizing, the issues may be summarized as follows. An important variable in the administrative relationship is the quality of the personal or affective interaction. Affectivity may be neutral (impersonal) or charged with meaning for the individuals involved (personal). Interactions are said to be impersonal when they are expected to have the same quality for all participants. In this sense, they are based upon constant behavioral norms, and the relationship between the participants is *universalistic*. Interactions are said to be personal when they are expected to have varying qualities depending on the identity of the particular participants. In this sense, they are based upon differential behavioral norms, and the relationship is *particularistic*. It is of course clear that, from the institutional point of view, administrative relationships must be based on universalistic norms transcending any personal needs or special circumstances—the primary consideration is what is best for the institution. From the individual point of view, administrative relationships must be based on particularistic norms specific to the given role incumbents—the primary consideration is what is best for the individual. As Parsons has suggested, in the particularistic relationship the important question is *who* is involved; in the universalistic relationship the important question is *what* is involved.

The Sanctions Variable. The fact that tasks for achieving the goals of a system are organized into roles implies that the roles serve as "norms" for the role incumbents. It is obligatory for each member of the system to behave more or less in accordance with the expectations of his role if the goals of the system as a whole are to be reached. But the mere existence of norms and expectations is of no consequence unless there is adherence to them. There must also be institutionalized ways of utilizing existing motivations for role performance (the optimum situation), or of creating such motivations, or, if need be, of enforcing adherence to the expectations. Accordingly, social systems have at their disposal controls, in the way of positive and negative *sanctions*, for insuring compliance to the norms, at least within broad limits. That is, one role incumbent has not only the opportunity but the obligation to apply appropriate sanctions to another role incumbent, depending upon the latter's success or failure in meeting his role obligations. For example, the teacher may give a student an A, a C, or an F, depending on the degree to which he exceeds, meets, or fails to meet expectations; a worker may be paid, raised, or fired, depending on the degree to which he meets, exceeds, or fails to meet expectations; and so on. Although we are discussing the problem of sanctions from the point of view of the superordinate member of a complementary role relationship, it is clear that both he *and* the subordinate member of the relationship have sanctions at their disposal: The student or his parent can complain about the teacher to the principal; the worker can seek redress for mistreatment in a grievance committee or form coalitions of power to take more drastic action.

So far we have been dealing largely with what may be called *extrinsic* sanctions—praise and censure, promotion and dismissal, increase and decrease in remuneration. In extrinsic sanctions the control of behavior by the institution and the feeling of satisfaction or dissatisfaction by the individual do not come from the role performance itself but as a by-product of it. In the case of the student, the negative sanction and the punishment are presumed to come not from the failure to learn but from the F; the positive sanction and reward are presumed to come not from the learning but from the A. In the case of the worker, the positive sanction and satisfaction are presumed to come not from the actual performance itself but from the consequences of the performance—it is not the skill or quality of the output but the measure of the external reward or punishment that is central.

There are other more subtle and ultimately more powerful and useful sanctions. These *intrinsic* sanctions are related not to the by-products of role performance but to the performance itself, not to the praise or pay but to the motives and satisfactions involved in what is actually being done. In the instance of the student, it is not the A but the learning that counts; in the instance of the worker, not the raise but the job well done.

In this connection, a useful distinction may be made between *labor* and *work*. In labor, energy is expended on the performance of a role for external purposes: one applies himself in order to gain something extrinsic to the role itself—say, in order to earn praise or money—and it really does not matter very much what one is doing or how well he is doing it. In work, energy is expended on performance of a role for intrinsic purposes: one applies himself because of the satisfaction inherent in the performance of the role itself, and it matters very much what one is doing and how well he is doing it.

This is not to say that praise, pay, promotion, and other positive sanctions (as well as negative sanctions) at the disposal of the system are unnecessary, but they are not sufficient. One *must* perform in order to have the necessities of life—obtained by labor; but one *wants* to perform in order to fulfill his deeper needs—achieved through work. When, for example, the creative writer has to turn out a "potboiler" in order to earn money, it is for him labor, and he begrudges every moment of the time devoted to it. When he is free to express himself as he will, the same expenditure of time and effort is seen as work rather than labor and in fact may have something of the pleasurable quality and absorption of play. In labor, the intrinsic value of the performance is secondary to the extrinsic value; in work, the reverse is true.

Hannah Arendt has put the distinction between labor and work rather nicely in the context of a crucial dilemma of our time:

> Whatever we do, we are supposed to do for the sake of "making a living"; such is the verdict of society, and the number of people, especially in the professions, who might challenge it, has decreased rapidly. The only exception society is willing to grant is the artist, who, strictly speaking, is the only "worker" left in a laboring society.... As a result, all serious activities, irrespective of their fruits, are called labor, and every activity which is not necessary for the life of the individual or for the life process of society is subsumed under playfulness.[27]

---

[27] Hannah Arendt, *The Human Condition*, Chicago, University of Chicago Press, 1958, pp. 126–127.

In effect, the performance of a role with a view to external rewards is labor and the performance of a role with a view to internal rewards is "playful" or, in the institutional setting, work. In this sense, gardening, learning, teaching, and writing may be either labor or work, depending on whether the sanctions invoked are predominantly intrinsic or extrinsic.

Three sources of intrinsic sanctions for the performance of institutional roles may be identified. One is in the need-dispositions of the role incumbent so that by meeting expectations one is also actualizing his needs; in this case role-personality congruence is at a maximum. A second is the interpersonal relations among role incumbents, so that to let anyone in the role-set down is personally painful; in this case group cohesion or belongingness is at a maximum. A third is in the integration of the role incumbent with the goals of the system, so that through socializations or other mechanisms the goals of the system itself have been introjected into the motivational and value structure of the individual; in this case identification is at a maximum.

In the framework of the present formulation of social behavior, the argument with respect to sanctions in the superordinate-subordinate relationship may be summarized as follows. Sanctions are contingent reaction patterns having positive (rewarding) or negative (punishing) characteristics as a function of the degree to which prescribed role behaviors are attained. Sanctions are either extrinsic or intrinsic: extrinsic when reliance is placed upon controls external to the person, intrinsic when reliance is placed upon controls internal to the person. Labor, which is the performance of a role for predominantly extrinsic sanctions, is distinct from work, which is the performance of a role for predominantly intrinsic sanctions. Since the institutional axis of behavior involves general external controls assumed to have equal force for all role incumbents, it is oriented toward labor. Since the individual axis of behavior involves specific internal controls assumed to have differential force for particular role incumbents, it is oriented toward work. Administrative emphasis on institutional considerations is likely to entail more extrinsic than intrinsic sanctions whereas emphasis on individual considerations usually entails more intrinsic than extrinsic sanctions.

The framework thus affords a set of relevant categories for the analysis of four important factors in the administrative relationship: the nature of the authority, the scope of the roles, the interpersonal affectivity, and the sanctions involved in the relationship. Conceptually the polar variables with respect to each of the factors—vested versus entrusted authority, functionally diffuse versus functionally specific role relationships, universalistic versus particularistic affectivity, extrinsic versus intrinsic sanctions—may be seen as characteristic of the institutional as against the individual ideologies of social behavior. Although in practice no situation quite coincides with the polar pure cases (any more than in practice pure introversion or extroversion, dominance or submissiveness, handsomeness or ugliness is found), the categories are fruitful as analytic devices for studying the superordinate-subordinate relationship, as we shall see in the analysis of leadership-followership styles.

LEADERSHIP-FOLLOWERSHIP STYLES

The terms "leadership" and "followership" have been variously defined in the administrative setting. Some people, in fact, would make a distinction between "leading" and "administering," "being administered" and "following."[28] Nothing would be gained by an extended discussion of the controversy here. We simply repeat here that to lead is to engage in an act which initiates a structure in interaction with others, and to follow is to engage in an act which maintains a structure initiated by another. We recall once more that the terms "leader" and "follower" in this usage are relative, for the follower is not altogether passive in the relationship and the leader is not entirely dominant. The nature of the relationship depends on the operating leadership-followership styles in the particular social system.

From the point of view of the present framework, three distinctive leadership-followership styles may be identified.[29] There is a problem here of referring to the styles without adding to the jargon of leadership nomenclature, yet without implying evaluation as in the case, say, of "authoritarian" (bad) and "democratic" (good) leadership. We shall term the three styles *normative*, referring to an emphasis on the institutional or role axis of behavior; *personal*, referring to the individual or personal-

---

[28] J. M. Lipham, "Leadership and Administration," in *Behavioral Science and Educational Administration*, Sixty-third Yearbook of the National Society for the Study of Education, Part II, Chicago, University of Chicago Press, 1964, pp. 119–142.
[29] Portions of the following are drawn from Getzels and Guba, "Social Behavior and the Administrative Process," pp. 423–441.

istic axis of behavior; and *transactional,* referring to alternate emphases on each. The three styles are represented in Figure 5–5.

In this conception the three styles of leadership-followership are three modes of achieving the same goal; they are not different images of the goal. We may examine the variations in the styles with respect to five major relational elements: (1) the proportion of role and personality factors in the behavior; (2) the differences with respect to the authority, scope, affectivity, and sanctions dimensions; (3) the relative weight given to effectiveness, efficiency, and satisfaction; (4) the nature of the predominant conflicts dealt with; and (5) the nature of the major mechanisms of institutional-individual integration.

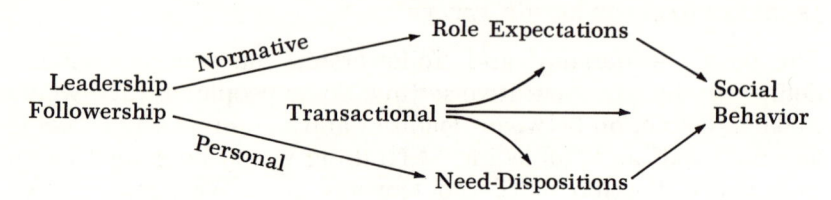

FIGURE 5–5. *Three leadership-followership styles. (Adapted from J. W. Getzels and E. G. Guba, "Social Behavior and the Administrative Process," School Review, 65 [1957], 436.)*

The Normative Style. The normative style places emphasis on the normative dimension of behavior and accordingly on the requirements of the institution, the role, and the expectations rather than on the requirements of the individual, the personality, and the need-dispositions. In the equation $B = f(R \times P)$, P is minimized and R is maximized. It is assumed that, given the institutional purpose, appropriate procedures can be discovered, perhaps through time and motion studies and the like, that will implement the purpose by conforming to the "right" procedures. These procedures are therefore included in the role expectations, and every role incumbent must adhere in minute detail to the expectations. If roles are clearly defined, and everyone is held responsible for doing what he is supposed to do, the desired outcomes will ensue regardless of who the particular role incumbents are, provided only that they have the necessary technical competence.

In the normative style of leadership-followership, the most expeditious route to the goal is seen as residing in the nature of the institutional structure rather than in any particular persons. In a sense, the people fulfilling the roles are as replaceable as the parts of a well-engineered machine. The obligation of the leader is to "write the program" for the machine, and the obligation of the follower is to "operate according to the program." In terms of the major variables in the superordinate-subordinate relationship, authority is vested rather than entrusted, the scope of interactions is diffuse rather than specific, the affectivity is universalistic rather than particularistic, and sanctions are extrinsic rather than intrinsic. The predominant conflict that is likely to be dealt with is role conflict, since this is immediately related to the institutional-role-expectation dimension of behavior, and any friction here is seen as threatening the structure of the system. The mode of individual-institutional integration is socialization of personality and adaptation rather than personalization of role and self-actualization. The standard of administrative excellence is effectiveness more than efficiency. The military during wartime mobilization is an example of this type of organization as a limiting case.

The Personal Style. The personal style of leadership-followership places emphasis on the personal dimension of behavior and accordingly on the requirements of the individual, the personality, and the need-dispositions rather than on the requirements of the institution, the role, and the expectations. In the equation $B = f(R \times P)$, R is minimized and P is maximized. This does not mean that the personal style is any less goal-oriented than is the normative style; it means that the most expeditious route to the goal is seen as residing in the people involved rather than in the nature of the institutional structure. The basic assumption is that the greatest accomplishment will occur not from enforcing adherence to rigorously defined expectations but from making it possible for each person to contribute what is most meaningful to him. Normative procedural prescriptions of the sort included in the minutely defined roles of the normative style are seen as restrictive and a hindrance rather than as a guide to productive behavior. The best government is the one that governs least—or better, hardly at all.

This point of view is obviously related to the particular individuals who fill the roles at a particular time. In the military, any one enlisted man or sergeant or officer is intended to be like any other—they are all GI—and nothing very much changes as one cadre leaves a given installation and another moves in. The standard operating procedures remain the same. This is not the case with a pure research laboratory. Scientists are not interchangeable, and one scientist is not easily replaceable by another. There are no standard operating procedures. Change the individual role incumbent of a laboratory, and in a very real sense you change with him the operating procedures and output, sometimes the very definition of the role itself. The pure research laboratory is an example of the personal leadership-followership style as a limiting case.

In terms of the major variables of the superordinate-subordinate relationship, authority is entrusted rather than vested, the scope of expectations is specific rather than diffuse, the affectivity is particularistic rather than universalistic, and sanctions are intrinsic rather than extrinsic. The predominant conflict that is likely to be dealt with is personality conflict, since this is immediately related to the individual-personality-needs dimension of behavior, and any friction here is seen as threatening to the functioning of the system. The mode of individual-institutional integration is the personalization of role and self-actualization rather than socialization of personality and adaptation. The standard of administrative excellence is efficiency more than effectiveness.

The Transactional Style. The preceding polarization of leadership-followership styles is not intended to imply that one style is inevitably good and the other bad. What is good and bad depends on the application in the particular case. The research laboratory could not be administered normatively without the danger of conformity and consequent loss in individual efficiency. The military organization could not be administered personally without the danger of anarchy and consequent loss in effectiveness.

The transactional style calls attention to the need for moving toward one style under one set of circumstances and toward the other style under another set of circumstances. In this sense it is intermediate—indeed, it moves from one style to the other—and is therefore least well defined. Since the goals of the social system must be carried out, it is obviously necessary to make explicit the roles and expectations required to achieve them. And since the roles and expectations are implemented by flesh-and-blood people with needs-to-be-met, the personalities of these people must be taken into account. But the answer is not as simple as might be indicated by saying that one should just hew to the middle course between expectations and needs, seeking a sort of compromise between them, for such procedure may very well compromise both the institutional role and the individual personality. Instead, the aim throughout is a thorough awareness of the limits of institutional and individual resources and demands within which administrative action must function. In the equation $B = f(R \times P)$, P and R are maximized or minimized as the situation requires. In terms of the variables of the superordinate-subordinate relationship, authority is either vested or entrusted, scope is either diffuse or specific, affectivity is either particularistic or universalistic, and sanctions are either extrinsic or intrinsic, depending upon the circumstances. There is sensitivity to all types of conflicts—role, personality, and role-personality conflicts being recognized and dealt with. The mode of individual-institutional integration is socialization of personality and adaptation, and personalization of role and self-actualization. The standard of administrative excellence is both effectiveness and efficiency.

That the transactional leadership-followership style is at once most often found or at least most usually desired and yet remains most nebulous and ill-defined illustrates the fact that at the present stage of knowledge the handling of administrative relationships must be considered as much an art as a science. The question of when to emphasize effectiveness and when efficiency, or whether to maintain relationships which are primarily diffuse or specific, or any other question relative to the factors at issue, can be resolved only by talented administrators with respect to particular circumstances. To suggest that such questions could be handled by mechanical manipulation of the kinds of variables proposed here is not the intent. This would be like suggesting that the success of a physician depends solely on his knowledge of the medical sciences—say, anatomy, physiology, biochemistry, and the like. Still, there is no gainsaying that such knowledge is of no little value in the practice of medicine. In much the same way, the application of relevant systematic variables from the behavioral sciences may help the administrator to sort out the problems which confront him, to study them in appropriate contexts, and to understand something of their internal dynamics. Such formulations, even though they may not provide generalized decisions for action and are perhaps of greater value for research than for application, may at least allow the administrator to understand why certain decisions and practices work whereas others do not.

On the dynamics of change in social systems

The study of any field tends to develop along certain lines. First comes the more or less random description of phenomena. Then elements of the phenomena are classified into sensible categories; taxonomies are constructed. Efforts are made to understand the relationships among the elements and between the classes; theoretical frameworks are conceived. Generalizations about the functioning of the parts in the whole are advanced, and predictions of future events are tested; systematic models capable of dealing not only with the existing structures but with *change* in the structures are formed.

The actual development is by no means as steplike and orderly as this schematic account suggests. One moves from the phenomena to the models and from the models to the phenomena. Nonetheless, there tend to be certain regularities. As Hagen has pointed out:

> As judged by the history of the physical, biological, and social sciences, study in any field is apt to begin with a none-too-ordered description of phenomena in the field, followed by a categorizing of them on the bases that seem to make sense. As understanding grows, the systems of classification become more closely related to the functioning of interacting elements. Gradually, generalizations about functioning are reached which are useful in predicting future events. As the generalizations gain rigor, they take the form of analytical models of the behavior being studied.[30]

That is, the models take the form of conceptual systems that may be applied simultaneously to describing the structures and the sources of change in the structures.

It is clear that organizations undergo change, and any model purporting to represent organizational behavior must deal, however imperfectly, with the phenomenon of change. The trouble is that no aspect of the behavior of social systems is less well understood than the sources of change or, for that matter,

---

[30] E. E. Hagen, "Analytical Models in the Study of Social Systems," *American Journal of Sociology*, 67 (1961), 144–151.

failure to change. Why does one social system change and grow, and another rigidify and decline? And what is the effect of differential administrative behavior in this process?

We may of course say simply that the one system had more creative personnel than the other. This is probably the case. But the "great man" explanation of change by itself only begs the question. Unless we wish to attribute change to a fortuitous meeting of genetic accident and situational circumstance, one question among many becomes: How was one system able to attract creative people and encourage creative behavior within the organizational framework, and the other not? Even the most innovative of individuals must have at least some stimulation and acceptability from the environment in order to make his mark. As someone has observed, "Had the infant Newton been cast among the Hottentots, would he have announced the laws of motion?"

We are nowhere near being able to deal at once with the complex issues of organizational structure and organizational change in any rigorous way. Yet we cannot remain forever bemused by the complexity of the phenomena and risk no attempt at some orderly classification and analysis, at least as a tentative approximation.

From one point of view an organization, conceived as a social system, seems a structure of cultural, institutional, and personal elements in apparently *fixed* relation to one another. But it must be reemphasized that the component elements are not static: The cultural values, the institutional expectations, the personalistic dispositions are *dynamic forces*. Each element is liable to alteration in itself and exerts pressure and counterpressure on the other elements. If one element changes, a series of pressures and counterpressures ensues. If the values change, institutional expectations previously congruent with the culture may cease to be so; should the expectations be changed in reaction to this, the personality dispositions previously congruent with the expectations may cease to be so; and so on. From this point of view an organization is not only a structure of relations but a *system in action*.

Assume specifically with respect to an educational system that, because of the impact of technology or a change in the composition of the community, the values undergo transformation so that the high valuation formerly placed on competence in the humanities is now placed on competence in the sciences. Or assume the reverse. In either case, the schools come under pressure for change. Roles may have to be reexamined, expectations redefined, individuals with other dispositions recruited. The administration itself may undergo transformations, and what Carlson has called a "place-bound" superintendent may be supplanted by a "career-bound" superintendent.[31] The former is typically a person employed from within a system who is expected to maintain the existing structure of the system; the latter is typically a person employed from outside the system who is expected to change it. The dispositions of the one are for retaining the status quo; of the other, for altering the status quo. But it is not a matter of personal dispositions alone, important as they are. The place-bound superintendent is required by the board of education to be responsive to its wishes and to the wishes of the existing staff. The career-bound superintendent receives a broad mandate from the board as to goals and is given wide latitude in methods for attaining the goals. Accordingly, he is able early in his tenure to make new rules (to redefine role expectations) and to add new members to the staff (to introduce new dispositions into the system).

But if the change in values sets off a chain of pressures for change, it also sets off a chain of counterpressures—that is, pressures against change. The existing structure of roles (the status quo) resists transformation. Individuals with particular dispositions ("the old guard") refuse to fulfill new expectations which are incongruent with their dispositions. The transforming values themselves reach stability so that institutional alterations outrun cultural support and reaction may set in. These factors place limits on how far and how fast the career-bound administrator can go before he must call a halt to his innovations or be superseded by a place-bound administrator who will consolidate the changes already made.

Our use of an alteration in values as the starting point for organizational change is only an illustrative case of the more general phenomenon. The initial force may come from the restructuring of a role-set which imposes new expectations in related role-sets. Or it may begin with the placement of a new individual with a particular set of dispositions in a strategic role in the system—say, the unintended recruitment of a career-

---

[31] Richard O. Carlson, *Executive Succession and Organizational Change: Place-Bound and Career-Bound Superintendents of Schools*, Chicago, Midwest Administration Center, University of Chicago, 1962.

bound superintendent who, because of his dispositions, may institute a redefinition of his own role (bring things up to date, he will assert), thus initiating a chain of reactions reaching not only through the immediate system itself but also into the community. If he changes the expectations within the school, he must "educate" the board and the parents to these transformations or fail to get support for what he is disposed to do. That is, he must attempt to alter the community values to conform to the institutional expectations. And in fact many superintendents claim that they must educate the community before they can educate the children.

As D. W. Allen has suggested, the issues raised in these illustrations may be generalized by reference to *vector* concepts.[32] The cultural values, institutional expectations, and personality dispositions are dynamic forces. They may be portrayed as vectors and the interactions among them as *vector relationships*. In such portrayal, the length of an arrow, that is, the "distance," between two interacting elements, represents the relative congruence or incongruence of the elements. Thus, Figure 5–6 shows a system whose elements are relatively congruent (the values, expectations, and dispositions are "close" to each other), and the behavior that satisfies the requirements of one element also meets those of the other elements.

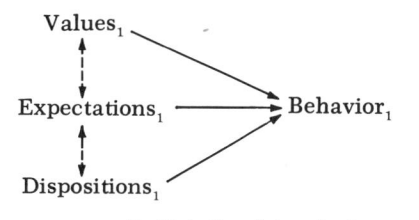

FIGURE 5–6. *Relationships before change in values.*

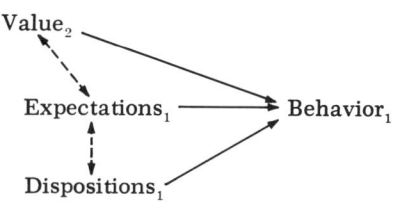

FIGURE 5–7. *Relationships after change in values.*

Assume that the values change. The expectations and dispositions and the values have become incongruent ("distant"), and the vector relationships are altered as in Figure 5–7. The behavior may still be efficient from the point of view of the

---

[32] Parts of this section and the figures are adapted from an unpublished paper by D. W. Allen ("Modelling Dynamic Social Structure"). We are grateful to Professor Allen for permitting us to use this material.

individual and effective from the point of view of the internal system itself, but the system is no longer congruent with the culture or with the other systems to which it is related. No organization—not even the most insulated of religious orders—can maintain such incongruence indefinitely and survive the consequent isolation. There will inevitably be pressure for response to the changed conditions, which may take the form of *reaction* or *accommodation* (or some combination of the two). Reaction operates to retain congruence by bringing the changing element back to where it was; accommodation operates to retain congruence by bringing the other elements into some appropriate realignment with the changing element.

If reaction is successful, the situation will return to the preceding state of equilibrium as portrayed in Figure 5–6. The danger of reaction is that it attempts to maintain equilibrium by rigidifying one of the elements—it might be the institutional expectations or the individual dispositions as well as the values in our illustration—and anchoring all other elements to it. This may provide short-term security but leads ultimately to organizational inflexibility: the system becomes static (closed) and unresponsive to emergent external or internal conditions.

Accommodation too entails some danger. For one thing, there may be a hasty and indiscriminate acceptance of change so that conformity to fads is mistaken for progress. For another, organizational change may become a matter of reshuffling roles and redefining expectations by administrative fiat—as is so often the case—without relation to the dispositions of the individuals involved, and the situation is altered as in Figure 5–8. The distance between the institutional expectations and cultural values has been decreased; that is, they have become more congruent. However, the distance between the individual dispositions and the institutional expectations has been increased; that is, they have become *less* congruent. The forthcoming behavior may still be effective from the point of view of the organization, and it will now conform to the cultural values, but it ceases to be efficient because it is divorced from the individual dispositions. Again there is disequilibrium and pressure for change, now for diminishing the distance between the dispositions and the changed role expectations. The distance may be diminished by altering (resocializing) the dispositions of the individuals already in the system or by recruiting into the system new individuals with already appropriate dispositions. This transforms the structure of relationships among the elements as shown in Figure 5-8 to those in Figure 5-9, which is formally like Figure 5-6, but is substantively a changed equilibrium: The values, the expectations, the dispositions, and the behavior have all undergone transformation.

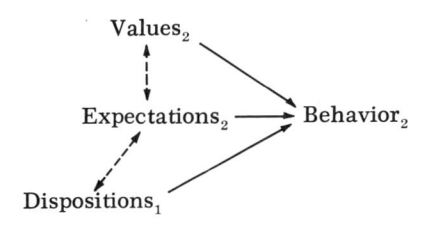

FIGURE 5-8. *Relationships after change in values and expectations.*

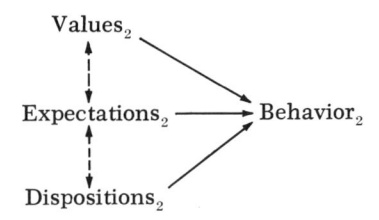

FIGURE 5-9. *Relationships after change in values, expectations, and dispositions.*

What has been suggested here with respect to values as a starting point of change holds also for a change in roles or in individuals. That is, each element may be viewed as a source of change, and a change in one element evokes pressures for or against change in every other element. The administrator must bear in mind that he is dealing with a system in continuous action, balancing, as the model suggests, cultural, institutional, and personalistic forces, each of which is itself in action. More than anyone else in the system, the administrator is located strategically to influence, although perhaps not to determine, the balance of forces for or against change.

Summary

In this chapter we considered a number of issues related to problems in administration: (1) the sources of organizational conflict, (2) the problem of adaptation and adjustment in social systems, (3) the meaning of effectiveness, efficiency, satisfaction, and morale, (4) the nature of authority and of leadership-followership styles, and (5) the problem of organizational change. We noted that these are recurrent issues—for example, the concepts of effectiveness and efficiency are from Barnard, the nature of leadership styles from Lewin—and argued that there are certain conceptual and methodological advantages in power and parsimony in dealing with these hitherto disjunctive issues in a single set of terms and relationships as given by our model. It must be borne in mind, however, that there are certain disadvantages as well. In the succeeding chapters we turn to illustrative empirical studies related to a number of the issues raised here.

6

Cultural differences and institutional expectations

That conflicting expectations are held for the schools hardly needs documentation. The school administrator beset by contradictory attacks from various individuals and groups is well aware that the culture at large consists of numerous subgroups, each apparently with varying expectations for the schools. But the crucial question remains: Are these differences in educational expectations haphazard or are they systematically related to the various subcultural groupings in our society?

We have already remarked upon the differences in values on the American scene which may be held by various subgroups. We also suggested in our general model that institutional expectations are inevitably related to cultural values. Accordingly, we would argue that differences in educational expectations are related, in however modest a degree, to the various subcultural groupings, and that any understanding of the crosscurrents in educational expectations must take into account these groupings.

Expectations for the schools: composite expectations and subcultural expectations

What should the schools be doing? is a question often raised but seldom satisfactorily answered. Responses range all the way from a general aphorism such as "teach the American way of life" or "hand down the best from the past" to a more specific injunction such as "teach the principles of American government" or "teach the three R's." Sometimes the response is more cynical—if cynical it is: "The schools should be doing everything the family, the church, and all the rest of us are doing badly or failing to do altogether for our children."

To provide at least a start toward a systematic answer to what Americans believe the schools should be doing, Downey, Seager, and Slagle[1] sought to determine the expectations held

---
[1] Lawrence W. Downey, "The Task of the Public School as Perceived by Regional Sub-Publics," Doctoral dissertation, University of Chicago, 1959; Roger C. Seager, "The Task of the Public School as Perceived by

for the schools as a social institution. They began their study by reviewing the notable statements of educational expectations from Horace Mann to the present. These statements were refined, ordered, and synthesized into four general dimensions, each with four representative school tasks:

A. Intellectual Dimensions
   1. Possession of Knowledge: A fund of information, concepts.
   2. Communication of Knowledge: Skill to acquire and transmit.
   3. Creation of Knowledge: Discrimination and imagination.
   4. Desire for Knowledge: A love for learning.
B. Social Dimensions
   5. Man to Man: Cooperation in day-to-day relations.
   6. Man to "State": Civic rights and duties.
   7. Man to Country: Loyalty to one's own country.
   8. Man to World: Interrelationships of peoples.
C. Personal Dimensions
   9. Physical: Bodily health and development.
   10. Emotional: Mental health and stability.
   11. Ethical: Moral integrity.
   12. Aesthetic: Cultural and leisure pursuits.
D. Productive Dimensions
   13. Vocational Guidance: Information and selection.
   14. Vocational Preparation: Training and placement.
   15. Home and Family: Housekeeping and family.
   16. Consumer: Personal buying, budgeting, and investment.[2]

On the basis of this framework a forced-choice, Q-technique instrument[3] was constructed permitting respondents not only to express their educational expectations but to assign priorities to each of the 16 representative expectations. The expectations of

Proximity Sub-Publics," Doctoral dissertation, University of Chicago, 1959; and Allen T. Slagle, "The Task of the Public School as Perceived by Occupation and Age Sub-Publics," Doctoral dissertation, University of Chicago, 1959. Major findings of these investigations have been summarized by Lawrence W. Downey, *The Task of Public Education*, Chicago, Midwest Administration Center, University of Chicago, 1960.

[2] Lawrence W. Downey, "Sub-Publics View the Task of Public Education," *Administrator's Notebook*, 8 (December, 1959), 1–2.

[3] Lawrence W. Downey, Roger C. Seager, and Allen T. Slagle, *The Task of Public Education Opinionnaire*, Chicago, Midwest Administration Center, University of Chicago, 1958.

1,286 educators and 2,544 noneducators in 15 selected communities in the Far West, the Midwest, the South, New England, and the prairie provinces of Canada were sampled. Members of service clubs, religious and patriotic organizations, labor groups, PTA's, and school faculties served as subjects. There is inevitably the issue of sampling in this type of study. No implication is made that the communities represent a cross section of all communities in the United States—that, for example, a suburb of Chicago is the same as a suburb of New Orleans—or that the 1,286 educators and the 2,544 noneducators are representative of all educators and all noneducators. To this extent the study, like most studies in social science, must be interpreted with caution. Nonetheless, the researchers were aware of the difficulties in sampling and took measures to obviate as many of them as possible. If the data are seen as illustrative of trends rather than as definitive, they make the point of differential educational expectations by various subpublics of the general American culture—for example, according to occupational status, educational level, geographic region, and so on. The data presented here are possibilities of which the educational administrator should be aware. Even if the methodological difficulties were not as real as they are, today's data in this domain might not hold tomorrow in view of the dynamics of current technological and social change.

COMPOSITE EDUCATIONAL EXPECTATIONS

The results for all persons who responded to the Task of Public Education Opinionnaire (as the instrument was called) gave an impressive vote of confidence to the intellectual dimension. Since the subjects were asked to respond separately for elementary and secondary schools, a comparison between expectations was possible. The data are presented in Table 6–1.

As is readily apparent, three of the four intellectual items were among the first four priorities for both elementary and secondary schools. First priority was given to the three R's—the basic skills for acquiring and transmitting knowledge. Second priority was given to the desire for knowledge—the cultivation of an inquiring mind and "love of learning." These two expectations received first and second rank, respectively, for both elementary and secondary schools and by both the educators and the noneducators. The creation of knowledge—the weighing of facts and applying them to the imaginative solution of problems —was ranked third for the secondary school and fourth for the elementary school. Cooperation in day-to-day relations with others—one of the social dimensions—was ranked third for the elementary school and fourth for the secondary school. At the bottom was the expectation for consumer education for the elementary school and the expectation for homemaking education for the secondary school.

Although there was substantial consensus, numerous and significant differences were found among the several subpublics. For example, the gross data presented in Table 6–1, even without further analysis, indicate several disagreements between educa-

TABLE 6–1

Means and Ranks of Expectations Held for the Elementary and the High School by Composite Educator and Noneducator Samples

| | ELEMENTARY SCHOOL || HIGH SCHOOL ||
Task dimension or item	Educator N=1,286 $\bar{x}$	Rank	Non-educator N=2,544 $\bar{x}$	Rank	Educator N=1,286 $\bar{x}$	Rank	Non-educator N=2,544 $\bar{x}$	Rank
Knowledge	3.32	11	3.32	13	3.08	14	3.20	13
Intellectual skills	6.27	1	6.02	1	5.48	1	5.51	1
Creativity	4.98	4	4.99	4	5.10	3	4.85	3
Desire for knowledge	5.29	2	5.14	2	5.40	2	5.17	2
Man to fellow man	5.17	3	5.00	3	4.64	4	4.54	4
Citizenship	4.38	6	4.24	6	4.41	6	4.34	7
Patriotism	4.05	8	4.07	7	3.96	10	4.00	9
World citizenship	3.65	10	3.34	11	3.98	9	3.96	10
Physical	3.65	9	3.57	10	3.22	12	3.27	12
Emotional	4.37	7	3.93	8	4.54	5	4.02	8
Ethical	4.62	5	4.70	5	4.34	7	4.38	5
Aesthetic	3.32	12	2.99	14	3.66	11	2.99	15
Vocation—selective	2.79	15	3.33	12	4.19	8	4.34	6
Vocation—preparative	2.92	14	3.75	9	3.15	13	3.76	11
Home and family	2.95	13	2.81	15	2.19	16	2.53	16
Consumer	2.29	16	2.80	16	2.88	15	3.17	14

SOURCE: Adapted from Roger C. Seager, "The Task of the Public School as Perceived by Proximity Sub-Publics," Doctoral dissertation, University of Chicago, 1959, p. 101.

tors and noneducators. At the secondary school level, aesthetic expectations are ranked eleventh by the educators (low enough, it would seem) but fifteenth or next to absolute bottom by the noneducators. At the elementary school level, vocational preparation is ranked fourteenth by the educators and ninth by the noneducators—a circumstance that is surely not without potential for conflict in the expenditure of educational funds in some communities. In addition, disagreements were found for numerous other subpublics, including those differing by occupational status, educational level, social class, geographic region, age, religion, and race. We shall turn to a brief examination of each of these, and of the differences between educators and noneducators, bearing in mind of course that there are significant interactions among the several characteristics.

OCCUPATIONAL STATUS, EDUCATIONAL LEVEL, AND EDUCATIONAL EXPECTATIONS

Occupational Status. What is the nature of the relationship between occupational status and educational expectations? To explore this issue, Slagle[4] classified the 2,544 noneducators who had responded to the Task of Public Education Opinionnaire according to the following occupational categories: professional, semiprofessional, managerial, clerical, skilled labor, and unskilled labor. He found systematic relationships between occupation and educational expectations. For example, there were significant differences in the priority given to aesthetics between the individuals in the professions and in each of the other groups, the professional persons ranking educational expectations in this domain higher. The expectations given relatively higher priority by those in the professions and lower by those in the unskilled occupations, to take only the extremes, were possession of knowledge, creation of knowledge, desire to learn, communication of knowledge, aesthetic appreciation, and emotional stability. Conversely, the expectations given higher priority by those in the unskilled occupations and lower priority by those in the professions were consumer education, vocational training, social skills, home and family training, physical education, and vocational guidance. Data regarding the relation between occupation and educational expectations are summarized for only the extremes of the occupational continuum in Table 6–2. The

---

[4] Slagle, *op. cit.*

TABLE 6–2

Significant Differences[a] in Expectations for the Public School Between Subpublics of Differing Occupations

School	Higher priority assigned by professionals	Higher priority assigned by unskilled laborers
Elementary	Possession of knowledge Desire for knowledge Creativity Intellectual skills	Vocational guidance Moral integrity Consumer skills Vocational preparation Home and family
Secondary	Aesthetic appreciation Emotional stability Creativity Intellectual skills	Physical development Consumer skills Vocational preparation Home and family living

[a] At the .05 level or higher.

SOURCE: Adapted from Allen T. Slagle, "The Task of the Public School as Perceived by Occupation and Age Sub-Publics," Doctoral dissertation, University of Chicago, 1959, pp. 107–108.

priorities of those in the managerial occupations were a selective combination of the professional and unskilled priorities.

Educational Level. Just as occupational status is a clue to an individual's educational expectations, so is his educational level. Because occupational status and educational level are interrelated, it may of course be anticipated that the educational expectations of those at the higher educational levels will be similar to the expectations of those in the professions, and the expectations of those at the lower educational levels will be similar to the expectations of those in the unskilled occupations. Nonetheless, it is of interest to explore the exact nature of the relations between educational level and educational expectations. Seager[5] classified the noneducator respondents by educational level as follows: 0–9 years of schooling; 10–12 years; 1–3 years of college; Bachelor's degree; and graduate training. He then observed the priorities given by these groups to the various educational expectations. For the groups at the extremes of the educational continuum, the data are summarized in Table 6–3.

The anticipated relationships were in fact found. Individuals with more schooling placed a significantly higher valuation

[5] Seager, *op. cit.*

TABLE 6-3

Significant Differences[a] in Expectations for the Public School Between Subpublics with Differing Amounts of Schooling

School	Higher priority assigned by those with graduate training	Higher priority assigned by those with 0–9 years of schooling
Elementary	Possession of knowledge Intellectual skills Aesthetic appreciation Desire for knowledge Creativity	Patriotism Physical development Moral integrity Consumer skills Vocational preparation
High school	Aesthetic appreciation Desire for knowledge Intellectual skills	Home and family living Patriotism Physical development Moral integrity Consumer skills Vocational preparation

[a] At the .05 level or higher.
SOURCE: Adapted from Roger C. Seager, "The Task of the Public School as Perceived by Proximity Sub-Publics," Doctoral dissertation, University of Chicago, 1959.

than did individuals with less schooling on all the intellectual expectations: possession of knowledge, desire to learn, creation of knowledge, and communication of knowledge. The aesthetic dimension and emotional stability also increased in priority as the level of education increased. Conversely, the importance of patriotism, moral standards, consumer education, specialized vocational training, and physical fitness as expectations for the schools decreased significantly as the educational level of the respondents increased.

These observations were supported in an independent study by Hartrick,[6] who also found that individuals with university degrees placed significantly greater value on aspects of education dealing with intellectual and cultural development than did individuals with less than high school education. The latter tended to place significantly greater value on vocational information and training, consumer management, moral standards, and social skills.

[6] Walter J. Hartrick, "Perceptions of the Task and Program of the Public High School," Doctoral dissertation, University of Chicago, 1961.

SOCIAL CLASS STATUS AND EDUCATIONAL EXPECTATIONS

Combining both occupational status and educational level into a two-factor index of social class position, Hills[7] studied in depth the relationship of social class and educational expectations. The essential data were gathered by interview and questionnaire in two communities contrasted for social class: community A, a residential, upper-income suburb consisting primarily of well-educated professional and executive families, and community B, an industrial, lower-income suburb consisting predominantly of less-educated operative and unskilled labor families.

A sample of 389 residents in the two communities responded to an educational expectations instrument which permitted them to rank the relative importance of items such as the following:

I expect high school teachers to encourage students to take courses that will add to their knowledge and understanding. (Intellectual Orientation)

I expect high school teachers to encourage the development of skills necessary to earn a living. (Vocational Orientation)

I expect high school teachers to encourage the development of the skills necessary to get along with people. (Social Orientation)

The upper-, upper-middle-, and middle-class respondents expressed a strong preference for an intellectually oriented curriculum with secondary emphasis on a socially oriented curriculum. The vocational aspects of education were minimized. In contrast, for the lower-class and lower-middle-class respondents, the social aspects of education were paramount, followed closely by vocational and intellectual expectations in that order. Despite the priority of the social orientation, the lower-class and lower-middle-class respondents still attached substantial importance to the vocational and intellectual expectations—much more than the relative emphasis given to vocational training by the upper-class respondents. Thus, the vocational educational expectations seem to Hills to be the greatest source of potential educational conflict between social class groups. The lower classes attach almost equal importance to vocational and intellectual expecta-

---

[7] R. J. Hills, "The Relationship Between the Educational Expectations of Social Class Groups and the Role Expectations Within the Public High School," Doctoral dissertation, University of Chicago, 1961.

tions for the schools whereas the upper classes tend to deprecate vocational expectations for the schools.

To obtain a qualitative check on the questionnaire data and to assess the nature of the differences in expectations in the two communities as viewed by the teachers, individual interviews were held with representative samples of teachers. The interviews also elicited expressions from the teachers regarding the kinds of pressures exerted upon them in the two communities.

Educational expectations in community A were sharply defined. Of the 23 teachers interviewed, 22 mentioned that the parents insisted on the school's providing a highly specialized college preparatory program. The following comment was typically revealing:

> A woman I know was worrying because her fifth grade daughter was doing only average work in school. She was afraid the girl would not be able to get into college when the time came.[8]

Nor would just any college do. According to almost half of the teachers, the parents were determined to have their children prepared for a prestige college. This comment was again typical:

> They want a college prep course so they can get into a prestige school—an Eastern school.... When parents contact you, it's because they are upset about grades—they're afraid their kids won't get into the right college.[9]

In contrast, only one of the 23 teachers in community B recorded any desire on the part of the parents for a college preparatory emphasis in the high school. Fourteen teachers agreed that the parents were satisfied with a terminal high school education. As one teacher put it:

> The great majority of parents don't take a particular interest. They want a high school diploma; they're not concerned about grades or averages. When they ask, "How's my boy doing?" they mean, "Is he passing or failing?"[10]

Only one teacher in community A indicated any such feeling on the part of the parents there. Instead, 15 of the teachers in community A called attention to the high degree of interest on the part of parents in school affairs, and 8 specifically mentioned

[8] *Ibid.*, p. 60.
[9] *Ibid.*
[10] *Ibid.*, p. 63.

the existence of pressure from parents on the educational procedures in the school. One teacher said:

In the school where I taught before coming here no one would dream of telling a teacher how to teach. That's not the case here.[11]

In contrast, 19 of the teachers in community B commented on the lack of parental interest in school affairs, and 12 noted the lack of pressure. In the words of one teacher:

There's no parental pressure here—Johnny gets what he deserves and parents stand behind the teacher. We get no pressure to give special privileges—people are willing to let the teachers run the school.[12]

A summary of the interview data is presented in Table 6–4.

In short, on the basis of both questionnaire data from the residents and individual interviews with the teachers, distinct differences in educational expectations were found between the two communities. Community A, heavily weighted toward the upper-social-class levels, had a high preference for college pre-

TABLE 6–4

Interview Responses of Teachers Indicative of Community Expectations for Schools

Response	SCHOOL A[a] No.	Percent	SCHOOL B[a] No.	Percent
Desire a college preparatory program	22	95.6	1	4.3
Satisfied with high school education	1	4.3	14	60.8
High degree of interest	15	65.2	2	8.6
Lack of interest	0	0.0	19	82.6
High degree of pressure	8	34.7	0	0.0
Lack of pressure	0	0.0	12	52.1
Emphasis on instrumental and social value of education	16	69.5	0	0.0
High degree of professional freedom	5	21.7	13	56.5

[a] N = 23 teachers.

SOURCE: Adapted from R. J. Hills, "The Relationship Between the Educational Expectations of Social Class Groups and the Role Expectations Within the Public High School," Doctoral dissertation, University of Chicago, 1961, p. 61.

---

[11] *Ibid.*, p. 62.
[12] *Ibid.*, p. 64.

paratory educational expectations. Community B, heavily weighted toward the lower-social-class levels, had a high preference for terminal, vocationally oriented educational expectations.

Despite the significant differences in educational expectations, it would be erroneous to assume that there was any less support for the schools in B than in A. The financial outlay in terms of expenditure per pupil was almost identical in the two communities. Indeed, although industry was an important source of revenue in community B, the tax rate was higher in B than in A.

But these are not the only and, from the point of view of administrative issues, perhaps not even the most important differences.[13] In addition to preferring a college preparatory program, the parents of community A insisted that such a program be provided and took an active part in exerting pressure in the affairs of the school. The parents of community B, despite their preference for a terminal vocational training program, made few demands that it be provided and took no active interest in exerting any pressure in the affairs of the school, even though this might be the last school their children would attend.

The high level of parental interest in the school as exemplified by community A, so obviously desirable in itself, is paradoxically felt by many school people to be not without serious dangers. It may readily be transformed into meddlesome and onerous pressure for special interest, and many able schoolmen tend to avoid such communities—much to their own and the community's loss. Only recently the placement officer of a large university observed that to his surprise three highly successful superintendents who had "active" credentials on file in his office had requested that their names not be submitted to the board of education of a nearby wealthy suburban district, although the position seemed in many respects to be an ideal step up in size and salary for each superintendent. As one of them said, "Thanks, but this is not for me. An extra $5,000 a year is not worth all the headaches involved in working with the upper-upper—or those who think they are."

---

[13] The identification of such differences is the focus of recent studies by F. Donald Carver, "Relationships Between Education Level, Family Income, and Expectations of Citizens for the Role of the School Board," Doctoral dissertation, University of Wisconsin, 1966, and Douglas S. Ritchie, "An analysis of Four Secondary Schools in an Urban Setting: Expectations, Effectiveness, and Innovation," Doctoral dissertation, University of Wisconsin, 1967.

There seems little doubt that educational expectations are systematically related to occupational status, educational level, and social class position.[14] Although these stratifications are probably less sharp than formerly,[15] cleavages remain in educational desiderata corresponding to the stratifications in our society. The existing cleavages still make for administrative dilemmas, for the more nearly the administrator meets one set of expectations the more he risks failing to meet another set. Indeed, even when he is able to conform entirely to a single set of expectations as in the case of community A or B, the expectations may still be at variance with his own dispositions. Like the teacher whom we cited, he may feel that he is acting under pressure rather than from conviction. In the terms of our formulation, his behavior may be effective but not efficient. At least some administrators will avoid such situations, for ultimately these situations may lead to failure in both effectiveness and efficiency.

DIFFERENCES IN EDUCATIONAL EXPECTATIONS BY GEOGRAPHIC REGION, AGE, RELIGION, AND RACIAL COMPOSITION

In addition to the cleavages in educational expectations by social stratification, several studies have found significant differences by geographic region, age, religion, and racial composition,[16] although again it must be borne in mind that there are certain interactions, so that, for example, the expectations held by Negroes are not independent of their generally lower socioeconomic class status.

Geographic Region and Educational Expectations. The Task of Public Education Opinionnaire was given to roughly comparable samples in four geographic regions in the United States and one in Canada. The responses revealed numerous differences in educational expectations by region. For example, respondents in New England placed a high valuation on moral training and education for world citizenship and less emphasis

---

[14] Cf. Daniel U. Levine, "The Relation Between Attitudes Concerning Education and Attitudes Concerning Government and Society," Doctoral dissertation, University of Chicago, 1963. Also, Daniel U. Levine, "Liberalism, Conservatism, and Educational Viewpoint," *Administrator's Notebook*, 11 (May, 1963), 37–53.

[15] W. B. Brookover and D. Gottlieb, "Social Class and Education," in W. W. Charters and N. L. Gage, eds., *Readings in the Social Psychology of Education*, Boston, Allyn and Bacon, 1963, pp. 3–11.

[16] Downey, Seager, and Slagle, *op. cit.*, pp. 37–53.

on education for social skills and physical development. Conversely, education for physical development was highly valued by respondents in the South, who gave much less emphasis to the intellectual and aesthetic aspects of education. Respondents in the West tended to give a high priority to education for social skills and civic responsibility, placing low emphasis on moral training and consumer education. Canadians held high educational expectations for intellectual and aesthetic development but minimized the physical and patriotic aspects of schooling. Midwestern respondents assumed a middle position; their priorities corresponded most closely to the average of the sample as a whole.

Of course, these findings are situationally general rather than specific and must be viewed with great caution in relation to any particular community. That is, a particular residential suburb of San Francisco might not be dissimilar from a particular residential suburb of, say, Boston or Chicago. But on the whole there seem to be significant differences along the lines indicated between California and Massachusetts, between Mississippi and Alberta, and so on.

Perhaps the important point of these studies is not the exact scale of differences in regional values with respect to education, but the fact that the differences exist and are manifest. If we assume, as our theoretical formulation does, that no social system exists in a vacuum but is related to the values of the culture in which it is embedded, then to understand the operation of any social system, we must be aware of the values of the culture. This is especially so in the case of the school.

When a superintendent moves from a school system in Maine to one in Nevada, he is more than changing climate, architecture of buildings, and scope of responsibilities. He must also bear in mind that at least in some respects he may very well be changing one educational ideology for another. He needs to be aware that moral training, with a relatively high priority in New England, may be of less importance in the West. Education for social skills on the other hand, which may have been of no consequence in his old community, may have very high priority in the new one.

Whether the superintendent should go along with community preferences in educational ideology as he finds them or try to transform them is not the issue here. In either case—whether he chooses to conform or transform—he must begin by understanding the situation as it is and the values with which the goals of his school must interact.

Age and Educational Expectations. The educator and noneducator respondents in the task of public education studies were divided by age into two groups: those over 45 years of age and those under 45 years. Notable differences were found between the groups. On the whole, older respondents tended to stress the importance of physical education, moral training, patriotism, and aesthetic appreciation more than did younger respondents. Conversely, younger respondents tended to stress the intellectual and world citizenship aspects of education more than did the older respondents.

For the most part, the findings are in accord with trends in the culture at large. For example, the younger group (including many veterans of World War II and the Korean conflict) placed greater emphasis on world citizenship and less on nationalistic patriotism; the older group placed greater emphasis on patriotism and less on world citizenship. Several of the findings, however, seem to run counter to popular notions about age differences and educational values, notably the finding that the younger group stressed intellectual values more than did the older group. It may of course be that the younger respondents were reflecting their current concerns about the learning skills of their own young children, and the older respondents were reflecting their current concerns about *their* children, who were obviously older. Therefore, the issue was not learning skills so much as other aspects of education—aesthetic appreciation, for example.

In any case, the question of age differences in connection with values is an inescapable issue, especially, as we have seen, in a period of rapid technological change. We shall return to it when we deal with specific role conflicts in the school situation. The important point here is not so much the precise nature of the obtained differences, which in any event are not likely to be of universal application, but the fact that there are systematic differences in values by age. The frequently observed disagreements between younger and older factions regarding educational policy may be due not to the "lack of experience of the young Turks" or to the "hardening of the intellectual arteries of the old fogies"—explanations often given for the disagreements by age groups—but to genuine ideological differences, which must be understood and taken into account by the administrator.

Religion and Educational Expectations. Significant differences in educational values and expectations were found between Catholic and Protestant respondents. At both the elementary and the secondary levels, Catholic educators tended to stress education for morality more than did Protestant educators, and Protestant educators tended to stress desire for knowledge and physical education more than did Catholic educators. And as the researchers point out, values do seem to have concrete consequences—at least in this case.[17] Associated typically with a Catholic school is the parish church; associated typically with other schools is an impressive gymnasium or library.

That differences exist in expectations held for the role of the school by members of certain religious groups is common knowledge. Presumably, a greater emphasis upon moral training is the *raison d'être* of the parochial schools, and both the extent to which parochial schools affect pupils' moral values and religiousness has received substantial attention in recent years.[18] The degree to which "shared time" and similar cooperative arrangements represent a viable approach to the inculcation of spiritual values is also an area for fruitful study. It is increasingly clear that recent federal legislation fosters cooperative arrangements not only in public, private, and parochial schools but also through cultural, recreational, and other educational agencies in order that the educational goals of society at large —as perceived by the members of the Congress, at least—may be attained.

Negro-White Differences and Educational Expectations. Several significant differences were found when the respondents to the task of public education studies were divided into Negro and white groupings. As a group, the Negro respondents consistently gave higher priority to physical training and to education for home and family skills than did the white respondents; the white respondents gave higher priority to creativity, desire

---

[17] Whether or not differences in religious orientations are systematically related to expectations for the schools is investigated further in a recent study by John F. Meggers, "Expectations for the Role of the Board of Education Held by Parochial and Public School Oriented Parents," Doctoral dissertation, University of Wisconsin, 1966.

[18] See Andrew M. Greeley, Peter H. Rossi, and Leonard J. Pinto, *The Social Effects of Catholic Education,* Chicago, National Opinion Research Center, University of Chicago, 1964; and Donald Erickson, "Do Schools Affect Student Values?" *Administrator's Notebook,* 9 (December, 1962), 1–4.

for knowledge, and world citizenship than did the Negro respondents. It need hardly be pointed out that these differences are related to economic and social factors and are of course not "racial" in origin. Nonetheless, as in the case of religion, they do seem to find tangible expression in action. The high representation of Negroes among the nation's outstanding athletes may well be a function at least in part of the observed high value placed on physical achievement.

Expectations for the schools: differences between educators and noneducators

We have examined some of the research dealing with similarities and differences in educational expectations among various subcultural groups—by occupational status, educational level, social class position, geographic region, age, religion, and race.[19] We noted a number of significant disagreements in expectations among the various groups suggesting areas of actual or potential conflict in the administration of the schools. However, a significant source of conflict may exist more specifically between the educational values held by the citizenry at large and the educational values held by the personnel in the schools. We turn to two sets of studies in this domain. One set deals directly with differences in expectations between educators and noneducators, the other with differences in the perception of the high school graduate held by the two groups.

DIFFERENCES IN EXPECTATIONS

Few social institutions are as open to pressure from outside individuals and other institutions as the school. Citizens who would not dream of prescribing how public health or safety facilities, for example, should deal with their problems readily enter into the affairs of the school through either individual or collective action. The same parent who could not conceive of telling a doctor in a public hospital—even the rankest medical student—how to treat his child as patient, or of telling the fireman how to deal with a fire, even when the fire is on his own property, will

---
[19] Numerous other meaningful subpublic cleavages could undoubtedly be identified. For example, see William H. Streich, "Political Party Identification and Expectations for Local Schools," Doctoral dissertation, University of Wisconsin, 1966.

often feel perfectly free and competent to tell the teacher—even the most experienced one—in great detail how to teach his child to read, what textbooks to use (or not to use), what discipline to apply, and in general how to manage the problems of education.

In a word, the schools are not only dependent for support upon public acceptance and approval but vulnerable to direct pressure, often of a contradictory nature, from the numerous publics they serve. The educational values of the community (what we called in our theoretical model the cultural dimension) interact quite closely with the procedures of the school (what we called the institutional dimension of the social system). A significant question then arises: What is the relation between the public's educational values or expectations for the schools and those of the educators themselves?

The task of education studies revealed substantial areas of agreement between educators and noneducators. But there were also significant differences. The relevant data with respect to the differences are summarized in Table 6–5. The results must of course be seen in the light of the data we have already presented regarding variations in expectations by occupational and educational status, geographic region, age, and so on. Nevertheless, in the aggregate, it is readily apparent that without exception the general public gave the *nonintellectual* expectations for the schools a higher priority than did the educators. The noneducators ranked vocational training, vocational guidance, and consumer education higher than did the educators. The educators consistently gave a higher priority to every one of the *intellectual* expectations—desire for knowledge, aesthetic appreciation, the learning skills, and so on. They also gave higher priority to education for national and world citizenship, and for interpersonal relations.

DIFFERENCES IN THE PERCEPTION OF THE HIGH SCHOOL GRADUATE

A more indirect but ultimately perhaps more revealing indication of the relation between the cultural values and the institutional expectations in education can be found in a study by Goldman[20] examining the real and the ideal perception or image of the high school graduate held by educators and by noneducators. The relevant issues raised by this investigation were: What qualities

---
[20] Samuel Goldman, "Sub-Public Perceptions of the High School Graduate and the Roles of Institutions in His Development," Doctoral dissertation, University of Chicago, 1961.

TABLE 6-5

Summary of Significant Differences[a] Between Educators' and Noneducators' Expectations for the Public School

School	More important for educators than noneducators	More important for noneducators than educators
Elementary	Intellectual skills Home and family living Patriotism World citizenship Desire for knowledge Emotional stability Aesthetic appreciation	Vocational guidance Vocational preparation Consumer skills
Secondary	Creativity Desire for knowledge Emotional stability Aesthetic appreciation	Home and family living Vocational guidance Vocational preparation Consumer skills

[a] At the .05 level or higher.

SOURCE: Adapted from Lawrence W. Downey, *The Task of Public Education*, Chicago, Midwest Administration Center, University of Chicago, 1960, p. 40.

do educators and noneducators perceive as characteristic of today's high school graduate (termed in the study the "real image"), and what qualities do the same educators and noneducators believe the high school graduate should ideally have (termed in the study the "ideal image")?

To permit respondents to select the qualities they believe actually characteristic of high school graduates and the qualities they believe should ideally be characteristic of high school graduates, the investigator designed an instrument representing ten common values previously used in a study of adolescents.[21] Items representing the values were expressed in terms of personal qualities as follows:

... is basically spiritual in attitude toward life. (religious)
... feels that the prime goal in life is to make as much money as possible. (economic)
... knows the political issues of the day and is willing to be involved in political activity. (political)
... enjoys cultural activities and has a taste for the finer things of life. (aesthetic)

[21] Haron J. Battle, "Application of an Inverted Analysis in a Study of the Relation Between Values and Achievement of High School Pupils," Doctoral dissertation, University of Chicago, 1954.

... will sacrifice personal comfort for the comfort of others.	(altruistic)
... is able to make new friends easily.	(social)
... feels that the prime goal in life is to have as much fun as possible.	(hedonistic)
... takes great interest in developing a good figure or a strong body build.	(physical)
... has outstanding character traits such as honesty and trustworthiness.	(ethical)
... has some knowledge of many things and a desire to learn more.	(theoretic)[22]

The instrument was given to a sample of 153 high school teachers and 224 parents drawn from three middle-class communities in the Midwest. Respondents ranked the items twice: first to describe their "real image" of the high school graduate and second to describe the "ideal image" of the high school graduate. The results were quite revealing.

For the real image, educators ranked the economic, social, and hedonistic values as most characteristic of today's high school graduate and the political, aesthetic, and altruistic values as least characteristic. For the ideal image, educators ranked the ethical, religious, and theoretic values at the top and the physical, hedonistic, and economic values at the bottom. Figure 6–1 presents the real and the ideal profiles as given by educators.

The rank order correlation between the real and the ideal value patterns was −.53. The qualities showing the greatest variation in ranking were the economic and hedonistic—these being placed respectively first and third for the real image but tenth and ninth for the ideal image. Almost as large discrepancies appeared for the ethical and social values, the one being first in the ideal ranking but sixth in the real ranking, the other being second in the real ranking but seventh in the ideal. These reversals and the generally negative correlation indicate that educators are seriously dissatisfied with the character of the high school graduate. But they also indicate that there are grave discrepancies between the values they would like to teach and perhaps try to teach and the values the high school student actually acquires.

The qualities which noneducators considered most characteristic were the social, theoretic, and economic; the qualities they considered least characteristic were the religious, political,

---
[22] Goldman, *op. cit.*, pp. 72–82.

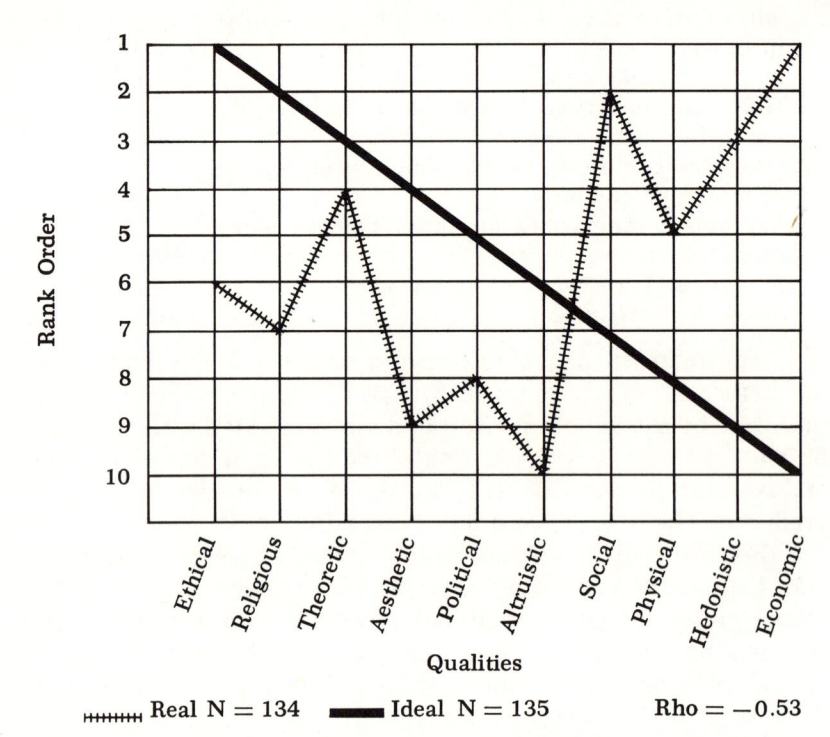

FIGURE 6-1. *Profile of the real and ideal image of the high school graduate by educators.* (SOURCE: *Samuel Goldman, "Sub-Public Perceptions of the High School Graduate and the Roles of Institutions in His Development," Doctoral dissertation, University of Chicago, 1961.*)

and altruistic. For the ideal image, noneducators ranked the ethical, religious, and theoretic orientations at the top and the physical, economic, and hedonistic orientations at the bottom. The real and the ideal profiles given by the noneducators are shown in Figure 6–2.

The rank-order correlation between the profiles is .15. The qualities showing the widest variation were the religious and economic values, the former being ranked second for the ideal image but eighth for the real image, the latter third for the real image but ninth for the ideal image. Perhaps most noteworthy is the difference between the real-ideal correlation of −.53 for the educators and .15 for the noneducators, suggesting some rather important disagreements between parental and teacher patterns of expectations.

The mean differences between the real and the ideal images

for each value orientation of the educators and the noneducators were computed and compared. In all cases the mean differences were higher for educators than for noneducators, and in six cases the discrepancy between educators and noneducators was significant at least at the .05 level. The largest discrepancies were in the economic and hedonistic values, with sizable discrepancies appearing also in the aesthetic, altruistic, physical, and social domains.

The study demonstrates that both teachers and parents tend to view today's high school graduate as having acquired economic and social values and rejected altruistic values. But within the present context it demonstrates something more: It highlights possible important differences between educators and noneducators with respect to what they believe the character of high school graduates should be and what it actually is.

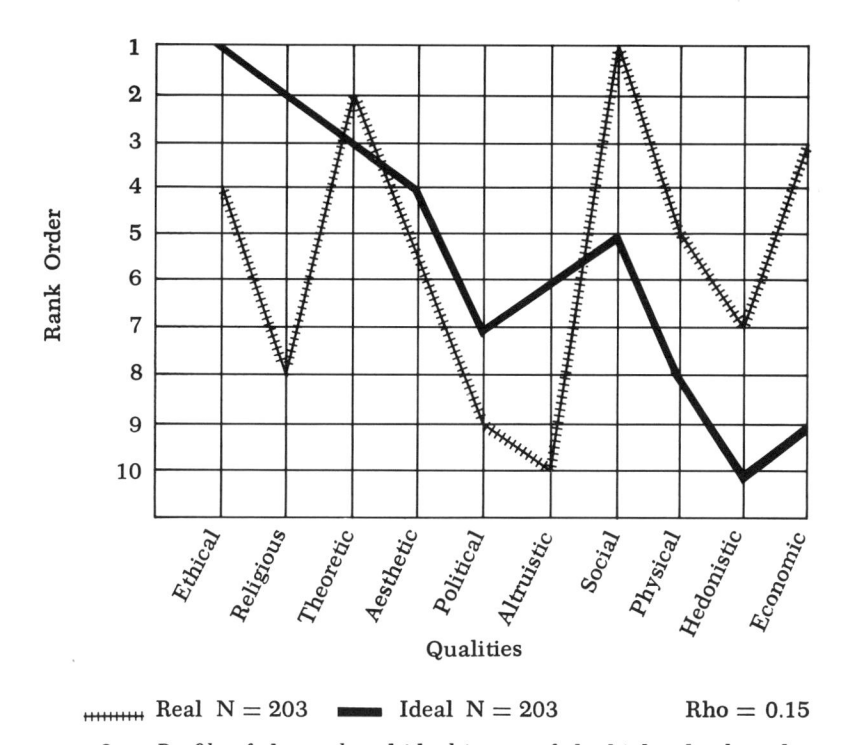

FIGURE 6–2. *Profile of the real and ideal image of the high school graduate by noneducators.* (SOURCE: Samuel Goldman, "Sub-Public Perceptions of the High School Graduate and the Roles of Institutions in His Development," Doctoral dissertation, University of Chicago, 1961.)

Toward further inquiry

These exploratory studies of educational expectations yield a number of implications for further inquiry along quite practical lines. There might be a more extensive and controlled investigation of the different expectations stemming from various sources, and the effect of these expectations on the operation of the schools. Consider, for example, the vociferous attacks upon the schools by certain individuals and groups, particularly those demanding that the schools "return" to stressing intellectual skills and creativity. The educators' response to the attacks has been largely defensive and apologetic. The criticisms may, however, well reflect the reactions of the critics to trends in the culture at large, with the schools made the unwitting scapegoat for what is primarily a cultural rather than a peculiarly educational state of affairs. It may be that the schools are necessarily (if unfortunately) only responding to the pressures of the community values upon educational expectations—pressures to which the schools may be accommodating against their own judgment. At least in the studies reported here—tentative as the conclusions must be—it is the noneducators rather than the educators who give the higher priority to the nonintellectual aspects of school activity, and the educators who give the higher priority to the intellectual aspects of education. Moreover, despite the accusations to the contrary, the educators show less complacency about the schools than do the noneducators; the former rather than the latter reveal the greater discrepancy between what they believe the high school student should be and what he actually is. How far can the school administrator go in *not* acceding to his patrons (note the word "patrons"), whom he presumably must serve under the American system of lay control of educational policy?

A second line of inquiry might be directed toward the forces making for agreement or disagreement between cultural values and institutional expectations. In education, the issue is often put more specifically as follows: Does closer contact between the public and the schools tend to make for greater agreement in educational expectations between educators and noneducators? The Task of Public Education studies sought to explore this relationship by asking respondents to indicate the extent to which they were involved in school activities (citizens' committees,

PTA's) and the nature and frequency of their contact with school personnel. The findings were quite clear: Contrary to what had been anticipated by the investigators, the extent of the contact with the schools made little difference in the expectations held by the noneducators. As we saw, a good many other factors, such as occupational status, age, and religion, *did* make a difference.

In view of these results, it is perhaps time for careful studies to be directed toward examining in detail the assumption that involvement of the public in school affairs automatically increases consensus between educators and noneducators—an assumption on which so much so-called community relations work is currently based. Or, what may be more significant, research might be directed toward reexamining the techniques that are utilized to involve the public (in view of the observed differences, should it not be the publics?) in the educational enterprise.

A further general line of inquiry deriving from the theoretical model might explore the extent of the congruence or discrepancy between institutional expectations and observed behavior in a social system.[23] In the school, it would take the specific form of assessing how much the educational expectations are implemented by day-to-day practices.[24] Indeed, at least one school has utilized the Task of Public Education Opinionnaire for exactly this purpose. As a first step, the teachers in the system took inventory of their educational priorities with the Task Opinionnaire translated into operational terms. Grouped by schools, grade levels, and subject-matter areas, the teachers then compared each educational expectation they had ranked as important with their habitual classroom behavior.

The crucial issue under investigation was, "Is there any evidence that classroom behavior is reflecting the operationally defined expectations to which the teachers had subscribed?" The results were revealing—and in many ways quite startling. The teachers of science and English, for example, had ranked creativity (discrimination and imagination in problem-solving) as an important educational expectation. Yet the analysis of classroom activities showed that far more time and effort was devoted to such other expectations as possession of knowledge and communication of knowledge. The issue of course is not

---

[23] Downey, *The Task of Public Education*, p. 77.
[24] Cf. Norris M. Sanders, *Classroom Questions: What Kinds?* New York, Harper & Row, 1966, p. 176.

whether creativity should or should not be an educational expectation or an expectation of high or low priority. The point is that these teachers gave it a very high priority yet, on analysis, discovered that they were not doing anything about it in practice. Similar discrepancies between professed expectations and observed behavior were found in other subject-matter areas and at other grade levels many times over.

As a result of theoretical analysis and empirical inquiry, attention was directed toward the need for increasing congruence between what is valued and what is practiced. At least in this school, the staff attested to the utility of such systematic self-study. One might well suggest that similar studies in other systems would be of both applied and theoretical significance.

Summary

The conceptual model suggested a number of administrative issues with respect to the general problem of educational expectations. One issue involved the contention that since various subpublics are presumed to have different values they also hold different educational expectations for the schools—a situation of which the administrator must be aware. It was also suggested that one source of conflict in the school setting lies in the differences between noneducators and the educators themselves in the expectations they hold for the schools—differences which may well underlie the manifest frictions such as dissatisfaction with a given curricular item, a particular teacher, or the superintendent himself.

The several empirical studies did in fact find differences in educational expectations by occupational, educational, and social class group and by geographic region, age, religion, and racial composition. There were also differences between educators and noneducators in educational expectations, and in beliefs regarding the real and ideal characteristics of high school students.

It is of course clear that the variations among population groupings are not independent. For example, whether the observed differences by social class groups are due to the concomitant differences in occupational status or educational level is hard to say, and the studies do not disclose whether the differences between the educators and the noneducators are due to some intrinsic peculiarity in the educators or to the circumstance that for the most part they are members of the middle class. It would be useful if subsequent studies undertook to determine the source of the observed differences with greater specificity.

Nonetheless, the point here is not so much the exact nature and source of the differences, which in any case may be changing, as the fact that the differences exist and must be taken into consideration in the management of the schools. The injunction that the school administrator must be the educational leader in the community is only a cliché unless the administrator is aware of his own educational values, the values of the community, and the amount of agreement or disagreement on the expectations held for the schools.

Admittedly, the most accurate assessment of the degree of disagreement in expectations does not settle such issues as whether the school should attempt to modify the culture or should merely mirror the prevailing values of the dominant groups within the culture, whatever these values may be. Our own inclination is to think that the school cannot passively reflect the expectations of the community and let it go at that. In some areas it must follow or, if nothing else, lose the support on which its very existence depends. But in other areas it must take the initiative even at the risk of being out of step with some community wishes. If the present studies are accurate, those who would give higher priority to the intellectual expectations for the school are the educators, despite accusations to the contrary, and those who would give higher priority to the nonintellectual expectations are the noneducators. In this case, the school must educate the parents as well as the pupils.

In any event, although the administrator may not be able to harmonize the various pressures emanating from individuals and groups urging what appear to be their special interests, he cannot afford to be ignorant of the actual and potential crosscurrents in educational expectations underlying the pressures. Differences among the various subpublics in the culture in which the institution is embedded, and differences between educators and noneducators, have a direct bearing upon the functional problems facing the administrator—problems not only of institutional purposes but also of operational policies, programs, personnel, plant, and provision for financial support.

7

Institutional expectations

Whenever a role incumbent is required to conform simultaneously to several expectations which are mutually exclusive, contradictory, or inconsistent, he is said to be in a situation characterized by a role conflict. Adjustment to a role-conflict situation is difficult, since fulfillment of one set of expectations makes fulfillment of the other set (or sets) uncertain, if not impossible. Obviously all roles are liable to conflict. But few seem so fraught with difficulty as roles in the educational setting.

Consider, for example, the position of a school administrator in a small Midwestern community. As superintendent of schools he was expected to assume leadership in numerous community activities. Accordingly, he found himself elected overseer of a Sunday school at the same time that he was serving as commander of a local patriotic organization. As he explained later, as superintendent he could not refuse to give help to a church function any more than he could refuse to lend a hand to a patriotic enterprise. But now the conflict: as Sunday school leader he was supposed to be a model in holding the Sabbath holy; as commander he was expected to direct the annual turkey shoot on Sunday to raise funds for worthy community projects.

Since effectiveness in a role depends on the degree to which behavior conforms to expectations, effectiveness cannot be forthcoming if the expectations are inconsistent, regardless of *who* the particular incumbent is. In this sense, role conflicts are situational givens and independent of the personality of the role incumbents. They are evidence of dislocation in the institutional axis of behavior.

Three types of conflict in the educational setting will be dealt with in this chapter: (1) contradiction between the expectations of two or more roles which an individual is attempting to fulfill simultaneously, or "interrole conflict"; (2) contradiction among several reference groups, each defining the expectations for the same role, or "interreference-group conflict"; (3) contradiction within a single reference group defining a given role, or "intrareference-group conflict."

Conflict between roles

As we observed, interrole conflict (or for brevity here, role conflict) has its source in the contradictory expectations of two or more roles which an individual is attempting to fulfill simultaneously. In some school systems, for example, the same individual must serve as a building principal and as the chief executive officer of the entire system, directly responsible to the board of education. People in this position testify that they often find themselves torn between getting the most for *their* building and dispassionately considering policy questions relating to the school community as a whole. In other systems the so-called teaching principal must often choose between the demands of his role as teacher and the demands of his role as administrator.

These organizational arrangements, handed down either historically or expediently, have frustrated if not utterly defeated many a potentially effective administrator (or teacher). In addition to intraorganizational conflicts, extraorganizational conflicts plague the administrator. We have already mentioned the superintendent who as director of the Sunday school was expected to keep the Sabbath holy and as commander of the patriotic organization was expected the same day to organize a turkey shoot. And we need hardly expand on such obvious role conflicts as attempting to be a devoted family man and a successful superintendent who must be out of the house three or four evenings a week. But another recent case, although trivial in itself, makes the point: The school administrator role may clash with *any number* of other roles. In this instance, as member of a civic club a high school principal was elected to the committee of the club's TV script-writing contest. This surely seemed innocuous enough, until it was discovered that the school board had passed a regulation forbidding such activity by school personnel. Now what? If the principal resigned from the committee, he would be seen as failing his colleagues in the civic club, who might not understand the reasons for the board's regulation. If he remained on the committee, he would be seen as failing the school board, who insisted on sticking by their regulation. Trivial? Of course. Yet out of the stuff of such conflicts often arise the most passionate of controversies. The important problem becomes not the wisdom of the particular educational policy or practice, but whether this group or that group should have its way. In the present case, whichever group won, in some measure at least the principal was bound to lose.

We have cited instances of role conflict for the school administrator. Similar types of conflict beset the school board member and the teacher. In this section we shall use illustrative empirical studies of board members, administrators, and teachers to examine somewhat more systematically than can be done from anecdotal data the nature and effect of such conflict.

ROLE CONFLICT AND SCHOOL BOARD MEMBERSHIP

The board of education, by its very nature, must mediate between the affairs of the organization and the concerns of the public. Thus it is neither wholly inside nor wholly outside the organization. Insofar as the board member's extraorganizational role affiliations are incompatible with the intraorganizational role expectations there is a potential for ambiguity and conflict. Assume, for example, that from the intraorganizational point of view all his decisions as a school board member are expected to be made in the light of the criterion "What is best for the school?" Can the board member who is a labor union officer disregard in his consideration of, say, the National Education Association versus the American Federation of Teachers that he *is* a labor union officer? Can the board member who is a realty association officer disregard in his consideration of a school tax issue that he *is* a realty association officer? Can the board member who is also a Knights of Columbus officer or a Masonic lodge officer disregard in his consideration of a church-school question that he *is* a Knights of Columbus officer or Masonic lodge officer?

Our point here is not whether they can or cannot do so or, even if they could, whether they should or should not. Nor is it that assuming several roles with differing expectations *necessarily* leads to poor performance in the roles. Rather, it is that the multiple role incumbencies of school board members may induce role conflict, and that it is important to understand its nature and potential effect.

An intensive study by McCarty[1] of the motives of school board members in seeking their office will help us do just this. In bringing to light the varied reasons why individuals try to obtain board membership, the investigation also reveals the

---
[1] Donald J. McCarty, "Motives for Seeking School Board Membership," Doctoral dissertation, University of Chicago, 1959.

extraboard affiliations of the members and the extent to which certain of them face discrepant demands from their extraschool board roles and their school board role. As we shall see, some of the members seem to be on the board in order to represent their other roles. In a choice between what is good for themselves, that is, as representatives of the other roles, and what is good for the schools, they may select the former as against the latter.

Detailed interviews were held with 52 people serving on boards of education in seven Illinois and Wisconsin communities to determine their motives for seeking board membership and to examine the relation of these motives to the operation of the boards. Community A was a single-industry, handsomely landscaped village of 500 homes built by the manufacturing company for its employees. Community B was an economically diversified metropolitan city, one of the nation's leading industrial centers. Community C was a heavily industrialized city of 60,000, three of every four employed persons earning their living in manufacturing establishments. Community D was a package suburb of 25,000, catering to young mobile executives who need a haven between transfers. Community E was a "Gold Coast" suburb, serving an upper-class elite clientele. Community F was a mature residential suburb, still a favored place to live but with an increasing number of lower-class ethnic groups infiltrating the district. Community G was a farm village of slightly over 3,000 people which becomes a tourist attraction in the summer.

Although representativeness of the sample for the nation as a whole is obviously not claimed, several of the descriptive variables, such as age of the board members and ratio of male to female members, are very similar to national board of education norms. There are some notable characteristics of the present sample. One is that fully a third of the board members do not have children in the schools with which they are associated. Another, and at least for the investigator perhaps the most striking descriptive finding, is that almost 10 percent of the board members send their own children to Roman Catholic parochial schools. The 10 percent come from only two of the school systems, but in one they comprise 2 of a total of 7 members and in the other, 3 of 14 members. Perhaps another noteworthy characteristic of the sample is the enormous range in income among the school board members taken en masse, and the homogeneity of income in certain communities. For example, in community C 4 of the 7 board members earn less than $7,500 and none more than $15,000; in community E all of the 7 board members earn more than $15,000. In general, the income level, although high, is not surprising in view of the fact that 3 of the communities are residential suburbs of a major city.

On the Motives of School Board Members. Among the interview questions were, "Why did you decide to run for the school board?" and "What do you think is the primary reason your colleagues sought membership?"[2] Even the *manifest* reasons given for seeking membership on the board, to say nothing of latent reasons that possibly were not verbalized, were complex. The subjects tended in the main to give a number of dissimilar motives almost in the same breath, several of which might in fact be quite contradictory. It was the investigator's impression that "some measure of contradiction in purpose seems ordinary," and that "all seven boards apparently have some members who sought election, in part, for their own personal aggrandizement."[3] Here is an excerpt from a characteristic interview:

> I ran because I had built up real pride in our school district and I had one child in the school which made me feel closer to the school. This prompted me to want to be helpful in making it a greater school. The secondary reason was more selfish—to gain knowledge. I wanted to know more about the educational field and the administration of a big institution. I knew and realized that our school was the biggest business in our community and the running of it would teach me something about big business. Also, I wanted to see what I could do in the local school election. I was fairly successful and polled the highest number of votes ever. The reason was that I had been active in other community affairs. I had been slugging away at some other things. Another thing, it is actually considered an honor to be a part of the management of our school because of its stature. You do not have to hide your head at all.[4]

Note in this statement the diversity of motives. There is public service: to make it a great school. Then the admission of self-interest: to gain knowledge. Then the hint of political ambitions: to see what he could do in a public election. And then the prestige: it is an honor to be a board member.

A summary of the various reasons given by the respondents for seeking board membership is given in Table 7–1. It is

---

[2] *Ibid.*, p. 148.
[3] *Ibid.*, p. 56.
[4] *Ibid.*, pp. 56–57.

TABLE 7-1

Reasons Given by Board Members for Seeking Election to the Board, by Frequency and Percent

Reasons given by board members	Frequency of mention	Percent of board members
Felt it to be a civic duty	24	46.2
Persuaded or pressured by friends	20	38.4
Interest in educational matters	15	28.9
Opportunity to learn something new	9	17.3
Recognition, honor, prestige	7	13.5
Satisfactions received from PTA work	5	9.6
Disapproved of the way the schools were being run	5	9.6
See that tax money was well spent	4	7.7
Personal admiration for superintendent of schools	3	5.8
Represent the Catholic religion	3	5.8
Enjoyment of board associations	3	5.8
New school had to be built	3	5.8
Represent section of school district	3	5.8
Wanted administrative experience	2	3.9
Interested in getting some experience in politics	2	3.9
Graduated from the school	2	3.9
Duty to the labor union	2	3.9
Chance to release energy	2	3.9
Ego gratification	2	3.9
Necessity to do something about convictions	1	1.9
Concerned about the kinds of people who were getting on the board	1	1.9
TOTAL	118	

SOURCE: Donald J. McCarty, "Motives for Seeking School Board Membership," Doctoral dissertation, University of Chicago, 1959, pp. 54–55.

immediately evident that although civic responsibility heads the list, at least some say openly that they are on the board because of pressure from others, or to represent their religion in school affairs, or they feel they owe it to their labor union. It is interesting that in telling why their colleagues sought board membership, they mention essentially the same motives—but with one notable exception: only 4 percent of the members give politics as a reason when describing their own motives, yet fully 25 percent mentioned politics as a motive of their colleagues. The complete data are shown in Table 7–2.

TABLE 7-2

Reasons Board Members Sought Election, According to Their Colleagues

Reasons given by colleagues	Frequency mentioned	Percent total
Felt it to be a civic duty	28	53.8
Persuaded or pressured by friends	14	26.9
Satisfy political ambitions	13	25.0
Recognition, honor, prestige	9	17.3
Interest in educational matters	7	13.5
Represent Catholic religion	4	7.7
See that tax money was well spent	4	7.7
PTA satisfactions	4	7.7
Represent section of school district	3	5.8
Disapproved of the way the schools were being run	3	5.8
Ego gratification	2	3.9
TOTAL	91	

SOURCE: Donald J. McCarty, "Motives for Seeking School Board Membership," Doctoral dissertation, University of Chicago, 1959, p. 55.

On Role Conflict and School Board Membership. On the basis of the interviews, the investigator divided the school board members into two groups. The "community-oriented" group was composed of those who responded to the role of board member *in its own terms*. As the investigator put it, "A community-oriented board member was defined as one who wanted the board experience in order to contribute to the best interests of the schools and all children in the community."[5] The "self-oriented" group was composed of those who responded to the role of board member *in terms of their membership in other roles*. In the investigator's words, "A self-oriented board member was defined as one who wanted the board experience for his own benefit or to represent a particular group."[6] The classification of board members into these groups was highly reliable, the consistency of coding by three independent judges exceeding .90.[7] The distribution of the groups in the seven communities is given in Table 7-3.

Perhaps most noteworthy is the relatively high proportion of community-oriented school board members in community E,

---
[5] *Ibid.*, p. 58.
[6] *Ibid.*
[7] *Ibid.*, p. 53.

TABLE 7-3

Motives of Board Members Classified as Community-Oriented or Self-Oriented

Type of motive	COMMUNITY							Total	Percent total
	A	B	C	D	E	F	G		
Community-oriented	2	3	4	3	5	4	3	24	46.2
Self-oriented	1	11	3	4	2	3	4	28	53.8
TOTALS	3	14	7	7	7	7	7	52	100.0

SOURCE: Donald J. McCarty, "Motives for Seeking School Board Membership," Doctoral dissertation, University of Chicago, 1959, p. 58.

the "Gold Coast" suburb, and the exceedingly high proportion of self-oriented members in community B, the large city. At least in the present study, one factor making for conflict in the school board role was type of community. Another seemed to be religion or, strictly speaking, the type of school the board member's own children attended. Specifically, McCarty found that Catholic members who sent their children to parochial schools tended to be more self-oriented than other school board members, including Catholics who did not send their children to parochial schools.

The interviews by McCarty provide numerous illustrations of role conflict and its effect on the person himself and on others. An especially vivid portrait is that of the Catholic board member in his role as member of the school board, and of the resentment engendered by the real or apparent dual allegiance in some of the non-Catholic board members. For example, asked why he sought board membership, one Catholic respondent said simply, "I felt and members of our church felt that we should have a Catholic on the board."[8] Or, asked what he hoped to accomplish as a board member, one explained:

Before I leave the board I want a report on how many Catholics have been promoted to administrative positions. We have only one. It doesn't seem reasonable to assume that there aren't some deserving Catholic candidates. Those things are hard to track down. They can say they were considered and were not qualified. That's why we want to get in a position where we can review the candidates for promotion.

[8] *Ibid.*, p. 61.

Then we can assure that Catholics aren't passed over because of religion.[9]

The Catholic board members who send their children to parochial school are often resented by the non-Catholic members. As one non-Catholic board member said, "I think a person has guts galore to be a board member and send his kids to a parochial school."[10]

These observations refer almost exclusively to Catholic board members who send their children to parochial schools. That is, these board members were seen as occupying two roles liable to incompatible expectations. Catholic board members who sent their children to the public schools were not differentiated from other board members. As the investigator states, "... a Catholic board member who sends his children to the public school will be just as likely to be community oriented as a non-Catholic member. Where the Catholic board member's children attend school is apparently the distinguishing factor...."[11] This finding is similar to the one by Gross, who found that only 24 percent of Massachusetts board members with children in parochial schools had "good" motivation.[12]

It must be emphasized that the incompatible demands cited here between certain religious and educational affiliations do not imply that a majority of the potential role conflicts of school board members are related to religious issues. On the contrary, McCarty found that many board members sought a position on the school board not only to serve the school but to further interests of a particular group—a labor union, a business organization, residents of a specific geographic section of the school district, or a political party. Some 54 percent of all board members in the sample expressed reasons classified by the investigator as "self-interested,"[13] that is, as wanting the board experience "for his own benefit or to represent a particular group." At a choice point in a conflict between the expectations of the one role (say, as representative of a particular labor or business or political group) and those of the other role (as representative of the school community as a whole), it is not at all certain which expectations will be fulfilled.

---

[9] *Ibid.*
[10] *Ibid.*, p. 61.
[11] *Ibid.*, p. 62.
[12] Neal Gross, *Who Runs Our Schools?* New York, Wiley, 1958, p. 80.
[13] McCarty, *op. cit.*, p. 136.

Role Conflict and the Operation of School Boards. An important issue confronts us: Does the fact that an individual is simultaneously fulfilling roles as a member of the school board and as a representative of some special interest or group make any difference in the operation of the board?

The problem of studying the operation of boards with their variety of community contexts and complex characteristics is formidable, and surely no definite answers can be forthcoming from any one investigation. Nonetheless, McCarty's explorations in this area are well worth examining.

A preceding study of the relation between the motives of board members and the operation of the board had been based on data provided by the superintendents about the conduct of the boards. A central conclusion had been that "The 'well-motivated' [board members] behave professionally; the 'badly motivated' behave unprofessionally."[14] McCarty suggested that since this measure of conduct was obtained from a single source —the superintendent—the evaluation might not be reliable. Accordingly, he defined board operation by the *specific mechanisms used by the board to establish consensus* and interviewed *all* board members on how decisions were reached at their board meetings. Inasmuch as each member was interviewed separately, the investigator felt that when the descriptions of the board meetings reinforced each other they were reasonably accurate accounts of what actually took place.

On the basis of the mechanisms used to reach decisions, the boards were classified into two groups, high-friction boards and low-friction boards. In high-friction boards, problems were usually solved by the sheer power of majority vote, or through the machination of splits and cliques, even though overt disagreement may have been avoided in formal board meetings. In low-friction boards, members characteristically settled disagreements through discussion until consensus was attained, without recourse to the power of majority vote or through the maneuvers of cliques.[15] Four boards—those in communities B, C, D, and G—were found to be high in friction, three—those in communities A, E, and F—low in friction.

The relevant question in the present context is, "Is there any relationship between boards categorized as self-oriented or community-oriented (that is, differing in extent of role conflict)

---
[14] Gross, *op. cit.*, p. 99.
[15] McCarty, *op. cit.*, pp. 104 ff.

and boards classified as high friction and low friction (that is, differing in type of board operation)?" McCarty found that three of the four community-oriented boards were low in friction and the three self-oriented boards were high in friction.[16]

Case Studies: A Low-Friction Board and a High-Friction Board. To put flesh on the tabular data, the investigator presented brief vignettes of the board members and the mode of operation of each of the boards. We cite here two such vignettes, one of a low-friction board (the one in community F, the mature residential suburb) and one of a high-friction board (the one in community C, the heavily industrialized small city).

A LOW-FRICTION BOARD[17]

Motives of board members. Mrs. Jorgensen, a housewife and active worker in the League of Women Voters, remarked that she had "an enormous sense of pride in being asked to help set educational policies for the community." Mr. Wright, the president of a small manufacturing company, stated that "it is my school and I have a personal interest in it." Mr. Fitch, an engineer, accepted because of "the satisfaction I got working with people in the grammar school PTA." Mr. Lloyd, a mechanical engineer, said that he had "a keen interest in education and the work is rewarding." Mr. Glock, another engineer, liked board work and also felt that "a person must serve his community if he expects it to grow and maintain high standards." Mr. Proctor, a merchandise manager for a department store, thought that he "might learn something and might contribute something due to past experience on elementary school boards." Mr. Parsons, a lawyer, was persuaded by the PTA committee, but also felt that "it was an obligation to accept the service."

Character of board operation. The board group works as a unit. The minor difficulties are straightened out by discussion; the more serious problems are tabled and carried over for investigation by a fact-finding committee. Most decisions are ultimately decided unanimously.

All members, except Mrs. Jorgensen, claimed that there were no forbidden topics. Note what the one woman on the board had to say:

> I think we should find the right kind of Negro teacher. This is a field where you can't push people very far. I would like to see the school do something in race relationships. It is always safer to talk about Greece and Rome. It would be interesting to

---
[16] *Ibid.,* p. 58.
[17] *Ibid.,* pp. 109–111.

bring this up. The superintendent wouldn't bring this up. The closest we have come to a fight is about girls' clubs. They choose their membership and they are chosen on a ruling clique basis. We are going to see if we can bring this closer to the democratic process. I feel that this is a wrong thing. I am against sororities and fraternities at the college level; at the high school level it is just too darn bad. I would like to force this issue a little faster; on this issue you have got to take a position.

As far as the data permit us to judge, the presentation of social objectives, such as those presented above, would not be likely to impede the operation of the board; the issue would be tabled or discussed until some sort of consensus was reached.

A HIGH-FRICTION BOARD[18]

Motives of board members. Mr. Kelly, a junior bank executive, sought board membership because his mother was a teacher and he had "heard education for so many years that it seemed like the natural thing to do." Mr. Scibelli, the financial secretary of a labor union, got "roped into it by union headquarters." Mr. Lynch, a department head in an industrial plant, ran because he was asked by a delegation of citizens who felt that "the radical element of labor had control of the board." Mr. Putzakuluch, a supervisor in a plant, thought he "could be of some help in solving problems." Mrs. Martinelli, an employee of the local radio station, wanted the position because she was "struck by the illogical kind of reasoning that governed decisions." Mr. Gottfried, an insurance agent, felt that there was "an utter lack of public relations between the public and the school system." Mr. Smith, an unemployed plant supervisor, didn't seek the position. He was requested to run by one of the non-partisan groups in the community because he had "an old name in the community and a highly respected one."

Character of board operation. In many places in the interviews, we find evidence that difficulties are overcome by resorting to the simple expedient of a majority vote. The quotation below is an excellent illustration of this procedure.

> Well, sometimes we cuss each other out. Usually if it gets to a four to three vote, the majority will say "let's move on to the next issue." We used to have a board member who went out and fought decisions openly. She was a crusader but she has somewhat got over that. At times we think one member of the board is stupid.

---
[18] *Ibid.*, pp. 112–114.

Each of the members stated that any issue could be brought before the board. Although the board was fraught with dissensions, no attempt was made to submerge potential centers of conflict; curiously the board members seemed to enjoy the internal struggles. The quotation below gives some idea of this attitude:

> I am too stupid to be afraid of any issue. If it would help the school system I don't care how hot it is. Sometimes the board wrangles without coming to a decision. I am not afraid of making a decision. Tomorrow I may change. Does that seem like a fair approach? If the superintendent can't get a decision, it is frustrating as hell. It is better to make one and find out if it is right or wrong.

Two final comments are in order. First, it must be recognized, as the investigator himself points out, that certain limitations in the data must be taken into account. In an interview study there may be some distortion of response in the direction of social acceptability; the criterion followed in selecting the sample was variety of community situations rather than representativeness of board members; open-ended questions do not lend themselves easily to quantification, and there may be bias in the content analysis of the qualitative material. Second, no attempt was made to determine which boards were ultimately more effective or which procedures led to the wisest decisions. Perhaps some conflict of interest is necessary in order to sharpen the decision-making process, and under certain circumstances it is the high-friction rather than the low-friction board which operates to better purpose. The function of conflict in board interaction is surely a fruitful topic for further study.

In any event, it seems that (1) there is a range of motives for seeking board membership; (2) many board members experience a certain amount of role conflict; (3) the extent of the conflict is at least in part a function of the type of community; and (4) the amount of role conflict in the membership is related to the nature of operation of the board: the greater the role conflict, the higher the friction in the board operation.[19] The administrator who would understand the operation of his board, then, must understand the type of community which is the context for his school and have some insight into the nature and

---

[19] Cf. Alan D. Osterndorf, "Expectations and Satisfactions of Effective and Ineffective School Board Members," Doctoral dissertation, University of Wisconsin, 1966.

extent of the role conflicts represented in the membership of the board.[20]

ROLE CONFLICT AND THE SUPERINTENDENCY

The school administrator is especially exposed to role conflict,[21] as we have already shown. We shall continue to examine this aspect of educational administration from differing points of view but at the moment wish only to cite some illustrative material from the well-known School Executive Studies.[22] It will be recalled that in these studies 105 superintendents in Massachusetts were interviewed on various phases of their work. Among the issues raised was the relationship of the superintendent to his position as father, as personal friend, as member of a local community association, and as member of a particular religious group.

Fully 48 percent of the superintendents reported conflicts between expectations deriving from their role as school administrator and expectations deriving from their role as father. That is, their children expected one thing from them, and others expected something quite different. As one superintendent described the situation:

> You know one of the worst things about this job that you never think of before you get into it is its effect on your children. You don't have time for your children. You have to be out every night and it just isn't fair to them. They don't like it; they resent it. And then the kids have a cross to bear. Either they get especially soft or especially rough treatment by the teachers. And the teachers are just waiting for you to throw your weight around.
>
> For example, my boy has told me certain things about one of his teachers—the way she behaves in the classroom. He's an honest

---

[20] For analyses of factors relating to school board-community interaction, see F. Donald Carver, "Relationships Between Education Level, Family Income, and Expectations of Citizens for the Role of the School Board," Doctoral dissertation, University of Wisconsin, 1966; and John F. Meggers, "Expectations for the Role of the Board of Education Held by Parochial and Public School Oriented Parents," Doctoral dissertation, University of Wisconsin, 1966.

[21] Administrative interns in training are likewise subject to role conflict, as is revealed in Leo A. Dorais, "Role Conflict in Internship: A Study of Administrative Residencies," Doctoral dissertation, University of Chicago, 1964.

[22] Gross, *op. cit.*; also Neal C. Gross, Ward S. Mason, and Alexander W. McEachern, *Explorations in Role Analysis*, New York, Wiley, 1958. The present section is based on Neal Gross, "Some Contributions of Sociology to the Field of Education," *Harvard Educational Review*, 29 (Fall, 1959), 275–287.

youngster so I have no reason to doubt him, and if I were not the superintendent you can be darned sure I'd raise a lot of Cain. But as the superintendent I'm not supposed to invade a teacher's classroom. So I try to support the teacher even though I know she is in the wrong. I feel pretty mean about this, but what can I do? I hope my boy will understand the situation better later on.[23]

Perhaps as great a source of personal and emotional strain is the conflict arising from the expectations of personal friends which are incompatible with those of the general public. Thirty-five percent of the superintendents reported conflicts of this kind.[24] Not only are there requests from personal friends for special personnel decisions and for allocation of contracts, but more often there are importunities for special consideration for their children. According to the superintendents, friends asked that teachers be reprimanded for treating their children unfairly, that their children be transferred to a school in another district, that their children be promoted against the best judgment of the teacher, that transportation be provided for children who were not entitled to it, and so on. Each of these "special consideration" expectations is incompatible with procedures which the superintendent is expected to follow by the school board, by the teachers, and by other parents who are not his personal friends. One superintendent described the dilemma this way:

[One of the] nastiest aspects of my job is bus transportation. Good friends of mine have the nerve to telephone me, the superintendent of schools, and ask that a bus pick up their children, when they know, and I know, and the bus driver knows, that they live within the one-mile limit. I tell them I don't drive the bus, I'm just superintendent of schools. Talk to the bus driver. They think I am saying okay, and I guess I am if you come right down to it. Someday I guess I'll get into trouble when someone who doesn't have the gall to come to me goes to the committee and says "so and so, the superintendent's friend, has his kids picked up. Why can't I have mine?" It's all in the game and sometimes the game is rough.[25]

The investigator rightly points out, "Undoubtedly there are many requests of this kind which superintendents automatically ignore or refuse and which they did not mention in the interview; it is when these requests come from personal friends and when these

---

[23] Gross, "Some Contributions of Sociology to the Field of Education," p. 285.
[24] *Ibid.*, p. 284.
[25] *Ibid.*, p. 285.

friends expect the superintendent to make particular concessions, that the superintendents describe them as role conflict situations."[26]

Eighteen percent of the superintendents found that incompatible expectations were held for them as members of a local community association and as chief executive officers of the community schools.[27] For example, on occasion certain local organizations to which the superintendent belonged expected him to allow students and staff to work on organizational business during school time, whereas the professional school staff expected him to resist such requests and protect the schools from this kind of "invasion." The investigator listed, among others, organizational demands that pupils be active in fund-raising activities, that the school band play in parades, and that the schools participate in youth activities. Surely, there is no harm in any of these activities in themselves, and it ought to be easy for the superintendent to go along with his colleagues in the associations. But the superintendent also knows, as the investigator points out, that a major complaint of the faculty is that this type of activity disrupts their planned school program. The conflict is exacerbated for the superintendent because it is not just a personal matter between him and some group he belongs to in his private capacity. If it were, he could just disengage himself from the conflicting organization. The situation is complicated by the fact that he is expected to be a member in good standing of a number of civic associations, since they are often influential in community affairs. For example, suppose a bond issue is coming up and the organization making the request has a powerful voice in the community at the same time that the faculty feels especially sensitive about classroom disruption from outside quarters. How does the superintendent proceed then? It is of the very nature of a role-conflict situation that, whatever one does, one set of expectations may be left unfulfilled.

Another source of role conflict for the superintendent must be mentioned, however briefly. Twenty percent of the superintendents interviewed reported facing incompatible expectations in being simultaneously a superintendent and a member of a religious group. Again, the essential point is that as superintendents they were expected to act one way and as members of a particular religious organization they were expected to act in

---

[26] *Ibid.*, p. 284.
[27] *Ibid.*, p. 285.

another way. We have already seen this type of conflict engendered in the case of school boards and membership in the Catholic church. But of course no church has a monopoly in causing this type of conflict. Similar incompatible demands are made by other denominations. A Protestant superintendent described his situation:

> [My] minister wants all kinds of special favors because I am a member of his church. He expected me to turn over our gym to the church basketball team. He wanted me to support his idea of giving out a Bible to each public school child. He told me that he thought I ought to see that more of "our people" get jobs in the school. None of these are fair requests. I'm supposed to represent all the people, and I want to use the criterion of "what's best for the schools," not "what's best for my church." I might give him the gym, but it would be worth my job to give in on the Bibles in this community. I try not to play favorites, but sometimes it's hard to know what is the right thing to do.[28]

ROLE CONFLICT AND THE TEACHER

The teacher faces role conflicts similar to those of other individuals centrally located in the educational system.[29] He too may be liable to incompatible expectations stemming from his role as teacher and from other roles he is attempting to fulfill simultaneously. Getzels and Guba studied certain aspects of these incompatible expectations and, in addition, raised the question of whether the ensuing conflicts were typical of all communities or occurred only in some.[30]

Specifically, the investigators posed the following issues: (1) What are the expectations held for teachers (as reported by the teachers themselves)? (2) How do these expectations accord with the expectations of other roles the teacher occupies? (3) In what ways are the several sets of expectations inconsistent? (4) How do the inconsistencies vary from one teaching situation to another?

Incompatible Expectations for Teachers. The initial attempt to answer these questions was based on extensive interviews with 41 teachers drawn from school systems in two Midwestern

---
[28] *Ibid.*, p. 284.
[29] Cf. Anne E. Trask, "Principals, Teachers and Supervision," *Administrator's Notebook*, 12 (December, 1964), 1–4.
[30] J. W. Getzels and E. G. Guba, "The Structure of Roles and Role Conflict in the Teaching Situation," *Journal of Educational Sociology*, 29 (September, 1955), 30–40.

states. Three major areas of conflict were identified, each stemming from a salient role a teacher performed in addition to the teacher role.

1. *The socioeconomic role.* Teachers are usually assumed to be members of at least a quasi-professional group having middle-class standards of living. But in comparison with persons who live according to similar standards, the teacher receives a salary inadequate to implement the expectations they entail. Many of the strains upon the teacher arise not only because he is underpaid but because he is supposed to maintain amenities of taste and living which are out of his financial reach. A typical comment describing this type of conflict might be, "Although the community expects a teacher to maintain the same standard of living as say a minor executive or a successful salesman, the salary typically paid a teacher is too small to make this possible."[31]

2. *The citizen role.* Most adults are assumed to be responsible citizens whose judgment regarding their own conduct can be trusted. But in some communities a teacher is not granted the same confidence. For example, he may have to participate with more vigor in church affairs or to conform more assiduously to community mores, but to put less vigor into political matters than his own beliefs dictate. Although the teacher resides in the community, he may have only second-class citizenship, since the expectations placed upon him in his role of teacher restrict the degree of freedom in his role as citizen. A typical comment from a teacher was, "While almost no one ever concerns himself with the conduct of the average individual unless he seriously violates the customs and conventions of the community, many people are constantly on guard to be certain that teachers behave appropriately at all times."[32]

3. *The professional role.* The teacher is expected to be a specially trained person with expertness in a particular field. Certification of this professional training and competence is required, and persons without such certification are not accepted as teachers. In practice, however, the teacher's professional standing and prerogatives may be challenged by almost anyone who has succeeded only in becoming a parent or paying a tax bill. Not only may the school administrator prescribe more or less minutely what the teacher may or may not do, but parents

---
[31] *Ibid.,* pp. 31–32.
[32] *Ibid.,* p. 32.

and others, as the teacher's "patrons," may dictate classroom procedures in direct opposition to the teacher's best professional judgment. The following statement concerning discipline may be taken as an instance of this type of conflict: "While many parents expect the teacher to discipline their children as well as to educate them, these same parents are often resentful of the disciplinary methods employed, even when these methods are justified."[33] The issue here is not whether the administrators and parents are in a better position to make classroom decisions than is the teacher. They may very well be. But consider the conflict from the teacher's point of view: He is expected to be a professional person with special competence; he is simultaneously expected to submit to others at crucial points in his own field of competence.

Role Conflict and the Teaching Situation. That these several kinds of conflict do in fact exist, at least to some degree, seemed amply documented by the interviews, although determination of the extent of such conflict must await nationwide study. Nonetheless, even within the limits of an available sample, the next question could be asked, if only as a point of departure for further theoretical and empirical work: Do the role conflicts vary from one teaching situation to another, and are these variations, if they exist, related to known differences in the several teaching situations under study?

On the basis of the interviews a group questionnaire comprised of 71 items getting at the indicated conflicts was developed, and the responses of 166 teachers in six varied school systems were analyzed. Among the school systems were (1) a secondary and an elementary system in rural Kansas, (2) two secondary schools and one elementary school in suburban Chicago, and (3) one private church-affiliated secondary school in Chicago.

The analysis of the responses, school by school and item by item, showed that the conflicts seemed to be distributed in three different patterns: *situationally independent, situationally variant*, and *situationally specific.*

1. *Situationally independent conflicts.* The situationally independent conflicts seemed to have equal impact in all teaching situations sampled and to be independent of local conditions. Almost all teachers in all schools agreed that the conflict de-

---

[33] *Ibid.*

scribed by the item existed in their teaching situation. For example, on a six-point scale from "practically no teachers would agree" (scale score 0) to "very many teachers would agree" (scale score 5), the item "While teachers understand that they act as parent surrogates, parents expect teachers to set a better example for the children than the parents themselves are willing to set" received a mean score of 2.8 for all schools. It received a mean of 3.0 in the highest-scoring school, and a mean of 2.6 in the lowest-scoring school.[34] That is, the mean score was quite high and essentially the same in all schools, indicating that this type of conflict was readily recognizable by the teachers, that it seemed to be inherent in the current teaching situation, and that it was independent of the specific conditions in the communities in the sample.

2. *Situationally variant conflicts.* The situationally variant conflicts seemed to have some impact in all teaching situations but to be substantially aggravated or alleviated by local conditions. In some schools the particular conflict was highly prominent, in others it was less so.[35] For example, the item "While almost no one would object if the banker occasionally stopped in a tavern for a drink, such conduct would be considered inappropriate for the teacher by the community" received a mean score of 2.7 in all schools, essentially the same as the situationally independent conflict. But the mean in the highest-scoring school was 3.8 and in the lowest-scoring school 2.2, a range of 1.6 scale points, whereas in the situationally independent conflict the range had been only 0.4 scale points.[36] That is, although the mean score for all schools was again quite high, it varied markedly from school system to school system. Moreover, the variation seemed to be related to the differential teaching situation. In the case of the item cited, the highest-scoring school was in a rural community where teacher visibility was high.

3. *Situationally specific conflicts.* The situationally specific conflicts seemed to be unrecognized in most teaching situations but to have considerable impact in a particular locality. For example, the item "Even though dancing may be an accepted form of social recreation in the community, the teacher who dances is often thought of as somewhat immoral" received the negligible mean score of 0.4 for all schools. But it had a mean score of 2.6

---
[34] *Ibid.,* p. 34.
[35] *Ibid.,* p. 35.
[36] *Ibid.,* p .36.

in one school.[37] Clearly items falling into this pattern represented conflicts which are not generally prevalent in the teaching situation as such but are a function of some particular school or community idiosyncracy. The high-scoring school with respect to the item cited here was one "where church attendance is 'taken for granted' and whose rules frown upon dancing."

We shall return to the problem of the role conflicts of teachers when we examine individual differences in reaction to such conflict. We shall show that one teacher, although acknowledging the existence of the conflict in his school, seems to be able to shrug it off without any personal involvement whereas another, acknowledging the existence of the same conflict, is greatly troubled by it. This is another dimension of the general issue. Here we wished only to point out that there are several kinds of role conflicts. Some have similar force in all teaching situations and are independent of local conditions. In a sense, they are indigenous to the role of teacher. Some conflicts have considerable force in all teaching situations but may be aggravated or ameliorated by local conditions. Some conflicts are unrecognized in most teaching situations but have relatively great force in particular situations. In a sense, these conflicts seem to inhere in the locality. The implications for the administrator are clear enough. If he is not aware of the different kinds of conflicts faced by his teachers, he may be puzzled as to why behavior that was no problem in one school system becomes a problem both for himself and for his teachers in another.

Conflict between reference groups

In the preceding section we examined a number of aspects of the situation in which the expectations of *two or more roles* held simultaneously by an individual are contradictory. Now we shall consider some aspects of the situation wherein two or more reference groups have different expectations for the *same* role, and these in turn differ from the expectations of the individual in the role.

THE SUPERINTENDENT AND HIS REFERENCE GROUPS

We have cited the case of the professor whose department chairman expects him to emphasize teaching and service to the de-

---
[37] *Ibid.*

partment and whose academic dean wants him to emphasize research and the attainment of prominence in his discipline. Consider now the school superintendent's position with respect, say, to collective negotiations—only one of a multitude of problems that lend themselves to this kind of analysis.

From the teachers' point of view the superintendent may be expected—and legitimately so—to support their plea to the board for maximizing salary increases. He is seen as the teachers' representative to the board. From the board's point of view—to say nothing of the point of view of some taxpayers' groups—the same superintendent may be expected to support their case to the teachers for minimizing salary increases. Here he is regarded as the board's representative to the teachers. Any decision he makes, even a negotiated compromise, will probably be viewed by either group or both as somehow letting them down, as not fulfilling their expectations for his role. In addition, of course, he has some expectations of his own for the superintendent's role.

Hencley[38] examined these crosscurrents in expectations for the superintendency as held by the incumbent and, what is more germane here, as held by various groups. Each of the groups felt it had at least some right to define the superintendent's role. One group was made up of other superintendents, as a "professional" reference group. In every case the superintendent had reason to believe the group in question did have such right, and in fact he made his decisions at least partly with the expectations of these groups in mind. The investigator broadened the scope of preceding studies in this area in two ways. First, he examined the expectations for the superintendency on the part of three different types of reference groups—an intraorganizational group (teachers and principals), an interstitial group (the board of education), and several extraorganizational groups (chamber of commerce, PTA council, labor council)—as well as of a number of superintendents themselves. Second, he examined disagreements, not only in such task areas as finance and business management, curriculum and program, staff personnel, school plant, pupil personnel, and school-community relationships, but also with respect to the generalized roles such as chief executive of the board, status leader of the organization, member of the community, and member of the educational profession.

---

[38] Stephen P. Hencley, "A Typology of Conflict Between Superintendents and Their Reference Groups," Doctoral dissertation, University of Chicago, 1960.

Utilizing a framework for the observation of administrative behavior developed at the Midwest Administration Center,[39] the investigator devised a 64-item questionnaire covering expectations for the superintendent's behavior in the indicated tasks and roles. Responses were obtained from 15 superintendents of schools in three Midwestern states, and from 102 board members, 776 teachers and principals, 425 business people, 310 PTA council members, and 194 labor council members in the school districts served by the superintendents. A comparison of the responses revealed sharp differences as well as similarities between the superintendent group and each reference group and among the reference groups themselves. We may illustrate the findings by referring to selected items in several of the task and role areas under study:

1. *Staff personnel.* One item here dealt with expectations regarding superintendent support of merit pay for teachers: "I expect the school superintendent to support the principle of merit pay for teachers." The respondents were required to indicate the strength of their expectations on a five-point scale from "strongly agree" (scale score 1) to "strongly disagree" (scale score 5). The mean score for the superintendent group was exactly 3.0 ("undecided"). The labor reference group agreed with this. But the other four groups differed substantially with the superintendents' position, and, perhaps more to the immediate point, the reference groups differed among themselves. The board member, parent, and business groups were considerably *more* in favor of superintendent support of merit pay than was the superintendent group whereas the teacher group was *less* in favor of superintendent support of merit pay than was the superintendent group.[40] Presumably the superintendent cannot maintain the "undecided" posture forever. But whichever way he moves, he is bound to disappoint at least one of his important reference groups.

Here is another item from the same set. Should the superintendent "insist that the board hire only those teachers that he recommends"? The mean scale score of the superintendent group was 1.5, between "strongly agree" and "agree." But the expecta-

---

[39] Staff Associates, *Observation of Administrator Behavior*, Chicago, Midwest Administration Center, University of Chicago, 1959.
[40] Hencley, *op. cit.*, p. 138.

tions of the reference groups deviated from this, and they differed in the strength of deviation from a mean score of 2.9 ("undecided") for the teacher group to 3.9 ("disagree") for the labor group.[41] One final item: Should the superintendent "keep a watchful eye on the personal life of his subordinates"? The mean score of the superintendent group was 3.8 ("disagree"). That of the teacher group was exactly the same. But each of the other reference groups indicated greater agreement with the expectation described in the item, that is, the superintendent *should* keep a watchful eye on the personal life of his subordinates.[42]

2. *Curriculum and program.* A number of interesting alignments among the reference groups are illustrated by the reactions to the items in this set. For example, "I expect the school superintendent to ask teachers to work on curriculum committees on their own time" received a mean score of 2.3 from the superintendent group. The board of education and the business groups agreed with that group. But all the other groups disagreed, the teachers being almost a full scale point and the labor group one and a third scale points less in favor of such a requirement.[43] In view of the nature of the item, this pattern of agreement among the reference groups is perhaps not surprising. However, a different and rather surprising alignment of reference groups occurred on the item "I expect the school superintendent to consult the public about proposed curriculum changes." The superintendent group endorsed this expectation. The labor group now agreed. But each of the other groups, including the parents, was less in favor of this expectation than were the superintendents.[44]

3. *Finance and business management.* Perhaps the most interesting item in this set read simply, "I expect the school superintendent to help the school board resist demands by teachers for higher salaries." The superintendent group "disagreed" with this expectation. The expectations of the parent, business, and labor groups were essentially the same as those of the superintendents. But the groups most directly involved in the issue—the school board members and teachers—deviated markedly. Moreover, they deviated in opposite directions, the

---
[41] *Ibid.*
[42] *Ibid.*
[43] *Ibid.*, p. 137.
[44] *Ibid.*

board group being *more* in favor of this expectation, the teacher group being *less* in favor.[45] This result comes as no surprise. Yet to see it in these empirical terms as a conflict between two reference groups does raise the issue more concretely than was hitherto the case: What *is* the role of the superintendent in the face of opposing reference-group expectations, especially if one of the groups is the board?[46]

The same problem is raised perhaps even more sharply by another item in this area—an item receiving the highest "strongly agree" rating from the superintendents in the entire questionnaire: "I expect the school superintendent to recommend that school sites be bought even if they will not be used for some time to come." Indeed, the mean score was 1.2, about as strong an endorsement as it was possible for an expectation to attain. All reference groups deviated from this, although again in varying degree—the parent group, for example, deviated fully 1.9 scale points, the board 0.55 scale point.[47]

What must be noted, if it has not already become clear, is that the superintendent group itself is a reference group for each superintendent. In a sense, it is the professional sounding board for his behavior. Here then is the same dilemma in somewhat different terms: In the face of his own convictions and the virtual unanimity of his professional colleagues in the expectations for one type of behavior, does the superintendent conform to the expectations of other reference groups who are not so sure of the wisdom of this behavior or who may even actively dissent from it? And if the answer to this is "Of course not," then what about his role as chief executive officer of the board, whose main function is presumably to administer board policy? Or take the problem to an extreme and assume that the expectations of the professional group, with which the superintendent agrees, and the expectations of the board are absolutely opposed. Then what? An examination of the responses to two items dealing with the expectations for the superintendent as "chief executive officer of the board" may help clarify the issue, although it will not settle it.

---

[45] *Ibid.*
[46] Charles A. Perry and Wesley A. Wildman, "A Survey of Collective Activity Among Public School Teachers," *Educational Administration Quarterly*, 2 (Spring, 1966), 133–151.
[47] Hencley, *op. cit.*, p. 126.

4. *Chief executive of the board.* Is the superintendent bound to defend the wisdom of the board of education? The specific item read, "I expect the school superintendent to defend board of education policies whether he agrees with them or not." The mean scale score of the superintendent group was 1.8—a very substantial endorsement. The board of education group perhaps not unnaturally agreed with the superintendents. But each of the other reference groups differed in the direction of *less* agreement with this expectation.[48] A second item was directed toward the question not only of defending disagreeable board policies but carrying them out: "I expect the school superintendent to carry out board decisions even though he thinks they are unsound." The mean score of the superintendent group was 2.3. The board of education group again agreed with the superintendents, as did the business group. But the teacher, parent, and labor groups tended once more to deviate in the direction of less agreement on this expectation.[49]

In effect, in the case of both items the superintendents and the boards of education, and in the case of one of the items the business group as well agreed that the superintendent should defend and carry out board policy whether he agrees with it or not. That is, to paraphrase Decatur's sentiment, "Our board! may it always be in the right; but our board, right or wrong." But teachers, parents, and labor were not at all certain that the superintendent should be activated by this sentiment. What might be seen by one reference group as "loyalty" could be seen by another as "rubber stamp."

We cannot conclude this section without making explicit that the issue is not as simple as this dichotomy might suggest. Nor, of course, are reference groups as divided in their expectations as the selected items imply. In response to another set of items of which the following two are typical, "I expect the school superintendent to use his own judgment in interpreting school board rules" and "to insist on having a free hand in putting board decisions into practice," the superintendent group scores were in the middle range of agreement, and there was virtual consensus among all reference groups with these ratings.[50] Apparently, although there is serious conflict among reference groups about

---
[48] *Ibid.*, p. 140.
[49] *Ibid.*
[50] *Ibid.*

the superintendent's place vis-à-vis the board in setting policy, there is no conflict over his place in carrying out the policy once it is made. Whether such nice division between "making policy" and "carrying out policy" can actually be maintained in practice is of course another question—one of considerable importance but beyond our present concern.

We have illustrated the problem of interreference-group conflict by adducing material from a study of the superintendency. Similar material exists for other administrative roles within the educational setting.[51] For example, Cheal[52] found that the secondary school principal seemed particularly subject to conflicts in expectations among various reference groups. Superintendents, teachers, students, and parents reported differing expectations for the principal's behavior in such areas as pupil discipline, instruction, staff personnel, and public relations. In another study of the principalship, Moser[53] found that superintendents expected the principal to conform to one set of expectations as leader while teachers expected him to conform to another set. According to his superintendent, the principal was "to lead forcefully, to initiate action, to accomplish organizational goals, to emulate the nomothetic behavior of his superior." His teachers expected the same principal "to keep things on an even keel, to cater to the individual needs of his subordinates, to defend them from unfair demands on the part of top management, to look to them for suggestions on what is to be done." In facing the superintendent and the teacher, the principal was almost in the position of balancing two different roles in two separate systems rather than acting in a single role within a unitary system. The investigator concluded from his observations: "Evidence in this study has illustrated that the principal is in a delicate position as a member of two organizational families. . . . He dare not exhibit his inner drive for upward

---

[51] A study of the role of director of instruction which utilized observation of actual on-the-job behavior, instead of a questionnaire, was completed by Emmett J. Duffy, "The Role of the Director of Instruction—Tasks, Interactions, and Processes," Doctoral dissertation, University of Wisconsin, 1965.

[52] John E. Cheal, "Role Conflict in the Principalship of the Composite High School," Master's thesis, University of Alberta, 1958.

[53] Robert P. Moser, "A Study of the Effects of Superintendent-Principal Interaction and Principal-Teacher Interaction in Selected Middle-Sized School Systems," Doctoral dissertation, University of Chicago, 1957.

mobility lest he lose the confidence of his teachers, but he needs to demonstrate that drive to lead or he suffers low effectiveness ratings from his superiors. . . . His behavior is viewed differently by superiors and subordinates."[54]

Conflict within a reference group

Contradictory expectations may occur within a single reference group defining a given role. That this is often the case in education as in other institutions hardly needs to be documented. One principal described his situation as follows:

> My school is split right down the middle and I can't seem to do a thing about it. The root of the trouble is an old athletics-music feud that gets mixed in with age, training, community newcomer-oldtimer, and what have you. Every vote is a 14 to 14 tie. This year we've had knock-down, drag-out fights over our study hall schedule, testing program, merit rating, team teaching—even the time and place of a faculty party. And all 28 will be back next fall raring to go at it again.

The knock-down, drag-out fights within the teaching group may be symptomatic of more basic differences than are involved in the question of the time and place of a faculty party. They may point to disagreement on the fundamental expectations regarding education and administrative behavior. Indeed, the preceding studies of variations in this respect among reference groups revealed serious clashes *within* the groups—within the teacher group no less than within the others. A crucial question may be raised: What is the effect of such differences—especially, in the present context, of differences *within a teaching group*— on the satisfaction of the teachers with their work situation?

A study by Moyer[55] provides some insight into this issue. He obtained a measure of the relative "solidarity" of expectations for the leadership behavior of principals in seven schools by having the teachers react to an 80-item, Q-sort instrument describing various possibilities from leader-centered attitudes (for example, "[The principal] should make the decisions and run the school

[54] *Ibid.*, pp. 140–141.
[55] Donald C. Moyer, "Teachers' Attitudes Toward Leadership as They Relate to Teacher Satisfaction," Doctoral dissertation, University of Chicago, 1954.

according to his best judgment") to group-centered attitudes (for example, "[The principal] should rely heavily upon his teachers for help with school problems"). In addition, he measured the teachers' satisfaction with the principal, with the other teachers in the school, and with the over-all work situation. Each person's Q-sort was correlated with everyone else's Q-sort in each school, and a number of relationships to the satisfaction ratings were examined.

We shall refer only to three of the findings that seem especially relevant here. First, and most obvious, there was a wide range of individual differences within the teacher groups in what they wanted from the principal as leader. Some teachers preferred leader-centered behavior, others group-centered behavior. The principal behavior that fulfills the expectations of one teacher may disappoint those of another teacher in the same school. Second, there were differences from school to school in the homogeneity of attitudes and expectations among the teachers. In one school, for example, the range of correlations between teachers on the 80-item Q-sort was from .72 to .37; in another school the range was from .76 to —.06.[56] That is, there seemed to be greater "solidarity" in teacher expectations for principal behavior in the one school as against the other, so that the same principal behavior would have a relatively similar teacher reaction in one school but a relatively heterogeneous teacher reaction in another. Third, and perhaps most important, there appeared to be a positive relationship between group "solidarity" within a school as measured by the Q-sort and the over-all measure of teacher satisfaction.[57]

To be sure, the study was done with rather small samples, and findings based on seven selected schools cannot be generalized to all schools without replication. Nonetheless, it seems that the extent of congruence in expectations for principal behavior within a school is a factor in teacher satisfaction fully as important as the type of behavior the principal actually exhibits. In this sense, the issue is not altogether whether an administrator is leader-centered or group-centered—authoritarian or democratic —which has been a central question in administrative research and practice. The issue is also how much those who are administered—in the present case the teachers in a particular school—

---

[56] *Ibid.*, pp. 107–108.
[57] *Ibid.*, p. 91.

agree or disagree among themselves on what they expect of the administrator.[58]

Toward further inquiry

An important problem here as elsewhere in social science is the generality of results. It is, for example, virtually impossible to do a study like McCarty's on a random massive scale. The same material would almost certainly not have been forthcoming to a checklist-type questionnaire or an opinion-poll-type encounter or even the usual kind of impersonal interview. To obtain the candor and detail that McCarty did required some familiarity with the respondents, the cultivation of their confidence, leisurely informal interviews, and perhaps even a particular type of person as interviewer. (Would a board member put down on a questionnaire or tell just anyone that the primary reason he sought board membership was that it was good for his contracting business?) Moreover, the board must *volunteer* to participate. The investigator cannot force the board to "cooperate" in his research as he can force, say, his sophomore college class to do so. What then about boards that refuse to volunteer and are therefore never part of the research sample? All this makes for selected rather than representative respondents, and although there is a gain in the depth of findings there may be a loss in the generalization of results.

It is clear from McCarty's study, for example, that a relation exists between type of community and board of education conflict. The bigger the community, apparently the greater the conflict. But is this true only of the particular city in McCarty's sample, or of other big cities as well? Of *all* big cities? *How* big? Does it make any difference whether the city is in Massachusetts or in Mississippi? What factors other than those present in the boards under immediate study might account for different patterns of school board role conflict? All boards in McCarty's sample were elected by popular vote. Would the same patterns of role conflict occur in boards appointed by the mayor, city

---

[58] Expectations for decision-making behavior within school systems constituted a major focus of a long-range study recently completed at the University of Wisconsin: Glen G. Eye *et al.*, "Relationship Between the Perception of the Locus of Administrative Decisions and Instructional Change," Washington, D.C., U.S. Office of Education, Research Project 1913, 1966.

council, or similar agencies? Our point of course is that studies like McCarty's are fruitful not only in the findings they produce but perhaps more in the direction they give to further work. Through the replication and accretion of such studies, using different samples and added factors within a well-mapped framework so that the results of one study may readily be related to those of another, we may approach a greater generality of understanding than we now have.

There is a second problem that needs additional investigation—again here as elsewhere in organizational research. This is the delicate problem of a criterion of organizational effectiveness. In the terms of the theoretical formulation within which we are working, it is assumed that severe role conflict may be expected to affect individual behavior adversely. Besides, it is suggested that excessive role conflict has certain deleterious effects on the functioning of the social system as a whole. But how do we evaluate these effects? To date most studies have used intermediate criteria such as teachers' ratings of the confidence they have in their administrator's leadership, or teachers' self-ratings of their own satisfaction in the teaching situation. But is individual satisfaction necessarily related to organizational effectiveness?

Sometimes a measure of interpersonal "friction" is used as the criterion of effectiveness. The greater the friction, presumably the less the organizational effectiveness. On the whole, this seems plausible. But, as we have already observed, is not a certain amount of friction needed in an organization to sharpen the issues, refine the decision-making process, and instigate the search for change and innovation? Is not necessity—dissatisfaction with the status quo rather than satisfaction with it—the mother of invention?

To point to such issues is in no sense to disparage the use that has been made of these secondary criteria. On the contrary, they are necessary variables at the present stage of our ability in this area. No one has argued that they are sufficient criteria, or even the necessary criteria under all circumstances. The search for an ultimate standard of administrative or organizational effectiveness in any domain, to say nothing of education, where the ultimate objective of the system itself is a matter of controversy, is a problem of almost insurmountable methodological and philosophical difficulty. Nonetheless, this is an area that must remain open for further inquiry.

In addition to the criterion problem, there are methodological issues in research on role expectations which call for caution in interpreting observations and indicate areas for inquiry. Charters points to two such problems.[59] One problem has to do with the definition of role expectations; the concept is multifaceted, and exactly what is being dealt with must be distinguished. A second problem has to do with the particular comparisons which are made, and from which the measures of agreement and conflict are derived.

Specifically with respect to the data to be compared, Charters delineates a number of distinctions that must be borne in mind. Among these are: (1) Normative versus predictive beliefs. There is a difference between phrasing the question whether a certain behavior "should" or "should not" occur, and whether it "will" or "will not" occur. Indeed, explicit distinctions have rightly been drawn between "expectation" and "anticipation"[60] and between "norm" and "expectation."[61] In the present studies the definition referred to "should" or "should not," and presumably respondents were answering accordingly, although whether they did so is more easily ascertained in interviews than in questionnaires. (2) Direction versus intensity of beliefs. An expectation may vary both in whether the behavior is proscribed or prescribed and in how strong the proscription or prescription is held. Research has most often dealt only with direction of belief to the neglect of intensity. (3) Situational specificity versus situational generality. A role definer's expectations may apply to behavior in a particular situation or to behavior regardless of the situation. (4) Detailed behaviors versus general functions. It seems clear that the level of behavior described in an expectation—say, the teacher "should direct learning" as against the teacher "should sponsor dances"—will affect the likelihood of finding agreement or disagreement in the defining population. (5) The attribution of role expectations. If the problems are already complex, the complexity is compounded, as Charters puts it, when studies involve the attribution of expectations by one person to another, and they mount even further when a person is asked to estimate the expectations for a whole group.

---

[59] W. W. Charters, Jr., "The Social Background of Teaching," in N. L. Gage, ed., *Handbook of Research on Teaching*, Chicago, Rand McNally, 1963, pp. 791–797.
[60] Gross, Mason, and McEachern, *op. cit.*, p. 59.
[61] B. J. Biddle, H. A. Rosencranz, and E. F. Rankin, *Studies in the Role of the Public School Teacher*, Columbia, University of Missouri, 1961.

Specifically with respect to the comparisons to be made, Charters delineates a number of problems. Among these are: (1) Conflict as distinct from disagreement. A useful distinction may be made between conflict referring to a contradiction between two expectations, and disagreement referring to a difference between two expectations. (2) Role consensus. Only rarely is there full agreement among a defining group on the expectations applying to a particular role. What, then, is the criterion for agreement? (3) The defining population. A related problem is determining the boundaries of the defining population for a role. As the boundaries are extended, the likelihood of discovering agreement diminishes. Differences in role expectations from one study to another may be due to differences in the boundaries of a defining population. (4) Types of conflict and agreement. There is an almost limitless number of ways in which conflict or agreement in expectations can be sought empirically. It is possible to study the difference or similarity between one role definer and other role definers, between expectations and needs, between an individual's own expectations and his attributions to others, and so on. Charters points out that many of the methodological issues here resemble those of research in interpersonal perception.[62]

We have dealt with three salient problem areas: the problem of sampling when one must necessarily depend on volunteers, the problem of a criterion of organizational effectiveness when the ultimate objectives of the organization itself may be a matter of controversy, and the problem of empirical role analysis when the conceptual and methodological issues are so complex. For each problem area we called attention to certain needs for further inquiry. But perhaps the single need mentioned most frequently by those working with problems of institutional role is for *longitudinal* studies. Cross-sectional and status studies, and even experimental work, cannot by their very nature provide the continuous observations required for tracing the transformation of roles and expectations, and the concomitant changes in role conflict over time. What, for example, is the effect of introducing a new administrator into an organization high in conflict? His immediate impact may be observed in the "single-shot" study.

---

[62] L. J. Cronbach, "Proposals Leading to Analytic Treatment of Social Perception Scores," in R. Tagiuri and L. Petrullo, eds., *Person Perception and Interpersonal Behavior*, Stanford, Calif., Stanford University Press, 1958, p. 355.

But the ultimate effect—and surely the *process* of the effect—must be examined sequentially. How do roles that are initially shaken up become reconstituted? How are new role-sets formed? And out of what do new conflicts emerge? There is something of the process of metabolism in the growth and decline, the disappearance and resurgence of organizational structures and conflicts. A faculty member speaking of a new dean put it this way recently: "Oh, he came in full of beans and was pretty hard to swallow at first. But it took a little time, and I think by now he is pretty well digested by almost everyone." By what process does "digestion" take place in an organization? Indeed, what is the "natural history" of a role or a conflict in roles or, for that matter, of a particular institution in a given social system? Issues of this kind may be dealt with only through historical or longitudinal inquiry.

From a somewhat different point of view, how do shifts in external systems affect the functioning of internal systems with which they are connected? For example, by what process do shifts in educational policy at the state and federal levels affect the organization of roles at the local level? More specifically, what is the effect on existing roles and role conflicts when organizational policy is changed from centralized control in the district office to autonomous control in each school building? It is important not only to observe the manifest products of change but to understand the processes underlying the change and the consequent products. And to this end longitudinal studies are needed, for through such studies changes in roles, alterations in role conflicts, and the institutionalization of new expectations may be traced.

There is another type of issue in the area of role conflict that requires yet another line of inquiry. This is the experimental or quasi-experimental investigation in which the investigator systematically manipulates the variables he wishes to study and observes the consequences of his manipulation under controlled conditions. In a subsequent chapter we shall consider an investigation of this kind in some detail and note the extraordinary power of the method for some purposes. Here we want only to give a brief illustration of a subject to which it is applicable. It has been argued that the frustrating effect of role conflict is a function not only of the existential contradictions in expectations but of the *poor communication* within the social system. Thus if the formal structure of roles in a role-set were left alone but communication in the role-set were encouraged, the debilitating effect of the existential inconsistencies would diminish, and individual satisfaction and group productivity would increase. The research issue then is: Would the effects of structural role conflict in fact diminish and satisfaction and productivity increase if communication within the system were encouraged?

Here it is necessary to manipulate the situation in some schools characterized by role conflict in such way that communication is encouraged and see whether the hypothesized consequences ensue, as compared with schools similarly characterized by role conflict but not subjected to such manipulation. As the question is put, probably neither the status study nor the longitudinal study would serve as well in investigating the issue as does the experimental method. To be sure, an experiment in an operating organization ordinarily lacks the neat control and precision of the laboratory experiment after which it is modeled. But surely this method must take its place next to the other methods in the systematic study of the nature, effect, and amelioration of role conflict in organizations.

Summary

Whenever a role incumbent is required to conform simultaneously to a number of expectations which are mutually exclusive, contradictory, or inconsistent, so that fulfillment of one set of expectations interferes with fulfillment of another, he is said to be in a role-conflict situation. This conflict, symptomatic of disorganization in the normative dimension of social systems, has three sources: (1) contradiction between the expectations of two or more roles which an individual is attempting to fill simultaneously (interrole conflict), (2) disagreement between two or more reference groups each defining expectations for the same role (interreference-group conflict), and (3) disagreement within a reference group regarding the expectations held for a given role (intrareference-group conflict).

With respect to interrole conflict, empirical studies were adduced to illustrate types of conflicts facing school board members, superintendents, principals, and teachers. Such conflicts may result, for example, from holding positions in organizations or groups whose purposes are at variance with the major goals of the given educational system. More specifically, in the case of boards of education, a relationship was shown between role conflict and friction in the operation of board meetings. In the case of teachers, it was shown that some role conflicts are situationally independent, some are situationally variant, and some are situationally specific.

With respect to disagreements among reference groups, the studies revealed that the administrative officer of a school system is in a particularly vulnerable position. The superintendent or principal is often caught between opposing expectations of board members and teachers within the immediate system and opposing expectations among such reference groups as the chamber of commerce, labor council, and parent associations outside the immediate system. Discrepancies in expectations were observed among the various internal and external groups in each of the major functional and leadership aspects of the administrator role.

With respect to disagreements within a reference group, the studies showed a wide range of differences within the teacher group, as an instance, regarding what they wanted from the principal as leader. Moreover, there were differences from school to school. Some schools were relatively homogeneous in their expectations and other schools relatively heterogeneous in their expectations. Furthermore, and perhaps most important, there appeared to be a positive relation between solidarity in expectations and teacher satisfaction with the teaching situation.

A number of limitations of the studies were discussed, and implications for further inquiry were suggested. Among the proposals for further work were the problems of the criteria for organizational effectiveness, the need for longitudinal studies, and the possibility of applying the experimental method to the study of the nature, effect, and amelioration of role conflicts in organizations.

8

Institutional role and individual personality

The relationship between the pattern of expectations attached to a given role and the pattern of need-dispositions characteristic of a particular incumbent of that role is of crucial importance to the administrator. One of his major functions is to integrate role and personality in the fulfillment of organizational goals, and in all organizations some discrepancy between role expectations and personality dispositions is bound to exist. Indeed, the administrator himself is not immune to role-personality conflict, as the following remarks by a school principal make clear:

> If I had it all to do over again, I would become a carpenter—or some kind of worker in the building trades. I enjoy outside work—you don't feel so hemmed in. I also get real satisfaction out of working with my hands. But on this job you catch it from all directions. Even when you do your best, the board of education or someone above will slam you down. Working with the petty problems of parents, teachers, and pupils is also a pain in the neck. I'd go back to my old industrial arts job in a minute, but financially I just can't afford it. I'm longing for the day when I can retire from this job, buy a school bell, let it ring, and ignore it.

This is not an atypical example of the mutual interference between normative expectations and personal dispositions. The individual cannot both meet his obligations as a principal and feel authentic as a person. He must choose between fulfilling institutional requirements and meeting individual needs. If he chooses to fulfill the institutional role requirements (it is not of course always a matter of conscious choice), he is in a sense shortchanging himself and is liable to failure in self-actualization; he is inefficient. If he chooses to fulfill his needs, he is shortchanging his role and is liable to failure in adaptation and unsatisfactory role performance; he is ineffective.

Many students of human behavior in general and of administration in particular have stressed the problem of conflict arising from the incompatibility of roles and personalities in a social system. Linton,[1] for example, pointed out that roles and statuses

---
[1] Ralph Linton, *The Study of Man*, New York, Appleton-Century-Crofts, 1936, p. 253.

exist apart from the individuals who must occupy them, and role performance may require adjustments and adaptations which cause some individuals to experience conflict. More particularly, with respect to executive responsibility, Barnard[2] suggested that the administrator must be aware of this problem, and that the executive cannot with impunity push employees into situations likely to cause them severe personal conflict. Simon[3] too has indicated the existence of a zone of acceptance within which an individual will behave according to the demands of the organization, but when organizational demands fall outside this zone, his personal motives will assert themselves. In protest against the decline of individualism in our society, which he attributes to the hegemony of the organization over the person, Whyte[4] has urged that the individual must learn to resist organizational demands. Argyris[5] similarly has viewed the organization as a threat to individual self-realization.

Whether the man makes the job or the job makes the man is a fruitless if recurring argument. But that the nature of the relationship between the job and the man is crucial in the functioning of an organization, and that the integration between the two is probably the critical task of the executive, is hardly open to question. Surprisingly, however, most studies of leadership and administration have tended to focus exclusively either on the definition of the role or on the assessment of the person without relating the one to the other. The early investigations of leadership and administration were primarily concerned with the "traits" of the good leader or administrator. Subsequently this *traitist* approach gave way to the other extreme—the *situationist* approach—with exclusive emphasis on the study of the good leadership role or administrative structure. Only recently have systematic attempts been made to resolve the traitist-situationist dichotomy by studying the *interaction* between individual characteristics and role requirements.

In terms of the theoretical model we have been using, it is of course clear that to understand organizational behavior, with the concomitant leadership-followership activities, both the insti-

---

[2] Chester I. Barnard, *The Functions of the Executive*, Cambridge, Mass., Harvard University Press, 1964, chap. 17.
[3] Herbert A. Simon, *Administrative Behavior*, New York, Macmillan, 1955.
[4] William H. Whyte, Jr., *The Organization Man*, New York, Simon and Schuster, 1956.
[5] Chris Argyris, *Personality and Organization*, New York, Harper & Row, 1957.

tutional role expectations and the individual need-dispositions must be taken into account interactively. Several investigations based on this model have utilized both role and personality variables to study organizational behavior and the nature of role-personality conflict. For purposes of reporting here these investigations are grouped somewhat arbitrarily according to two dominant research strategies: One strategy, which for reference we may call the "personality-assessment method," utilizes primarily personality variables to describe both the individual and the role, and the relationship between them; the other strategy, which we may call the "role-definition method," utilizes primarily role-expectation variables to describe both the role and the individual, and the relationship between them.

The study of role-personality relations: the personality-assessment method

The personality-assessment approach to the study of role-personality relationships describes the organizational role in terms of psychological variables (needs) usually applied to the description of personality patterns. Then, through appropriate assessment techniques, an evaluation is made of the extent to which a given role incumbent exhibits the pattern of personality characteristics compatible with the role expectations, already defined *in the same terms*. Psychologists and personnel specialists have long utilized this general approach for selection purposes. Only recently, however, have research studies of administrative relationships been undertaken along these lines. Two complementary investigations, a study of business executives and a study of school administrators, both deriving directly from the model, seem to us despite their exploratory nature to have important implications for practice and for further research.

ADMINISTRATIVE ROLE-PERSONALITY RELATIONS AND PROMOTABILITY IN A BUSINESS ORGANIZATION

Many organizations use their nonadministrative personnel as a major source of administrative personnel. Salesmen become managers, professors become deans, bank tellers become vice-presidents, insurance underwriters become executives, and so on.

For any given organization, the following questions may then be raised.

1. What are the expectations for the administrative role as seen by those who seek personnel to fill the role? Or, put another way, what characteristics are regarded as differentiating between individuals considered promotable to this role and individuals considered not promotable to this role, even though both groups are perfectly satisfactory at the non-administrative level?
2. What characteristics, identified through the use of selective measures of personality, distinguish the promotable from the nonpromotable individuals for the administrative role?
3. What is the relation between the characteristics identified in question 1, that is, the role expectations, and the characteristics identified in question 2, that is, the personality dispositions?

A study by Malo[6] sought answers to exactly these questions in a large-scale business organization. The subjects were underwriters in one of the largest casualty and property damage insurance companies and the executives who regularly choose the individuals for promotion to administrative positions from among these underwriters. As a first step in the study, Malo asked the executives to classify 125 underwriters in four branch offices as promotable to an administrative position, using the criteria they habitually applied when making their selections.

To be included in the study, the underwriters had to have a minimum of two years' experience in the company, there had to be agreement as to their promotability or nonpromotability, and the promotable and nonpromotable groups had to be equated in chronological age, mental ability, and formal education. From the total of 125 underwriters serving as a pool for the selections, the procedure produced a group of 22 promotable and 17 nonpromotable subjects for individual study.

The investigator then asked each executive who had done the rankings to describe the behavioral characteristics of each individual he had chosen as promotable to an administrative position. These unstructured "off-the-cuff" comments were recorded verbatim and subsequently content-analyzed according to Murray's needs taxonomy.[7]

---
[6] Albert H. Malo, "Personality Variables Related to Administrative Potential," Doctoral dissertation, University of Chicago, 1959.
[7] Henry A. Murray *et al.*, *Explorations in Personality*, New York, Oxford University Press, 1938.

The Expectations for the Administrative Role as Seen by Executives. The answer to the first research question (on the nature of the expectations attaching to the administrative role) was obtained from the executives' descriptions of the promotables. In discussing the reasons for their choices, the executives were of course describing the expectations for behavior in the administrative role, at least as they saw them. The content analysis of these descriptions provides a clear portrait of the role of administrator expressed in personalistic need terms.

The expectation most frequently mentioned by the executives was the ability to coordinate thinking and acting, to analyze and to take action, and to operate in a purposive and coherent manner. This characteristic was regarded as an asset in 18 of the 22 promotable subjects; its absence was regarded as a limitation in 16 of the 17 nonpromotable subjects. In effect, the executives were saying that from their point of view a most important requirement of the administrative role is, in Murray's need terminology, "conjunctive" behavior.[8] The complete data are presented in Table 8–1.

Typical of the statements describing this variable with respect to the promotables and nonpromotables were these.

TABLE 8–1

Frequency Distribution of Promotable and Nonpromotable Subjects According to Strength or Deficiency in Characteristics Attributed to Them by Their Superiors

Characteristic	Promotable (N = 22) High	Promotable (N = 22) Low	Nonpromotable (N = 17) High	Nonpromotable (N = 17) Low
Conjunctivity	18	0	0	16
Intensity	12	0	0	9
Social ability	18	3	4	11
Orientation to reality	13	2	1	9
Achievement drive	13	1	0	10
Endurance	13	0	4	1
Understanding	11	3	1	4
Superego integration	10	4	3	6

SOURCE: Adapted from Albert H. Malo, "Personality Variables Related to Administrative Potential," Doctoral dissertation, University of Chicago, 1959, pp. 71–74.

[8] *Ibid.*

Conjunctivity, Promotable Subjects:
>He organizes his work well.
>
>He shows an increasing capacity for being able to analyze and take action.
>
>He's good at looking at the broad picture and seeing things that have to be done.
>
>He looks at today's work as a step to tomorrow's.

Conjunctivity, Non-promotable Subjects:
>He's inclined to follow a set pattern and not look for better ways of doing things.
>
>He lacks analytical ability.
>
>He lacks initiative.
>
>I was inquiring about his planning for the week and he said his supervisor hadn't suggested anything, so he hadn't planned anything.[9]

A second expectation is intensity. According to Murray, "various aspects of this factor may be represented by the following common words: power, strength, force, gusto, zest, eagerness, enthusiasm, emphasis, vividness, loudness, demonstrativeness."[10] The executives in this study tended to stress enthusiasm, power, and zest rather than loudness or demonstrativeness. These characteristics were mentioned with respect to 12 of the promotable subjects and none of the nonpromotable subjects. Typical of the statements regarding this quality were:

Intensity, Promotable Subjects:
>He bubbles over with enthusiasm and interest in his job and in the things going on around him.
>
>He does the work of two people.
>
>He's very much interested in his work.

Intensity, Non-promotable Subjects:
>He's a slow worker.
>
>He doesn't have enough drive.
>
>Lethargy bordering on laziness.[11]

In addition to conjunctivity and intensity, a number of qualities were descriptive predominantly of the promotables and from the comments of the executives may be taken as expecta-

---

[9] Malo, *op. cit.*, pp. 48–50.
[10] Murray, *op. cit.*, p. 208.
[11] Malo, *op. cit.*, pp. 50–51.

tions for the administrative role. These qualities were social ability, orientation to reality, achievement drive, endurance, understanding, and superego integration. We present brief descriptions of each of these, in Murray's terms, and some illustrative statements from the interview protocols:

1. *Social Ability:* the ability to affiliate and associate successfully with others.

    He knows a lot of people and gets along well with everybody.

    He pays attention to relationships with people.

    He's a likeable guy.

2. *Orientation to Reality:* the ability to be interested in practical results, to adapt to the world as it stands, and to be without illusions.

    He has good judgment. Doesn't overstress technicalities.

    He's smart, observant, and a thinker—not hidebound in his attitudes.

    He's not arbitrary. Doesn't try to bull his way through. He weighs facts before making decisions.

3. *Achievement Drive:* the tendency to be ambitious, to seek responsibilities, and to take on new assignments.

    He realizes that study of procedures is important so he asked to be considered for transfer as much as two years ago.

    He would like to have more responsibility.

    There is evidence of wanting to grow.

4. *Endurance*: persistence and sustained effort. Whereas intensity expresses "how hard a person works," endurance expresses "how long one works."

    He has shown a willingness to take outside studies, to put in extra time, to stay down nights cleaning up work, to share the extra burden during peak periods.

    He comes early and leaves late.

    The work is tedious, but he takes it in stride as a job that has to be done.

5. *Understanding:* interest in theory, the tendency to ask or answer general questions, and the inclination to analyze events or generalize.

    He's done a damn good job on work that was new to him.

    He shows a willingness to learn.

    He's still going to school nights.

He's inquisitive. Wants to know why he's doing something. He likes to learn new things.

6. *Superego Integration:* a sense of responsibility, security, loyalty, faithfulness, and confidence.

His attitude toward the company is good. I feel he's not using us as a stepping stone.

He's very conscientious. He tries to do the right thing at all times. He's very happy with what he's doing.

He's a steady, good, loyal person.[12]

An ancillary, albeit not insignificant, observation was that the executives made an average of less than one nonpromotable statement per promotable subject, and exactly one promotable statement per nonpromotable subject. Obviously, there is a halo in these kinds of judgments which may introduce error into the particular descriptions. Taken individually, therefore, no single judgment is an adequate description either of promotability or of the administrative role. Taken collectively, however, the descriptions, and the relative frequency of mention, provide a promising characterization of the executive role in personalistic terms, at least for further exploration.

Personality Characteristics of Those Considered Promotable and Nonpromotable to the Administrative Role. To provide an answer to the second research question—What personality characteristics distinguish the promotable from the nonpromotable individuals?—a number of personality instruments were given to the two groups of subjects: an adjective checklist, two forms of the Sentence Completion Test, and the Thematic Apperception Test. The results revealed numerous differences in personality structure between the promotables and the nonpromotables. Moreover, similar patterns emerged regardless of the particular terminology in which the instruments were scored. The findings for two of the instruments serve as examples of the personality differences between the two groups.

1. *Sentence Completion Test.* Two forms of the Sentence Completion Test—a direct and an indirect form—were used.[13]

---

[12] *Ibid.*, pp. 53–69.
[13] The use of this procedure to discover the extent of inflation of scores due to the halo with which an individual surrounds himself is treated in J. W. Getzels and J. J. Walsh, "The Method of Paired Direct and Projective Questionnaires in the Study of Attitude Structure and Socialization," *Psychological Monographs: General and Applied*, 72 (1958), 2–4.

The direct form consisted of items stated in the first person, and the indirect or projective form consisted of the same items stated in the third person. The items were written to prompt responses in a number of significant areas of psychological functioning relevant to the administrative role, including the following:

a. *Activity drive:* to move forward purposefully; to direct strong mental or physical effort toward the solution of problems.
b. *Achievement drive:* to do one's best; to improve one's competencies through general and specialized study; to become a leader of groups.
c. *Social ability:* to associate successfully with others in the solution of problems; to participate in friendly groups.
d. *Feelings of security:* to view family relationships with pride and satisfaction; to view authority figures as serving constructive purposes.
e. *Emotional control:* to assess environmental conditions objectively and realistically; to adjust well to irritations, confusion, and criticism.

Typical items in each of these areas were as follows:

1. *Activity Drive:*
   Having solved the problem, he (I) . . .
   While they were urging Frank (me) to make up his (my) mind, he (I) . . .
2. *Achievement Drive:*
   Ten years from now, he (I) . . .
   When they asked him (me) to be in charge, he (I) . . .
3. *Social Ability:*
   Working with others all of the time made him (me) . . .
   When he (I) spoke to strangers . . .
4. *Feelings of Security:*
   Having told a humorous story, he (I) . . .
   Given complete independence, he (I) . . .
5. *Emotional Control:*
   When he (I) was put under pressure, he (I) . . .
   As the opposition increased, he (I) . . .

Responses to the stems did not always fit into the category anticipated for the particular stem. The response was then scored for the category in which it did fit. Thus, if the response to "Ten years from now, I . . ." was "will be able to retire successfully," it was scored in the category Feelings of Security. For the purpose of quantitative analysis, responses were assigned a value ranging from 2 to − 2, depending on the direction and strength of the response. Thus, to the item "When they asked him to be in charge, he . . ." the response "shuddered and refused" was given a − 2, and the response "was happy and took over" was given a 2. The scoring was found to be highly reliable.

Both the direct form and the projective form tended to differentiate the promotables from the nonpromotables at encouraging levels of significance, the projective form being somewhat more discriminating. Moreover, regardless of the form used, the results were quite systematic, and the promotables tended to score higher than the nonpromotables in activity drive, achievement drive, social ability, feelings of security, and emotional control. The area that did not show any significant difference on either form of the instrument was mobility drive, and although emotional control differentiated significantly on the third-person form it did not on the first-person form. The data for the projective form are given in Table 8–2.

TABLE 8-2

Scores of Promotable and Nonpromotable Groups for Variables Measured by the Sentence Completion Test

	MEAN SCORES			
Variable	Promotable group (N = 22)	Non-promotable group (N = 17)	t	P
Activity drive	15.14	10.35	1.98	.10
Achievement drive	3.68	1.88	1.96	.10
Social ability	4.41	1.35	2.94	.01
Feelings of security	3.27	− 0.65	5.94	.01
Emotional control	− 1.23	− 5.94	2.71	.02

SOURCE: Adapted from Albert H. Malo, "Personality Variables Related to Administrative Potential," Doctoral dissertation, University of Chicago, 1959 p. 101.

2. *Thematic Apperception Test* (TAT). The subjects responded to selected cards from the Thematic Apperception Test. Although the stories were used primarily for qualitative analyses, it was possible to score them quantitatively as well for each of the variables listed for the Sentence Completion Test. The results

corresponded closely with the findings from the sentence completion instruments—indeed, the TAT proved to be a somewhat more powerful instrument than the others.[14]

Comparison of the Executive Descriptions and the Personality Assessments of Promotables and Nonpromotables. To evaluate the extent of agreement or disagreement between the characteristics executives considered essential for the administrative role and the personality variables identified through personality-assessment procedures, summations were made of the instances in which descriptions made by the executives either agreed or disagreed with the scores made by the subjects on the corresponding variables as measured by the relevant tests. The agreement between executive descriptions and sentence completion data for the promotables was 70.8 percent with the direct form and 68.3 percent with the indirect form; for the nonpromotables it was 69.8 percent with the direct form and 64.4 percent with the indirect form. For the TAT, the agreement was 65.4 percent for the promotables and 79.3 percent for the nonpromotables.

As the investigator points out, it would seem that the personality patterns of the promotable individuals, as evaluated by personality-assessment procedures, are similar to the personality patterns held essential to effective compliance with the expectations for the administrator role, as judged by executives responsible for promotions to administrative positions in an actual business organization.[15] But there is in addition a more general theoretical point made by this study: Organizations tend to minimize the dangers of what we have called role-personality conflict by this matching of individual characteristics and institutional expectations—whether the matching is done by preinduction screening through personality-assessment procedures or by postinduction screening through internal personnel redistribution or promotional procedures.

ADMINISTRATIVE ROLE-PERSONALITY RELATIONS AND EFFECTIVENESS IN A SCHOOL SYSTEM

The expectations held for the educational administrator's role are usually expressed in terms of an inventory of tasks, responsibilities, duties, and rights, such as enforcing the rules and regulations promulgated by the board of education, preparing the

---
[14] Malo, *op. cit.*, p. 106.
[15] *Ibid.*, p. 171.

school budget, supervising the teaching personnel, speaking to community groups, and so on. Sometimes the expectations are expressed in terms of the administrative process: planning, decision-making, organizing, communicating, and evaluating. On the basis of the theoretical model and the preceding work by Malo, Lipham[16] argued that the role of the educational administrator also could be described in terms of a number of crucial expectations of a more personalistic kind. Thus the administrator might be expected, for example, to exert himself energetically; strive for achievement and higher status; relate successfully to other people; view the future with confidence, the present with understanding, the past with satisfaction; and adjust well to frustrations, irritations, and criticisms in pressure situations. Individuals having a basic personality structure characterized by such needs and dispositions will suffer less strain in fulfilling the administrative role and will therefore be more efficient and effective than those whose needs and dispositions are in conflict with the role expectations. Specifically, it was hypothesized that effective administrators would tend to rank higher than ineffective administrators on the following personal variables: activity drive, achievement drive, social ability, feelings of security, and emotional stability. Malo used the same variables in his study in a business organization, it will be recalled, and the present study is therefore not only an extension into the educational setting but also an attempt in a sense at partial replication.

A wide range of personality-assessment instruments were utilized: self-report measures including an adjective checklist and the Edwards Personal Preference Schedule; quasiprojective techniques including the Sentence Completion Test used by Malo; and a focused individual interview and observation of approximately two hours in duration designed to provide both verbal and nonverbal data on drives, motives, attitudes, and manifest behavior.

The subjects for study were 84 school principals in a large Midwestern city. To secure a measure of effectiveness—that is, of the extent to which the principals met expectations for the administrative role—they were ranked on this criterion independently by the superintendent of schools and four assistant superintendents, all of whom had direct contact with the subjects. Correlations among the independent ratings ranged from

---

[16] James M. Lipham, "Personal Variables Related to Administrative Effectiveness," Doctoral dissertation, University of Chicago, 1960.

.55 to .73, with a mean correlation of .67. Total ranks for each subject were used to select the top and bottom quarters, providing two samples of 21 principals each—one termed "effectives" and the other "ineffectives."

The central research issue was, of course, Would the two groups differ in the indicated personality variables? The results may be presented in two categories, one based on the verbal test and interview data, the other on the nonverbal observations.

Personality Differences of Effective and Ineffective Principals. The personality tests revealed significant differences between the effective and the ineffective principals. In each of the five relevant variables on the first-person form of the Sentence Completion Test, scored by the procedures used by Malo, the effective group differed from the ineffective group. Three of the differences were significant at the .05 level and one was significant at the .10 level; the other showed a strong tendency in the hypothesized direction. What is perhaps most noteworthy about these results is that they replicate the findings of Malo on the individuals who were promotable and nonpromotable to the administrative role in the business organization. The complete data are given in Table 8–3.

Similarly, the interview protocols, content-analyzed independently for the same categories, revealed differences between the two groups in each of the experimental variables. The data are presented in Table 8–4. In addition to the quantitative results,

TABLE 8–3

Scores of Effective and Ineffective School Principals for Variables Measured by the Sentence Completion Test

Variable	EFFECTIVE GROUP (N = 21) M	SD	INEFFECTIVE GROUP (N = 21) M	SD	t	P
Social ability	4.29	3.83	0.52	4.08	3.09	.01
Emotional control	−2.05	3.57	−4.86	3.62	2.53	.02
Feelings of security	1.90	3.31	−0.29	2.91	2.28	.05
Activity drive	10.81	5.79	7.33	5.96	1.92	.10
Achievement drive	1.62	2.97	0.81	1.95	1.05	—

SOURCE: Adapted from James M. Lipham, "Personal Variables Related to Administrative Effectiveness," Doctoral dissertation, University of Chicago, 1960, p. 65.

Institutional role and individual personality

TABLE 8-4

Scores of Effective and Ineffective School Principals for Variables Assessed During Individual Interviews

Variable	EFFECTIVE GROUP (N = 21) M	SD	INEFFECTIVE GROUP (N = 21) M	SD	t	P
Feelings of security	1.19	1.00	−.96	1.07	6.71	.01
Achievement drive	1.10	1.30	−.39	1.02	4.13	.01
Activity drive	1.05	0.80	.24	0.89	3.09	.01
Emotional control	1.19	1.10	.14	1.28	2.84	.01
Social ability	1.19	1.20	.33	1.16	2.36	.05

SOURCE: Adapted from James M. Lipham, "Personal Variables Related to Administrative Effectiveness," Doctoral dissertation, University of Chicago, 1960, p. 106.

the investigator summarized the qualitative analysis of the interview material for each of the following variables.

1. *Activity drive.* The effective principal is inclined to engage in strong and purposeful activity. While on the job he seems particularly sensitive to the pressing responsibilities of the principalship. He evidences a high degree of concern for the appropriate use of time and finds curbs to activity such as physical illness most unpleasant. He looks forward to continuing his present high level of activity at retirement. During leisure hours he participates in the activities of a large number of organizations and holds many leadership positions in these groups.

The ineffective principal, on the other hand, is inclined to be deliberate and slow to act. At work he engages in numerous random behaviors, serving as errand boy, report maker, substitute teacher, and "baby-sitter" with disciplinary cases. He looks forward to a reduction in activity at retirement. During leisure hours he participates in a limited number and range of activities; he prefers viewing television to more active forms of recreation.

2. *Achievement drive.* Keen achievement and mobility drives are characteristic of the effective principal. He has set specific goals for further study, stresses better job performance as a goal in life, and views the school superintendency as a desirable ultimate vocational objective. Responses of effective principals to the question "Toward what objective do you plan to

do additional study, if any?" were "Study school finance," "Complete a Six-Year Diploma" and "Work toward my Ph.D. at ———— University so I can become a school superintendent."

In contrast, the ineffective principal evidences little concern for undertaking a planned program of further study, holding positions of leadership, or attaining any position higher than his present job assignment. His aim in life is "To set a good example for youth," "To hold a steady job," "To accumulate enough money to return to the classroom," or similar reflections of status maintenance.

3. *Social ability.* The effective principal is high in social ability. He associates successfully with others in the solution of problems. He feels that he obtained his initial principalship because of his ability to relate well to others and that his present relationships with teachers, central office personnel, and parent groups are satisfactory. Helping teachers with problems of instruction is his greatest job satisfaction. Typical comments were as follows:

> If you help a teacher who is struggling with an instructional problem and you see him accept a suggestion and become more effective, then it gives you a real warm feeling.

> The thing I enjoy most is a "jam-up" in-service activity that stirs the teachers' enthusiasm.

> Helping teachers improve so that I do not have to unload them on someone else at the end of the year gives me a real feeling of accomplishment.

By contrast, the ineffective principal experiences frequent conflict with teachers, parents, and central office personnel. If he were now twenty years of age, he would probably enter some field requiring less contact with people. Apparently he is more secure in the presence of children than teachers, since he derives his greatest job satisfaction from helping children—as evidenced by reactions such as the following:

> I like for children to speak to me when I see them on the streets or downtown.

> I'm something of a "mother-hen," I suppose. I especially enjoy playing baseball with the kids. They tell you their troubles and you can help them.

> I like to bring a handicapped child to the office, work closely with him, and watch him "blossom out."

4. *Feelings of security.* The effective principal is secure in his home and work environments. He views family relationships with pride and satisfaction and regards authority figures as friendly and serving constructive purposes.

Typical of the ineffective individual, however, are severe home difficulties ("My mother dominates every detail of my life" or "My wife is seriously ill with a blood disease") and such job-related problems as feeling the groups of teachers or members of the central administration are "down" on him. He feels further that his own mental, emotional, or physical weaknesses may prevent the attainment of his life goals.

5. *Emotional control.* In reacting to frustrating, confusing, and irritating situations, the effective principal exercises greater emotional control than does the ineffective principal.

> I enjoy making decisions—the knottier the problems, the better.

> I like working with the rough and tumble situations—also the feeling of responsibility that comes from knowing that so much of this school's program depends on me.

The ineffective individual tends to clash frequently with others, feels that actions by other people are likely to drive him to distraction, and engages in self-pity and similar strong emotional reactions in conflict situations. The following examples of job dissatisfaction were indicative of negative emotional control:

> I have a fourth-grade teacher who was shipped off onto me. She's real bossy—particularly to other teachers. "Please" and "May I" are simply not in her vocabulary. She literally hates my guts, and we're driving each other nuts.

> There are two cliques in this school—each with its own ringleader. One is the "old guard," the other is "either lazy or modern." One prefers rigid discipline, the other pandemonium. I'm not strict enough to suit the old and I'm too strict to suit the new. I lose my temper with both.

Behavioral Patterns of Effective and Ineffective Principals. Noting after Halpin that "the muted language of non-verbal communication is a rich source of cues in determining the course of interpersonal relations,"[17] the investigator took the opportunity provided by the interview situation to observe certain behavioral

---

[17] Andrew W. Halpin, "Muted Language," *The School Review,* 68 (Spring, 1960), 97.

patterns, which he was able subsequently to categorize for quantitative analysis. At the time the observations were made, he had no knowledge either of the effectiveness rankings or of the scores on the personality measures of the individuals being observed. To be sure, the observations may have been influenced by the verbal interchange during the interview, and to this extent the data are probably not free from some halo effect. Nevertheless, they are worth reporting, at least as an indication of the rich possibilities for further research in nonverbal behavior, a domain that is now largely neglected. In the present study significant differences were observed between the effective and the ineffective principals in each of the following behavior patterns, the former tending to manifest the indicated behavior, the latter not.

1. Meeting the interviewer at the door of the office.
2. Offering to take the interviewer on a tour of the building or to observe classroom teachers.
3. Hanging up the coat and hat of the interviewer or arranging for a secretary to do so.
4. Having in the office some item of interest, such as a paperweight of unusual design, a drawing, a citation, or some other objects not obtainable in an office supply store.
5. Arranging a private place for the conference—instead of talking in the presence of secretaries, teachers, or pupils.
6. Seating the interviewer at the side of the desk instead of directly across the desk.
7. Having few interruptions, either directly or by telephone.
8. After the conference, walking with the interviewer to either the door of the office or the outside door of the school—instead of remaining behind his desk.

By itself, each item seems innocent enough and hardly noticeable until pointed out. But consider the cumulative image projected by a person who meets a visitor at the door, as against one who lets him walk across the room to greet him; arranges a private room or office for the conference, as against one who does not take the trouble to make any such arrangement and is forced to use whatever space happens to be available; courteously escorts the visitor to the door, as against one who remains behind his desk and lets the visitor make his way out alone. That most of these differences relate primarily to the social-ability variable does not detract from their significance for the administrative situation. It is surely not our intent to suggest that any administrator who imitates this image will automatically become more effective. However, we would argue that the extent of the conflict between an individual and his role as indicated, at least in this case, by assessment techniques may become apparent also through his habitual interpersonal acts, to which he pays no attention. Indeed, the "muted language" of unpremeditated behavior may be louder than carefully measured speech, not only in reflecting the congruence or conflict between any institutional role and the role incumbent's personality, but in determining the effectiveness or lack of effectiveness of the administrator in fulfilling the institutional and individual goals for which he is responsible in the social system.[18]

In sum, the major relevant findings of this study may be stated as follows:

1. There is greater congruence between role expectations and personality dispositions of principals who are rated effective by their superiors and greater conflict between role expectations and personality dispositions of principals who are rated ineffective by their superiors.

2. This finding replicates the findings with respect to individuals promotable and nonpromotable to an administrative role in a business setting. In the latter case there was greater congruence between role expectations and personality dispositions for the promotables, greater conflict for the nonpromotables.

3. In both cases, significant differences between the comparison groups were found in the following variables: activity drive, achievement drive, social ability, feelings of security, and emotional control. The effective principal was inclined toward strong and purposeful activity, concerned with achieving success and positions of higher status, able to relate well to others, secure in interpersonal relationships, and stable in the face of frustration. The ineffective principal was deliberate and occupied with speculative reasoning, accepting of his present level of achievement and not concerned with reaching a higher status, lacking in skills essential for working with adults but anxious to give assistance and consolation to children, highly dependent on others for support, and likely to exhibit strong emotional reactions in the face of frustration.

---

[18] James M. Lipham and Donald C. Francke, "Non-Verbal Behavior of Administrators," *Educational Administration Quarterly*, 2 (Spring, 1966), 100–109.

4. In addition to these findings from personality assessment techniques such as tests and interviews, significant differences in the manifest behavior of effective and ineffective principals were observed.

5. Perhaps most important, systematic relationships in the hypothesized direction were demonstrated among the three experimental variables under inquiry: the ratings in administrative effectiveness or ineffectiveness, the congruence or conflict between administrative role expectations and personality dispositions as evaluated by assessment techniques, and certain aspects of observed manifest behavior.

Taken together, the two studies, as well as other work deriving from the same concepts,[19] provide valuable empirical data regarding the administrative role expectations expressed in personalistic terms, the relation between the expectations and the personal dispositions of role incumbents, and the consequences of conflict or congruence between the expectations and dispositions and the ratings by superiors of promotability to the administrative role and effectiveness in the performance of the role.

The study of role-personality relations: the role-definition method

A serious difficulty in studying personality and role relationships in the administrative setting is that there are no commonly accepted concepts for expressing and relating the sociological or role variables and the psychological or personality variables in the same terms. As Guba, among others, has noted, "This state of affairs points very directly to what seems . . . to be the next step in the development of administrative science."[20]

A number of studies of role-personality conflict deriving from the present framework have moved toward the resolution

---

[19] See Bryce M. Fogarty, "Characteristics of Superintendents of Schools and Centralization-Decentralization of Decision-Making," Doctoral dissertation, University of Wisconsin, 1964; and Joseph J. Semrow, "Role Conflict in the Superintendency and Its Relationship to Personal Variables and Effectiveness," Doctoral dissertation, University of Wisconsin, 1965.
[20] E. G. Guba, "Research in Internal Administration—What Do We Know?" in Roald F. Campbell and James M. Lipham, eds., *Administrative Theory as a Guide to Action*, Chicago, Midwest Administration Center, University of Chicago, 1960, p. 129.

of this problem. In these studies the roles are defined in substantive terms, and the terminology is used to construct measures of the dispositions of the role incumbents toward the specific expectations in which the role was defined. We have designated this research strategy as the "role-definition" method in the study of role-personality relations and conflict.

TEACHER ROLE-PERSONALITY RELATIONS

Applying the theoretical model to the problem of teacher conflict, Merton Campbell[21] argued that certain expectations are attached to the role of teacher and that in a given school the principal is the logical person to define at least one set of legitimate expectations for the role. To the extent that teacher dispositions for behavior in the role are not congruent with the expectations prescribed by the principal, the resulting role-personality conflict should have certain consequences for both teacher and principal, and for the evaluation of the one by the other.

Specifically, the following relationships were postulated between the degree of this type of role-personality conflict and the satisfaction of the teacher in the school, his feeling of competence as a teacher, his confidence in the leadership of the principal, and the principal's rating of the teacher's effectiveness:

1. Teachers with a low degree of role-personality conflict will rate themselves higher in *teaching satisfaction* than will teachers with a high degree of role-personality conflict.
2. Teachers with a low degree of role-personality conflict will rate themselves higher in *teaching competence* than will teachers with a high degree of conflict.
3. Teachers with a low degree of role-personality conflict *will express greater confidence in the leadership of the principal* than will teachers with a high degree of conflict.
4. Teachers with a low degree of role-personality conflict *will be rated by the principals as more effective* than teachers with a high degree of conflict.[22]

The investigation was conducted in eight elementary and seven secondary schools located in southern Wisconsin and

---
[21] Merton V. Campbell, "Self-Role Conflict Among Teachers and Its Relationship to Satisfaction, Effectiveness, and Confidence in Leadership," Doctoral dissertation, University of Chicago, 1958.
[22] *Ibid.*, pp. 12–13.

northern Illinois. Fifteen principals and 284 teachers participated in the study. School size ranged from 182 to 735 pupils. Care was taken by the investigator to insure that so far as possible the sample of teachers was representative of the national population of teachers on such variables as academic preparation and marital status, although of course no claim for total representativeness can be made.

To obtain data regarding the expectations of principals for the teacher's role, an instrument containing sixty statements involving various types of teacher behavior was administered to each principal, who was asked to indicate by ranking the items what he expected (that is, wanted) his teachers to do. Sample items from the instrument are:

I expect teachers to . . .
Take community opinion into account in matters of personal behavior, even if it means being more circumspect than most.
Maintain impartiality in the face of parental pressures for special favors and privileges, realizing that the teacher has an equal obligation to the parents of all students.
Talk freely to other teachers about their problems, since what is important to them is important to the school.
Adapt curricular guides to the needs and interests of pupils.[23]

Within the limits of the items, a principal's responses to the instrument provide a measure of his expectations for teachers in his school.

The same instrument was given to each teacher, but with a change in directions. The teacher was asked to respond to the items in terms of *his own* needs, wants, and inclinations in the teaching situation. Thus, the same list of items which provided a measure of the principal's expectations for the teacher's role was also used to provide a measure of the teacher's dispositions in the role. Conflict was defined as the item-by-item difference (squared) between the principal's score on an item and the teacher's score on the same item.

Using a standard-type rating scale consisting of both specific and global items, each principal rated the effectiveness of each of his teachers. In addition, each teacher rated his own satisfaction, effectiveness, and confidence in the leadership of his prin-

---

[23] *Ibid.*, pp. 154–159.

cipal. From these data it was possible to (1) determine the extent of agreement or disagreement between the principal's expectations and the teacher's dispositions; (2) rank the teachers on the degree of agreement or disagreement between the expectations and dispositions; and (3) assess the relationship between the degree of such agreement or disagreement and the teacher's feeling of satisfaction and effectiveness in the teaching situation, his expression of confidence in the leadership of his principal, and the principal's rating of the teacher's effectiveness.

The results are discussed with respect to each of the hypotheses in turn:

Role-Personality Relations and Teacher Satisfaction. The first hypothesis was that teachers low in role-personality conflict would express greater satisfaction in the teaching situation than would teachers high in role-personality conflict. The results were quite clear-cut. When the teachers showing the greatest agreement between their dispositions and the principal's expectations (*low* in role-personality conflict) were compared with the teachers showing least agreement between their dispositions and the principal's expectations (*high* in role-personality conflict), the former expressed significantly greater satisfaction with teaching.[24]

The observed relation does not of course give the direction of causality. However, the result is in keeping with other studies of employee satisfaction.[25] An extensive study by Chase,[26] for example, provides a number of conclusions related to role-personality conflict and teacher satisfaction. First, teachers want to participate in policy-making with respect to salary schedules, working conditions, and the educational program. Participation in policy-making gives the individual a sense of creating the role to which he must conform in the organization, and thus instills it with his own dispositions. In present terms, the consequence of such participation is greater agreement between institutional requirements and individual needs. Along similar lines, the factor that was rated as a source of satisfaction by all teacher

---

[24] *Ibid.*, p. 83.
[25] See Nels H. Havens, "The Relationships of Organizational Characteristics and Personal Characteristics to Job Satisfaction," Doctoral dissertation, Stanford University, 1963; and Sister Mary Georgita Griffin, "Job Satisfaction of Lay and Religious Teachers in Catholic Elementary Schools," Doctoral dissertation, University of Chicago, 1963.
[26] Francis S. Chase, "Factors Productive of Satisfaction in Teaching," Doctoral dissertation, University of Chicago, 1951.

groups was freedom to plan one's own work—that is, in present terms again, to be able to express one's own dispositions in the context of one's role in the organization. Another relevant finding was that teacher satisfaction is related to the clarity with which the aims and objectives of the school are defined and whether they are considered attainable by the teachers. In present terms, these are factors tending to decrease possible sources of strain between principal expectations and teacher dispositions, i.e., role-personality conflict.

In addition to using checklist questionnaire items, Campbell asked the teachers to write statements giving the reasons for their satisfaction ratings. A content analysis of these statements showed that teachers low in role-personality conflict and high in satisfaction almost unanimously referred to the fine qualities of the principal and hardly mentioned other factors. In contrast, teachers high in role-personality conflict and low in satisfaction generally failed to mention the principal but tended instead to focus on disagreeable conditions such as shortage of equipment and materials, onerous extracurricular duties, friction among teachers, unwanted teaching assignments, lack of pupil interest, the nature of the community, and even the character of the principal's wife.

Typical of these statements were:

Teachers high in satisfaction

My satisfaction in the situation is related to (1) the challenge of building a school policy, curriculum, etc., and (2) the general competency, scholarly attitude, and personal qualifications of the administrator. The principal goes to a great deal of trouble to make each teacher feel worthy. Most of our teachers are new. I'm not, so I know how other principals are.

I consider it good because of the guidance, without interference, given by our principal.

The school is ideal in size—the community is a very pleasant one to live in—and I personally like the way Mr. _____ operates the school. He makes it easy, or rather not so difficult, to teach as he maintains order.

The personality of the principal overshadows any pet peeves or minor dissatisfactions.

Great patience and understanding have been shown me as a beginning teacher in my field. I doubt if such genuine courtesy would have been extended elsewhere by an established administration.

Teachers low in satisfaction
> I feel at present that three classes of kindergarten are too much for one teacher; it is too tiring. It is difficult to remain patient when so many come (one group after another) with little time away from them. I cannot teach kindergarten the way I would under normal conditions.
>
> I rather like the teaching of English but am most unhappy with general science.
>
> I feel that there is too much inter-staff competitiveness and not enough cooperation between staff members.
>
> I base my answer on personal reasons such as having to live within the district and turning in contracts before stipulated state law.
>
> I like the school and the administrator fine. However, the other teacher in my department has been here for eleven years and she and I don't get along. This makes the teaching situation somewhat undesirable.
>
> I do not fit into a small town, but my return to teaching at a late age barred me from anything better.
>
> Position and community fine, but principal's wife teaching in the system somewhat complicates things in my particular instance.[27]

These findings are similar to those of Worthy,[28] who concluded from a study in an altogether different context that if employees are discontented they seize upon and magnify any inconveniences arising from their working conditions. The concrete complaints of the dissatisfied group may very well be symptomatic of deeper underlying disaffections, salient among which may be the conflicts between the role expectations and need-dispositions to which we are pointing.

Role-Personality Relations and Teacher Feelings of Effectiveness. Campbell utilized two measures of teacher effectiveness: self-ratings by the teachers and ratings by the principals. The hypothesis with respect to effectiveness was that the teachers low in role-personality conflict would rate themselves higher in teaching effectiveness than would those high in such conflict. Although there was a tendency in the hypothesized direction,

---

[27] Campbell, *op. cit.*, pp. 109–111.
[28] James C. Worthy, "Factors Influencing Employee Morale," *Harvard Business Review*, 28 (January, 1950), 61–73; and James C. Worthy, "Organizational Structure and Employee Morale," *American Sociological Review*, 15 (April, 1950), 169–179.

both the lows and the highs for the most part rated themselves about the same—at the average—and the hypothesis was not substantiated.[29]

The statements by the teachers regarding their self-ratings provide some insight into the reasons why these ratings were not discriminating.

Typical of the statements were:

> I have never had any means of evaluating my effectiveness as a teacher from the standpoint of a critical evaluation by a qualified supervisor. I can only assume that so long as I have never received any adverse criticism, my effectiveness must be at least satisfactory.
>
> I feel I could be more effective if I were left more time and energy to *teach* rather than do clerical work, outside sport activity supervision, curriculum work, attending time-consuming teachers' meetings, etc. Do not misunderstand, I do believe those things are necessary, but *too* much time is being consumed on them.
>
> My behavior is determined by my own values rather than by others. I think teachers should reflect professional standards in their behavior.
>
> I do the best job I am capable of. I am going to night school most of the time to improve myself. It is my aim, as I further educate myself and gain experience to be among the *most* effective.[30]

As might be anticipated, these statements suggest that the observed difficulties in self-ratings were due to diffidence in making extreme judgments about oneself for good or for ill, ignorance of a criterion against which to judge one's own performance, modest assessment against some generalized high standard, and seeking the safety of a rating in the middle. In any case, the result was a compromise self-evaluation of "average," prohibiting reliable differentiation.

Role-Personality Relations and Confidence in the Administrator's Leadership. The teachers were asked to rate their degree of confidence in their principal's leadership. In a sense, such rating is an evaluation of the principal in terms of the teacher's conceptualization of the ideal principal. The hypothesis was that the level of confidence would be related to the congruence of the principal's expectations for the teacher's role and the teacher's dispositions in the role. Teachers low in role-personality conflict

---
[29] Campbell, *op. cit.*, p. 83.
[30] Campbell, *op. cit.*, pp. 111–113.

did in fact express more confidence in the leadership of the principal than did teachers high in role-personality conflict.[31]

It need hardly be stressed that the principal is the key administrator in the school, and it is essential that teachers have confidence in his leadership. Otherwise he is in a poor position to initiate structures to achieve either institutional or individual goals, for although he may lead, his teachers may not follow. If lack of confidence in an administrator is related to role-personality conflict, as the data seem to show, one constructive way to alter the situation is to minimize the conflict.

Role-Personality Relations and Principal Ratings of Teacher Effectiveness. So far we have dealt with the relationship between role-personality conflict (as measured by teachers' expressions of their dispositions and principals' expressions of their expectations for the teacher) and the teacher's rating of his own satisfaction and effectiveness and of an aspect of the principal's effectiveness. What about the relation between this type of conflict and the *principal's rating of the effectiveness of his teachers?* It will be recalled that the study was designed so that each principal rated his teachers in effectiveness. This design made it impossible to obtain a measure of interrater agreement. Using a standard-type rating form, however, each principal, as contrasted with the teachers in their self-rating, did differentiate between effective and ineffective teachers, although it is of course impossible to judge the validity of the ratings. The hypothesis that teachers low in role-personality conflict would be rated as more effective teachers than those high in such conflict was substantiated.[32]

This finding points to an important practical issue. If a teacher's rating in effectiveness is likely to be lowered when his dispositions for teaching methods and materials differ from the expectations of the principal, how are change and innovation in the school to be instituted? To ask teachers to take the initiative in this process is to ask them to risk negative judgments from the administrator—at least in some school systems. It would seem then on the whole, as Campbell points out, that if change is to occur in the school, it must in large measure originate with the principal.[33] To be sure, this is an extreme position and, as we

---

[31] Campbell, *op. cit.*, p. 83.
[32] *Ibid.*
[33] Merton V. Campbell, "Teacher-Principal Agreement on the Teacher Role," *Administrator's Notebook,* 7 (February, 1959), 4.

shall show, other forces make for change despite the principal. Nonetheless, if innovations contrary to the principal's expectations are instituted by the teachers, the result may be only lowered ratings in teacher effectiveness and the consequent discrediting of both the teacher and the innovation. Indeed, one aspect of the current controversy regarding the merit rating of teachers may well involve precisely this fear—that instead of encouraging teacher initiative it will make the teacher even more dependent upon conformity to the principal's expectations.

In any event, the role-definition approach to the study of role-personality relations, as exemplified by this investigation, provides information, in however modest a degree, on the conditions which are related to the satisfaction of teachers, their feelings of confidence in the administrator's leadership, and the administrator's ratings of their effectiveness.[34]

Toward further inquiry

The observed significant relationships between role-personality conflict and teacher satisfaction, effectiveness, and confidence in the administrator's leadership highlight the importance of two aspects of social behavior in the administrative setting. In formulating role expectations, at least as he sees them, the administrator must be concerned with the task specifications and functions of the role in the achievement of institutional goals. But he must also be aware of the needs and dispositions of the individuals who will inhabit the roles and be required to fulfill the expectations. He must formulate the expectations to make room for autonomous as well as the required compliant behavior. Moreover, in selecting and assigning personnel, he must bear in mind that behavior in a social system is a function of both role and personality variables, and that the interaction between the variables is related to the satisfaction and effectiveness of those

---

[34] That agreement on role definitions relates to numerous factors other than satisfaction, effectiveness, and confidence in leadership is also apparent. The impact of agreement regarding role definitions on interpersonal interaction was recently investigated by Eugene W. Tornow, "A Study of Teachers' Perceptions of Decision Points and the Interactions of the Superintendent of Schools, the Director of Instruction, and the High School Principal," Doctoral dissertation, University of Wisconsin, 1965.

who are administered and to their confidence in his administration.[35]

The studies we cited directed attention to one source of strain in the administrative setting—that between role and personality—and to several of its apparent consequences. But these studies must be viewed as only a modest beginning; additional investigations are needed. Bakke,[36] for example, suggests no fewer than sixteen specific research areas involving role-personality conflict in industry. Several instances of such research with special reference to education may be mentioned as illustrative of further directions for inquiry in the school setting.

Inquiry into the recurring notion of an "administrative personality" compatible with the administrative role no matter what the specific field—whether public administration, business administration, hospital administration, educational administration, and so on—might proceed at three levels: (1) Findings from existing studies in the several fields might be compared and synthesized. (2) Studies using the same set of concepts and terms could be carried on across fields. (3) Student and intern exchange programs might be instituted. The recent emphasis of commonalities among fields of administration ("an administrator is an administrator") notwithstanding, little systematic research has been directed at the presumed similarities, and it might have important implications for both theory and training in administration. It is not inconceivable, for example, that the personality prerequisites for effective performance in the school superintendent's role are more like those for the city manager's role than for the school principal's role.

A second line of inquiry might be directed toward the process through which roles become modified to suit individuals and individuals become modified to fit roles.[37] This is of course the problem to which we referred as the personalization of roles and the socialization of individuals in a social system. Issues

---

[35] An exploratory investigation of these relationships also was conducted by Harold G. Stewart, "Criteria Used by Superintendents in the Selection of Beginning Principals in Certain Wisconsin Schools," Doctoral dissertation, University of Wisconsin, 1963.

[36] E. W. Bakke, *The Fusion Process*, New Haven, Labor and Management Center, Yale University, 1953, pp. 30–34.

[37] See Sister Mary St. George Thompson, B.V.M., "Modifications in Identity: A Study of the Socialization Process During a Sister Formation Program," Doctoral dissertation, University of Chicago, 1963.

such as reassignment of personnel or dropping and adding functions in a given office are often dealt with in terms of such time-honored concepts as line-and-staff, span of control, or flat-pyramidal structures, which have proved of limited usefulness. For example, the question "Why did this school district add a business manager?" elicits responses ranging all the way from "Because the superintendent got tired of meeting salesmen" to "Because student enrollment exceeded 1,000." Studies in this area might also shed light on the frequently observed phenomenon that whenever an administrator retires he seems to be replaced by from two to five other administrators.

A converse series of inquiries might be directed toward the impact of specific roles on the personality of the role incumbents. Does an individual indeed tend to acquire, as it is said, a "military personality" with his military bearing while in service? The studies would focus on the factors making for personality change as a function of role behavior. That such studies are fraught with methodological difficulties of extraordinary magnitude is evident. Nonetheless, it is something of an anomaly that, although the literature abounds with investigations of personality change during childhood, adolescence, and at retirement with old age, the problem of personality change during the middle, occupationally productive years is largely ignored.

Implicit in most studies of role-personality relationships is the assumption that a minimum of role-personality conflict—ideally none—is desirable for individual satisfaction and presumably for institutional effectiveness. Systematic inquiry might well raise this assumption to an explicit level and subject it to test. It is conceivable, for example, that at extremes of employee satisfaction the organization becomes rigid and insensitive to changing conditions, any attempted innovation being seen as a threat to the prevailing satisfaction. Those who are dissatisfied are often the ones to provide the stimulus for re-examining organizational policies and procedures which are merely taken for granted by those who are satisfied. If this is the case, the morale level in terms of satisfaction, or what has been called the "happiness index," may not be the best criterion to assess the organization's well-being. In somewhat oversimplified form, the issue for inquiry might be: Is there an *optimum*, rather than the assumed absolute *minimum*, level of role-personality conflict in a social system?

Finally, we must reiterate that both the studies already conducted and those that still need to be conducted in the domain of role-personality relationships are subject to severe methodological difficulties—difficulties that are endemic to research not only in administration but in social science generally. One is the lack of an adequate terminology to relate phenomena that are dealt with separately in sociological and psychological schemata, to say nothing of anthropological, economic, and other formulations which may also be relevant. But even within each schema there is the problem of choosing the most fruitful concepts and terms. In the absence of an appropriate theory of personality, for example, Malo and Lipham were forced to utilize a taxonomy of needs which, although immediately useful for their purpose, is a far cry from a satisfactory conceptualization of role-personality functioning. Similarly, Campbell's adaptation of a role instrument to permit individuals to express their wants, again useful as it was for his purpose, is by no means a measure of teacher personality dispositions in any ultimate sense.

A second difficulty involves the ubiquitous criterion problem. Since research in administration almost always entails implicitly or explicitly some measure of competence, on what criterion is such measure to be based? At the most general level, in industry the competence of one executive can perhaps be indicated by comparing his profit and loss statement with that of a competing executive, although this is by no means a foolproof standard. But at the same level, what is the appropriate criterion in education? In a university, for example, is it growth in the number of students? Increase in endowment? Excellence of teaching? Output of pure research? Contribution to the solution of immediate state and national problems? And if it is, say, excellence of teaching, how is one to measure *that*? The resort then most frequently is to rating an administrator in general terms like "confidence in his leadership." This is defensible, at least for want of anything better. But such judgments by one group in a social system are known to correlate imperfectly with the judgments of another group in the same system. And of course the same issue may be raised about the judgment of teacher effectiveness by principals. What if the pupils, parents, and peers do not agree with the principal? The arguments regarding the criterion problem in educational administration are endless and, if not futile, surely have so far not proved very profitable. Instead of arguing *who* is ultimately to judge administrative effectiveness, perhaps more effort should be devoted to searching for more meaningful observations of administrative behaviors which lead to the accomplishment of organizational and individual goals. But this too is easier said than done. In any event, in view of our preceding findings regarding differential educational values held by different reference groups, the demand for a value-free criterion of administrative effectiveness in the educational setting—a criterion which would hold equally for all reference groups—is perhaps not unlike asking for value-free values.

That the model has served to call attention to the difficulties and limitations in the present work on role-personality relationships—our own as well as that of others—is no less useful than that it has itself stimulated investigations in this area.[38] The studies we have cited represent a modest beginning to the understanding of a crucial aspect of the relation between role and personality in the administrative setting.

Summary

Role-personality conflict was described as a function of discrepancies between patterns of expectations attaching to an institutional role and patterns of need-dispositions characteristic of the incumbents of the role. Since a primary function of the administrator is to elicit goal-directed behavior that is institutionally useful and individually satisfying, the nature and extent of conflict between role and personality are of crucial concern. In terms of the model, both the normative and the personal dimensions of behavior must be considered if behavior in the social system is to lead toward achieving both institutional and individual goals.

Two approaches to the investigation of role-personality relationships were cited: (1) the personality-assessment method, which utilizes personality variables to describe the relationship of the individual to the role, and (2) the role-definition method, which utilizes role-expectation variables to describe the relationship of the role to the individual. Studies using the first approach found positive relationships between promotability to and effec-

---

[38] For a review of the literature regarding these relationships see James M. Lipham, "Organizational Character of Education: Administrative Behavior," *Review of Educational Research*, 34 (October, 1964), 435–454.

tiveness in the administrative role and such personality characteristics as the disposition for activity and achievement, social ability, feelings of security, and emotional control. Studies employing the second approach showed that the satisfaction of individuals in the work situation, ratings of their effectiveness by the administrator, and their expression of confidence in the administrator's leadership were related to the degree of role-personality conflict. Specifically, teachers with smaller discrepancies between the expectations held for their role by the principal and their own dispositions toward the role tended to be more satisfied with the teaching situation, were rated by their principal as more effective teachers, and in turn indicated greater confidence in the principal's leadership than did teachers with greater discrepancies.

Although these studies are useful, they are only a small step toward needed empirical inquiry into the interaction between role and personality in the administrative setting and the consequences of different patterns of such interaction. A number of additional inquiries were suggested in the form of issues for investigation. To cite an example or two, it is a basic assumption of much administrative theory that organizational effectiveness increases as role-personality conflict decreases. There is reason to believe that this is not necessarily the case. A basic research issue might be: Is there an *optimum*, rather than the assumed absolute *minimum*, level of role-personality conflict in a social system? Again, it is more and more assumed that there is a so-called administrative personality suitable for the administrative role no matter what the field, whether industrial or educational. This too may not be the case. A basic inquiry might be directed toward a crossinstitutional study of administrative roles and their incumbents.

Finally, we pointed to two major methodological difficulties in the systematic study of administration—not only in the field of education but in social science generally. One is the lack of an entirely satisfactory conceptual system and terminology for dealing simultaneously with different levels of observed social behavior. The other is the ubiquitous and crucial problem of the criterion of administrative effectiveness.

9

Individual personality

Just as a role is an *institutional given* that may be conceived of as existing before anyone occupies it and independent of any role incumbent's particular personality, so personality is an *individual given* that may be thought of as existing before any role is occupied by the individual and independent of the role. As the model suggests, within a social system behavior may be understood as a function of the interaction between the personality variables and the role variables. It is with the nature, variation, and effect of personality factors on certain aspects of behavior in the school system that we are concerned in this chapter.

We shall examine the general problem in the context of several prototypical studies involving (1) the relation between teacher personality and subject taught, and the effect of this relationship on teacher-administrator interaction; (2) the relation between certain personality variables and felt conflict in the teaching situation; and (3) the relation between personality variables and the reaction to different types of supervision in the educational setting.

The relation between teacher personality, subject matter taught, and teacher-administrator interaction

Ask a group of school administrators, "Which teachers are hardest to get along with?" Their answers will reveal two interesting phenomena, a tendency to group teachers by subject matter taught and an inclination to impute to each group some characteristic personality patterns. Thus one administrator may respond, "Mathematics and science teachers. They're a cool and calculating lot." "No, art teachers—they're hopelessly disorganized," says another. "You don't know empire-building music teachers," says a third, thinking of the pressure for a bigger band, more baton twirlers, and more colorful uniforms. "No," asserts still another, "coaches and physical education people get my vote—they're miserable teachers, who value brawn over brain." And so on.

To be sure, the comments are stereotypic. It is nonsense to assume that *all* science teachers are *this* by personality, and *all* art teachers are *that* by personality. Yet are there not certain personality characteristics that differentiate scientists from artists, and artists from athletes, at least as groups? May there not be similar differences among different teacher groups? And should not the administrator be sensitive to such differences, and be aware of their possible effects upon him and his effect upon them?

Two salient issues may be raised for empirical investigation:

1. If secondary school teachers are grouped by subject-matter field, do the resulting groups differ in mensurable personality characteristics such as needs, values, and attitudes?
2. If there are such differences, are they related to factors of direct concern to the administrator, such as satisfaction in the teaching situation and feelings of excessive pressure for conformity to administrative expectations?

TEACHER PERSONALITY AND SUBJECT MATTER TAUGHT

The central hypothesis of a study by Andrews[1] was that "subject-matter field groups of secondary teachers differ from one another in personality needs, values, and educational attitudes."[2] To obtain the necessary data, the investigator administered the Edwards Personal Preference Schedule and the Allport-Vernon-Lindzey Study of Values to 564 secondary teachers in eight large high schools in Illinois, Indiana, and Wisconsin. He also used the Kerlinger Educational Scale, the Minnesota Teacher Attitude Inventory, a measure of situational satisfaction, and a measure of pressure to conform to administrative policies.

The basic hypothesis of psychological differences among teachers according to subject matter taught was confirmed. For example, on the Allport-Vernon-Lindzey Study of Values, an analysis of variance revealed significant differences for both male and female teachers according to subject-matter field on four of the six value scales. The complete data are presented in Tables 9–1 and 9–2.

---

[1] John H. M. Andrews, "Administrative Significance of Psychological Differences Between Secondary Teachers of Different Subject Matter Fields," Doctoral dissertation, University of Chicago, 1957.
[2] *Ibid.*, p. 80.

TABLE 9-1
Values of Male Principals and Teachers by Subject-Matter Groups

Group	N	THEORETICAL Mean	SD	ECONOMIC Mean	SD	AESTHETIC Mean	SD	SOCIAL Mean	SD	POLITICAL Mean	SD	RELIGIOUS Mean	SD
Commerce	18	39.00	3.87	46.22	7.87	34.50	9.89	36.22	5.75	41.67	6.56	42.39	8.50
English	38	49.87	6.89	36.24	8.94	42.68	9.17	36.82	7.48	39.29	5.84	44.11	8.90
Industrial Arts	51	43.37	5.13	43.55	6.25	33.37	7.01	35.94	6.66	40.31	6.11	43.45	7.82
Mathematics	29	46.55	6.33	40.69	7.66	32.28	7.30	35.48	6.11	38.66	5.81	46.03	8.25
Physical Education	30	42.30	5.84	43.37	7.72	33.07	6.56	36.37	5.40	42.33	5.44	42.47	7.61
Science	55	50.42	6.08	38.11	8.98	32.78	8.04	35.80	5.86	38.75	5.14	43.84	9.31
Social Studies	47	41.94	6.73	38.43	8.21	36.15	8.03	37.81	5.91	42.28	6.15	43.43	8.91
Fine Arts	16	39.81	5.60	38.63	9.58	48.25	10.12	34.00	4.53	37.88	5.80	41.44	10.09
Principals	11	42.45	5.18	36.45	7.23	35.27	5.69	38.63	6.53	38.36	5.20	48.82	8.07
TOTAL	295	43.84	6.93	40.12	8.53	35.71	9.03	36.34	6.18	40.12	5.90	43.78	8.64
Significance		.001		.001		.001		NS		.01		NS	

SOURCE: John H. M. Andrews, "Administrative Significance of Psychological Differences Between Secondary Teachers of Different Subject-Matter Fields," Doctoral dissertation, University of Chicago, 1957, p. 82.

TABLE 9-2
Values of Female Teachers by Subject-Matter Groups

Group	N	THEORETICAL Mean	SD	ECONOMIC Mean	SD	AESTHETIC Mean	SD	SOCIAL Mean	SD	POLITICAL Mean	SD	RELIGIOUS Mean	SD
Commerce	19	37.26	8.01	42.32	6.05	38.68	4.92	37.37	5.88	40.16	5.40	44.21	10.70
English	67	37.04	7.27	34.96	8.76	43.91	6.68	38.97	6.26	37.60	5.50	47.40	9.29
Foreign Language	23	35.78	5.12	36.96	7.02	45.61	7.68	40.30	5.76	35.91	5.64	45.39	6.13
Home Economics	21	39.10	6.50	41.90	5.89	38.24	6.34	38.10	6.32	35.76	5.55	46.43	7.95
Mathematics	19	41.79	5.25	39.58	7.74	36.16	7.18	39.68	8.92	34.21	4.60	48.42	6.02
Physical Education	20	38.75	6.07	41.60	4.33	36.90	5.78	36.25	4.81	37.45	7.50	47.05	9.00
Science	17	44.29	6.85	35.18	7.59	41.94	6.17	36.94	5.57	34.59	5.97	46.47	8.43
Social Studies	33	38.30	6.89	36.48	7.54	41.39	7.03	38.48	7.36	42.06	6.26	43.58	8.35
Fine Arts	15	39.07	7.60	36.13	6.53	50.20	3.93	36.87	5.63	33.80	6.58	43.87	9.78
TOTAL	234	38.49	7.02	37.62	7.79	41.99	7.28	38.37	6.42	37.35	6.29	46.08	8.63
Significance		.01		.001		.001		NS		.001		NS	

SOURCE: John H. M. Andrews, "Administrative Significance of Psychological Differences Between Secondary Teachers of Different Subject-Matter Fields," Doctoral dissertation, University of Chicago, 1957, p. 89.

We may call attention to one or two of the systematic variations among the male groups. It is readily apparent that teachers of commercial subjects are highest in economic values and lowest in theoretical values; teachers of science are lowest in economic and highest in theoretical values. Fine arts teachers are highest in aesthetic values and lowest in political (power) values; physical education teachers are lowest in aesthetic values and highest in political (power) values. Similar differences may be observed among the female groups. Other personality differences were found on the Edwards Personal Preference Schedule. In need order, for example, the female home economics teachers were highest and the female science and fine arts teachers lowest; in need exhibition, the science and fine arts teachers were highest and the female home economics teachers lowest.

The point of the study here is not so much the discovery of unanticipated personality characteristics of teachers. On the contrary, it is perfectly sensible that the fine arts teachers be higher in aesthetic values than the physical education teachers, and that the commercial teachers be higher in economic values than the science teachers. But the demonstration of these differences in empirical terms makes concrete the issue of the possible administrative problems of personality cleavages among various groups within a single institution. As the investigator himself concludes, "If teachers differ in personality needs, dominant values, and educational attitudes according to their subject-matter fields, then sectionalism and conflict of interest between groups within a high school is a potential danger."[3]

TEACHER PERSONALITY AND TEACHER-ADMINISTRATOR INTERACTION

The investigator pursued further the possibility of institutional sectionalism as a function of personality cleavages among groups in the educational setting. He reasoned as follows:

In a high school there is a general culture whose norms are oriented toward education. This is the in-group in the school. Members of the group are teachers of particular subjects but they identify not with their subjects but with education. Around the fringes of this central culture in the school are a number of sub-cultures—one for each of the subject-matter fields. Members of these subject-matter field cultures identify with their own particular subject matter rather than with education as such. A member of the chemistry sub-culture,

---

[3] John H. M. Andrews, "A Deterrent to Harmony Among Teachers," *Administrator's Notebook*, 6 (March, 1958), 2.

for example, is distinctively a chemistry teacher rather than one who is primarily a teacher and secondarily concerned with chemistry. Of the chemistry teachers in a high school, then, some are members of the education culture and others members of the chemistry subculture. The same is true of the other subject-matter field groups.[4]

On this basis, it was hypothesized that teachers in the subject-matter culture, that is, those who are strongly identified by personality characteristics with a particular subject-matter field, would feel themselves in an unsympathetic environment relative to the teachers in the education culture, that is, those who are not so strongly identified by personality characteristics with a particular subject-matter field. Their alienation would result in lower satisfaction in the teaching situation, feelings of excessive pressure to conform to administrative policy, and a tendency to leave one job for another.

To examine this possibility empirically, the teachers were divided into two groups with regard to personality differences: those whose personality pattern was more like that of the teachers in their particular subject-matter field, and those whose personality pattern was more like that of the average of all teachers. The former were designated members of the "subject-matter culture," the latter members of the "education culture."

The findings for the male teachers were quite straightforward. There were significant differences between the two groups in educational background, locus of teacher preparation, teaching preference, and, more important in the present context, certain factors of preeminent significance to the administrator, such as turnover rate, satisfaction in the teaching situation, and feelings of pressure from the administrator.

Specifically with respect to background variables, (1) education group teachers had more semester hours of courses in education than did subject-matter group teachers; (2) education group teachers more commonly were trained in teachers colleges or university departments of education, subject-matter group teachers in liberal arts colleges and university subject-matter departments; and (3) subject-matter group teachers more commonly desired to teach the subject of their training, as opposed to some other subject, than did education group teachers. Specifically with respect to administrative variables, (1) subject-matter teachers moved from one job to another more than did

---
[4] *Ibid.*, p. 2.

education group teachers; (2) subject-matter group teachers expressed lower over-all satisfaction with teaching than did education group teachers; and (3) subject-matter group teachers felt under greater pressure to conform to the educational policies of the school administration than did education group teachers.[5] The latter finding incidentally is a very nice empirical demonstration of the effect of excessive discrepancy between the personality dispositions and role expectations in a social system as conceived in the present general theoretical formulation.

The investigator sums up the findings of this aspect of his study as follows:

> Differences in personality needs, dominant values, and educational attitudes which have been shown to exist between the different subject-matter field groups of male secondary teachers have also been shown to be of more than theoretical interest to the study of educational administration. These differences formed the basis for dividing teachers into two categories which have been explained as two opposing reference group orientations. This categorization has been shown to have practical significance in that the categories are related to variables which are eminently important to the study of administration and to the actual operation of schools. The three variables of administrative consequence which are related to the categories are Tenure Index, Global Satisfaction, and Conformity Pressure.[6]

The existence of a dominant education culture and a number of subsidiary subject-matter subcultures in the school, and the observed effect of membership in these cultures on such factors as tenure, satisfaction, and reaction to administrative policy, raises an important issue regarding the handling of conformity and freedom in the social system. On the one hand, administrators are quite properly urged to permit teachers the greatest freedom and initiative, since teaching is a creative activity which can best be performed in an "open" organizational climate. On the other hand, administrators are urged to stress commonality of goals, purposes, and practices, since there are necessary continuities between grades and subjects and the individual classroom is not—and cannot be—an independent unit. No single set of meaningful rules or, as they are sometimes called, guidelines for action can be set forth that will hold under all circumstances. But one general principle may be stated with

---
[5] *Ibid.*, pp. 3–4.
[6] Andrews, "Administrative Significance . . . ," p. 136.

confidence: The administrator must understand the underlying deterrents to organizational harmony inherent in the cleavages in teacher values, needs, and attitudes if he is to deal with central causes rather than with peripheral effects.

Two other issues may be raised. The first revolves about the question of why the reported results held for male teachers but not for female teachers. The investigator suggests with reason that the social or role context of the school is different for the two groups.[7] For example, the administrative threat of blocked promotion in the system is not as highly salient for female teachers as for male teachers, and teaching is not a low-status profession relative to other female professions as it is relative to other male professions. These obvious variations in role definition, to mention no others, would make a difference in the relation between the personality and role variables under study, although the nature of the differences cannot be specified in the present case. All that may be said with certainty is that the entire question of sex differences in role and personality in the educational system would make a fruitful area for further theoretical and empirical analysis.

The second issue revolves about the question of which type of teacher is more desirable, the one oriented to education or the one oriented to subject-matter field. The easy answer is a teacher who is oriented equally and of course maximally to subject matter and to education. But easy answers do not solve grave problems. The fact is that no one quite knows how to turn out such balanced teachers in great numbers—perhaps the current Master of Arts in Teaching programs are a step in the desired direction. As things stand the administrator must apparently deal with teachers of opposing orientations. Depending, then, on one's view, the subject-matter-oriented teacher may be looked upon as a scholar become victim of the anti-intellectual atmosphere of the high school, or as a teacher who is preoccupied with his own specialty at the expense of a deep interest in children and a grasp of the educational process.[8] Conversely, the education-oriented teacher may be regarded as a dedicated educator of children become victim of an overly specialized subject-matter emphasis, or as a teacher who is preoccupied with children and instructional method at the expense of dedication to his subject matter and grasp of the field of his presumed expertness. In

---

[7] Andrews, "A Deterrent to Harmony . . . ," p. 4.
[8] Ibid.

either case, name-calling is surely not the solution. It may be hoped instead that serious conceptual and empirical consideration of the problem of the scholar as teacher and the teacher as scholar will lead in the short term to a greater understanding by the administrator of the cleavages in his school, and in the long term to teacher preparation programs that will do away with the cleavages themselves.

The relation between personality and role conflict in the teaching situation

As we have already indicated, endemic to social systems short of utopias are numerous forms of role conflict. The conflict may arise because the institutional roles are poorly defined, inconsistent expectations are held by different individuals in the role-set, a person may be occupying two roles making conflicting demands upon him, a single role may be so structured that there are contradictory expectations for behavior, and so on. In any case, the individual is faced with inconsistent expectations for performance in the social system.

The critical issue for the social system is that such role conflict is symptomatic of institutional disorganization. The critical issue for the individual is that he must cope with the conflict, and that it may engender feelings of ambiguity, frustration, and threat to him as a person. However, the same existential conflict seems to engender varying degrees of ambiguity, frustration, and threat in different individuals. In a sense, the existential institutional conflict is differentially represented in individually *felt* conflict. Some people can withstand, and in fact appear to thrive under, the same conflictual conditions that drive others "wild." These variations in reaction to conflict are said to be a function of differences in personality.

In cases of severe personality disorder, such frustrations may lead to observed functional breakdowns so that existential objects and events come to have minimum representation in the private world of the person. The roles are detached from the institutional setting and used to work out personal needs, however inappropriate these may be to the organization. The effect is to keep the individual at odds with the social system either because he cannot maintain a stable relationship to a given role or because his autistic tendencies impel him to misperceive the expectations placed upon him. The paranoid, for example, reacts to the world about him as a carefully laid plot directed against his well-being.

But the effect of personality on behavior is not restricted to the readily observed extremes of deviance. It is pervasive. Many differential reactions to the environment generally and to role conflict specifically, well within the range of "normal" behavior, may also be understood in relation to the personality and other characteristics of the role incumbents. If these differences are not so manifest or striking as those at the extremes, they are nonetheless real and of concern to the administrator.

We shall proceed to a more concrete consideration of the relation between personality and role conflict in the context of two specific empirical studies: (1) a study of the relation of personality to role conflict in the military setting as a type case of an extreme conflictual teaching situation, and (2) a study of the relations of certain individual characteristics to role conflict in the more usual public school situation.

PERSONALITY AND ROLE CONFLICT IN A MILITARY TEACHING SITUATION

Getzels and Guba[9] posed the question directly: "Is there a systematic relationship between the degree of *felt* conflict and certain identifiable personality variables?" Theoretically, the felt conflict should be greater for individuals characterized by "nervousness," "feelings of inferiority," "depressiveness," "intolerance of ambiguity," and "overreaction to frustration" than for those in the same situation but not possessing such traits of personality. The investigators attempted to test this assumption in an empirical study of instructors in a highly conflictual educational situation.

The setting for the study was the Air Command and Staff School of Air University, Maxwell Air Force Base. The school was staffed by some 300 officer-instructors and supervisory personnel, who provided advanced training to several thousand officers a year. Individual interviews with a sample of the instructors revealed that a major source of dissatisfaction was the conflict between the officer role and the instructor role, and this was selected as the role conflict for study in relation to personality functioning. The nature of the conflict and the setting itself

---

[9] J. W. Getzels and E. G. Guba, "Role Conflict and Personality," *Journal of Personality*, 24 (September, 1955), 74–85.

provided an excellent opportunity for investigating the problem in a real-life situation for at least three reasons: (1) The roles and role expectations were defined with an explicitness not usually found in nonmilitary educational settings, thus permitting highly reliable observations. (2) The roles of teacher and officer were clearly at odds as the situation was structured. (3) The subjects under study were available for extensive testing and examination, a circumstance not readily found in other educational settings, and one that is of no mean importance in real-life situation rather than laboratory research. The disadvantage that the substantive data might not be applicable to nonmilitary educational situations was not a primary consideration, since the intent was to investigate a general theoretical relationship between personality and role conflict rather than to provide predictive data with respect to specific personality tests and scores for universal application.

On the basis of the individual interviews a 46-item role-conflict questionnaire was constructed for group administration. Represented in the items, which were taken directly from statements in the interviews, were four areas of conflict between expectations attaching to the officer role. The following are the conflict areas and sample items from the questionnaire:

1. *Procedures*. The items here reflect conflicts when officers wearing the mark of their "hierarchical" position in clear sight are required as teachers to be "democratic" in the classroom without regard to the visible differences in military status.

   The mixture of democratic and military procedures at Air University leaves the instructor in the ambiguous position of never knowing when to act on his own initiative and when to be guided by S.O.P. (Standard Operating Procedures).

2. *Rank*. The items here reflect conflicts arising from the circumstance that although all officer-instructors from colonel to warrant officer at Air University are expected to function equally as teachers in the classroom, their ultimate responsibility, authority, privilege, and salary derive not from their equal educational status but from their differential military rank.

   It frequently happens at Air University that competent teachers have low military rank while poorly qualified teachers have high military rank.

3. *Career.* The items here reflect conflicts arising when professional Air Force officers are required to perform an academic assignment they may not visualize as contributing to their primary career as military personnel.

In spite of a good record as a teacher, an instructor at Air University with no overseas or combat experience has little chance for promotion.

4. *Assignment.* The items here reflect conflicts arising when officers subject to the assignment regulations of military service find these regulations applied to their assignment in the educational setting.

Although an officer is trained in military planning, it does not follow that he is equipped to do the kinds of educational planning such as curriculum making, which Air University requires of him.[10]

The subjects under study were required to respond to each item on a six-point scale, indicating at one extreme that they felt free from concern over the conflict described in the item and at the other extreme that they felt greatly troubled by the conflict. Fully 204 of the total number of 234 officer-instructors responded to the questionnaire. Approximately the top quarter in felt conflict (55 officer-instructors) were identified as the high-conflict group, and approximately the bottom quarter in felt conflict (53 officer-instructors) were identified as the low-conflict group. Comparison could then be made between the personality patterns of the two groups.

Three standard instruments, each intended to measure a significant aspect of personality, namely, *adjustment, authoritarianism*, and *reaction to frustration*, were administered: (1) the Guilford-Martin Inventory of Factors GAMIN and STDCR, a "direct" instrument designed to measure individual differences in *adjustment*, including such variables as "nervousness," "feelings of inferiority," "masculinity," "cycloid disposition" (mood swings), "introversion," and so on; (2) the California Fascism (F) and a subsection of the Ethnocentrism (E) Scale, an "indirect" measure of individual differences in *authoritarianism*, including such variables as "rigidity" and "intolerance of ambiguity"; and (3) the Rosenzweig Picture-Frustration Study, a "projective" instrument designed to measure individual differences in *reaction to frustration.* Mean scores for the high- and

---

[10] *Ibid.*, pp. 79–80.

low-conflict groups were computed for each measure and the relevant comparisons made. The results were quite straightforward and may be presented most simply with respect to each of the aspects of personality and instruments in turn.

Personality Adjustment and Role Conflict. Table 9–3 provides the pertinent data regarding role conflict and personality adjustment as measured by the Guilford-Martin Inventory. It is

TABLE 9–3

Mean Scores of High- and Low-Conflict Groups on the Guilford-Martin Inventories of Factors GAMIN and STDCR

Variable	High-conflict mean scores (N = 55)	Low-conflict mean scores (N = 53)	t	P
G—General activity	13.255	12.491	1.001	.30–.40
A—Ascendancy	24.473	25.849	1.155	.20–.30
M—Masculinity	23.091	26.000	3.632	.001
I—Inferiority (lack of)	34.182	40.038	3.830	.001
N—Nervousness (lack of)	27.145	32.736	4.358	.001
S—Social introversion	12.964	9.830	2.199	.05
T—Thinking introversion	25.891	23.396	1.975	.05
D—Depression	15.618	7.642	4.407	.001
C—Cycloid disposition	20.364	11.755	4.594	.001
R—Rhathymia	33.000	34.396	0.876	.30–.40

SOURCE: J. W. Getzels and E. G. Guba, "Role Conflict and Personality," *Journal of Personality,* 24 (September, 1955), 82.

clear that on three of the five GAMIN factors there are significant differences between the high- and the low-conflict groups, the high group obtaining lower scores in masculinity, lack of inferiority feelings, and lack of nervousness. These findings conform to the hypothesized relationships between personality and role conflict at a place like Air University. Since the expectations in a military setting are predominantly for masculine interests and behavior, an individual with relatively nonmasculine personality characteristics would have greater difficulty in meeting these expectations than would his more masculine colleagues. Similarly, an officer-instructor with greater feelings of inferiority and nervousness would find the ambiguity and potential frustration of the role-conflict situation more disorganizing than would his colleagues with lesser feelings of inferiority and nervous tension and accordingly would feel greater conflict. In addition, significant differences were found on four of the five STDCR factors, the high-conflict group being more socially and intellectually introverted, more depressive, and more prone to mood swings ("cycloid disposition"). This too is in line with the hypothesized relationships. The expectations in a military setting are for anything but introversion, moodiness, and temperamental instability. An individual with these dispositions would be more likely to react negatively to existing role conflicts than would his more stable colleagues.

In short, the suggested relationship between personality adjustment and individual liability to role conflict is clearly confirmed by the obtained data. It is all the more noteworthy because, with the single exception of the factor of thinking introversion, both the high-conflict and the low-conflict groups had scores typical of "better adjusted" individuals according to Guilford-Martin criterion norms. The Air Force officer, especially the officer-instructor assigned to Air University, is of course a carefully screened individual. The fact that highly significant relationships were obtained on seven of a possible ten personality factors with such a homogeneous sample in adjustment is striking evidence of the significance of personality factors in relation to liability to role conflict.

Authoritarian Personality and Role Conflict. The relationship under examination here was that the high group would be more authoritarian, rigid, and intolerant of ambiguity, that is, they would score higher on the California Ethnocentrism and Fascism Scale, than would the low-conflict group. The underlying hypothesis was that the authoritarian individual is under particular stress in a setting which has ambiguous, if not contradictory, expectations typical of a role-conflict situation. He finds it difficult to choose one set of expectations in preference to another without feelings of guilt or anxiety. Or, lacking personal flexibility, he cannot shift readily from one set of expectations to the other as the situation demands. In Air University, for example, he cannot move easily between the roles of teacher and officer. In contrast, the same problem does not entail the same difficulties for the nonauthoritarian individual, who is at once more flexible, less conventional, and more tolerant of ambiguity.

As the data in Table 9–4 indicate, this relationship was in fact found, the high-conflict group scoring significantly higher on the E and F scales than the low-conflict group.

TABLE 9–4

Mean Scores of High- and Low-Conflict Groups on the E and F Scales[a]

Variable	High-conflict mean scores (N = 43)[b]	Low-conflict mean scores (N = 43)[b]	t	P
E—Ethnocentrism (9 items)	21.535	18.512	2.009	.05
F—Fascism (full scale)	67.116	53.512	3.505	.001

[a] Values shown in the table are total scores adjusted by the addition of constants (E Scale—20; F Scale—90) to facilitate computation.
[b] Subjects for whom the data were available.
SOURCE: J. W. Getzels and E. G. Guba, "Role Conflict and Personality," *Journal of Personality*, 24 (September, 1955), 83.

Reactions to Frustration and Role Conflict. A person in a role-conflict situation cannot ordinarily escape a certain amount of disequilibrium, since conformity to one pattern of expectations will result in nonconformity to the other pattern. Thus, role conflict inevitably involves some frustration. Behavior is to a great extent a function of the individual's characteristic reaction to frustration. To the extent that this reaction is (in the terms of the Rosenzweig Picture-Frustration Study) *extrapunitive*, that is, primarily concerned with placing blame for the situation and expressing hostility, the conflict will not be resolved and may indeed be augmented. To the extent that the reaction is *impunitive*, that is, not primarily concerned with placing blame and expressing hostility, the individual is freer than his extrapunitive colleague to do the best he can under the circumstances, even if he cannot alter the essential conflict. The same is true with what Rosenzweig calls the *ego-defensive* and *need-persistent* types of characteristic reactions to frustration. The ego-defensive individual is primarily concerned with avoiding personal devaluation; he magnifies the conflict as a potential threat to his being. The need-persistent individual views the conflict as an external barrier to be overcome in order to achieve a desired goal. The one expends his efforts on avoiding blame for the conflict, the other on reaching his ends despite the conflict.

The hypothesis under examination was that the high-conflict group would be more extrapunitive and ego-defensive and the low-conflict group would be more impunitive and need-persistent. As the data in Table 9–5 indicate, substantial verification of the hypothesis was found. The high-conflict group was indeed significantly more extrapunitive and more ego-defensive, and the low-conflict group significantly more impunitive and need-persistent. The latter group was also found to be more intropunitive, although this variable was not among the stated hypotheses.

TABLE 9–5

Mean Scores of High- and Low-Conflict Groups on the Rosenzweig Picture-Frustration Study

Variable	High-conflict mean scores (N = 41)[a]	Low-conflict mean scores (N = 35)[a]	t	P
E—Extrapunitive	53.537	40.951	3.790	.001
I—Intropunitive	23.537	28.600	2.779	.01
M—Impunitive	22.927	29.429	2.697	.01
PD—Obstacle dominance	18.146	19.114	0.565	.50–.60
EG—Ego defensive	47.585	42.029	1.918	.05–.10
NP—Need persistence	24.171	29.514	2.148	.05

[a] Subjects for whom the data were available.
SOURCE: J. W. Getzels and E. G. Guba, "Role Conflict and Personality," *Journal of Personality*, 24 (September, 1955), 84.

In sum, role and personality are two crucial constructs for the understanding of organizational behavior. The present study investigated the relationship between certain aspects of personality and certain aspects of role expectations within an ongoing educational setting. When officer-instructors at a military school were divided into two groups, one more conflict-prone and the other less conflict-prone, the following differences in personality were found: (1) The more conflict-prone were less masculine, less free from feelings of nervousness, more socially and intellectually introverted, more depressive, and more temperamentally unstable than the less conflict-prone. (2) They were more authoritarian and intolerant of ambiguity. (3) Their characteristic reactions to frustration were more extrapunitive and ego-defensive, less impunitive and need-persistent. That is, where the one group tends to seek solutions to the frustrating situation by avoiding blame for themselves and placing it on others, the other group tends to avoid placing blame but strives instead to work toward a constructive goal despite the conflict.

It must be emphasized that all the observations were made through verbal instruments, and the results are necessarily to be viewed with the caution due in all such studies. It may of course be that certain "response sets" to verbal material operated to give the data a greater consistency than would be found through other types of observations. Nonetheless, the instruments were *not* only of the *self-report* type, said to be readily liable to "respondent-faking" or response sets which might produce the observed consistency. Indirect and projective instruments like the Rosenzweig P-F Study were also applied. And, as we have already pointed out, the fact that the study was done in a military setting rather than in a public school setting must be considered with reference to the specific findings. Yet, as the following study will show, there are certain systematic relationships between individual differences in *nonverbal* characteristics (such as the sex of the teacher) and individual differences in reaction to role conflict in a *public school* setting as well.

PERSONALITY AND ROLE CONFLICT IN A PUBLIC SCHOOL SITUATION

As part of the role-conflict study already reported in some detail in Chapter 7, Getzels and Guba asked the question, "Are there significant differences in the personal reactions of teachers to the role conflicts in their schools, and if there are such differences, are they related systematically to the personal and social characteristics of the teachers?"[11]

A measure of the individual differences in reaction to conflict in the teaching situation in a number of public schools was obtained through a procedure similar to the one used in the military school. Specifically, 168 teachers in 6 Midwestern school systems responded to each of 71 items of a role-conflict instru-

---

[11] J. W. Getzels and E. G. Guba, "The Structure of Roles and Role Conflict in the Teaching Situation," *Journal of Educational Sociology*, 29 (September, 1955), 30–40.

ment by indicating on a 6-point scale how *troubled* they felt by the situation described in the item. Typical items were:

> While many parents expect the teacher to discipline their children as well as to educate them, the same parents are often resentful of the disciplinary methods employed, even when these methods are justified.
>
> While the plumber who operated a shoeshine shop in his spare time would be lauded by the community as an energetic citizen and a good provider, the teacher who attempted to emulate his example would be severely criticized for conduct unworthy of his social position.
>
> While the introduction of any religious influence into the schools is often viewed with alarm by the community, there is still an insistence that the teacher be a churchgoer; in fact, that he attend what is for the community an "approved" church.

Some teachers, although acknowledging the existence of the conflict in their school, seemed able to shrug it off as of no personal consequence. They said, "Yes, the conflict exists, but it does not bother me." Other teachers not only acknowledged the existence of the conflict but also stated that they were troubled by it. The research issue was whether these differences were related systematically to the individual characteristics of the teachers.

Accordingly, in addition to the role-conflict data, four other types of data were collected for each teacher: (1) descriptive characteristics, such as age, sex, teaching experience; (2) socio-economic conditions, such as number of dependents and part-time jobs; (3) extent of integration with the community, such as membership in churches and clubs and degree of similarity between present community and home community; and (4) extent of integration with the teaching profession, such as membership in professional societies and satisfaction with teaching as a career. The relationship between these characteristics and reaction to role conflict were examined as follows: Comparison groups were formed for each personal characteristic, either by dividing the distribution at the mean for continuous variables (such as age and length of teaching experience) or by taking advantage of natural groupings found in the categorical items (such as sex). A mean role-conflict score was computed for each comparison group, and the scores were then tested for significance by appropriate statistical techniques.

The following personal characteristics were found to be associated with significantly *higher* conflict scores:

1. Male teachers, as compared with female teachers.
2. Teachers with one dependent, as compared to teachers with no dependents or with more than one dependent.
3. Teachers who have part-time jobs in addition to their teaching duties, as compared to teachers who do not have part-time jobs.
4. Teachers who come from communities which they perceive to be different from the community in which they teach, as compared to teachers who come from communities which they perceive to be similar to the one in which they teach.
5. Teachers who feel restricted in their social lives, as compared to teachers who do not feel restricted.
6. Teachers who have fewer friends among persons in the community than they would like to have, as compared to teachers with a sufficient number of such friends.
7. Teachers who feel that certain groups of their fellow teachers have a more personal influence with the administration than do other groups, as compared to teachers who do not so feel.
8. Teachers who feel that their relationships with the administration are not as adequate and satisfying as they might be, as compared to teachers who do not so feel.
9. Teachers who would not again enter the teaching profession if they had such a choice, as compared to teachers who would again choose to teach.[12]

Clearly, there are systematic relationships between certain personal characteristics of teachers and their liability to role conflicts in the teaching situation. Of critical importance is the fact that the observed relationships seem to be logical and meaningful. Consider, for example, the sex difference. Since teaching is often thought of as a woman's profession, it is not surprising to find that men are more liable to conflicts in the teaching situation than women. For women, teaching is a respected occupation often representing a top-level vocational goal. They can be more tolerant of the inconsistencies in expectations. In any case, many of the constraints represented by the expectations are already placed upon females, qua females. Incidentally, the findings of sex differences here corroborate and clarify the similar results in the independent study by Andrews, who also found significant differences between teachers grouped by sex with respect to other incompatibilities in expectations. This agreement

[12] *Ibid.*, p. 38.

of the two studies is of not only substantive but methodological significance, for it points to the value of applying a single framework, so that the conclusions from one study may be juxtaposed with those from another study in comparable terms and concepts.

Consider the two items dealing with economic status: number of dependents and part-time employment. Obviously a teacher who must seek a part-time job in order to make ends meet is more likely to feel conflict in a situation that pays little but requires a relatively high standard of living than is one who for whatever reason does not need the extra income. It is interesting too that less conflict is felt by those with no dependents or with more than one dependent. The teacher with no dependents is usually single and is quite able to maintain expected standards on his salary. The teacher with several dependents is older, probably higher on the salary scale, and likely to have learned to make the necessary compromises. It is the younger person with one dependent trying to set up appropriate standards of living who feels the burden of the conflict most keenly.

Similarly, for the three items dealing with community relationships, it seems logical that teachers who do not identify with the community in which they are teaching, who find it difficult to make friends within the community, and who feel most restraint in their social life would find themselves most troubled as measured by the role-conflict instrument. Again, the relationship between the teacher ingroup and outgroup, so far as the administration is concerned, and the extent of liability to role conflict is consistent. The outgroup members might logically be expected to score higher in role conflict, and indeed they do. Finally, it is the dissatisfied teacher, the one who "would not again enter the teaching profession," who might be expected to feel more conflict.

In a number of the reported findings the observed relationships do not in themselves specify which factor is the antecedent and which the consequent, especially in the case of satisfaction and conflict. It may very well be that the conflict does not induce the dissatisfaction but that a teacher dissatisfied on other grounds is more sensitive to the conflict or uses it as a rationale for his dissatisfaction. Moreover, the characteristics studied do not exhaust the possible factors influencing differential reactions of teachers to incompatible expectations. Considered in conjunction with the work in the military school, however, the observations in the public school situation do point to systematic relationships between personal characteristics and reactions to the teaching situation. It need hardly be added that these relationships are of direct concern in understanding the dynamics of the interaction of the teacher and the school, and of course of the teacher and the administrator.

Personality and reaction to supervision

At the most general level, the model suggests that behavior in a social system reflects the individual's attempts to cope with an environment composed of patterns of expectations in ways consistent with his own pattern of personality dispositions. In a unique *experimental* study, Brown investigated the interaction among three specific factors: tension-inducing supervisory expectations, selected personality characteristics, and effectiveness of classroom teaching behavior.[13]

Psychological stress or at least tension is likely to ensue in the supervisory relationship when the teacher interprets the supervisor's comments as incongruent with his own structure of dispositions, emotional makeup, and intellectual self-image. If this stress acts as a force directing his energies toward better performance, the supervision is constructive and raises the teacher's level of effectiveness. Surely this is the intent. But the same supervision that makes for more effective performance in one individual often makes for less effective performance in another in which case it is destructive. The critical question may be raised: How is it that the same manifest supervision, that is, supervision by the same person using exactly the same words, can have such disparate results—in the one case increasing effectiveness, in the other decreasing effectiveness?

ON THE CURVILINEARITY OF THE RELATIONSHIP BETWEEN STRESS AND PERFORMANCE

Here Brown makes a distinct theoretical contribution to the model. The model, he points out, or at least preceding derivations from the model, seems to imply that the relation between conflict and effectiveness is linear or monotonic—the greater the conflict or tension, the less the effectiveness. This, he suggests, is in

---

[13] Alan F. Brown, "The Differential Effect of Stress-Inducing Supervision on Classroom Teaching Behavior," Doctoral dissertation, University of Alberta, 1961.

error. The relation between tension and performance may be curvilinear rather than linear. Performance does not necessarily deteriorate under conditions of increased conflict (or increased tension). It may go either up or down or remain unchanged depending upon individual differences in personality. Conflict may produce a decrement in effectiveness if it pushes the individual past his point of optimum drive, but it may produce an increment in effectiveness if it brings him up to his point of optimum drive. Whether there will be increment or decrement depends on at least three specific aspects of personality: (1) degree of neuroticism or anxiety, (2) level of scholastic aptitude or general intelligence, and (3) strength of need for achievement.

Briefly stated, the rationale for the assumed operation of each of these factors is as follows. Neuroticism is a proneness to breakdown under stress. This characteristic, therefore, tends to determine the extent to which an individual develops a state of "disorganization" or of "restriving" in the face of conflict. Scholastic aptitude not only is a measure of pure intellectual functioning but may also represent self-expectations built up through experience of success or failure in intellectual performance. When administrative behavior is seen as deprecating this self-structure, there is a feeling of severe threat with concomitant deterioration in behavior. Performance is likely to deteriorate more for an individual with high scholastic aptitude than for one with low scholastic aptitude. Need for achievement is reflected in a desire to do a good job, to succeed in one's endeavor. Perceived failure or threat of failure causes greater frustration in a person possessing a strong need for achievement than in one lacking such need; accordingly, change in effectiveness under stressful supervision depends on the relative strength of the need to achieve.

The three personality factors combine to form what Brown calls *drive arousability*, an attribute varying from person to person from a low to a high intensity. This is the internal or individual drive potential for performance in a situation. There is also an external or institutional drive potential or, as Brown calls it, an *objective drive stimulus* for performance in a situation. Brown puts it this way:

> There is a certain amount of stress present in every task (this is certainly true of teaching) which may be referred to as the normal

challenge of the job—this is part of the *objective drive stimulus* or factors within the environment that are reasonably constant for all individuals within a given class or activity. The objective drive stimulus is increased if, during individual supervision, a situation is created which could normally be regarded as stressful. . . . These two classes of factors—the internal and the external, the individual and the institution, the personality and the role-expectations, the drive arousability factors and the objective drive stimuli—combine (whether summatively or multiplicatively does not matter for this treatment) to form the total *effective drive potential* which varies (as a result of its component variables) from low to high.[14]

One other concept must be introduced. This is *effective reaction potential*, and it refers to an individual's potential for producing behavior that is effective relative to the task in the particular situation. It too ranges from low to high. It is a dependent variable and, if individual differences in ability to accomplish the task are held constant, varies *curvilinearly* with the drive potential. The essential relationship is shown in Figure 9-1.

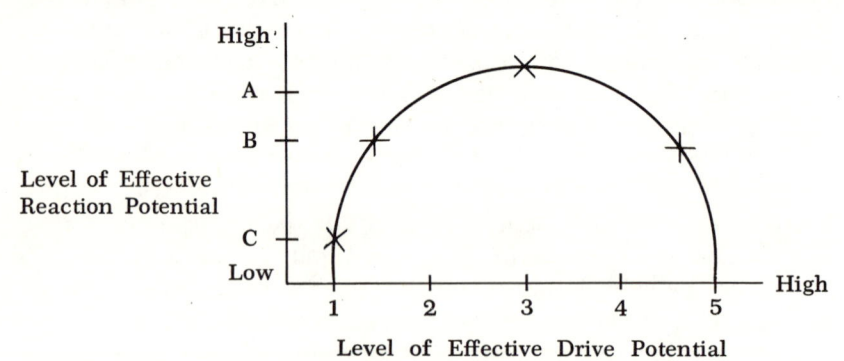

FIGURE 9-1. *Curvilinear relationship of drive level to effective performance on complex tasks. (Adapted from Alan F. Brown, "The Differential Effect of Stress-Inducing Supervision on Classroom Teaching Behavior," Doctoral dissertation, University of Alberta, 1961.)*

Here effective reaction depends on effective drive potential, which is a combination of drive-arousable factors (neuroticism, scholastic aptitude, need for achievement, and possible others) and objective drive stimuli (normal challenge and frustration of the task; other externally induced states such as stress-inducing supervision). For example, in Figure 9-1, the per-

---
[14] *Ibid.*, pp. 89-90.

formance of an individual whose level of effective drive potential was optimum for the task (fell at point 3) would *deteriorate* if his drive level were increased (moved toward 4 or 5). Conversely, a person with a low drive (say, at point 1 or 2) might, under conditions that increased the over-all drive, *improve* his performance. In effect, with increased tension the one would move downward on the curve and away from optimum performance, and the other would move upward on the curve and toward optimum performance.

If this is the general theoretical scheme, the empirical questions then become: Assuming the possibility of studying this phenomenon systematically, what will actually be observed in the performance of people as the conflict in a situation is increased? Will the performance of some of them in fact go up, of others go down, and of still others remain the same? For the administrator the more significant question perhaps is: Exactly who goes which way, and why?

It is precisely to these questions that Brown directed his inquiry by formulating the following hypotheses for experimental test:

1. Teachers placed under conditions of stress-inducing supervision will, relative to control conditions, vary both in degree and direction of change in teaching effectiveness; some will deteriorate to different degrees, some will improve to different degrees, and some will remain the same.
2. Increasing the external stress stimulus through ego-threatening or failure stress will depress the effectiveness of high-neuroticism subjects and will enhance the effectiveness of low-neuroticism subjects.
3. Increasing the external stress stimulus through ego-threatening or failure stress will depress the effectiveness of subjects evidencing experience of high scholastic aptitude and will enhance the effectiveness of subjects evidencing experience of low scholastic aptitude.
4. Increasing the external stress stimulus through ego-threatening or failure stress will depress the effectiveness of subjects possessing a strong need for achievement and will enhance the effectiveness of subjects possessing a weak need for achievement.[15]

THE EXPERIMENT

The hypotheses were tested in an experiment with 78 student-teachers at the University of Alberta during their regular teach-

---
[15] *Ibid.*, pp. 100–101.

ing activities in the public schools. The advantage of using student-teachers rather than regular teachers was that controls would be achieved over such obvious variables as age, experience, professional training, and institutional environment. Two types of data were needed: (1) observations differentiating the students by neuroticism, scholastic aptitude, and need for achievement; and (2) observations of teaching performance under usual and under supervisory stress-inducing conditions from which a "change in effectiveness" measure could be derived.

The first type of data was obtained through relevant instruments—the Maudsley Personality Inventory for neuroticism, the American Council on Education Psychological Examination for scholastic aptitude, the Edwards Personal Preference Schedule for need achievement, and the California Psychological Inventory for achievement via conformity and for achievement via independence. The second type of data was obtained through observing the actual performance of the students in the teaching situation. The subjects were visited by experimenters in the guise of faculty advisers who observe student teaching. Since such advisers regularly supervise and evaluate student teaching, the experimental "faculty advisers" were able to establish a realistic superior-subordinate relationship with students, so far as the latter were aware. Each experimenter observed two consecutive lessons: the first, a usual (or control) lesson; the second, the stress (or experimental) lesson.

Each teacher's behavior was recorded and evaluated on the standard form utilized by the university for grading student-teachers. Regardless of the quality of the performance, at the end of the first lesson the "faculty adviser" made the following series of comments designed to induce stress:

Miss _____, I'd like to make a comment about the lesson you have just taught. You are in the degree program, aren't you?

In the Bachelor of Education program we expect a high standard of student teaching. Your lesson fails to measure up to these standards. That is, you would have to receive a failure rating for this lesson.

These lessons are rather important, you know. For your sake, they help to determine your success or failure at the university and your suitability for teaching. For the sake of the pupils, they are deprived of regular instruction from their own teacher when you take over. That's why I want you to be aware of this now, before you go on with the next lesson.

You see, there are quite a number of things that you should watch out for. Your last lesson was disappointing on each of several aspects; in fact, all those things that really go to make up good teaching.

But you go ahead with the next lesson now and we'll go over these points afterward.[16]

During the lesson immediately following these comments stress was maintained by the continued evaluating presence of the "faculty adviser." The direction and degree of change in teaching effectiveness was noted on a seven-point scale (D-score) ranging from marked deterioration (-3) through zero change to marked improvement ($+3$). At the end of the second lesson a number of prescribed steps were taken to extinguish the stress.

Supervisory Stress and Teaching Effectiveness. The first hypothesis, it will be recalled, suggested that under conditions of stress the performance of some teachers will deteriorate, of some will improve, and of others will remain the same. The findings were quite clear-cut: The performance of 35 (45 percent) of the teachers deteriorated, that of 23 (29 percent) improved, and that of 20 (26 percent) remained the same.[17] *On the average*, of course, there was a deterioration of performance under supervisory stress. But the point is that apparently some individuals react to stress as if it were added motivation to do better, and others remain unaffected. Are these observed differences in reaction due to some artifact in the data, or are they systematically related to the hypothesized factors—individual differences in neuroticism, scholastic aptitude, and need for achievement?

Supervisory Stress, Neuroticism, and Teaching Effectiveness. The second hypothesis suggested that supervisory stress will tend to depress the performance of high-neuroticism subjects but enhance that of low-neuroticism subjects. On the basis of the scores obtained on the Maudsley Personality Inventory, the 78 teachers were divided into three equal groups, high, medium, and low in neuroticism. The relationship between change in effectiveness (D-score) and the neurotic classification of the subjects was then observed. Results are presented in Table 9–6.

The basic hypothesized relationship between supervisory stress, neuroticism, and teaching effectiveness receives strong

---
[16] *Ibid.*, p. 145.
[17] *Ibid.*, pp. 158–160.

TABLE 9-6

Distributions of D-Scores of Three Subpopulations of Teachers Classified by Level of Neuroticism (MPI-N) (N = 78)

Level	Low neuroticism	Medium neuroticism	High neuroticism
D-Score	f	f	f
+2	3	1	0
+1	8	9	2
0	7	7	6
−1	5	4	8
−2	2	4	8
−3	0	2	2
N	25	27	26
$\bar{x}$	+0.200	−0.259	−1.077

SOURCE: Adapted from Alan F. Brown, "The Differential Effect of Stress-Inducing Supervision on Classroom Teaching Behavior," Doctoral dissertation, University of Alberta, 1961, p. 172.

support from these data—at least with respect to the effect of stress of the one group relative to the other. The average change in teaching effectivenesse from the nonstress to the stress situation was + 0.2 for subjects with low scores in neuroticism, − 0.259 for subjects with medium scores, and − 1.077 for subjects with high scores. Put another way, although only 2 (7 percent) of the 26 subjects high in neuroticism improved in effectiveness and 18 (69 percent) deteriorated, 10 (33 percent) of the 27 mediums improved and 10 (33 percent) deteriorated, and 11 (45 percent) of the 25 lows improved and only 7 (28 percent) deteriorated. An analysis of variance disclosed that the difference in the discrepancy scores for the three subgroups was statistically significant at beyond the .001 level.

Supervisory Stress, Scholastic Aptitude, and Teaching Effectiveness. Given stressful conditions in the school situation, who would be more likely to improve in performance, who more likely to deteriorate in performance—student-teachers with higher scholastic aptitude or those with lower scholastic aptitude? Brown suggests that equally appealing but diametrically opposed conjectures could be made.[18] On the one hand, it might be hypothesized that the more able the individual intellectually, the

---

[18] Alan F. Brown, "Conflict and Stress in Administrative Relationships," *Administrator's Notebook,* 10 (March, 1962), 2–3.

better he could adjust to the changing conditions of increased stress. In this case there should be greater deterioration in performance for the less able group than for the more able group. On the other hand, it might be hypothesized that students with lower scholastic aptitude, having experienced failure under test conditions more often, might adjust more readily than the scholastically superior students, who presumably have not experienced failure so often. In this case there should be greater deterioration in performance for the more able group than for the less able group.

It is in fact the latter hypothesis that received support in the investigation. Teachers whose ACE scores were in the highest third for the group as a whole declined most in teaching effectiveness; those in the middle third declined somewhat less; those in the lowest third actually improved slightly. These findings apparently could not be attributed to regression effects or other artifacts. The data are presented in Table 9–7. The analysis of variance disclosed that the differences in discrepancy scores among the three groups were statistically significant at the .035 level.

Supervisory Stress, Need for Achievement, and Teaching Effectiveness. The fourth hypothesis was that increasing the

TABLE 9–7

Distributions of D-Scores of Three Subpopulations of Teachers Classified by Level of Scholastic Aptitude (ACE) (N = 78)

Level	Low ACE	Medium ACE	High ACE
D-Score	f	f	f
+2	4	0	0
+1	6	8	5
0	9	4	7
−1	3	9	5
−2	4	5	3
−3	0	0	4
N	26	26	26
$\bar{x}$	+0.115	−0.423	−0.846

SOURCE: Adapted from Alan F. Brown, "The Differential Effect of Stress-Inducing Supervision on Classroom Teaching," Doctoral dissertation, University of Alberta, 1961, p. 175.

supervisory stress stimulus will depress the effectiveness of subjects possessing a strong need for achievement and enhance the effectiveness of those with a weak need for achievement. The data obtained did not support this hypothesis. When the student-teachers were divided into three groups by strength of need for achievement, as had been done with neuroticism and scholastic aptitude, no differences in the effect of stress supervision on their classroom effectiveness were found. Brown offers a plausible and experimentally instructive explanation. The attempt to control for a number of nonexperimental variables had the side-effect of preventing the selection of cases at random with respect to the experimental need-achievement variable itself. As Brown puts it:

> It is ironical that the attempt to achieve a homogeneity that would control a number of non-experimental variables probably resulted in a sample that was too homogeneous for the free operation of the particular experimental variable of need for achievement.... In addition to this, the plan of the experimental procedure probably resulted in an increased uniformity of need for achievement, at least situationally. The subjects were placed in observations, were told that it was important to do a good job, and—as with observation lessons generally—saw this as a critical situation demanding a high level of motivation. The inference is drawn by the present investigator that both selective and situational factors hindered the free operation of the need-for-achievement variable in the experimental sample so that there was insufficient opportunity for the effects of the stress stimulus to discriminate between different levels. The "levels" were simply not that different.[19]

Supervisory Stress, Drive Arousability, and Teaching Effectiveness. The theoretical orientation posited at least three components of the internal drive dimension: neuroticism, need for achievement, and scholastic aptitude. These elements of personality were presumed to combine to form the drive arousability level of an individual, which, together with factors in the external world, constitutes his drive potential for a given situation. It was hypothesized that a marked increase in objective drive stimuli (such as supervisory stress) would result in differential effects upon performance, and these in fact were found in the case of neuroticism and scholastic aptitude.

---

[19] Brown, "The Differential Effect of Stress-Inducing Supervision . . . ," pp. 182–183.

The dependence of performance upon each of the two main variables under study was established when the factors were studied independently. But the theory further suggested that the differential effects would also depend on their combination, and that there was a curvilinear relationship between the effective drive potentials and effective reaction potentials. Specifically, the following hypothesis was tested with *positive* results: There will be a greater degree of performance change (incremental or decremental) shown by subjects who are at the upper and lower extremes of the personality variables than by subjects who are in the middle range. Brown summarizes his conclusions from the investigation in this outline:

A. the method of supervision does have a significant effect upon teaching behavior,
   1. the nature of the effect is predictable when elements of the teacher's personality are known,
      (a) bright neurotics deteriorate significantly when the supervision is stress-inducing,
      (b) the less intelligent but more stable personalities improve under conditions that most would regard as stressful,
      (c) those in the middle range deteriorate only slightly.
B. this effect can be explained in terms of the teacher's drive level (combined personality elements) and the drive potential of the setting, including the direct supervision,
   1. under conditions of stress, net effectiveness shows an inverse linear relationship to level of drive arousability intensity,
   2. the relationship of total effective drive potential (internal factors plus objective stimulus) is curvilinearly related to effective reaction potential: when total effective drive potential is increased through stress-inducing supervision those that were initially low on this variable move upward toward the optimum level and those that were initially high move down from the optimum.
C. stress-inducing supervision affects several components of the teaching process differentially,
   1. the more personal aspects of teaching (use of personal qualities, contact with pupils) deteriorate the most,
   2. the more "bookish" aspects of teaching (evidence of preparation for lesson, lesson plans, evidence of subject-matter knowledge) deteriorate the least, and, in fact, improve,
   3. the more traditionally pedagogical aspects of teaching (classroom management, presentation of lesson) deteriorate to an extent somewhere between the other two, approximately to the same degree as general teaching effectiveness,

4. the more intelligent the teacher, the more she deteriorates in effectiveness of classroom management and contact with pupils.[20]

IMPLICATIONS OF THE STUDY OF ROLE STRESS, PERSONALITY, AND BEHAVIOR: DIFFERENTIAL SUPERVISION AND GROUPING

From at least one point of view, what is most pertinent about this experiment is that it was derived from the model and contributed to it by clarifying a number of relationships. In this sense, the study demonstrates the fruitfulness of the formulation as heuristic for further theoretical and empirical work.[21] From another point of view, the experiment provides some implications relevant to practical problems of administrative supervision. We turn briefly to these latter issues.

It is somewhat ironical that a school administrator will urge his teachers to devote ever greater attention to individual differences among their pupils but at the same time assert the absolute necessity of "always treating all teachers exactly alike." As Brown notes, it is perhaps time for administrators to take a leaf from the books of the very persons they supervise. He writes:

> To attempt to improve supervision with the cook-book approach, or to prescribe general procedures supposedly suited to "teachers-in-general," is to overlook the individual nature of both the supervisor and the supervised. The particular characteristics of both the classroom teacher and his administrative superior will interact in a manner that uniquely influences teaching proficiency. This interaction need not produce a total absence of stress-arousing conflict in every instance for proficiency to be enhanced. Unless bland conformity is the aim, administrators must reject the naive notion that complete harmony between institutional expectations and individual predispositions must be maintained. Keeping a bovinely satisfied teaching body implies failure to provide effective stimulation where it is needed....
>
> An unvarying style of leadership discloses a lack of alertness to the human element of the task. Whether directly through individual supervision or indirectly through policy, reputation, and administrative "climate," the supervisor will have an inescapable effect upon the quality of learning. Because of variations among teachers, his

---

[20] *Ibid.*, pp. 261–262.
[21] For an application of the theoretical model to research relating to small groups of teachers, see Robert D. Gilberts, "The Interpersonal Characteristics of Teaching Teams," Doctoral dissertation, University of Wisconsin, 1961. Also see Judson T. Shaplin and Henry F. Olds, Jr., eds., *Team Teaching*, New York, Harper & Row, 1964, pp. 66–70.

effect may be other than intended; his best assurance lies in the continual readjustment of his professional activities in keeping with the differential needs and abilities of his heterogeneous staff. The discovery and accommodation of these individual characteristics is a responsibility he must be prepared, as an administrator, to assume.[22]

The problem of the heterogeneity of staff and the need for differential supervision raises the general issue of grouping individuals for maximum organizational efficiency. In a series of studies which deal with grouping in the classroom but which have implications for interpersonal relations in all manner of role-sets, Thelen describes three methods of forming groups more effectively.[23] This does not mean that supervisory stress or conflict is done away with but rather that there is greater understanding of the sources of tension and hence the possibility of more productive behavior.

The first method, *compatibility* grouping, emphasizes the goodness of "fit" or congruence in personality between teacher and student or between administrator and administered. It is based on research showing that the greater the similarity in values and attitudes among individuals, the more effective the communication among them. A second method, *homogeneity* grouping, is similar to the first one but emphasizes the commonality or "fit" within the students or the administered group without reference to the teacher or administrator. This is the method used when students are grouped according to achievement or ability. Such a group, of course, may be as heterogeneous as random groups with respect to some other criterion—social interaction, for example.

The third approach to grouping, *complementation*, takes account of differences rather than similarities among individuals. It recognizes that people tend to be threatened by one sort of individual and supported by another. When a person is with those who threaten him, even though they are quite unaware of their effect, he is inhibited and preoccupied with defending the self. Supervision under these conditions inevitably becomes stressful and anxiety-provoking in the extreme, with consequent deterioration in effectiveness. When a person is with those who support him, he is more open and less concerned with self-defense. Supervision under these conditions can raise the level

---

[22] Brown, "Conflict and Stress in Administrative Relationships," p. 4.
[23] Herbert A. Thelen, "Classroom Grouping of Students," *School Review,* 67 (Spring, 1959), 60–76.

of motivation without producing excessive anxiety and stress. Psychological complementation takes into account the threat and defense structure of individuals and of groups and their consequent reaction to supervisory stress.

In most classroom situations some combination of the several grouping strategies is used. Whatever the nature of the particular grouping, Thelen urges (1) that a more precise definition of the situation be developed, and (2) that more meaningful information about the individual be obtained[24]—or, in the terms and methods of the present model, that additional information be obtained about both the institutional role expectations and the individual personality dispositions. And what is urged for the classroom is applicable to other administrative groupings—councils, committees, departments, and so on. In placing individuals in working groups and in supervising their activity, the administrator must take into account not only the demands of the organization but the nature of the individuals—their drives, needs, aspirations, temperament, and intelligence.

To return to Brown's comments about the implications of his study:

> Perhaps the most important practical implication is the need for what has been called "differential supervision." Just as the weight of research on the teaching-learning process has led teachers to observe individual differences among pupils and adapt their instruction accordingly, so now the research on specific administrative relationships indicates the need for supervisors to be alert to individual differences in personality and aptitude among their teachers and to individualize their supervisory procedures.[25]

Toward further inquiry

At least three major issues for further inquiry emerge from the studies presented in this chapter. First and perhaps most obvious is the need for synthesizing the many studies currently available on the personality characteristics associated with prevailing roles in the educational system—the roles of teacher, principal, and superintendent. To what extent is there overlap or discrepancy among the personality correlates of these roles? Teachers be-

---

[24] *Ibid.*, pp. 66–73.
[25] Brown, "The Differential Effect of Stress-Inducing Supervision . . . ," pp. 272–273.

come principals, and principals become superintendents. But the demands upon the teacher and presumably his personality characteristics are very different from those of the principal, and we venture to say that the demands upon the principal and perhaps his personality characteristics are rather more different from those of the superintendent than one is likely to think. Yet induction into the superintendency is almost exclusively through the principalship, and induction into the principalship is almost exclusively through the teachership. How does this induction channel operate in the school system, and what are the consequences of such hard-and-fast induction procedures for educational administration? Is it possible that there is an inverse relationship between the personality characteristics required for teaching and those required for administering, and that the best person is lost to the superintendency, since he never aspires to be a teacher? We need hardly state that to raise these issues for inquiry is in no way to prejudge the answers.

A second issue calling for systematic investigation is the nature of what we may call the centrifugal and centripetal interactions between individuals because of their personality characteristics. If organizations are to function effectively, the constitution of the component face-to-face groups—the committees, work gangs, councils, departments—cannot be left to chance. Some individuals placed together tend to act cohesively, others disruptively. What is true of the group as a whole seems to be true also for the interaction between the supervisors and those they supervise. Supervisory stress does not affect all individuals quite the same way but seems related to the drive arousability potential of the persons involved. Two types of studies are indicated: (1) studies of the relative effectiveness of groups varying in composition by personality characteristics, and (2) studies of the supervisory interactions between individuals varying in drive arousability potential.

The third issue to which inquiry might be directed is the assessment of the efficiency of individuals in an organization. In the terms of the model, efficiency is the relationship between behavior and need-dispositions, and effectiveness is the relationship between behavior and role expectations. Even though equally effective, an act may be done efficiently, that is, with a minimum of psychological strain and energy, by one individual and inefficiently, that is, with a maximum of psychological strain and energy, by another. Usually the measurement of organizational productivity is against the criterion of effectiveness without reference to the criterion of efficiency. So long as the work gets done, who cares what the cost is to the individual psychologically? But there are uncounted costs to the institution that do not get into the measure of effectiveness—costs in emotional breakdown of personnel, interpersonal friction, organizational tension, and, at a more immediately tangible level, high blood pressure and ulcers.

The assessment of efficiency in relation to effectiveness poses some difficult methodological problems. For one thing, there is the already remarked upon conceptual confusion between institutional criteria and individual criteria of productivity. For another, efficiency cannot be measured apart from the particular need structure and psychological cost to the individual, and these are hard to measure. One can get an idea of how much "physical sweat" a certain act costs, but how is one to figure out how much "psychological sweat" the same act exacts? Nonetheless, despite the obvious difficulties, this is in many ways a crucial and, we venture to think, a fascinating issue—one well worth attention. A measure of efficiency in relation to effectiveness would not only channel the study of administration into fruitful theoretical directions but help refine current techniques in the selection and placement of individuals in the role structure of an organization.

Summary

The nature, variation, and effect of personality factors on selected aspects of administration in the school system were dealt with in this chapter. The general problem was examined in the context of empirical studies involving (1) the relation between teacher personality and the subject taught, and the effect of this relationship on teacher-administrator interaction; (2) the relation between certain personality variables and felt conflict in the teaching situation; and (3) the relation between personality variables and reaction to supervisory stress.

With respect to the relation between teacher personality and the subject taught, evidence was presented that teachers do in fact differ in personality according to subject-matter taught, and that the differences not only create cleavages within the school population but bear directly on such factors as satisfaction in the teaching situation and pressure to conform to organizational policies. With respect to personality differences in relation to conflict, studies in military and public school situations revealed systematic relationships between certain personality variables and reaction to role strain. In the military situation, for example, teachers high in conflict were found to be less emotionally stable, more authoritarian, and more extrapunitive than teachers low in liability to the same role strains. With respect to the interaction between personality variables and supervisory stress, the relationship between certain drive states, supervisory stress, and teaching effectiveness turned out to be *curvilinear*. That is, performance does not necessarily deteriorate under conditions of stress. It may go either up or down, or remain the same, as a function of what may be called the level of effective drive potential, which includes at least two personality factors, neuroticism and intelligence. A number of implications of the model and these findings for administrative behavior and further inquiry were discussed.

10

Value orientations and selective perception

We have conceived of a prescribed role relationship—say, the relationship between a teacher and a principal, or between a superintendent and a consultant—as being enacted simultaneously in two private situations, one embedded in the other. Each role incumbent selectively perceives and organizes the relationship in terms of his own goals, experiences, and information. These private situations are connected through whatever aspects of the existential objects, symbols, and values are present in the perceptions of both individuals. When we say that two complementary role incumbents understand each other, we mean that the area of this overlap is maximal; when we say that they misunderstand each other, we mean that the area of overlap is minimal.

In accordance with the concept of *selective perception*, the thesis may be advanced that irreconcilable difficulties in organizational relationships arise not so much from direct differences (that is, disagreements that are out in the open) as from complexities and differences in underlying values (that is, disagreements that are underground and liable to misperception). The precise way in which normative role relationships are perceived idiosyncratically is not altogether clear. Nor is it clear how needs, dispositions, and values influence perceptual processes and, consequently, interpersonal relationships. But that they do have powerful effects, and that greater understanding is called for in this domain, is emphasized among others by Bruner and Tagiuri, who put the matter as follows: "If there is to be a science of interpersonal behavior, it will rest upon the cornerstone of social perception. If for this reason only, far more effort must be expended on the task of discovering how people come to perceive other people as they do."[1]

The present chapter will explore both the nature of the value orientations of individuals in a number of role-sets in the school system and the effect of these values on the relations

---

[1] J. S. Bruner and R. Tagiuri, "The Perception of People," in G. Lindzey, ed., *Handbook of Social Psychology*, Cambridge, Mass., Addison-Wesley, 1959, vol. II, p. 650.

among the individuals involved. Included in the studies to which we shall refer were citizens, superintendents, educational consultants, principals, teachers, and pupils. We shall begin with individual value orientations and their relation to certain school variables, then turn to some aspects of selective perception as related to problems in administration.

Individual value orientations in the school system

The values people hold affect their definition of institutional roles and their perception of institutional events. More particularly, in the terms of the general model, it may be hypothesized that the nature and extent of differences in values among complementary role incumbents will have systematic effects on how they view each other and therefore on relevant administrative relations.

Consider a commonplace instance with regard to the procurement and disposal of resources: A school principal committed to "economically liberal" values finds himself working with a school superintendent committed to "economically conservative" values. Each time the principal requests an item requiring a major expenditure of funds a serious struggle ensues. As one principal remarked recently, "This language lab is a great idea. Now if we can only convince the superintendent and the board. Even with NDEA paying for half of it they're so conservative they back away each time you mention a dollar—much less several thousand." Obviously, such disagreement in basic value orientations affects the interpersonal and administrative relations within the school system.

PUPIL, TEACHER, AND PRINCIPAL VALUES

It may be instructive, by way of introducing the general matter of value orientations in the school setting, to consider in concrete terms a number of questions regarding the values held by pupils, teachers, and principals: (1) Do the values held by pupils and teachers differ by type of school? (2) Are the values held by pupils related to such variables as school performance and career choice? (3) Are there systematic variations in the values of teachers and of principals by variables such as age?

The instrument used to answer these questions was constructed by Prince.[2] On the basis of the formulation of traditional and emergent values already described, he developed the Differential Values Inventory (DVI), a forced-choice questionnaire containing 64 pairs of items, one item in each pair representing a traditional value, the other an emergent value. The respondents were required to choose the more *desirable* alternative. Here are some sample items:

A. Feel that "right" and "wrong" are relative terms.
B. Feel that I should have strong convictions about what is right or wrong.
A. Choose to work with people I like in a job I don't like.
B. Choose to work with people I don't like in a job which I like.
A. Say what I think is right about things.
B. Think of the effect on others before I speak.
A. Feel that happiness is the most important thing in life.
B. Feel that being respected is the most important thing in life.

The instrument was scored by summing the number of traditional alternatives chosen, so that a high score represented traditional value orientations and a low score emergent value orientations. We may briefly discuss the data obtained by Prince and others with respect to each of the questions raised.

Pupil and Teacher Values. To explore possible differences in value orientations of pupils and teachers by type of school, Prince administered the DVI to representative groups of freshmen, seniors, and teachers in sixteen public high schools, four religious high schools, and two private high schools. On a priori grounds, the private schools were thought to be most "progressive," the religious schools most "conservative," and the public schools "in-between." As Table 10–1 shows, substantial differences were found for both pupils and teachers by type of school. With the exception of the differences between public and private school freshmen, all differences between schools were statistically significant at the .05 level or better. The differences between teachers, seniors, and freshmen in the same type of school were all small and not statistically significant. Although a discussion of the function of the school in changing student values would take us far afield, it seems clear that differences in values

---
[2] Richard Prince, "A Study of the Relationships Between Individual Values and Administrative Effectiveness in the School Situation," Doctoral dissertation, University of Chicago, 1957.

TABLE 10-1

Value Patterns of Teachers and Students in Three Types of Schools

Type of school[a]	TEACHERS N	Mean DVI	SENIORS N	Mean DVI	FRESHMEN N	Mean DVI
Public	75	33.50	420	33.78	439	31.71
Religious	15	38.56	88	37.47	78	36.67
Private	10	27.50	61	30.31	40	30.90

[a] All differences among schools significant at the .01 level, except between public and private seniors significant at the .05 level, and between public and private school freshmen not significant. The differences among teachers, seniors, and freshmen within each type of school are not statistically significant.

SOURCE: Adapted from Richard Prince, "A Study of the Relationships Between Individual Values and Administrative Effectiveness in the School Situation," Doctoral dissertation, University of Chicago, 1957, p. 106.

are found *among* the different types of schools, showing that the instrument did differentiate among groups. However, *within* each type of school there were no significant differences between the values held by freshmen and the values held by seniors. One reason may very well be that, if values are acquired by a process of identification with significant others, the possible others available in the school setting as represented by peers and by teachers tend to have the values already held by the freshmen when they come to the school.

Pupil Values, School Performance, and Career Choice. If the values held by individuals do affect their behavior, then it could be hypothesized that students with a traditional value pattern, which includes the work-success ethic and future-time orientation, ought to perform better than those with an emergent value pattern, which includes the ethic of sociability and present-time orientation. Accordingly, Prince classified the high school students into superior and inferior achievement groups and compared their DVI scores. There were 109 students with superior grades and 82 with inferior grades. The mean DVI score of the superior students was 36.86; of the inferior students, 30.48. Since these results could be obtained through the operation of a number of factors, such as social class differences, Prince separated the 131 middle-class students from the 191 students composing the total superior and inferior achievement groups, divided these into superior and inferior achievement subgroups, and compared their DVI scores. The results were the same: The superior group was significantly more traditional in value orientation than the inferior group. The data are given in Table 10-2.

TABLE 10-2

Relationship Between Student Values and Grades, Holding Social Class Constant

Grades of students in middle social classes	N	Mean DVI	t	P
Superior	67	36.45	3.812	.001
Inferior	64	30.77		

SOURCE: Adapted from Richard Prince, "A Study of the Relationships Between Individual Values and Administrative Effectiveness in the School Situation," Doctoral dissertation, University of Chicago, 1957, p. 119.

Although this analysis controlled for social class, it did not control for such factors as age, sex, and intelligence. A succeeding study by Stone[3] attempted to control for the latter factors. He compared three 24-person groups of "traditional," "emergent," and "middle" students, matched for age, sex, social class, and intelligence on two criteria of achievement: a single year's average and cumulative grade averages. The findings were the same. For example, with cumulative grades as the criterion, in the traditional group 29 percent were high, 54 percent average, and 17 percent low in achievement; in the emergent group 4 percent were high, 42 percent average, and 54 percent low in achievement.

There are at least two possible explanations for these results. One is that the criterion was teacher grades, which quite possibly were predicated on the degree of similarity or difference between the value orientations of the pupils and of the teachers. Battle[4] had, in fact, demonstrated in a preceding study that higher grades were given by teachers to pupils with values like their own. Since, as we shall see, older individuals typically have

---

[3] Shelley C. Stone, "A Study of the Relationship Among Values, Family Characteristics, and Personality Variables of Adolescents," Doctoral dissertation, University of Chicago, 1960.

[4] Haron J. Battle, "Application of an Inverted Analysis in a Study of the Relation Between Values and Achievement of High School Pupils," Doctoral dissertation, University of Chicago, 1954.

more traditional values, the traditional child is more likely to resemble his teacher in values and hence, with the grading bias found by Battle, to receive the better grade. A second explanation resides in the DVI itself. A traditional score represents a belief that people "ought to" work hard and delay present gratification for future gratification; an emergent score represents a belief that people "ought to" be sociable and enjoy present gratification without considering the future. To the degree that individuals act in accordance with their stated beliefs, the differences in school performance between traditional and emergent students are quite understandable.

That the values represented by the DVI are operative in the second as well as in the first sense is supported by data on the relation between values and choice of courses in school and career in life. Prince[5] compared the DVI scores of 320 high school seniors who had chosen the college preparatory course and 279 who had chosen general, vocational, or terminal courses. He also compared the DVI scores and the course choices of some 686 high school freshmen. In both cases students choosing college preparatory courses were more traditional in values. Stone[6] made similar observations with respect to career choice and found that traditional students chose much higher occupational levels than did emergent students. These relations between values and academic and career choice, although interesting, must be viewed with caution because they are obviously affected by school achievement. But Stone[7] showed that there were also perhaps more fundamental differences in career styles and goals between the two groups that could not so readily be attributed to educational experience alone. For example, using questions from the Cornell Student Questionnaires, he showed that students high in traditional values more often than students high in emergent values tended to prefer "altruistic" careers.

Teacher and Principal Values. Prince[8] administered the DVI to the principals and a sample of 100 teachers of varying ages in 20 schools. The mean value score for all teachers was 33.28 and for all principals 35.55. Thus Spindler's[9] hypothesis that teachers are more emergent than principals may be well

---

[5] Prince, *op. cit.*, pp. 115–116.
[6] Stone, *op. cit.*, pp. 76–79.
[7] *Ibid.*, p. 133, pp. 80–84.
[8] Prince, *op. cit.*, pp. 84–90.
[9] G. D. Spindler, "Education in a Transforming American Culture," *Harvard Educational Review*, 25, no. 3 (Summer, 1955), 145–156.

taken. Of greater interest to Prince, however, was the relation between values and age. Dividing the teachers into four age levels—under 30, 30 to 39, 40 to 49, 50 and over—he found that there was a significant difference between teachers under 30 and teachers of 50 and over, the latter being more traditional. Similarly, when he divided the twenty principals into the ten youngest and the ten oldest, the cutting point being age 47, the difference in values was also significant, the older principals being more traditional.[10]

Again we wish to emphasize that these and the preceding observations are more suggestive of further work than definitive in themselves, although there is considerable evidence corroborating the findings. McPhee,[11] for example, found a similar relation between age and value for a sample of 498 respondents under 50 years of age and 133 respondents over 50 years of age, and Abbott[12] did the same for some 200 school board members. Abbott did not find the indicated relationship for a small sample of superintendents. His study revealed, however, that school board members were more traditional in values than parents, citizens, and superintendents, again in keeping with Spindler's hypothesis that school board members are more traditional than other school-related reference groups.[13]

Value orientations and relations in role-sets

There seems hardly any question that individuals constituting a role-set may differ in values, and an important question arises: What specific effects follow the differences in values between pupils and teachers, teachers and principals, school superintendents and board members, school superintendents and citizens?

PUPIL-TEACHER RELATIONS

Prince[14] raised the issue: How do differences in values between pupils and teachers affect the pupils' relation to their teachers? For example, would Student A, with a value pattern similar to

---

[10] Prince, *op. cit.*, pp. 86, 89.
[11] Roderick F. McPhee, "The Relationship Between Individual Values, Educational Viewpoint, and Local School Approval," Doctoral dissertation, University of Chicago, 1959.
[12] Max G. Abbott, "Values and Value Perceptions of School Superintendents and Board Members," Doctoral dissertation, University of Chicago, 1960.
[13] Spindler, *op. cit.*, p. 151.
[14] Prince, *op. cit.*, pp. 91–93.

his teacher's, rate this teacher higher in effectiveness than would Student B, whose value pattern is unlike the teacher's? Prince administered the DVI to some 550 high school seniors and to 100 of their teachers, asking the students to describe their teachers on a "What Does Your Teacher Do" scale in each of eight areas such as classroom management, "putting across" subject matter, handling students "who get out of line," and so on. From their descriptions a teacher effectiveness score from 1 to 5 could be derived. These scores could then be compared with the relative difference or similarity in pupil-teacher values. It turned out that there were 171 teachers with high effectiveness ratings (score 1–1.49) and 169 teachers with low effectiveness ratings (score 3.50–5.0). Comparison of the pupil-teacher values in the two groups suggested a greater difference in pupil-teacher values in the low-teacher-effectiveness group than in the high-teacher-effectiveness group. That is, in our example, Student A, whose values were similar to his teacher's, described his teacher more favorably than did Student B, whose values were dissimilar to his teacher's. And it must be noted that these findings held even though the students observed the *same* behavior of the *same* teachers. Thus the same teacher behavior may elicit different pupil reactions depending on the "fit" between pupil and teacher values. As we shall see, findings of this type have numerous implications for the administrator in the recruitment, selection, and assignment of teachers.

TEACHER-PRINCIPAL RELATIONS

Just as the relation between pupil and teacher may be affected by the undercurrent of value orientations, so is the relation between teacher and principal likely to be similarly affected. Consider the case of a teacher with one set of values who brings a student who has misbehaved to a principal with another set of values. The teacher believes that such a student is a *troublemaker* and *should be punished*. The principal feels that he is *troubled* and *should be understood*. Without thinking of the effect on the teacher, the principal says, "There must be some good in the boy; let's find out what it is." Afterward the teacher reports to his colleagues, "I took Johnny to see Mr. _____, and as usual he did nothing—absolutely nothing—about it."

On the basis of the model, Prince[15] hypothesized that there would be a relationship between teacher-principal values and

---
[15] *Ibid.*, pp. 95–97.

teacher confidence in the principal's leadership and evaluation of his effectiveness. He administered the DVI to the principals of 20 schools and to a sample of 100 of their teachers. In addition, the principal rated the effectiveness of the teachers, and they rated their confidence in his leadership, his effectiveness as a principal, and their own satisfaction. When the five schools with the greatest difference in teacher-principal values were compared with the five schools with the smallest difference in teacher-principal values, it was found that the teacher ratings of confidence in the principal's leadership and of his effectiveness were higher in the second than in the first set of schools. That is, teachers with emergent values tended to have most confidence in and perceive as most effective a principal who also had emergent values. Teachers with traditional values tended to have most confidence in and perceive as most effective a principal who also had traditional values. It is not the values themselves but their fit in the role-set that seems important in the teacher's estimate of principal performance.

CITIZEN-SUPERINTENDENT RELATIONS

At least in more or less closely related role-sets—those between pupil and teacher and between teacher and principal—there are systematic effects between the fit in broad value orientations and the relations of the role incumbents. The question then arises: Would similar effects be found when the interactions are more distant, as in the case of relations between the citizenry and the superintendent? It is apparent that success in the superintendency depends in no small measure on community approval of the educational program. Would the similarity or difference in values held by the citizens and the superintendent, then, be related to approval or disapproval by the citizens of what was being done in the schools?

McPhee[16] explored various aspects of this problem, using 632 subjects in four Midwestern communities who responded to two instruments in addition to the DVI. One instrument was Bullock's General Educational Problems Scale, which, in contrast to the broad value orientations of the DVI, focuses on educational orientations. The other was Bullock's Your Schools Scale, a measure of school approval or disapproval.[17] The Educational

---

[16] McPhee, *op. cit.*, pp. 123–140.
[17] Robert P. Bullock, "School-Community Attitude Analysis for Educational Administration," Doctoral dissertation, Ohio State University, 1956.

Problems Scale is a 12-item instrument assessing "traditional" or "modern" viewpoints with respect to school practices, a modern viewpoint being defined as acceptance of the educational goals more commonly held by teachers than by nonteachers. The validity of the scale was determined by its ability to discriminate between teachers and nonteachers. Typical items are:

All children who fail to come up to the minimum passing grade in a subject should be required to repeat the subject until they learn it.

In school a child should be made to be and act as much like a miniature adult as he can.

In general, book-reading, drill, and recitation are more effective educational activities than performing experiments, taking trips, or watching demonstrations.

The Your Schools Scale is a 20-item instrument designed to elicit the relative approval or disapproval of schools in a community by having the respondent react along a five-point continuum from strongly agree to strongly disagree with such statements as:

Our schools are effective in teaching good work habits.

Our schools are doing a good job of teaching children social skills.

The more important basic skills and knowledges are being effectively taught in our schools.

The investigator undertook a variety of analyses, but central to our interests here are the tests of four specific hypotheses: (1) Respondents with emergent values will have more modern educational viewpoints than will respondents with traditional values. (2) Citizens with modern educational viewpoints will tend to approve the schools more than those with traditional educational viewpoints. (3) Citizens with emergent values will tend to approve the schools more than those with traditional values. (4) Citizens whose values and educational viewpoints are similar to the values and educational viewpoints of the superintendent will express a higher degree of school approval than citizens whose values and viewpoints differ from those of the superintendent.

The results for the first two hypotheses were quite straightforward. With respect to hypothesis 1, respondents with emergent values did have more modern educational viewpoints.

The data were highly significant with extreme groups, and further analysis showed that the general relationship held over the entire range of respondents. With respect to hypothesis 2, respondents with modern educational viewpoints did tend to be higher in approval of the schools than those with traditional viewpoints. Here, however, caution in generalizing from the findings is indicated, for it is not inconceivable, as McPhee points out, that in some situations the relationship would not exist. For example, if a school system were itself traditional, citizens with modern educational viewpoints might well be lower in approval than those with traditional educational viewpoints because the prevailing practice would run counter to their beliefs about desirable school practices. Further work with various types of communities is needed.

With respect to hypothesis 3, the data did not support the logic of the prediction. Despite the systematic relationship between broad values and specific educational viewpoints, and between the educational viewpoints and evaluation of the schools, such relationship was not found between the broad values and the evaluation of the schools. In effect, the individual's specific educational viewpoints seemed to have a direct bearing on his opinion of the schools, but his general values did not. It may well be that the general values are not sufficiently focused, so that, although they are related to educational viewpoints, they are not sufficiently nuclear to education, as McPhee says, to have an appreciable effect on the way an individual responds to questions about the local schools. Again, further work is needed.

Finally, with respect to hypothesis 4, although the data on values were in the hypothesized direction, they did not reach a statistically significant level, but the data on educational viewpoints were both in the hypothesized direction and statistically significant.[18] That is, the more congruent the educational viewpoints of the citizen and the superintendent, at least at the extremes, the more likely is the citizen to express approval of the schools. To be sure, the relation was weak, and the effect must not be overemphasized. Nonetheless, when taken with the previously noted effects for pupil-teacher and teacher-principal relations, it is well worth further consideration.

A word ought to be said, if only as suggestive of further

---

[18] McPhee, *op. cit.*, p. 77.

inquiry, about why the broad DVI-type values were operative in the other cases but only the more specific educational viewpoints were operative in this instance. We may speculate that the difference resides in the proximity of or distance between the role incumbents involved in the several types of role-sets. In the pupil-teacher and teacher-principal role-sets the relations are proximate—eye to eye, as it were—and the general values of those involved are wittingly or unwittingly communicated and brought to bear on each other. In the citizen-superintendent role-set, the relations are usually distant—almost never eye to eye; the superintendent's values remain unknown or at best guessed at. However, his educational viewpoints are of course communicated through speeches, newspaper articles, and school publications and do become a matter of issue. Citizens can compare their own beliefs with his, and the extent to which they agree or disagree may affect how much they approve of the schools he administers.

Perception of roles

Conflict and misunderstanding in a social system are often—and appropriately—dealt with as a function of existential contradictions in values, in personal need-dispositions, or in expectations for role performance. With regard to role expectations, we study the *actual* differences between the views of two or more reference groups as to what is appropriate behavior in a given role, or the *actual* contradictions between the views of the role incumbent and those of one or more of the reference groups. But conflict and misunderstanding can also rise from another source. The differences may not be existential but *perceptual*. The role incumbent may believe that he and his reference groups have significantly different views when they are actually the same, or conversely that they are the same when in fact they are different. In either case, conflict is a result not of any real differences in expectations but of perceived differences in expectations.

These two issues are central in this domain: (1) Are there identifiable types of error in role perception, and if so, what is the extent of these errors in an educational organization? and (2) In what way is error in the perception of roles related to performance in the roles? We shall consider these issues in turn.

TYPES OF PERCEPTUAL ERROR

That the school superintendent must know his community hardly needs reiteration. That there are various subpublics in the community with specific expectations for the superintendent's behavior, and that his effectiveness depends at least in some measure on their support, is also self-evident. But the superintendent's perception (or misperception) of the actual expectations held by the several subpublics is by no means known in any systematic way. Accordingly, Hencley[19] explored the relationship between the expectations of a number of the salient subpublics (school board members, school personnel, and various citizen groups in the community) and the superintendent's perception of these expectations. In all, the subjects under study were 15 superintendents of schools in Indiana, Illinois, and Wisconsin, 102 school board members, 776 school personnel, 425 business people, 310 PTA council members, and 194 labor council members.

The investigator devised a 64-item questionnaire dealing with typical expectations for superintendent behavior in the areas of curriculum development, pupil personnel policies, financial and business management, and so on.[20] Each item could be marked "strongly agree" (that is, insist that the expectation be fulfilled as stated) to "strongly disagree" (that is, insist that the expectation not be fulfilled as stated). Three types of responses were secured: (1) the superintendent's expression of his own expectations, (2) the superintendent's perception of the expectations of each subpublic or reference group, and (3) the actual expectations of each reference group. Three sets of comparisons were then made for each item: (1) a comparison of each superintendent's expectations with his perception of each reference group's expectations, (2) a comparison of each superintendent's perception of the expectations held for him by the reference groups with the reference groups' actual expectations, and (3) a comparison of each superintendent's own expectations with the expectations of each reference group.

Attention has already been called to the conceptual and methodological complexities in this type of study (pp. 213–215).

---

[19] Stephen P. Hencley, "A Typology of Conflict Between Superintendents and Their Reference Groups," Doctoral dissertation, University of Chicago, 1960.

[20] Staff Associates, *Observation of Administrator Behavior*, Chicago, Midwest Administration Center, University of Chicago, 1959.

However, the investigator was aware of the difficulties and did take certain precautions. He was consistent in phrasing his questions in normative terms, not confusing them with predictive terms; he delimited the boundaries of his defining populations; he posed his questions with reference to a particular situation. But several difficulties remain and cannot be resolved. For example, although the defining populations were asked to state their expectations for a particular superintendent, the superintendent himself was asked to make estimates for a whole group. It is difficult to say what such estimates mean, for even within carefully defined populations there is inevitably a range of expectations. Nonetheless, the possible categories of disagreement between a superintendent and five of his reference groups as derived by Hencley are well worth considering.

Comparisons of the superintendents' responses with those of the five reference groups on each of the 64 items presented the possibility of 320 instances of agreement or disagreement. There were 233 disagreements (or "conflicts") and 87 agreements (or "congruences"). Further analysis revealed that 82 percent of the 233 disagreements could be accounted for by three basic errors categorized by the investigator as follows:

1. *Trouble-seeking*, accounting for 22 percent of the disagreements. In this type of error the superintendent's own expectations and his perception of the reference group expectations were significantly different, when in fact his expectations and the actual expectations of the reference group were *not* significantly different. In effect, the superintendents were "trouble-seeking"—they thought their expectations were different from those of their reference groups when in actuality their expectations were the same.

2. *Innocent*, accounting for 32 percent of the disagreements. This is the reverse of the preceding type of error. Here the superintendent perceived no differences between his own expectations and those of the reference group when in fact there were significant differences between his own expectations and the actual expectations of the reference groups. In effect, the superintendents were "innocent"—they thought their expectations and those of their reference groups were the same when in actuality their expectations were different.

3. *Keen*, accounting for 28 percent of the disagreements. In this type of conflict the superintendent's perception and the

actual expectations of the reference groups did not differ, but a significant difference did exist between the superintendent's own expectations and the actual expectations of the reference groups. That is, the perceptions of the superintendents were essentially "keen"—they described the expectations of the reference groups accurately, albeit these expectations did not agree with their own.[21]

In addition to these three major types of error or conflict, four others accounting for the remaining 18 percent of disagreements were identified. In the investigator's terminology, these were (1) "cautious semikeen" (the superintendent perceived an existing conflict but underestimated its magnitude); (2) "bold semikeen" (the superintendent perceived an existing conflict but overestimated its magnitude); (3) "overlooked support" (the superintendent and the reference group were in essential agreement but the former failed to recognize his strong reference group support); and (4) "reversed polar" (the reference group expectations were the exact opposite of what the superintendent perceived them to be).[22]

It will be recalled that there were five reference groups: school board, school personnel, parents, business, and labor. What was the relative magnitude of disagreement between the superintendent and each of these groups? The investigator's initial hypothesis was that the magnitude would increase systematically from intraorganizational groups (school personnel) to interstitial organizational groups (school board members) to extraorganizational groups (parents, business, labor). The data did not entirely substantiate the hypothesis. Although the magnitude of both the actual and perceived disagreement was in fact greatest for the extraorganizational groups, there was no appreciable difference between the school personnel and the school board members in this respect. The data are presented in Table 10-3.

Perhaps most noteworthy is the unanticipated finding that the superintendents seemed to perceive the business group as most divergent from their own views when in fact the parent group was most divergent. The number of *actual* differences was greatest for the parent group; the number of *perceived* differences was greatest for the business group.

---

[21] Hencley, *op. cit.*, p. 49.
[22] *Ibid.*, pp. 73–74.

TABLE 10-3

Number of Disagreements Perceived by Superintendents Compared with the Number Actually Identified

Reference group	CONFLICT PERCEIVED[a] (Number of items for which SA and SP are significantly different)	CONFLICT IDENTIFIED[b] (Number of items for which SA and RGA are significantly different)
Board of Education	22	31
Teachers	23	30
Parents	33	42
Business	41	35
Labor	30	34

[a] This is the discrepancy between the superintendent's actual expectations (SA) and his perceived expectations (SP) for each of the indicated reference groups.
[b] This is the discrepancy between the superintendent's actual expectations (SA) and the actual expectations of the indicated reference groups (RGA).

SOURCE: Adapted from Stephen P. Hencley, "A Typology of Conflict Between Superintendents and Their Reference Groups," Doctoral dissertation, University of Chicago, 1960, p. 53.

It is possible to pose this issue in a more powerful way, that is, in terms of the relative *trust* and *distrust* the superintendent has in the several reference groups with which he must deal.[23] Distrust is implied in the trouble-seeking, overlooked support, and bold semikeen types of error, whereas trust is implied in the innocent and cautious semikeen types. In the one case, the actual expectations are the same but the superintendent is suspicious or distrustful and believes them to be different; in the other, the actual expectations are different but the superintendent is unsuspicious or trustful and believes them to be the same. In Table 10-4 the data are ordered in terms of the trust-distrust dimension.

This analysis brings to light a provocative finding—one well worth further investigation. Superintendents seem most distrustful of the business reference group and most trustful of the parent group, even though, as is shown in Table 10-3, the greatest actual disagreement is with the parents. In the investigator's own words, "This striking finding merits restatement: although superintendents are most suspicious and least trustful

[23] *Ibid.*, p. 53.

TABLE 10–4

Conflicts Characterizing Superintendent Trust and Distrust of Reference Groups

Characteristic	Board	Teachers	Parents	Business	Labor
Distrust[a]	9	15	11	22	10
Trust[b]	20	20	22	12	21

[a] Combines trouble-seeking, overlooked support, and bold semikeen conflicts occurring with each reference group.
[b] Combines innocent and cautious semikeen conflicts occurring with each reference group.

SOURCE: Adapted from Stephen P. Hencley, "A Typology of Conflict Between Superintendents and Their Reference Groups," Doctoral dissertation, University of Chicago, 1960, p. 54.

of the business group, the real source of conflict in their social system is with the parent group."[24]

A further caution with respect to this study must be observed, as the investigator himself points out. Although a variety of expectations and situations were sampled, and a number of conflicts between superintendents and others were found, there is no way of assessing the generality of the findings without additional investigation. We cannot say whether the superintendents here were especially high, low, or only average in any of the types of conflict, or whether the relation between these superintendents and their reference groups is typical in situations elsewhere. There are no standards or norms for comparison. But having pointed to the possible empirical restrictions on the data, we may add that they do not detract from the conceptual usefulness of the observed types of disagreement or conflict and of the issues raised for further study by the application of the proposed taxonomy.

Numerous other studies from a variety of points of view attest to the prevalence of disagreements in the perception of expectations and role behavior in the educational setting. Sweitzer,[25] for example, found differences both in the definition of desirable behavior and in the perception of the actual behavior of superintendents by principals, teachers, school board mem-

---

[24] *Ibid.*, p. 54.
[25] Robert E. Sweitzer, "The Fulfillment of Role-Expectations and Teacher Morale," Doctoral dissertation, University of Chicago, 1957.

bers, and the superintendents themselves. Brottman[26] likewise found many significant differences in the perception of the principal's behavior by parents, teachers, central office personnel, and the principals themselves. Halpin, in a notable study, reported significant lack of consensus among board of education members, teachers, and superintendents in the perception of the superintendent's behavior in the "initiating structure" and "consideration" aspects of leadership activity. He suggested that the role the superintendent adopts when working with board members may be very different from the one he adopts when working with his staff.[27]

Whether the observed variation in the perception of the same role by different members of a role-set is due to personality differences, whether the variation in perception is due to the circumstance that the administrator adopts different miens when dealing with different reference groups, whether the reference groups are simply in different positions to view the same administrative behavior and therefore obtain different perceptions of it, or whether some combination of all these is operative, the important fact here is that extensive disagreements in the perception of administrative role behavior in the educational setting do exist.

EFFECT OF AGREEMENT OR DISAGREEMENT IN ROLE PERCEPTION

Although there is hardly any question that differences in the perception of mutual expectations exist, a major issue may be raised: Is agreement or disagreement in the perception of complementary role expectations related to the effectiveness of the interaction between the role incumbents?

Perhaps the most revealing observations in this domain come from studies of the interaction of consultants and school administrators. Ferneau,[28] for example, investigated the working relationships of consultants in state departments of education with school administrators in the local setting. His basic hypothesis was that consultation services will be ineffective if

---

[26] Marvin A. Brottman, "The Administrative Process as Perceived in the Behavior of Elementary School Principals," Doctoral dissertation, University of Chicago, 1962.

[27] Andrew W. Halpin, *The Leadership Behavior of School Superintendents*, Chicago, Midwest Administration Center, University of Chicago, reprinted, 1959.

[28] Elmer F. Ferneau, "Role-Expectations in Consultations," Doctoral dissertation, University of Chicago, 1954.

the administrator and the consultant do not perceive the complementary role expectations along the same lines.

From an analysis of consultation services,[29] the investigator identified three patterns of expectations, each defining a distinct type of consultant service:

1. The consultant as *expert*. In this pattern, efforts are directed at arriving at the "right" answer to the particular problem in the specific situation. The consultant is presumed to have expert knowledge which the consultee does not have—knowledge based on absolute principles. The best use of the consultant's time is to get the right answers from him, and to apply this answer to the given problem in order to arrive at the correct solution at the earliest possible moment.

2. The consultant as *resource person*. In this pattern, efforts are directed at providing a variety of relevant information so that the individuals involved in the situation can have a choice of alternatives applicable to the solution of the problem. The consultant is presumed to possess a wide range of experiences, either vicarious or direct, on which the consultee may draw. The best use of the consultant's time is to permit him to provide information but to let the consultee himself consider the material in relation to the specific problem.

3. The consultant as *process person*. In this pattern, efforts are directed toward developing a method of working together in order to bring about needed changes so that those involved in the problem will be able to arrive at their own solution. The consultant is presumed to have special skills in human relations, and the best use of his time is to allow him to work in such way as to make the consultee more competent to handle not only the particular problem but similar problems in the future.[30]

To assess the overlap in expectations between consultant and administrator, a hypothetical but typical circumstance for a consultation was formulated:

An administrator wanted to make revisions in the curriculum and program of instruction because of high rate of drop-outs, truancy, and apathy to the school. He was faced with a faculty which was indifferent or hostile to such change and an apathetic community. Since he felt inadequate to handle this situation he called upon the state department of education for assistance and it sent a consultant to help him with his problem.[31]

---

[29] William W. Savage, *Consultative Services to Local School Systems*, Chicago, Midwest Administration Center, University of Chicago, 1959.
[30] Elmer F. Ferneau, "Which Consultant?," *Administrator's Notebook* 2 (April, 1954), 2.
[31] *Ibid.*

Series of ten statements of possible expectations of a consultant and ten statements of possible expectations of an administrator with respect to the consultative situation were devised. The statements dealt with such issues as kind of planning before the consultation, methods for identifying the problem, and steps in arriving at an acceptable solution. Each statement was phrased in three ways: according to "expert" expectations, "resource" expectations, and "process" expectations. Thus, the final instrument contained sixty paired-comparison items permitting a consultant or an administrator to make choices which resulted in a description, in expert, resource, and process terms, of what, if he were an administrator, he expected of a consultant, and vice versa. The overlap between any given administrator and consultant, at least with respect to these patterns, could then be examined, and the relation of agreement or disagreement to other variables, such as evaluation of the success of the consultation, could be observed.

The instrument was given to 132 school administrators in Kansas, Michigan, Nebraska, and Wisconsin who had received consultative services, and to 43 consultants who had provided the services. In addition, each respondent was asked to evaluate the outcome of the consultation.

The results confirmed the basic hypothesis. When an administrator and a consultant agreed on the expectations, they tended to rate the actual consultation favorably; when they disagreed, unfavorably. And apparently the evaluation of success and failure was in a measure independent either of the particular expectations or of the manifest behavior. The critical variable was the extent of overlap in the participants' perception of the expectations, whatever they were.

Although both administrators and consultants definitely preferred the process approach, there was no evidence that any one type of consultant, expert, resource, or process, was more successful than another. The crucial factor was that consultants and administrators had to perceive the complementary expectations along similar lines if the consultation was to be effective—at least as judged by both the consultant and the consultee.

We shall consider later the implications of these findings for further conceptual and empirical work. Here we wish only to indicate the implications of the study for practice as stated by the investigator. Even if the consultant's behavior is the preferred mode of operation—as a process person—his performance is by no means likely to be judged effective unless the consultee conceives of his role in the same terms. In Ferneau's words, "The consultant who operates as a 'process' person is usually destined to fail if he agrees to give assistance to an administrator who conceives the role to be that of the 'expert.' Or, if he operates as an 'expert' when the administrator looks upon the consultants as 'resource' or 'process' persons, he is again limiting very severely the chances of success in the consultation."[32]

Again, the residual issue of this study, as of others, is how easily the conclusions can be generalized from the particular situation involving consultant relationships to other situations involving other types of role relationships. Theoretically, the observed relationships between role perception and role interaction should be quite general. Indeed, another study along the same theoretical lines, but dealing with a different substantive area, reached conclusions similar to those of the study of consultants. Moyer examined the relationship between the expectations of teachers and of administrators for leadership in the educational setting and the effect of congruence or discrepancy in the perceptions upon teacher satisfaction.[33] He found that the greater the agreement between the teacher and the principal in their respective expectations, the more favorable are the teacher's attitudes toward the actual work situation. In effect, what seems to emerge from these studies is this central conclusion: At least so far as the judgment by the participants in a complementary role relationship as to the success of the interaction is concerned, the important issue is not the extent to which one of the participants conforms to some absolute principle of desirable behavior but the extent to which there is overlap in the perception of the complementary expectations for the interaction.

Self-role perceptions

The problem of adjustment for a given individual in a social system, and more specifically between a teacher and principal,

---
[32] *Ibid.*, p. 4.
[33] Donald C. Moyer, "Teachers' Attitudes Toward Leadership as They Relate to Teacher Satisfaction," Doctoral dissertation, University of Chicago, 1954.

may be viewed from two vantage points. As an outside observer might see it, conflict arises from the incongruence between the principal's expectations for the role of teacher and the teacher's own needs in the teacher role. The greater the incongruence, the greater the conflict. Thus, the teacher may be disposed to form particularistic relations with pupils whereas the principal expects the role of teacher to call for universalistic relations with pupils. Certain relationships may be postulated between the degree of this type of disagreement and the teacher's satisfaction, effectiveness, and confidence in the administrator's leadership. Such conflict has been dealt with in Chapter 8.

Conflict can also be viewed, within the terms of the present model, from another, more subtle and ultimately perhaps more important standpoint. That is, it may be seen as having its source in the *perceptions* of the teacher. This approach focuses on the congruence or incongruence between what the teacher perceives as the principal's expectations for the teacher role and the teacher's own dispositions in the role. The assumption is that the principal's role definition for teachers will be perceived differently by various teachers in the same school. Each teacher will hold to be real that which he perceives and will behave according to what he perceives. Here too there may be discrepancies—discrepancies between the teacher's needs in the teacher role and his perception of the principal's expectations for the role. Certain relationships may be formulated between the degree of this type of conflict—that is, what we may call self versus perceived role conflict—and the teacher's confidence in the administrator's leadership, teacher satisfaction, and teacher effectiveness. It is with this type of conflict and the concomitant relationships that we are concerned here.

SELF-ROLE PERCEPTIONS OF TEACHERS

Merton Campbell[34] made the assumptions we have indicated, and formulated four hypotheses regarding the relation between the self-role perceptions of teachers and a number of self-ratings and ratings by principals:

1. Teachers with a low degree of conflict between self and perceived role will express greater confidence in the leadership of the principal than will those teachers with a high degree of conflict.

---

[34] Merton V. Campbell, "Self-Role Conflict Among Teachers and Its Relationship to Satisfaction, Effectiveness, and Confidence in Leadership," Doctoral dissertation, University of Chicago, 1958.

2. Teachers with a low degree of conflict between self and perceived role will rate themselves higher in teaching satisfaction than will those teachers with a high degree of conflict.
3. Teachers with a low degree of conflict between self and perceived role will rate themselves higher in teaching effectiveness than will those teachers with a high degree of conflict.
4. Teachers with a low degree of conflict between self and perceived role will be rated by the principal as more effective teachers than will those teachers with a high degree of conflict.

This phase of Campbell's study deals with "perceived" expectations and is a complement to the phase described in Chapter 8, which dealt with "actual" expectations. The problems of the representativeness of the sample, the nature of the effectiveness ratings, and the type of instrumentation have already been discussed. There is in addition the problem that data regarding the level of conflict and the ratings of effectiveness (whether of oneself or of others) are often obtained from the same subjects—in this case the teachers—and are thus not independent. In the present work, data regarding conflict and effectiveness were obtained not only from the teachers themselves but ratings of the teachers' effectiveness were also given independently by their principals. This, of course, does not abolish the manifold complexities in this type of study (see pp. 213–215)—for example, the validity of these ratings. But it is a step in the right direction.

Measures of the degree of conflict between self- and perceived role were obtained from a comparison of the teachers' expressed needs in the teaching situation and their perceptions of their principal's expectations for the teacher role. Using a modified Q-sort technique, the investigator asked teachers to rank sixty items of possible teacher behavior (for example, "develop and use a detailed lesson plan, because good planning means good teaching," "maintain the classroom in whatever state of order and appearance is personally felt to make teaching easiest," and so on) in two ways: first, according to what they thought the principal expected them to do, and second, according to what they wanted to do. In addition, the teachers filled out a self-rating form on various aspects of their satisfaction in the teaching situation, their effectiveness as teachers, and their confidence in the principal's leadership. The principals rated each of their teachers in teaching effectiveness. The instruments provided the following measures for a sample of 284 teachers in

15 elementary schools in Illinois and Wisconsin: degree of self- versus perceived-role agreement or disagreement, teacher ratings on their own satisfaction and effectiveness as teachers, their confidence in the principal's leadership, and the principal's rating of the teachers' effectiveness.

The hypotheses were then tested by dividing the teachers into an upper quarter and a lower quarter in self- versus perceived-role conflict and comparing the groups in their own ratings of satisfaction, effectiveness, and confidence in the principal's leadership, and the principal's rating of their effectiveness.

The first hypothesis was that low-conflict teachers would express more confidence in the principal's leadership than would high-conflict teachers. The hypothesis was substantiated.[35] The second hypothesis was that low-conflict teachers would rate themselves higher in teaching satisfaction than would high-conflict teachers. This hypothesis was also substantiated.[36] One explanation for these results is that perception of the principal's expectations as opposing the teacher's own dispositions thwarted the teacher's self-expression, causing frustration with consequent decrements in confidence in the principal and satisfaction in the teaching situation. Another line of argument suggests that one cannot say anything about the direction or the meaning of the relationships. The observed data are artifacts resulting from the fact that the measures of relative congruence and of relative confidence and satisfaction are based on the verbal responses of the teachers themselves. The first explanation may be too "pat," but the second, although it may be a plausible alternative, cannot be accepted out of hand in light of the observed relationships to the ratings of effectiveness—one by the teachers themselves and the other by their principals.

The third and fourth hypotheses, it will be recalled, dealt with the relationship between this type of conflict and two separate ratings of teacher effectiveness—self-ratings by the teachers and ratings of the teachers by their principals. The hypothesis that teachers low in conflict would rate themselves higher in teaching effectiveness than those high in conflict was *not* substantiated.[37] As we have already indicated in Chapter 8, virtually all teachers rated themselves about average, thus prohibiting

---

[35] *Ibid.*, p. 114.
[36] *Ibid.*, pp. 107–111.
[37] *Ibid.*, pp. 111–113.

any differentiation with respect to other variables. However, the principals were able to make distinctions in the effectiveness of their teachers, permitting a test of the hypothesis that teachers low in conflict would be rated more effective by their principals than those high in conflict. This hypothesis *was* substantiated.[38] It is noteworthy that these results are based on the measure of conflict obtained from the teachers and a measure of effectiveness obtained from their principals. To be sure, certain qualifications in the results must be borne in mind. The strength of the effect is not the same in all schools; there are situational variations. But this point may be made: in the interaction between the administrator and the teacher, or more generally among members of a role-set, the crucial issues may be not the actual expectations involved but the perceived expectations.

On the process of perception

It is impossible to enter here into any extensive exploration of the problems and processes of perception. But in view of the powerful effect of perceptual differences on administrative interaction, a brief account of at least one point of view regarding the issues and mechanisms of perception is in order.[39]

By the time we are ready to react "meaningfully" to an object, message, or event, we are ready to react to it in a particular way. We have some attitude or set—in the terms of the present model, some *disposition*—toward the object, message, or event. The attitude or set determines in some degree what we will see and hear, what we will remember and forget, what we will think and say, and what we will do. Its significance is that it "predisposes" each individual to react in a particular personal way to the apparently same public situation. In this sense, as we have seen, the same expectations of a role may be perceived idiosyncratically by the different members of a role-set. Granted that individual dispositions affect perception and consequently manifest behavior. How do they do so?

Suppose a certain amount of redness—say, a blotch of red paint on a white card—is shown at rapid exposure times. If the observer is not color-blind, fairly soon he will identify it as some-

---

[38] *Ibid.*, pp. 113–114.
[39] The discussion in this section is drawn largely from J. W. Getzels, "Attitudes at Work," *Adult Leadership* 5 (February, 1957), 245–246, 256.

thing red. Suppose now that the same amount of redness is shown under exactly the same conditions, but in the shape of an ace of spades. What is seen? Evidence from an experiment of some years ago[40] suggests that one might have trouble seeing anything in the second situation, or at least identifying the color correctly and rapidly as red. The experimental subjects tended to say in this situation that the color was brown, or purple, or black and red mixed, or lighter than black, or blacker than red. Why the difference between the two events? Presumably the amount of redness in the stimulus is the same. Why is seeing the right color more troublesome in the one instance than in the other?

One answer may be found in the effect of sets and personal dispositions founded in past experience. We have difficulty seeing *red* because when something is in the shape of an ace of spades we are prepared to see *black*. The internal private disposition affects the way we tend to perceive the public event or "reality." In the particular instance, we may make a perceptual compromise between the disposition and the reality by "seeing" *brown* or *purple* or *black and red mixed*.

The effect of personally held values on perception that we observed in the study of administrators and board members may be demonstrated with somewhat greater precision by reference to a classic laboratory experiment by Postman, Bruner, and McGinnies.[41] A number of college students were given the Allport-Vernon *Study of Values*, on the basis of which they were divided into six value groups, each composed of individuals scoring highest on one of the following values: religious, political, social, economic, aesthetic, and theoretical. The students were then shown for a fraction of a second each of 36 words, 6 representing the religious value, 6 the political value, 6 the economic value, and so on.

The experimental question was: Would there be a systematic relationship between the value profile or disposition of the individual and the kinds of words he recognized most quickly

---

[40] J. S. Bruner and L. Postman, "On the Perception of Incongruity: a Paradigm," *Journal of Personality* 18 (1949), 206–223.

[41] L. Postman, J. S. Bruner, and E. McGinnies, "Personal Values as Selective Factors in Perception," *Journal of Abnormal and Social Psychology* 33 (1948), 142–154. An alternative interpretation of the results to the one given by the authors and described here may be found in R. W. Solomon and D. W. Howes, "Word Frequency, Personal Values, and Visual Duration Thresholds," *Psychological Review*, 58 (1951), 256–270.

and correctly? Would, for example, a person high in economic values tend to recognize the economic words more readily than, say, the social words? Conversely, would a person high in social values tend to recognize the social words more readily than the economic words?

The results were highly significant. There was a systematic relationship between the values held by the individual and the ease with which he recognized the relevant value words. A subject highest in economic value and lowest in social value tended to perceive the economic words most easily, the social words least easily. A subject highest in social value and lowest in economic value tended to perceive the social words most easily, the economic words least easily. The values and dispositions acted as differential "sensitizers" to environmental phenomena, emphasizing some events and deemphasizing others.

Moreover, as the experimenters pointed out, a value or disposition held by an individual does more than this: it actively distorts the reality to conform with the way he is "disposed" to see it. For example, confronted with the word "sacred," a subject low in religious value gives the following sequence of responses at successive exposure: "sucked," "sacked," "shocked," and only then "sacred." Another subject, low in aesthetic value, confronted with the word "elegant," sees "hypocrisy." Individual perception here provides almost a critical commentary on the object to be perceived.

We refer finally to an experiment illustrating the tendency to "distort" reality to conform to the way the individual is disposed to perceive it. This is the famous study by Else Frenkel-Brunswik.[42] Children in the sixth, seventh, and eighth grades were given a series of tests, on the basis of which they were divided into two groups. One group was characterized by relatively prejudiced and authoritarian attitudes or dispositions, the other by relatively unprejudiced and democratic attitudes and dispositions. The same story was read to all the children. It dealt with how pupils in a certain school reacted to some newcomers to their neighborhood. After an interval, the children were asked to reproduce the story.

In the context of the present inquiry, we may conceive of the story as a message and ask how the perceptual and memory

---

[42] E. Frenkel-Brunswik, "Intolerance of Ambiguity as an Emotional and Perceptual Personality Variable," *Journal of Personality 18* (1949), 108–143.

processes of children with different dispositions toward certain aspects of reality may change the message. Three noteworthy results were reported: (1) The story as told mentioned that one of the newcomers was "the son of a Negro who worked in a hotel." That is all that was said of this particular newcomer. In reporting what they had heard, or in any case remembered, the prejudiced children tended to describe the newcomer in an unfavorable light much more frequently than did the unprejudiced children. (2) This negativistic tendency in the perceptual and memory processes of the authoritarian children was not limited to the description of the boy with the minority status. The authoritarian children in general recalled more undesirable than desirable qualities of *all* the newcomers. That is, although they remembered correctly, they remembered *only one side*. (3) The story included mention of a fight, though it was by no means the focus of the story. Nevertheless, 43 percent of the authoritarian children proceeded to make the fight the central point of the story. Eight percent of the democratic children did the same. In short, one group of children with one set of dispositions tended to keep to the facts in retelling the story; the other group, with another set of dispositions, tended to distort the story to conform to their attitudinal preconceptions.

Here we see past experience, beliefs, attitudes, and dispositions at work on ongoing perceptual and cognitive processes. The subjective reality of past experience with the ace of spades gained ascendance over the immediate objective reality of the color red. The subjective reality of a particular set of beliefs and attitudes toward Negroes imposed itself on what was actually said about the Negro in the message. An individual is likely to emphasize or deemphasize words that are congruent or incongruent with his values.

What are the mechanisms through which individual perceptual processes act selectively to regularize and to distort, to emphasize and to deemphasize certain aspects of the common environment? An analysis of the investigations permits us to identify at least four relevant mechanisms, which, we need hardly add, by no means exhaust the possibilities:[43]

---

[43] For a further discussion of these and other mechanisms, see, in addition, F. C. Bartlett, "Social Factors in Recall," in H. Proshansky and B. Seidenberg, eds., *Basic Studies in Social Psychology*, New York, Holt, Rinehart and Winston, 1965, pp. 32–39; and G. W. Allport and L. J. Postman, "The Basic Psychology of Rumor," *Basic Studies in Social Psychology*, New York, Holt, Rinehart and Winston, 1965, pp. 47–58.

1. *Assimilation.* A disposition exerts a powerful attractive force upon phenomena. It provides the subjective context for making objective events significant. It gives meaning and cohesion—even if false meaning and spurious cohesion—to what might otherwise be contradictory and puzzling. For example, the color red was assimilated to the preconception that something in the form of an ace of spades must be black. The prejudiced children assimilated the neutrally described Negro newcomer to their subjective negative image of the Negro and gave him unfavorable characteristics nowhere mentioned in the story (message) as actually presented.

2. *Rationalization.* When a set or attitude is in operation, the facts opposed to it may be rationalized even into their opposite in order that the opposed evidence will conform to the pre-existing belief or disposition. For example, the word "elegant," which is opposed to the individual's dominant attitudes toward the environment, becomes "hypocrisy." If a Negro is said to be working in a hotel, and no specific occupation is mentioned, he is not conceived of as a manager or clerk but as a porter or dishwasher. To the prejudiced individual, the object of the prejudice may not be seen in a different light even when he is explicitly defined in other terms. Accordingly, a Negro who is described as "poor" is so because he is "lazy," but a Negro who is described as "rich" is so not because he is hard-working but because he is "uppity." A Negro who is described as "dirty" is "the way all Negroes are," but if he is described as "clean," he is only "the exception that proves the rule."

3. *Simplification.* If the varied phenomena of reality are to be assimilated to a given attitude and placed without loose ends into the preconceived context, the complexity of the real data must be simplified. A common denominator equable to the value orientation or the disposition must be found. Recalcitrant facts are either distorted until they fit or rejected altogether. The result of this simplification is of course the typical one-sidedness and rigidity of the dogmatist, who sees everything in either-or terms. The experiment in communication provides an excellent illustration of this mechanism in operation. The authoritarian children learned only one side of the newcomer's characteristics—the negative side matching the hearers' dispositions.

4. *Accentuation.* Just as simplification acts selectively to play down everything that threatens personal belief or disposition, accentuation acts selectively in the opposite direction. It

emphasizes phenomena supporting the personal belief or disposition. A particular element of reality that happens to fit especially well into the preconception is exaggerated out of proportion to its true importance, and the individual accepts this caricature of the phenomenon as if he were dealing with its entirety. The authoritarian individual, with his preconception of the world as a hostile place, tends to accentuate the incidental mention of a fight until it becomes the focus and point of the whole message.

To summarize this brief account of one view of perception: Involved in the act of perceiving are our beliefs, attitudes, values, and dispositions. In a sense, these are the prisms through which reality is filtered into experience through the mechanisms of assimilation, rationalization, simplification, and accentuation. It is in terms of such mechanisms that we may understand at least some of the individual differences that were found in the perception of the same role by the different members of a role-set. It is perhaps also in these terms that we may gain some knowledge of why we do not learn as readily from the new as from the old, why facts, however obvious, are often of little consequence in changing opinions, and why the past may be more important than the present in shaping administrative policy for the future. This is not to say that actual structural and organizational factors are not significant in understanding administrative relationships —as preceding chapters have shown, they are very significant indeed. But as the studies in this chapter suggest, individual dispositional effects must also be included.

Toward further inquiry

The studies cited in this chapter must be considered exploratory investigations important not so much because of the data presented or of any unalterable conclusions they provide but because they bring to light significant issues for further speculation and systematic inquiry. There is, for example, an obvious need to repeat the studies with samples drawn from other types of organizations and for different organizational levels.

Also needed are studies founded on direct observation rather than on observations derived from paper-and-pencil instruments. And needed perhaps most of all are longitudinal rather than cross-sectional investigations. These would permit the observation of changes in perception that occur over time. Among the questions that might be raised are the following: When the patterns of structure and communication of an organization are altered, are there concomitant alterations in the patterns of perception among the members of a role-set? Do perceptual errors increase or decrease? Would specific attempts to diminish discrepancies in the perceptions of a given role-set increase the effectiveness of the relationships among its members? Suppose knowledge of the nature and extent of perceptual error were fed back into an organization—would systematic change ensue? Would the different types of error—say, the trouble-seeking and the innocent errors—be affected differentially?

The data for the investigations reported in this chapter were obtained from ongoing school systems. Many of them wanted "feedback" of the results, and in fact in a number of the schools this apparently was given. It is regrettable that no attempts were made to observe the possible effects (or lack of effects) of the knowledge when communicated to the schools. In the case of the studies of consultant relationships, for example, would the superintendents and the consultants now try to ascertain each other's expectations for the relationship as they had apparently not done before? And would this make any difference in the outcomes? Would principals and teachers try to gain a more explicit awareness of each other's role expectations? And would such awareness make any difference in, say, the confidence of the teachers in their principal's leadership?

Two other lines along which work in this domain might be extended ought to be mentioned. Nearly all studies thus far have explored single variables such as value or expectation, and for the most part with the implicit assumption that the relationship between variables is linear. Studies of the interaction among several relevant variables in multivariate designs need to be undertaken. Also, most studies have used role as central to the problem of perceptual error in an organization. Work might be done on the perception of personality in the administrative relationship. Nearly everyone has had the experience of getting a first impression of another individual and then the difficulty of shaking this first impression despite evidence to the contrary. What factors determine first impressions in the administrative interaction, and what mechanisms make these impressions so impervious to change?

Summary

This chapter has focused on a number of perceptual problems in administrative relationships. Studies involving values revealed that individuals tend to be selective in their perceptions. One's own values influence his perception of the other members of a role-set.

Studies in the perception of roles gave rise to a taxonomy of perceptual errors made by the superintendent. Some errors may be categorized as trouble-seeking—the superintendent perceives the expectations held for him by one of his reference groups as significantly different from his own when in actuality they are the same. Other errors may be categorized as innocent—the superintendent perceives the expectations held for him by the reference group as essentially the same as his own when in fact they are significantly different. These misperceptions tend to bear systematic relationships to certain administrative interactions. The congruence or discrepancy of a teacher's expressed needs in the teaching situation and his perception of the expectations for the teacher role as held by the principal were shown to be related to his level of satisfaction, his effectiveness in teaching as judged by the principal, and the teacher's expression of confidence in his principal's leadership. In all, the several studies lend support to the basic notion that malfunctioning in a social system and important problems facing the administrator may have their source not only in structural strains deriving from actual inconsistencies among expectations in the component roles but also in perceptual conflicts deriving from inconsistencies in the views of the same component roles by the various members of a role-set, even when the actual expectations are not inconsistent.

Finally, we dealt briefly with the general problem of perception, at least from one theoretical point of view, indicating a number of the mechanisms that account for individual differences in seeing the same role or event. We suggested some directions for further inquiry in this domain with special reference to the problems of administration.

In the ensuing three chapters we explore a number of implications for administrative practice of the conceptions and research discussed in the preceding chapters. We focus especially on problems of staff, board, and community relationships.

11

Staff relationships

As was stated previously, a school or college may be conceived of as a social system. A social system is purposive, peopled, structured, normative, and sanction bearing. Administration within a social system is based on the assumption of a hierarchy of superordinate-subordinate relationships, which are seen as the locus for allocating and integrating roles and facilities in order to achieve the goals of the social system. Implications for administrator-staff relationships growing out of this framework will be suggested in the present chapter.

Entrance into teaching

Since teachers represent the largest single professional group in the nation, the recruitment, selection, training, and certification of personnel for teaching and allied positions constitute an enormous task. The new supply of teachers each year numbers about 200,000. The framework presented here is applicable to the process by which these people become members of school and college staffs.

ROLE COMPATIBILITY

Prospective teachers, as well as those who control entrance into teaching, are concerned with the problem of role compatibility. Role, it will be recalled, refers to the dynamic aspects of positions, offices, or statuses within the social system—in this case the school or college—and each role has its set of norms or expectations. For instance, a biology professor was discharged from a Midwestern university for advocating premarital sex relations because he was violating the expectations held for professors at that institution.

In schools and colleges, since there are many positions, there are many roles. School directories, for example, list superintendent, business manager, director of pupil personnel, supervisor of music, counselor, elementary school principal, secondary school principal, elementary teachers by grade level from kindergarten through sixth grade, and secondary teachers by subject area—English, history, foreign language, science, mathematics, music, art, home economics, industrial arts, business, and others. College faculties are usually even more differentiated and characterized by additional specialization.

Furthermore, numerous school systems and institutions of higher education have their own unique expectations. What is expected of teachers in Scarsdale and New Trier is quite different from what is expected of those in many other high schools of the nation. The research expectations held for professors in major graduate schools are quite different from the teaching expectations held for professors in undergraduate divisions of colleges and universities. In view of this diversity in positions and among institutions, a wide range of people probably can be recruited and trained for education, but a position in a school or college is obviously not suitable for everyone.

An examination of possible role conflicts, as suggested by the framework, may help us understand the importance of role compatibility. Each teacher has a number of reference groups—the most obvious are his administrative superordinates, his fellow teachers, the parents and patrons, and the students—and each group expects certain things of him. On some matters the expectations may be in agreement, but on others they may differ sharply. For example, the principal may expect the teacher to serve on a school committee dealing with the revision of the curriculum and spend time after school meeting with that committee. The teacher's peers, however, may frown on any committee meetings that extend beyond school hours. The teacher in this situation is caught in a role conflict between reference groups.

Role conflicts also emanate from different expectations within a single reference group. If the principal of an elementary school and the supervisor of mathematics in the central office of the school district differ in their ideas about how arithmetic should be taught, a role conflict exists because of the varying expectations held by the administrative superordinates, a single reference group for the teacher.

A third type of role conflict may be present when a teacher or administrator is asked to assume two roles—to wear two hats, as we commonly say. The music teacher who must double as an English teacher, the counselor who must also serve as disciplinarian, the teaching principal who instructs pupils part of the day and directs a staff the other part may experience the conflict stemming from two different roles.

Those who expect to become teachers should know that some role conflict is probably inherent in the job. Those who help select and train teachers should do their best to induct into the profession people who can "take" a certain amount of role conflict. Apparently some people are better able than others to accept and to work with conflicting role expectations.

PERSONALITY COMPATIBILITY

It will be remembered that the personal or idiographic dimension of the model was concerned with people's need-dispositions, including their cognitive styles and abilities, and that need-dispositions are driving forces within individuals. These forces may not be fully perceived by the person himself, and most of us who observe others' behavior are not fully prepared to recognize and cope with their need-dispositions. Even so, enough is known about them to suggest that severe personality conflicts make acceptance of the teaching role most difficult.

As was indicated in Chapter 9, some of the line officers at Air University found it very hard to perform in the teaching role.[1] Officers who were high in felt conflict had greater "feelings of inferiority" and were more "nervous," "introverted," "depressive," "rigid," "stereotyped," "extrapunitive," and "defensive." Since standard personality instruments were used to detect these characteristics, it may be that such instruments will be of assistance in the selection and training of future teachers.

Implications growing out of a concept of role-personality compatibility for teaching have relevance for a number of institutions, including school systems, colleges and universities, state departments of education, and the organized teaching profession. School systems can help in the recruitment of prospective teachers and often provide the laboratory for student teaching. Teacher education is a specific function in a great variety of colleges and universities. Certification of teachers has been placed, legally, almost entirely in the hands of state departments of education. If these agencies are to coordinate their efforts in the selection and training of teachers, with particular reference to understanding the teaching role and the personality demands upon those who would fill that role, the organized teaching profession must show the way in terms of increased knowledge and appropriate action.

[1] J. W. Getzels and E. G. Guba, "Role Conflict and Personality," *Journal of Personality*, 24 (September, 1955), 74–85.

Employment and assignment

In the area of staff relationships, activities having to do with the selection, employment, and assignment of personnel occupy a prominent place. These functions are generally decentralized in American schools and colleges; each school system and each college or university seeks personnel and allocates duties among those who join the organization. The chief executive, be he superintendent or president, usually retains a certain amount of responsibility for these functions. However, in some school systems they are largely delegated to the principals of individual schools, and in colleges and universities department chairmen frequently have considerable voice in deciding who shall be added to the staff and what the duties of staff members shall be. In large school systems, employment is often delegated to a director or an assistant superintendent in charge of staff personnel. Whatever the administrative arrangements, personnel have to be hired and assigned in every school and college.

In some cases, particularly in large city school districts, the employment function has been routinized and made highly impersonal. Such procedures reflect, quite unintentionally perhaps, a view of administration that was best set forth by Taylor and Bobbitt. In that view, organizational demands were the sole criterion for employment, and candidates were assessed in terms of those demands. Actually, teachers who accepted employment were seen as interchangeable parts to be put in organizational slots as needed. The present model has quite different implications for the employment and assignment of personnel.

JOINT EXPLORATION

The point at which anyone, particularly a professional person, explores the possibility of joining a school or college faculty is a most significant juncture for both the person and the organization. It is at this point that spokesmen for the organization should clarify its purposes, procedures, and expectations. Indeed, they would ordinarily do well to invite the prospective faculty member to visit the school or college to confer with administrative personnel and with future colleagues. A number of public school systems report that teachers can do more to help possible candidates decide for or against joining the organization than can administrators. Communication between employees and prospective employees of an organization is both verbal and nonverbal; what people are may speak more loudly than what they say.

Similarly, many colleges and universities have found that members of a particular department can give a prospective member of that department the best view of what life is really like in the institution in which appointment is being considered. Institutional purposes as reflected in teaching loads, quality of students, time for research, and demands for service to the field can and should be explored with the officials of an institution, but they should also be discussed with present staff members. Since both administrators and staff are subject to selective interpersonal perception, as noted in Chapters 4 and 10, a true assessment of the values and expectations of an institution is possible only as one notes how they are seen by people who occupy different places in that institution.

Although it is important to the organization and to the prospective employee to clarify organization purposes, procedures, and expectations at the point of employment, it is equally necessary to clarify the strengths, needs, and inclinations of the person seeking employment. Organizations achieve their goals only through people. Organizations are more productive if their workers derive personal satisfaction from the kind of activity required for the achievement of those goals—that is, if there is congruence between the organizational expectations and the individual's cognitive and affective dispositions. This congruence, as we have seen, is the substratum for satisfaction in the terms of the model.

The most strategic time to match man and job is at the point of employment. Some organizations have sufficient flexibility to adjust to many personal idiosyncracies of employees; other organizations are much less flexible. Schools have less flexibility than colleges, and colleges less than major universities. Among institutions in each of these categories there is considerable range, however, and the predispositions of the prospective employee must be viewed in terms of the expectations or range of behavior likely to be found acceptable in the institution in which he is interested.

For example, many educational institutions are not set up to encourage staff members to theorize, to do research, and to write. To bring into these organizations teachers whose inclination is toward these activities not only would be dishonest but would result in inefficiency for the individual and impair the effectiveness of the system. We recall a brilliant scholar, although one with a number of idiosyncracies, who joined the staff of a state university. After two years he was notified that his term appointment would not be extended. Why? The man had impugned the program of the institution, disparaged the work of many of his colleagues, and scoffed at the values held by many people in the state. But his disposition to be critical of the culture, of institutions, and of colleagues was known at the time he was considering joining the faculty. Moreover, the culture of the state and the nature of the university were well known. We suspect that a more careful assessment of the temperament of the man in question and of the expectations of the situation would have predicted conflict from the beginning and might have prevented an unfortunate experience on the part of both university and professor. This same scholar, by the way, without change in his dispositions or behavior, was eminently effective in another institution where the role expectations were different, the chief criterion of performance being what the man was contributing to his field of scholarship.

To reiterate, the time of employment is an opportunity for joint exploration of the organization and the man—the organization, for its expectations; the man, for his predispositions. When this is well done, the prospects for the organization to achieve its goals and for the individual to gain personal satisfaction from participation in its work will be enhanced. When employment is approached in this manner, initial assignment in the organization becomes obvious. Over time, subsequent assignments should be approached in the same way.

SITUATIONAL LIMITS AND DIVERSITY

Our next point, already alluded to, is that the prospective employee should be matched with the permissive limits of the organization. Organizations characteristically have rather well-defined role expectations for employees. Or, to put it differently, nearly every situation has givens, conditions that must be met, limits beyond which certain behavior will not be acceptable. For example, the president of a church-related college reported recently that in seeking new staff members he tried to get the best assessment possible from the chairman of the division and the academic dean. Then he added, "We also get evaluations from at least three people in the field regarding their academic preparation and their views regarding the church." Clearly, in this situation views regarding the church was one of the givens. Only when college and candidate were compatible on this point could other factors relevant to employment be taken into account.

But there is another equally important point. Organizations should seek, within limits, diversity in the personality structure of individuals even in the same role-set. In schools and colleges these limits are somewhat wider, we suspect, than in some other kinds of organizations. To demand little diversity among individuals would tend to make life within the organization rigid and probably militate against innovation. Rigidity and the status quo might actually be fostered in certain organizations such as the military, but in most schools and colleges a more stimulating and innovative climate is desirable. Disagreements may be a forerunner of destructive conflict. But they may also be the spur to fruitful dialogue with consequent constructive change.

Despite our predilection for conditions which encourage innovation in an organization, we recognize that many individuals prefer stability to innovation. Hemphill and others[2] found that teachers in elementary schools rated principals who tended to *maintain* conditions more highly than they did those who attempted to *change* the organization. Perhaps all of us cling to that which we know and fear that which is unknown. Even so, we still think that an organization made up of people who are sufficiently diverse in background, viewpoint, and disposition to assure some consideration of alternatives at decision-making points will be a more stimulating and a more productive one.

This discussion of organizational limits and staff diversity is made more meaningful when two concepts pertaining to role adaptation, as noted in Chapter 5, are employed. In any organization the process of socializing the personality of staff members is always at work. For instance, in his study of elementary school principals Bridges[3] found that the diversity among principals new in the position tended to disappear among principals old in the position. Apparently the longer people remained in the same role,

---

[2] John K. Hemphill, Daniel E. Griffiths, and Norman Fredericksen, *Administrative Performance and Personality*, New York, Bureau of Publications, Teachers College, Columbia University, 1962, p. 328.

[3] Edwin M. Bridges, "Teacher Participation in Decision Making: Interaction of Personal and Situational Variables," Doctoral dissertation, University of Chicago, 1964.

the less they differed. The other process of adaptation is the personalization of role. Most organizations allow a staff member some leeway to give personal expression to a given role. Thompson[4] found that this was the case even in a religious order in which many role expectations are well established and often minutely prescribed.

Socialization of personality is premised on the presence of some flexibility in the individual. Personalization of role is premised on the presence of some flexibility in the organization. Both people and organizations vary in degree of flexibility, a factor, as we have already indicated, which needs to be assessed at the point of employment. An approximate fit at the time of employment gives promise that a tolerable congruence between the normative and personal dimensions may be sustained while the individual is a member of the organization.

We have suggested that employment and assignment activities are strategic ones in the life of an organization. We have noted that, since their direction is largely decentralized in schools and colleges, many administrators are involved in planning and implementing employment procedures. And we have also noted the importance, both for the individual and for the organization, of joint exploration at this juncture.

Supervision and work conditions

The model, it will be recalled, is built on the assumption that every organization has superordinates and subordinates. The superordinate is ordinarily expected to supervise, in some fashion, the subordinate, and conversely the subordinate is expected to accept some form of supervision. The superordinate is also assumed to have some control over the work conditions which exist in the organization. But it must always be borne in mind that the subordinate is not merely passive in this situation. Although the role of the superordinate has received considerable attention, the role of the subordinate has been largely ignored. These factors, and other aspects of the model, may suggest to the practicing administrator a number of implications pertaining to supervision from both points of view.

---
[4] Sister Mary St. George Thompson, "Modification in Identity: A Study of the Socialization Process During a Sister Formation Program," Doctoral dissertation, University of Chicago, 1963.

SELECTIVE INTERPERSONAL PERCEPTION

The phenomenon called selective interpersonal perception described in Chapters 4 and 10 is relevant here. The reader will remember that each individual perceives his situation idiosyncratically. Inevitably, events taking place in an organization have different meanings to the members of the organization. For example, in one university recently, faculty retirement provisions were being reconsidered. One change under discussion was designed to give the university administration some discretion in deciding who should be retired at age 65 and who might be asked to remain beyond that age. To the administration this flexibility appeared to be highly desirable, but many faculty members felt that it bespoke undue administrative control and even indignity toward professors.

In part, these differential perceptions by administration and faculty resulted from the different placements of each in the organization. The administration was required to view the total operation, to think of all faculty members as they neared retirement age, to come up with a retirement plan which would assure vigorous and productive scholars. The faculty members inevitably saw the problem from a much more personal orientation. "How will this new plan affect me? My colleagues?" were questions of real moment to them.

Of equal importance with placement in the organization as a possible explanation of differential perception is the fact that each organization member brings a unique experience and background—and his own set of cognitive and affective dispositions—to his understanding of phenomena. The teacher with a middle class background, for instance, usually has some difficulty in recognizing worth in lower-class children, whereas the principal who comes from a lower-class family may be more tolerant of their behavior. These differences in perception could easily reach into the area of pupil control or discipline. The teacher might regard profanity as a type of pupil behavior calling for reprimand, or even more severe punishment, and expect support from the principal in administering it. The principal might recognize that for some pupils profanity is customary speech and does not necessarily imply disrespect or other improper conduct.

Many institutional practices in our society ignore the existence of selective interpersonal perception. Our courts, for example, operate on the assumption that two witnesses to the same event would see the same things. Were the reports of the two witnesses to vary appreciably, the courts would assume that at least one was *deliberately* falsifying the truth. Actually, a number of studies, including some reported in Chapter 10, have demonstrated that people tend to see what they are prepared to see. Much of what anyone perceives is in his own eyes. An administrator would do well to recognize that any two members of an organization, even if he is one of them, may see an event quite differently. Each brings his own background to the scene; neither is necessarily dishonest. A basis for understanding is reached when these differences can be discussed as differences in perception.

CLARIFICATION OF ROLE EXPECTATIONS

A second concept suggested by the model providing illumination in the area of supervision has to do with clarifying the expectations the organization has for each member. By definition, the superordinate is the spokesman for the organization. In a high school, for instance, the principal may expect the teacher to meet five classes every day, to sponsor the debating club, to participate in faculty meetings, to attend PTA meetings, and to be conservatively groomed and dressed. If he does not make these expectations clear, or if he has one perception of them and the teacher another, the basis for difficult relations between them has been laid. Even minor deviations from expected behavior on the part of the teacher, such as the growing of a beard or the wearing of sport shirts in the classroom, may displease the principal. Obviously, the superordinate needs to make organizational expectations clear to the subordinate.

In some organizations there are conflicting sets of expectations, and even an official spokesman for each set. In one school district where the programs of the elementary schools were organized on a departmental basis the cental office included a supervisor for each department—language arts, social studies, science, mathematics, and so on. Over the years these supervisors had in a sense become line officers for the content areas they supervised. They might more properly have been designated assistant superintendents for language arts, for social studies, and for each of the other areas.

Each teacher in the elementary schools found that he had as many bosses as there were supervisors. Moreover, the supervisors did not completely agree on the expectations they held for teachers. The science supervisor was quite certain that too much of the pupils' day was being devoted to English and social studies and too little to science. The mathematics supervisor expected all teachers of mathematics to enroll in an in-service education program to learn the new mathematics. Many teachers looked upon such a requirement as an imposition, and a number of supervisors in other areas were not convinced that the program was needed.

To make matters even more complex, some of the elementary school principals thought that they had an obligation to coordinate the *total* instructional program within their own buildings. These principals, in effect, encouraged their teachers to disregard the subject-matter supervisors from the central office when their instructions were in conflict with the whole program developed for the building or advocated by the principal. Many teachers were thus confronted with conflicting sets of expectations held by the principal and by a supervisor and even differential expectations held by different supervisors.

There appear to be certain ways to reduce this conflict in role expectations. One possibility would be more coordination of the programs represented by the several supervisors. The superintendent of schools or an assistant superintendent might work with supervisors as a group toward the end of bringing the content fields into some kind of rational total curriculum. Or the role of the central office supervisors might be changed from a line function to that of a staff or advisory function. If this change were understood and accepted by all members of the organization, teachers would feel more freedom to accept or reject ideas offered by supervisors. The change in role for the supervisor would also require a change in role for the principal. Each principal would need to work with his staff of teachers and with the resource people from the central office to build a coordinated instructional program for the pupils of the school.

To be sure, a redefinition of the role of supervisors and of principals is not an easy task. Supervisors who have relied heavily on the power of status and office may have real difficulty in learning to rely upon the power of prestige and influence.[5] As

---

[5] This distinction is explicated by E. G. Guba, "Research in Internal Administration—What Do We Know?" in Roald F. Campbell and James M. Lipham, eds., *Administrative Theory as a Guide to Action*, Chicago, Midwest Administration Center, University of Chicago, 1960, chap. 7.

was noted in Chapter 5, vested authority is quite different from entrusted authority. Moreover, principals who have been essentially custodians of buildings will often find it hard to exercise leadership in curricular matters. Some supervisors and some principals may find it possible to adjust to these new roles. In other instances, new people may have to be found who can meet the adjusted expectations. The reduction of role conflict on the part of teachers would seem to justify even rather extreme measures in terms of administrative staffing, assignment, and training.

The critical place of communication in an organization is reflected in much of what has been said here. Obviously, communication is dependent upon the communicator, the communicatee, and the nature of the message being transmitted from one to the other. Mere transmission of a message by the communicator, in either oral or written form, is not communication. Only when feedback from the communicatee suggests common understanding regarding the message can it be said that there has been communication.[6]

The need for feedback provides the best possible support for two-way communication within an organization. Only with two-way communication can the superordinate be sure that the expectations he has expressed for the organization are understood by the subordinates. Clearly, since two-way communication is easiest in a face-to-face relationship, superordinates should engage in face-to-face relationships with the members of the organization. The case for breaking the organization into subunits which permit this kind of interaction seems strong.

One university, recently faced with problems growing out of inadequate communication between the administration and the faculty, has attempted to remedy this matter in a number of ways. Some schools and departments have been divided so as to make each unit small enough to permit more two-way communication. The president and his chief assistants have begun attending the meetings of the faculty council regularly. Membership in the president's cabinet has been enlarged to include not only his chief assistants but also the president and president-elect of the faculty council. These devices appear to be of assistance

---

[6] For a more complete discussion see Jack Culbertson, "Recognizing Roadblocks in Communication Channels," *Administrator's Notebook*, 7 (March, 1959).

in clarifying many aspects of university operation, including role expectations held for the faculty and for the administration.

MAXIMIZING PERSONAL SATISFACTION

The personal dimension of the model, it will be recalled, suggests that each member of an organization is motivated by his own set of need-dispositions. One person may have need for dominance and achievement, another for submissiveness and love, and still another for nurturance. To be sure, these needs cannot be seen; they must be inferred from overt behaviors. Nor can every administrator be presumed to be an expert at inferring the psychological needs of his subordinates. At the same time, an understanding of the concept that each person is motivated, in part, by his own unique need-dispositions will provide an administrator with certain insights into the behavior of his associates.

At a less basic but probably related level, administrators can discover something about the desires, aspirations, and preferred activities of staff members. Some teachers, perhaps too many, prefer the lecture situation. Others prefer and are skilled in a nondirective counseling situation. Some teachers seek frequent and continuous direction from their superordinates. Others would rather have complete freedom and independence. Many teachers prefer youngsters who follow directions and do not raise embarrassing questions. A few teachers can cope with and find satisfaction in the mental forays of gifted students. Many teachers like to "hand out" the facts that are known about a content area whereas some favor a situation characterized by the search for new knowledge.

All this suggests that each unit in an organization should be small enough to permit the immediate superordinate of that unit to become well acquainted with each member, and acquaintance will come through formal and informal means—by listening to what people say, but even more by observing what they do. Thus, the principal, assistant principal, department head, and other supervisors in schools and colleges will find themselves in a continuous assessment of the dispositions, the aspirations, the strengths, the limitations of their staff members. Each person will soon emerge as unique, as motivated by a somewhat different combination of need-dispositions, as probably having a particular place to fill in the total effort of the organization.

To maximize both *effectiveness* and *efficiency* in the organization, the administrator is constantly faced with making the best possible assignments of his staff members. Without wishing to oversimplify the matter, we may surmise that teachers who are motivated by a strong nurturance need will find teaching in the primary grades more to their liking. Teachers who seek achievement will perhaps find great satisfaction in coaching one of the sports, in directing plays, or in sponsoring the debating team. Teachers who like to lecture may take particular pleasure in serving as the lecturing member of a teaching team. Teachers who can "take" bright youngsters may find an honors class in literature or creative writing the bright spot of their day.

The point is that every organization has a variety of tasks to be performed and a variety of workers to perform them. If the administrator knows his staff and is convinced that task and person should be matched as closely as possible, he can ordinarily establish some compatibility between particular role assignments and individual dispositions. We are not suggesting that compatibility will be perfect. Most organizations have some jobs that must still be done even though they are distasteful to all staff members, but even these become more palatable when interspersed with tasks from which one derives particular satisfaction.

An insightful administrator may actually be able to see a place for a staff member in an organization that the staff member himself does not see. In one university department an assistant professor was engaged in so much routine counseling, which tended to preclude his giving attention to his research interests, that his promotion was being jeopardized. The chairman of the department, perhaps sensing the situation more clearly than the assistant professor and recognizing his latent scholarly competence, sought to relieve him of his counseling tasks, to provide him with an office near a senior colleague in a related field, and to adjust his load to provide him adequate time for research. At first the assistant professor offered some resistance to these proposals; he apparently derived considerable satisfaction from the counseling activities. In time, however, he agreed to try out the new arrangement. In a few years the man became a productive scholar, his promotion was accomplished, he was recognized as an effective teacher in his special field, and he was sought as a counselor by graduate students. The staff member now has an established place in a university department, whereas at one time he was performing peripheral tasks, many of which could be handled by people with less potential ability. The initial push for the change in assignment came from the chairman, not the assistant professor. Here is an instance in which the attempt to maximize institutional effectiveness also succeeded in maximizing individual efficiency.

We have noted that the model provides insights which appear to have relevance for supervision in an organization. To begin with, the supervisor must recognize that organization members, because of their unique backgrounds and unique positions, will have differential perceptions regarding people and events in the organization. Armed with this knowledge, he may need to exercise considerable care to clarify organizational expectations and to be assured that communication about these expectations has "taken." Finally, ways can ordinarily be found to effect some compatibility between individual dispositions and role assignments and thus to increase the satisfaction of organization members.

Evaluation of staff performance

In most formal organizations, including schools and colleges, the superordinate is called upon to evaluate the performance of subordinates. Few issues in education are more explosive than the evaluation of teaching and of teachers. Some concepts, included as part of the model, appear to provide insight into evaluating staff performance.

BUILDING AGREEMENT ON PURPOSE

Much of what has been said about the clarification of role expectations has relevance at this point. Role expectations for various members of an organization can be clarified only within the framework of the purpose or mission of the organization. For instance, for years there has been controversy over the purpose of the high school; is the school to be a selective institution or is it to serve all youth? To be sure, this question may have been settled in the official written documents of most high schools, but many disagreements between teachers and principals and among teachers in high schools reflect a basic difference in perception concerning the purpose of the high school. If agreement on organizational purpose is to be reached, the organization must provide its members with some type of orientation.

This factor, when understood, does much to remove the consideration of goal as superordinate and subordinate think of it from the realm of personal relationships to one of an organizational norm. In other words, it is not merely a personal whim on the part of a principal when he expects a first-grade teacher to help 6-year-olds learn to read. Rather, it is a purpose of the school, often explicitly stated and reinforced by the larger society, to which the principal is giving expression. A school principal does a member of his faculty no service to equivocate about a purpose which the school and its culture have established.

Understanding and agreement about purpose by a school or college would seem to require a good deal of interaction among members of the organization. Some of this interaction might occur in formal meetings, some in less formal settings. Public expression of purpose, such as that found in college charters and school laws, should be clarified. Statements of governing boards as they refer to purpose should be explained. Administrative interpretations and faculty tradition as related to purpose should be considered. In other words, the aims of an organization or the expectations attached to the component roles at any particular moment form one of the givens in that organization and provide the framework within which the contributions of its members are to be judged. To be sure, purpose need not be static, and when it is changed, a new framework of role expectations within which to assess work performance has come into being.

The crucial nature of agreement on institutional purpose and its reflection in role expectations as a precondition to evaluating work performance is illustrated in the following incident involving an institution which was just evolving from a college into a university. Until recently, teaching had been its chief purpose, but now a new liberal arts dean and a few department heads thought research should become a major function. This shift had not been clarified by the controlling board, and the president and his assistants were also somewhat ambivalent about the matter. In the meantime, staff members without Ph.D. degrees were being discharged, presumably because they were not prepared to contribute to the evolving research purpose of the institution. Little wonder that staff members who were able instructors, many of their colleagues, and even a number of alumni had difficulty understanding or accepting the rationale behind the insistence by the new dean and department heads upon the resignation of instructors who were not research-oriented.

RECOGNIZING DIFFERENTIAL ROLES

The evaluation of work performance is relatively simple in some organizations. On the assembly line the workman is to keep up with the specific tasks assigned to him. In a sales operation the volume of sales is a relevant criterion. But in educational organizations, and all others in which many professionals are employed, the question of expertise complicates the problem. Who can really understand how to teach reading except other teachers of reading? Who can really understand the teaching of calculus except other teachers of calculus? To the extent that organizations employ professionals, just to that extent must expertise be taken into account in the evaluation of work performance. This circumstance has caused some students of organizations to suggest that line and staff personnel have exchanged roles in work groups made up of professionals.[7]

Obviously, no school or college administrator can be an expert in the content fields or the specialized areas with which he must deal. Nevertheless, he is the spokesman for the institution, and indeed his own role requires that he view the total institution, doing his best to understand how the work of each staff member, esoteric though it may be, fits into the broader purpose. The administrator does have help available in this task. First, he can listen as a staff member describes his own work and how it contributes to the entire effort of the institution. This exposition should help him realize the extent to which the staff member understands and is being guided by the goals of the system as a whole, the purposes of his role-set within the system, and the expectations of his particular role.

A second source of help may be found in the clientele of the school or college. Particularly as students become more mature, their reactions to their instructors may be taken as one indication of how the instructors are doing. Students readily characterize an instructor as one who "knows his stuff," "is a big bluff," "demands lots of reading," "falls for all the dames," and by other terms even more colorful. These appraisals, to be sure, may not deal with the total contribution of a staff member and should be judged accordingly, but they can hardly be ignored.

A third source of help to the administrator who must evaluate the work performance of professional staff members is found

---

[7] See Amitai Etzioni, "Authority Structure and Organizational Effectiveness," *Administrative Science Quarterly*, 4 (June, 1959), 43–67.

in their colleagues, some of them within the same institution. Thus, an English instructor works with other English instructors and often with the head or chairman of the English department. Since these people usually have insight into the expertise of the instructor in question, a way needs to be found to tap their understanding. Of course, interpersonal relations (particularism) may color and even override professional insights (universalism). If the administrator recognizes these phenomena, he will know how to interpret what he hears from the immediate colleagues of an instructor.

In universities particularly, the expertise of a staff member may have become known to a much wider group of colleagues. Through publications and participation in professional meetings, sociologists, for instance, become acquainted with other sociologists. The university administrator who must judge the contribution of a sociologist can ordinarily get some help from these (to him) outsiders. Even here, however, the appraisals must be tempered for, as Caplow and McGee have pointed out, some professors are institution-oriented and some are discipline-oriented.[8] If an institution were in need of visibility to be derived from a discipline-oriented professor, it would be poorly served by an institution-oriented one. A similar phenomenon is discussed in Chapter 9, where findings by Andrews revealed that some public school teachers are discipline-oriented and others are profession-oriented.

RECOGNIZING DIFFERENTIAL STYLES

Anyone called upon to evaluate the performance of his subordinates will probably find it helpful to recognize that people employ different styles when working on the same task. One teacher, for example, may be quite formal in dealing with students, another quite informal. One teacher may be permissive in student relationships, another directive. In part, these styles derive from the psychological characteristics of the teacher including his own need-dispositions. A teacher with a great need for dominance will probably have difficulty in conducting a highly permissive classroom. Conversely, a teacher with a great need for nurturance will no doubt be less directive in his teaching style.

We have already presented in Chapter 9 some evidence to show that teachers of science and mathematics and teachers of

---

[8] Theodore Caplow and Reece J. McGee, *The Academic Market Place*, New York, Basic Books, 1958.

social studies have different psychological characteristics. It may be that one kind of person is attracted to the relatively precise areas of study and another to the more speculative and value-bound areas of study. In any case, since people do differ in personal dispositions, it is folly to expect them to behave in identical fashion as they deal with students.

Recently, another line of reasoning which supports differential styles of teaching has developed. Bruner,[9] for instance, has pointed out that each subject has its own structure, which should determine how the subject is taught. If this is the case, the teacher of history is required to learn about the structure of history so that he may teach his subject effectively. Likewise, the teacher of chemistry should be guided by the unique structure of the subject of chemistry. In any event, the supervisor may find it desirable to be chiefly concerned with student achievement and less exercised over teacher style.

JUDGING EFFECTIVENESS

Clearly, the evaluation of teaching and administrative effectiveness is a difficult task. Small wonder that hundreds of school districts have found the problem of merit rating an insurmountable one. Teachers' organizations generally resist merit rating programs, whereas many boards of education insist that the work of school personnel be evaluated. Most of us would agree that if an organization is to be made more effective, appraisal of its present performance must be attempted, and in this process some examination of the performance of its members seems inevitable.

The concept of effectiveness, as suggested in Chapter 5, has relevance here. Effectiveness is seen as the congruence between behavior and expectations. Thus, if teachers are expected to be strict disciplinarians they will be judged effective when they act as strict disciplinarians. If teachers are expected to encourage inquiry among students they will be found effective when they in fact do so. A principal committed to the idea of nondirective counseling may think that a nondirective guidance counselor is effective whereas a principal who has reservations about nondirective counseling may consider the same counselor ineffective.

These illustrations make it apparent that in any organization the expectations need to be clearly stated. A major problem

---

[9] Jerome S. Bruner, *The Process of Education*, Cambridge, Mass., Harvard University Press, 1961.

in many situations in which merit rating has been tried is the lack of clarity in expectations. Often criterion statements have been unavailable or have been kept at such a level of generality that raters and rated have perceived their meaning differently. In the appraisal of work performance, organizations need to make explicit the expectations held for staff members.

With effectiveness seen as a function of the relationship between expectations and behavior, it seems obvious that the same behavior may not be construed as equally effective in different situations. Thus, a school principal who spends most of his time keeping records and reports would be thought by one superintendent to be effective. Yet another superintendent, who expected more leadership of staff and community by the principal, would look upon the report-bound principal as ineffective. Attempts to find universal measures of effectiveness will succeed only to the extent that there is universal agreement on expectations—a condition not likely to obtain.

We have suggested in this section that the model may provide an administrator with useful insights as he tries to evaluate the work of his staff members. Clearly, work performance should be approached within a framework of common purpose for the organization. Members of the organization need to recognize that they have differential roles to perform, and as organizations make greater use of professionals, the expertise surrounding each role becomes more extensive. We also noted that people employ various styles to achieve their ends. Finally, we pointed out that effectiveness can be determined only as expectations and behavior are related.

Reassignment and dismissal

If employment and assignment practices are influenced by some of the considerations dealt with here, reassignment and dismissal of personnel will diminish in importance as a problem. Even at best, however, the fact that some members of an organization are unproductive necessitates some adjustment in their status. Outright dismissal of an employee for unsatisfactory work is probably the simplest measure to invoke, but it may be unnecessary, and wasteful both to the individual and to the organization. Moreover, in many school and college situations tenure provisions make dismissal difficult and in a sense force administrators to examine other alternatives. We think the model provides some assistance with respect to the various alternatives available.

ASSESSING ROLE-PERSONALITY RELATIONS

Unsatisfactory work performance on the part of an employee may well raise a number of questions, the first of which has to do with role clarification. This point has been discussed already, but it seems appropriate to reiterate that whenever a supervisor of personnel, such as a school principal or a college department chairman, becomes convinced that a member of his organization is doing unsatisfactory work he should try to discover whether the employee really understands what is expected of him. Obviously, no adequate answer to this question can be had unless it includes feedback from the employee regarding the job demands as he perceives them.

A second question has to do with the need-dispositions of the employee. Although we recognize that administrators cannot be clinical psychologists, the fact remains that they must make the best appraisal they can of the needs, aspirations, strengths, and weaknesses of their employees. If the administrator has become well acquainted with the employee and his work and possesses even minimum psychological insight, he will have verbal and behavioral evidence of what the staff member likes to do, what he does well, and what he does poorly.

Assessment of institutional expectations and individual need-dispositions will permit the administrator to estimate the amount of incongruity between these two dimensions. If the discrepancy is great, reassignment or dismissal may indeed be called for. We do not suggest, of course, that all conflict between role and person can be resolved. Actually some conflict between institutional demands and individual propensities appears to supply a dynamic in an organization. Only when this conflict becomes intolerable are personnel transfers or dismissals necessary. Under these circumstances there appear to be three alternatives.

PERSONALIZING THE ROLE

The first alternative is to change the role to fit the employee. In this case the conflict has been used as a stimulus to look at the role, the role-set, and even the total system. Chapter 4 treated the balance between role and person as found in various organizations and suggested that the military was dominated by role expectations with little opportunity for personal discretion, whereas an artists' colony had few role expectations and permitted extensive personal discretion. Schools and colleges appear to be located between these two extremes. Thus some organizations have more leeway for the redefinition of jobs than do others. An assessment of the leeway possible in a particular organization seems to be necessary as consideration is being given to changing the role expectations for a particular employee. Such a procedure may set a precedent in the organization that will become most difficult to manage, may seriously affect "job definitions" of other employees, and may even result in malfunction of the system as a whole. On the other hand, job redefinition may suggest an organizational change that would be welcomed by many employees and actually make the system more effective.

Let us try an example. For two or three decades many elementary schools have been organized on a self-contained basis, which in most cases means that each teacher in kindergarten through grade six is responsible for the total program of a particular group of youngsters. This form of school organization is the result, to some extent, of a reaction from the platoon school and other departmental arrangements prominent in the 1920s. Some elementary school teachers and possibly more professors of elementary education came to look upon the self-contained classroom as a part of the sacred birthright of every child. Only by such an arrangement, they contended, could the whole child be adequately nurtured.

Recently, in a certain school with self-contained classrooms there was a sixth-grade teacher who did an excellent job with music, who handled language arts and social studies in barely passable fashion, but whose instruction in science and mathematics was deplorable. Moreover, this school was in an upper-middle-class suburb where the high school and community had responded to all of the national programs stressing improvement in the teaching of science and mathematics. Clearly, students in the sixth-grade section in question were not prepared for the seventh-grade programs in science and mathematics, and their ability to carry English and history courses in grade seven was dubious. In short, the work performance of the sixth-grade teacher was unsatisfactory.

Examination of what was happening by way of music instruction among the other teachers of the elementary school revealed that no one else had quite the skill in music instruction as the teacher in question. Actually, eight of the remaining nineteen teachers taught music in a perfunctory fashion or neglected it altogether. They looked upon other areas of the curriculum as more important than music, had little background in music, and seldom found personal enjoyment in music.

These circumstances suggested that if all areas of the curriculum were to receive suitable attention some form of departmentalization was necessary. Inadequacy on the part of one teacher in the areas of science and mathematics brought the problem to the foreground. A look at music teaching in the entire school provided further evidence that teaching might be subjected to a degree of specialization.

The staff of the school was able to discard the doctrine of the self-contained classroom and organize grades four through six on a modified departmental plan. An important place for the sixth-grade teacher was found; he took over the music instruction for five of the sections, organized an all-school chorus, and served as music consultant to teachers who continued to teach their own music but who needed some help with the program. To be sure, this reorganization was not effected merely to permit one teacher make optimum use of his special skill. Rather, the great discrepancy between his capacity to teach music and his capacity to teach arithmetic set in motion a reconsideration of the school organization to which other relevant data were added. Personalizing the role of a single member and possibly creating changes in the entire organization is an alternative requiring an open mind, some capacity for invention, and courage actually to try new practices. It need hardly be said that personalizing the role in the instance cited was not intended merely to create convenient teaching positions or to establish novel curricular arrangements, but to ensure the best possible instruction for each child, for this is the ultimate purpose of educational administration.

REASSIGNING ROLES

Sometimes employees who are found to be unsatisfactory in work performance can be reassigned in the organization. Many schools and most colleges have positions which represent considerable variety in terms of role expectations. Again, the object is not to find a shelter for incompetent people but to find a post for which the employee has appropriate strengths. The procurement and indoctrination of personnel is a costly process for both the organization and the individual. We are suggesting that an organization do everything it can to keep productive employees who have been through this process before deciding that it must seek new personnel and initiate them into the life of the organization.

Perhaps a report of an actual situation will illustrate what we have in mind. In a city school district an elementary school principal was judged by the superintendent to be ineffective. The man seemed to have difficulty in personal relations with faculty and students and even more with patrons of the school. At the same time, he was bright, he was well informed, and he raised provocative questions with the superintendent about various aspects of school operation. Sometimes these inquiries actually nettled the superintendent because a number of long-established practices in the district were called into question. The superintendent was ready to fire the principal.

At the same time, sensing that the district was called upon to make many decisions with inadequate information upon which to base them, the superintendent wished to establish a research department in the central office. Although the major purpose of the proposed research department was seen as the collection and analysis of status information, the plan was at least the beginning of an important development in that school system. Initially, the research department was to be staffed with one professional person and one secretary, and the possibility of transferring the principal to the new post was raised. At first the superintendent was doubtful; his discomfort with the principal in his present role was clearly evident. The superintendent did acknowledge that the man was alert, inquisitive, and skillful in organizing and writing material. A check with the university where the principal had taken his master's degree revealed that he had dealt adequately with a rather complex problem in his thesis, and that he had some background in research design and statistics.

The superintendent invited the principal into a conference where the idea of setting up a research department was discussed, and the interest of the principal in taking the new position was assessed. The principal acknowledged that there were aspects of his present role which annoyed him and which he probably handled poorly. He saw the need for the research department and was enthusiastic about the possibility of directing it. The outcome was the creation of the research department and the appointment of the principal to head it.

To be sure, not every difficult situation can have such a happy ending. Had no new position been brought into being, the solution in the case cited would have been harder. We would point out, however, that in many organizations, resignations and retirements provide roles to be filled even when no additional positions are being created. If the principal had not possessed the dispositions and training needed for the new role, the solution reported would not have been feasible. Far from suggesting the blind transfer of personnel, we are advocating a discriminating examination of possible reassignments.

DISMISSAL

Under some conditions role expectations and personal dispositions are so far apart that separation of a person from the organization seems to be the only solution. The organization may take the initiative and dismiss the employee, or the employee may take the initiative and resign. In the best of circumstances the decision for separation might actually be a joint agreement between an official of the organization and the employee in question.

Before any decision is made, in the interest of both parties at least three conditions should be met. First, a reasonable period of time should be provided so that the staff member has a genuine opportunity to demonstrate his worth to the organization. In many school districts this is called the probationary period antecedent to a tenure appointment, and it may be as long as three years. In colleges the probationary period provided by term contracts may vary from three to six years. Second, there should be established during the probationary period a plan for supervision and counseling. A teacher, for instance, during his three-year probationary status should confer frequently with his principal and other superordinates concerning the adequacy of his work performance and ways to improve it. Third, the possibility of changing the role, or reassignment, in the organization should be considered.

When these conditions have been met and separation still seems necessary, the officer of the organization should do what he can to help the employee see the need for the separation. In some instances at least, both parties are able to recognize that role expectations and personal dispositions are seriously at odds and that separation is clearly indicated. In all cases in which the employee has strengths that may be useful in other organizations or other types of employment, these possibilities should be explored by both the officer and the employee. Whenever appropriate, the officer should extend help to the employee in securing a more appropriate placement.

Not long ago we knew an assistant professor in a graduate school of a major university where great emphasis was placed on research and scholarly productivity. This man seemed to be oriented more toward teaching than toward research. He and the dean met several times to discuss his teaching and the development of possible research interests, and in the second year of his three-year term a small committee of professors was also formed to appraise the assistant professor's progress and potential and to advise the dean. In the end, it seemed plain that although the man was a thoughtful, stimulating teacher he had no genuine research interests and in all probability would not be a scholar in the area of his specialty.

About this time the assistant professor received an invitation to join the faculty of another university. He and the dean discussed quite frankly the long-range possibilities at both institutions. It became evident that the expectations of the second university were much more in keeping with the dispositions and abilities of the assistant professor than was the case in his present situation. With this recognition the dean was able to support strongly the candidacy of the assistant professor to the officials of the second university. Months before his three-year term at the first institution was up, the assistant professor accepted the offer from the second institution, the appointment to become effective at the expiration of his contract.

Time has confirmed the wisdom of the decision described. Even so, we suspect there was some pain on the part of the assistant professor in the realization that he did not quite "pass muster" at the first university. But it must also be understood that in a sense the university did not "pass muster" with the individual. We would further suggest that both the first university and the individual gambled on the appointment and lost. Dismissal is a little like surgery—short-term pain to prevent long-term misery and even death.

In summary, we have proposed that the institutional and personal dimensions of the model have implications for the consideration of the reassignment and/or dismissal of cmployees.

We noted three alternatives open to most organizations at the time when possible separation of the employee from the organization is being considered: redefinition of the role, reassignment in the organization, and dismissal. Even dismissal, we suggested, can be handled humanely. At best, both the organization and the person pay a price for dismissal, but that price is ordinarily less than an extension of an untenable partnership which yields little to the organization and breeds hostility in the person.

The administrator in a transactional role

This chapter has been written from the vantage point of the administrator. Now we would like to deal with the administrator in his transactional role as he attempts to reinforce organizational expectations on the one hand and empathize with organization members on the other.

REINFORCING ORGANIZATIONAL EXPECTATIONS

By the very nature of his role the administrator is expected to reinforce organizational expectations. To use the language of the model, he is expected to interpret the normative dimension or norms of the organization. In Walton's opinion,[10] the administrator is supposed to discern and clarify the goals and purposes of the organization. We go farther than Walton and suggest that the administrator actually helps formulate the goals and purposes, first when he recommends to the controlling board and the community what they should be, and again when he interprets them and attempts to implement them with the staff. To reiterate, we think the administrator influences, discerns, clarifies, and interprets the goals, policies, and expectations of the organization in which he works.

We would emphasize that in this role the administrator is an organizational spokesman, not a personal spokesman. He is required to understand the cultural values of the supporting community, to interpret the policy positions of the controlling board, and to appraise the norms held by staff members. To be sure, his own values and perceptions will influence what he thinks is the position of community, board, and staff, but if his personal dispositions prohibit him from being a fairly faithful spokesman

---

[10] John Walton, *Administration and Policy Making in Education*, Baltimore, Johns Hopkins Press, 1959.

for his major reference groups he will, in time, be removed from his administrative post.

This is not to suggest that the community, board, and staff are always in agreement concerning their expectations for the organization. Actually, as was suggested in earlier chapters, these reference groups may hold quite disparate views of the purpose of an organization. We know of a superintendent of a high school district in an upper-middle-class suburb in which the board and the community had deliberately adopted the policy of keeping their district among the top 5 percent of school districts in the nation. This superintendent reported that some years ago they had a German language instructor who was about a B or C teacher, not good enough for their district. After several conferences with the instructor the superintendent decided that his contract would not be renewed. A number of the instructor's colleagues felt that the superintendent was wrong to let the German teacher go, but, as the superintendent remarked, "It's the close ones that are hard to call. I guess at times the administrator has to be the rejector, the gatekeeper."

In his transactional role, every administrator must at times live by the book—in the military, by Standard Operating Procedure. Even in the face of the conflicting expectations, and occasionally equivocal positions, of major reference groups, the administrator must do his best to reflect the norms of the organization he represents—never forgetting, however, that he can and sometimes must be a force for changing the norms.

EMPATHIZING WITH ORGANIZATION MEMBERS

There is another side of the coin. Not only does the administrator reinforce organizational expectations, but he also empathizes with organization members. In terms of the model, we have now shifted to the personal dimension.

For the administrator to empathize with staff members, he must first conceive this to be one aspect of the administrative role. Second, he needs to develop some understanding of personality and of the concepts represented by the term "need-dispositions," and in order to do so he must be available and he must listen. Again, the necessity emerges for breaking large organizations into subunits so that administrators can be available and can take time to listen.

The importance of listening to staff members was illustrated in an interview we had with a high school principal. After speaking of his role in improving instruction and his role in fiscal management, he said:

> My third role has to do with working with individuals. I serve as a Father Confessor, a listener, an encourager; I hear difficulties; I am a kind of counselor, a human maintenance person. This role takes about one third of my time, and yet it is so important that it cannot be delegated. I find myself saying to a Latin teacher that not all Latin teachers have to approach the teaching task in the same way and I show that I am interested and I do give encouragement. Many times in this role I have to say very little because the people just talk it out when they have a chance.

We have suggested that as the interpreter of organizational expectations the administrator has to "use the book" or take a *universalistic* approach. Yet to empathize with organization members he will often have to "throw the book away" or use the *particularistic* approach. In the latter case he is constantly faced with determining the degree to which extenuating circumstances should alter normal expectations. For instance, does a severe accident to a staff member justify a recommendation that sick leave provisions be extended? Or does the obvious artistic talent of a certain teacher justify his retention even though a full teaching load, as defined in the regulations, is not possible? These and similar problems require the administrator to exercise judgment and discretion.

When to reinforce organizational expectations and when to temper them because of extenuating circumstances is a question with which the administrator is always confronted. This capacity to emphasize the normative, the personal, or some combination of the two was designated as the transactional style of leadership in the discussion of the model. It takes a rather able administrator to make the judgments and effect the behaviors that this style entails.

SELF-UNDERSTANDING AND SELF-CONTROL

If the administrator is to serve as mediator or as transactional leader, still another requirement is suggested: some understanding of his own need-dispositions and the ability to exercise a large measure of self-control in his relationships with other people in the organization. As to self-understanding, an administrator's great need for dominance, for instance, may cause him to try to push community, board, and staff harder than they will be pushed and thus create insurmountable problems for the organization. If the administrator understands his own dispositions in this regard, he may be able to recognize more quickly the danger signals in the responses of the people with whom he is working.

Finally, we think that a mediator must demonstrate considerable stability or self-control as he works with members of the organization. He will confront staff members who are excited, enthusiastic, despondent, angry. If he shares the emotion of the staff member fully, his usefulness as a listener may be reduced. He should be in the position of hearing an outburst and then being able to ask whether there are not other possible explanations and alternative solutions. Although the administrator must be sympathetic to individual problems, there are times when he has to apply universalistic rather than particularistic criteria in decision-making.

Summary

The implications dealt with in this chapter can in no sense be viewed as prescriptions in the area of staff relationships. Nor do we pretend that all staff relationships have been covered. We have ignored, for instance, the growing problem of negotiating with teachers' organizations but will give some attention to that matter in the next chapter. We have supplied a number of illustrations that may help administrators view their functions through the perspective of administration as a social process. This perspective, we think, can be suggestive to administrators in numerous situations, for the model permits situational differentials to be taken into account. The framework elucidated here permits an administrator to use administrative theory in the only way theory can be useful to the practitioner—as an aid to his understanding of the situational and personal processes with which he must deal.

12

Board relationships

Although the controlling board of a school or college has a position in the organization quite different from that of the staff, the board is a part of the total social system. Thus many of the concepts of the model also have relevance to an examination of board-executive relationships, the central focus of this chapter. We shall discuss the nature of the board, the selection of board members, motivations of board members, the selection of the chief executive, working relationships between board and executive, and the relationships between the board and the staff.

The nature of controlling boards

Parsons has suggested that an organization may be viewed as having technical, managerial, and institutional levels.[1] In our model, Parsons' "institutional level" is somewhat comparable to the cultural milieu within which the organization is embedded. Between technical and managerial and between managerial and institutional levels there must be articulation. The controlling board of an educational organization, while functioning at both managerial and institutional levels, is a major articulating device between the two levels. In other words, the board relates the work of the chief executive and his immediate staff (who function primarily at the managerial level) to the larger society of which the organization is a part. In this sense the board is an interstitial body, part in and part out of the organization itself.

INTERSTITIAL POSITION OF THE BOARD

This very interesting location of the controlling board makes it a natural depository for cultural-institutional conflicts such as were dealt with in Chapter 6. Board members come from the larger society, are charged with representing it, and in doing so tend to reflect the values of their constituents. When the people of a school district become convinced that schools should place more

---

[1] Talcott Parsons, "Some Ingredients of a General Theory of Formal Organizations," in Andrew W. Halpin, ed., *Administrative Theory in Education*, Chicago, Midwest Administration Center, University of Chicago, 1958, chap. iii. (Reprinted, 1967, New York: Macmillan.)

emphasis on academic competence, they elect board members of the same conviction who can and will be spokesmen for this emphasis. Moreover, the citizens tend to keep checking their representatives to see that the positions held by the larger society are being faithfully espoused. By the very nature of their selection and continuation in office, board members are expected to reflect the values of their community.

Board members soon find, however, that they are indoctrinated into the expectations held by the organization. Some of these expectations may have a legal foundation not fully understood by the member prior to his induction to the board. For instance, a school district may not be eligible for certain state and federal funds unless it conducts a particular type of educational program and actually makes available for that program local revenues in specified amounts. Other organizational expectations grow out of the nature of the work of the organization and the expertise of the people who do the work. Thus, laboratory classes, because of space limitations and supervision requirements, may be limited to twenty students, a condition that perhaps was not understood by the board member. Still other expectations, such as salary levels and sick-leave provisions, may have resulted from hard bargaining between the staff and the board, and no easy way to alter the agreements seems available.

In some cases the values held by the community and the expectations held by the organization will not differ greatly and the board member will find his role an amiable one. More frequently, we think, the board member will discover some genuine differences between what the community, or at least some segments of the community, wants for the school or college and what the organization wants for itself. At this point, board members may feel frustrated, board sessions may become long and burdensome, and acrimonious debate may take place in and out of board meetings. Instead of facing up to the conflict, the board may strike out against the administrator or the entire staff. Boards have been known to take the position that if teachers do not like conditions in their school district they are free to go elsewhere.

THE BOARD AND ROLE CONFLICT

The relationships between a controlling board and its chief executive provide a perfect setting for developing role conflict between role incumbents. To begin with, state school codes and college charters give controlling boards broad powers over their respective organizations. Most school codes, for instance, let the board determine much of the curriculum, employ the teachers, build the buildings, adopt the budget, and exercise such other powers as are necessary for the operation of the schools. The same state codes say little about the function of the superintendent of schools.

In the Illinois code, one of the more explicit provisions regarding the superintendent empowers the board

to employ a superintendent who shall have charge of the administration of the schools under the direction of the board of education. In addition to the administrative duties, the superintendent shall make recommendations to the board concerning the budget, building plans, the locations of sites, the selection of teachers and other employees, the selection of textbooks, instructional material and the courses of study. The superintendent shall keep or cause to be kept the records and accounts as directed and required by the board, aid in making reports required by the board, and perform such other duties as the board may delegate to him. (10-21.4)

In Illinois, and in most other states, the superintendent does those things which the board of education delegates to him. Legally, final responsibility for school operation rests with the board.

In practice, in all but very small districts superintendents are expected to exercise great discretion in school operation. Many board members and superintendents alike, as Bowman[2] has shown, expect the superintendent to make minor decisions without reference to the board. And on major questions board members also expect superintendents to provide them with information and to make recommendations for action.

Despite considerable agreement between board members and superintendents regarding the superintendent's participation in the decision-making of the board, particularly in larger school districts,[3] troubling possibilities remain. How is the superintendent to know which are the minor questions that he need not take to the board? Information in what quantity and from what sources should be taken to the board? Upon what questions should the superintendent make definitive recommendations and upon which should he simply supply information? There is

---

[2] Thomas R. Bowman, "The Participation of the Superintendent in School Board Decision-Making," Doctoral dissertation, University of Chicago, 1962.
[3] *Ibid.*

evidence to suggest that as board members increase their tenure on the board they prefer the superintendent to make fewer decisions on his own and to make fewer recommendations to the board.[4]

In a more global study of school boards and superintendents, Gross found that board members and superintendents frequently disagree regarding their respective roles, as is noted in the following excerpt:

> Many school board members who are well motivated have ill-defined or hazy notions about their jobs. In some school systems school board members spend most of their time dealing with trivial matters and display little interest in the more crucial school problems such as curriculum improvement. Some school board members act as if they as individuals had the right to make decisions, which is the prerogative of the entire school board. Some school board members act as if they, rather than the superintendent, had the right to administer the policy decisions of the board. Superintendents and school board members frequently disagree over their respective rights and obligations.[5]

Not only do legal prerogatives give cause for differences in the perceptions of roles on the part of board members and superintendents, but their respective reference groups also contribute to the confusion. The major reference group for the board member is composed of his constituents, those who placed him in office. Often the major reference group for the superintendent is represented by the profession—fellow administrators and professors of administration. In the language of Gouldner, the board is often "local" in orientation whereas the superintendent may be "cosmopolitan" in orientation.[6] Stated otherwise, the board member is ordinarily concerned with what is "good" for his particular community, the superintendent with what is "good" professional practice.

Nor do the reference groups for the board member and the executive just stand by while their representatives seek to compose their differences. Actually, the values of each group are rather continuously reinforced. A citizen may say to the board member, "I thought we were going to get rid of some of that

---

[4] *Ibid.*
[5] Neal Gross, *Who Runs Our Schools?* New York, Wiley, 1958, p. 139.
[6] Alvin W. Gouldner, "Cosmopolitans and Locals: Toward An Analysis of Latent Social Roles," *Administrative Science Quarterly*, II (December, 1957), 283–306.

deadwood in the faculty when you got on the board." Or, "What have you done about that merit pay plan you stood for when you were running for election to the board?" The executive, on the other hand, may insist that appropriate criteria be established for the evaluation of the work of any faculty member, "deadwood" or otherwise. He may also resist a merit pay plan unless it can be worked out over a period of time with the understanding and support of a majority of the faculty. The seeds of discord are present.

Potential conflict between board members and the executive is found in the value orientations of the community and the organizational expectations. It is also found in the way the roles of board members and the executive are perceived by the respective incumbents. The incompatibility of legal language and the practice of board delegation to the chief executive give ground for role conflict, as do the reference-group orientations of the board and the executive. Such conflict often prevents the achievement of a partnership between the board and the executive, a condition necessary to the most effective operation of the organization.

Selection of board members

The United States has approximately 24,000 operating school districts.[7] There is no detailed report of the operating procedures as they pertain to school boards in all of these districts. One survey[8] does describe practices found in over 4,000 school districts, about 90 percent of all districts enrolling 1,200 or more pupils and accounting for about four fifths of the pupils in the nation. Basic data used here are taken from that study.

ELECTION OR APPOINTMENT

In the 4,000 school districts 86 percent of the board members were elected and 14 percent were appointed. These percentages, however, varied considerably in terms of size of district and region. In small districts (1,200–2,999 enrollment) 90 percent of

---

[7] Research Division, *Estimates of School Statistics*, Research Report, 1965-R17, Washington, D.C., NEA, December, 1965, p. 6.
[8] Alpheus L. White, *Local School Boards: Organization and Practices*, OE-23023, Bulletin 1962, No. 8, Washington, D.C., U.S. Government Printing Office, 1962.

the school boards were elected whereas in large districts (25,000 or more enrollment) 73 percent were elected. In the Northeast, North Central, and West regions 90 percent of the boards were elected, but in the South this percentage was 62. Where school boards were appointed, a variety of procedures was used. In large city school districts appointment was frequently made by the mayor or the city council. In the South appointment was often by county boards of supervisors, the governor, or the judges of the district court.

Since most school board members are elected, nomination procedures are important aspects of the election process. In 44 percent of the districts electing board members nomination was by petition, signed by a specified number of local electors. In 23 percent of these districts nomination could be achieved by individual announcement. Thus, in two thirds of the districts an individual himself or an individual and a few of his friends could have his name placed on the school board election ballot.

In only 3 percent of the districts employing the election process was the caucus procedure used to secure board nominees. In something over 100 districts community agencies were invited to send representatives to a caucus at which nominees for the school board were selected. Relatively homogeneous suburban communities appear to have made most extensive use of caucus nomination. Actually, the method is usually extralegal, and all legal requirements for nomination must be met in addition to the caucus. Those who advocate the caucus method of nomination see it as a way of inducing citizens to stand for board election who would hesitate to seek nomination in other ways.

This description of the nomination and election of school board members should not blind us to the subtleties often present in the process. In the case of the appointment of board members a crucial question may be: Who has the ear of the appointment officer? Often special interest groups have sufficient influence to control the ultimate selection of the board members. Where board members are elected, several practices not written in the law books may also be applied. In some communities members resign a few months prior to the expiration date of their term of office so that a successor to fill out the term can be appointed by the school board. The appointee then runs for the office at the ensuing election. This practice ordinarily results in making the board-selected candidate better known and thus enhances his chances of election. Often school elections are nonpartisan and are even held on special election dates. Since special elections draw frequently but a small percentage of the electorate to the polls, under these circumstances any well-organized minority can control the election. Even teachers have been known to control the selection of school board members.

The fact remains, however, that most communities, when aroused, can control who sits on the board of education. Even when board members are appointed, as was demonstrated some years ago in Chicago,[9] a determined citizenry can change the membership of the board of education. Under election procedures, despite the desires of some boards to be self-perpetuating and of special interest groups to control board membership, the people of a community can, when they insist, name their own board members. In spite of the fact that citizens are often lackadaisical in the exercise of their franchise, the possibility of its exercise stands as a constant reminder to board members and to those interested in the behavior of board members. These circumstances give substance to the position taken here that board members tend to reflect the values of the community and that they see the community as their major reference group.

But most communities are not homogeneous. The larger ones, particularly, are likely to have diverse populations holding pluralistic values. To reflect these values is often a most difficult task for the board member and contributes to his problems and those of the organization, as will be shown later.

In passing, we would point out that methods used to secure controlling boards for colleges and universities vary even more than among public school districts. The fact that colleges are both public and private affects the selection of board members. In major private universities the boards are often self-perpetuating. Church-related colleges are commonly controlled by boards appointed by the church body. Boards for public institutions of higher education are most often appointed by the governor of the state with the approval of the state senate. In a number of states, however, board members are elected. Board members for public and church-related institutions can be influenced in somewhat the same fashion as public school boards. Board members in major private universities are somewhat more insulated, but even

---

[9] See National Commission for the Defense of Democracy Through Education, *Certain Personnel Practices in the Chicago Public Schools*, Washington, D.C., NEA, 1945.

these institutions must continue to merit the financial support of the larger community or they cannot exist.

SOCIOECONOMIC STATUS OF BOARD MEMBERS

Many years ago Counts found that most school and college board members were drawn from the managerial and professional groups in our society. This being so, he concluded that these people would "be defensive and conservative rather than creative and progressive."[10] Other studies confirm the findings of Counts with respect to the occupational groups from which board members are drawn, but they show that Counts had little evidence for his conclusions. Indeed, the matter is much more complex than he led us to believe.[11]

For the 24,000 board members serving the 4,000 school districts, to which reference has been made,[12] 48 percent were college graduates as compared to 8 percent for the general population; 35 percent came from the business and managerial groups, 27 percent from the professional groups, and 12 percent were farmers, most of whom were also managerial people. Thus, about three fourths of the board members come from the managerial and professional groups in our society and about half of them are college graduates. These data seem consistent with what one would expect in an industrialized society.

Level of schooling and type of occupation seem to affect the way people see the educational task. For over 2,500 lay citizens, as reported by Downey,[13] these two variables were found to be most closely associated with the educational viewpoint of the respondents. People with more schooling, who are relatively high in occupational category, saw the intellectual tasks of the school as much more important than the social, personal, and vocational tasks.

It appears that board members who serve communities where educational and occupational levels are high will find the

---

[10] George S. Counts, "The Social Composition of Boards of Education," *Supplementary Educational Monographs*, Chicago, University of Chicago Press, 1927.

[11] For instance, see Roald F. Campbell, "The Social Implications of School Board Legislation," Doctoral dissertation, Stanford University, 1942.

[12] White, *op. cit.*

[13] Lawrence W. Downey, *The Task of Public Education*, Chicago, Midwest Administration Center, University of Chicago, 1960. See also chap. 6 in the present book.

views of their constituents and their own views rather compatible. On the other hand, board members in more diverse communities may find considerable lack of congruence in the educational viewpoints of many of their constituents and their own viewpoints. Under these circumstances the expectation that the board member represent his entire community may become most difficult to fulfill. The relevance of this point will become more apparent as the motivations of board members are discussed.

Motivations of board members

It is hard to describe the motivations of other people. Even so, as we have shown in Chapter 7, McCarty was able, through extended interviews, to identify board members as community-oriented or self-oriented in terms of the motives they mentioned as salient. A self-oriented board member, it will be recalled, was defined as one who was interested in achieving his own personal goals or the goals of a special interest group. A community-oriented member was defined as one who was interested in advancing the objectives of the school system to benefit the community generally. Using these categories, the investigator found that 46 percent of the board members had community-oriented motives and 54 percent had self-oriented motives. Although we must be cautious in generalizing from one study, we can probably say the assumption that board members are all devoted public servants is unwarranted.

SELF-ROLE CONFLICT

Perhaps the problem is even more complex than McCarty's conclusions suggest. Those who appear to yield more to satisfying personal desires as well as the special interests of some particular reference group are probably the self-oriented board members reported by McCarty; those who appear to support most frequently organizational expectations are probably community-oriented. We suspect every board member is often pressed to decide between actions that represent his personal interests or preferences and actions that appear to be necessary to the welfare of the total organization. Thus there is the possibility not only of reference-group conflict but also of self-role conflict.

For instance, a board member sees a term on the board of education as the first step in a political career. But he is also genuinely interested in helping the school system provide an adequate educational program. Personal dispositions and role expectations need not be incompatible, at least not in the abstract.

Now suppose the question of open attendance at all schools for any pupil within the city comes before the board. Under such a plan, Negro students will leave all-Negro schools and go across the city to attend all-white schools. The proposal may include the demand that the board provide free transportation to facilitate this type of integration of the student body.

Such a proposal has many ramifications. It seems to violate the neighborhood school concept. It imposes an additional cost for transportation. It appears to be an effort to solve all socioeconomic problems, including those of job opportunity and housing, through the schools. On the other hand, crowded conditions in Negro schools may be relieved without new construction if all available space in the school district is used. Then, too, many Negro parents know intuitively, if not explicitly, that their children will learn more if the classmates of their children include middle-class pupils. There is also the implementation of equal educational opportunity, a condition difficult if not impossible to achieve in a "separate but equal" school, as was suggested in the Brown case.

Few board members will find a decision within this welter of forces easy. For the board member who hopes to advance politically, the nature of his constituency may be the deciding factor. If most of his constituents oppose open attendance, self-interest is likely to propel him toward that view. If most of his constituents favor open attendance, his need for future political support will probably push him toward that view. In most situations an apparently defensible argument can be developed for either position, and the possible rationalization need not allude to the actual motivations to which the board member is responding.

Let us change the illustration slightly. Were the board member interested in attaining a place on the federal bench, his motivations on the civil rights questions before the board might be somewhat different from what they would be if he were seeking a place in a state legislature from an all-white constituency with reservations about integration. In both cases self-interest might govern the board member in positions he took on integration questions, but the positions could be quite different.

We do not wish to be cynical in this matter. Most social questions are complex; any decision may seem to be 51 percent "right" and 49 percent "wrong." Firm personal convictions or, as we have suggested, compelling motivations may easily reverse these percentages. Frequently board members experience self-role conflict. Their own need-dispositions, even when not made explicit, affect the intensity of this conflict.

ROLE CONFLICT

Board members may also experience role conflict. McCarty referred to this when he spoke of the board member who represented a special interest or reference group as contrasted to one who represented the entire community. In other words, the board member, particularly if elected, is placed in the role of representing a "constituency" to the organization. Yet the school board literature makes much of the point that the board member should represent the entire community and not some segment of it.

It is most difficult to represent all of the people. For example, the coreligionists of a particular community may band together and elect a board member. Such a member may experience genuine role conflict as he tries to speak for the religious group and as he also comes to recognize an obligation to all groups in the community. Again, this problem becomes severe only as one goes from the general to the specific. If the public school is being requested to join in a "shared-time" program such as admitting parochial school pupils to the public schools for certain laboratory classes, the role conflict of, say, a Catholic board member is joined. His colleagues on the board may insist that the program violates the "wall of separation" between church and state. They may also point out the budget demands of the program and the problems inherent in administering it. His Catholic constituents at the same time may be emphasizing the point that science is a secular and not a religious subject, that the additional expense to which the public school is put is a minor one and is entirely legitimate, and that adequate administrative arrangements can be evolved. To which group does the board member respond? His Catholic constituents expect him to be their spokesman. At the same time he cannot remain oblivious to the predominant view in the community and to his colleagues on the board who express that view. His dilemma is clear; in his role as a board member he must decide whether to serve as a representative of the Catholics or of the entire community.

But role conflict does not arise only from religious differences in the community. As already noted, most board members come from the professional and managerial groups in our society. They can be expected to place great value on the college entrance aspects of the school program. But a majority of high school students in most cities will not go to college; actually, a substantial percentage of them drops out before finishing high school. These two groups constitute a large proportion of the people who are unemployed. More vocational, technical, and adult education is obviously required if the noncollege group is to acquire salable skills. Can the college-oriented board member represent equally the noncollege and college-going segments of his community? For some this may present a genuine role conflict.

Nor is role conflict limited to board members for public schools. Many governors in appointing trustees to college boards try assiduously to select people who represent various groups, often dominant minorities, in the state. Thus, care is taken to include representatives of certain economic, religious, and political interests. One sometimes gets the impression that group representation is more important to the governor and his advisers than the welfare of the institutions of higher education. In any case, board members so selected will experience role conflict as they confront special group interests and total group interests.

We have noted that board members have varied motives for wishing to serve and that these motives may create conflicts. Those who want to understand and work with board members will do well to recognize these circumstances. As McCarty suggested, the resolution of such conflicts would seem to require a community orientation rather than a self-orientation on the part of the board members.

Selecting the chief executive

It is commonly recognized that selection of the chief executive of the organization is the most important single task performed by school and college boards. In effect, the board is selecting a partner who will help determine policy for the organization and then see that it is implemented. But in the scope of his duties the chief executive is no ordinary partner. To fill this strategic role the board seeks a person who has professional knowledge and insight about educational institutions, their functions, and their operation. For superintendents of schools, particularly, most states have special training and certification requirements designed to help provide school boards with the kinds of people needed for administrative positions. Even among such people there is great diversity, and thus the problem of selection is a very real one for school boards. College boards ordinarily have greater freedom in the selection of a president.

We shall not detail the process of selection here. It should be noted, however, that usually the more successful board establishes some criteria to govern its search (defines broadly the role expectations as it sees them), seeks candidates, appraises them by means of written credentials and in interview situations, and then selects the individual whose dispositions seem most congruent with the expectations. College boards frequently invite faculty representatives to help set up criteria, make nominations, and participate in preliminary screening of candidates. School boards seldom use faculty representatives in this way, but they may invite university personnel to help in the selection process. With or without assistance, however, the decision of who shall be the chief executive rests with the controlling board. At the point of decision a number of incipient conflicts may still remain.

ROLE CONFUSION

In establishing criteria for the selection of the chief executive and in considering candidates for the position, the board often finds that there is confusion about the role of the superintendent and its own role. The cliché is that the board makes policy and the superintendent executes it, but in practice it seldom works this way. Allison[14] found that board members generally look to the superintendent for help in policy formation. The executive influences policy by furnishing information to the board and actually recommending policy. The board cannot remain out of the administration of policy, for, by law, it is an administrative body and is required to legitimize administrative decisions such as the employment of staff, the approval of expenditures, and the adoption of books to be used in instruction. Specific examples of the overlap and differences in the roles of superintendent and board member were discussed in Chapter 7.

If there is no easy distinction between policy and administration, then, the setting for confusion between the role of the board and the role of the executive is clearly established. At the same time, if, as was shown, board members are being encouraged by

---

[14] Howard C. Allison, "Professional and Lay Influences on School Board Decision-Making," Doctoral dissertation, University of Chicago, 1965.

their community constituents actually to "run" the school, or if board members take their legal prerogatives literally, they may, perhaps not consciously, seek in their prospective executive a man who will respond easily to board direction, a Mr. Milquetoast. On the other hand, candidates for the executive position, particularly those who have professional training and consequently a strong professional reference group, and who understand the necessity for delegation of authority by the board to the chief executive, will see themselves as playing a major role in board decision-making—in a sense, using the board as a "rubber stamp."

These propensities of board members and prospective executives affect every selection process. As long as this role confusion is not recognized or remains implicit, it cannot be dealt with. Once the situation becomes explicit, a rational approach to the problem can often be evolved. The board-executive relationship has to be nurtured by good will and faith on both sides. Partnership begins with dispelling or at least recognizing the fact of role confusion at the time the executive is selected.

ROLE USURPATION

The conflict between board members and the potential executive at the time of his selection may amount to more than role confusion. Some board members will feel no confusion at all but a deep-seated personal desire to exercise the prerogatives that are ordinarily delegated to the chief executive. We once had the task of examining board-superintedent relationships in a city school district. In response to the question of what seemed to be at the bottom of the problem, the secretary of the board, who had been in his post 25 years, replied, "We have seven men on the board who want to be superintendents." Further examination of the situation suggested that this was a rather sage observation.

Board members, like staff members, as noted in Chapter 11, have different need-dispositions. The board member who has a great need for dominance will probably find it difficult to delegate substantial decision-making authority to the chief executive. He may endorse such delegation intellectually, but his personal needs will make it extremely hard for him actually to feel that it is proper. This distinction is subtle and may not always become apparent at the time the chief executive is being selected. One wonders what would be the effect on board-superintendent relations if the data presented in Chapter 7 were actually made the subject of discussion between board and superintendent.

Perhaps the prospective executive would do well not only to discuss board-executive relationships with his potential employers but also to ascertain from people who have worked closely with them how board members have actually behaved. A dominant board member may readily accept a general statement of policy, such as that the superintendent shall recommend all employees to the board of education. Yet, in the actual implementation of this policy, the board member may resist approving appointments to major positions if the people he thought should have them were not nominated by the superintendent. Accurate reports on the behavior of board members is probably a more reliable index of future actions than intellectual acceptance of generalized modes of behavior.

But prospective executives too may have self-role conflict leading to role usurpation. An executive with a great need for dominance will not only accept the authority delegated to him but actually seek even more authority. To put it otherwise, in his role as chief executive he must inevitably exercise, on many occasions, a firm hand. If, in addition to accepting these role expectations, his need-dispositions require him to exercise even greater control over people, his behavior may become intolerable to the board and to the staff of the organization.

There is, of course, the other type of executive—the man whose need for deference is so great that he cannot assume the decision-making role which most administrative posts demand. His behavior vis-à-vis the board is characterized by a refusal to make many "determinations," as Bowman[15] called them, and recommendations. With his staff his behavior is often characterized by warmth and concern, a belief in "democratic" administration, and a refusal to give direction to the enterprise. Like board members, prospective executives may not recognize fully their own need-dispositions. Thus, if board members wish to ascertain something about the administrative style of the prospective executive they would do well, in addition to discussing it with him, to examine how he has behaved in other situations.

A study by Carlson[16] on executive succession has some relevance at this point. He found that place-bound superintendents —those selected from within the organization—had high commitment to a specific community, had less influence with the school

---

[15] Bowman, *op. cit.*
[16] Richard O. Carlson, *Executive Succession and Organizational Change*, Chicago, Midwest Administration Center, University of Chicago, 1962.

board, had less influence with staff members, and tended to have long tenure in office. Career-bound superintendents—those selected from outside the organization—tended to secure a mandate from the board at the time of employment. They commanded higher salaries, they saw themselves as expendable, and both board and staff expected them to make changes in the organization. These findings suggest that many place-bound superintendents find it difficult to exercise the authority incumbent in an administrative post, particularly if the organization is at a point of rapid growth or is in need of substantial change. Such difficulty would seem to reside, at least in part, in the need-dispositions of the place-bound superintendent.

To achieve the desirable fit between board and executive, it seems necessary at the time of selection that the self-role conflicts of board members and prospective executives be assessed. This can be done to some extent in conference where board-executive relationships are considered frankly. Even more pertinent, however, would be consideration by both parties of the behavior of the other in previous situations.

PERCEPTUAL DIFFERENCES

The model, it will be recalled, deals with the phenomenon called selective interpersonal perception. This means that each person in an organization brings his own experience and information to the organization. Indeed, he cannot do otherwise, his own experience being the only one that he knows. But each person's experience is somewhat unique, and since the members of an organization must interpret each event in the organization in terms of their own experience, it is no wonder that identical events mean different things to different people. These differential meanings, important at the time the chief executive is being selected, may relate to value orientations, to role definitions, or to other social-psychological phenomena.

The model says much about role perceptions of different people in the social system. When the board is selecting an executive, this concept provides another basis for examining compatibility between the prospective partners. If, for instance, board members think of the superintendent as a "strong" executive with little need to consult his staff before making decisions, and the candidate believes in broad participation of the staff in decision-making, these differences should be elaborated at the time of selection and not remain unexposed until after employment.

We would like to say explicitly that the way people perceive the world is fully as important in determining relationships in an organization as the way the world actually is. At the time of executive selection, then, perceptions of both parties should be fully explored to the end that a modicum of compatibility is reached or the impossibility of achieving it is ascertained. Fortunately, there need not be complete compatibility between board and executive if the differences are understood.

We have noted that a number of possible conflicts are inherent in the situation when a controlling board seeks a chief executive. There is possible confusion between the role of the board and the role of the executive. There is also the likelihood that board members and prospective executives experience self-role conflict. Finally, board members and potential executives will all perceive the world as their own backgrounds permit. Resolution of these conflicts, if possible at all, requires much exploration at the point of employment.

Relationships of board and executive

Even with careful attention on the part of the board and the chief executive at the time of employment, working relationships between them after employment must still be established and maintained. The model provides certain implications for these relationships, now to be explored.

AGREEING ON PURPOSES

The chief executive and the controlling board must constantly work toward agreement on the purposes of the organization, just as administrators and staff must too, as we discussed in the preceding chapter. In a sense these purposes reside in the normative dimension of the organization. Purpose or goal should give direction to policy, norms, and expectations. Thus, a city school district may decide that every effort will be made to revitalize its slum schools. This objective, when shared and understood, will make a difference in terms of budget allocations, teacher assignments, employment of specialized personnel, and in many other ways entailing additional expenditures. In fact, real conflict between a board and the executive will almost certainly result on these latter items unless there is agreement on purpose.

At the college level the controlling board and executive may agree to maintain a first-rate school of business. Again, this agreement will say much for budget allocation, personnel assignment, and addition of physical facilities. We recently consulted with a board for higher education serving an institution where courses in business had been augmented and personnel in the business field had been added to the staff without clear agreement on purpose. A crisis had developed in the relationship between the board and the executive. As is usually the case, the crisis was reflected in staff uncertainty and lack of confidence throughout the university.

It is at the point of policy formulation that the controlling board has a genuine contribution to make to the organization. Ordinarily made up of laymen, the board does not have the specialized knowledge to suggest how purpose may be implemented, nor, since it delegates most of the administrative role to its chief executive, can it properly assume the role of implementation. But as the articulating body between the organization and society, it does have the obligation to help establish purpose for the organization. The board, even more than the executive, can speak for the larger society served by the organization.

The executive, to be sure, also influences purpose. It is in this interplay between board and executive that agreement on purpose evolves. Once agreement is established, the board has the further function of interpreting such agreement to the larger society. Although the executive may assist with this task, the board can usually interpret purposes to the community even more effectively than the executive. The latter can, of course, interpret purposes to the organization more effectively than the board. Thus, agreement on purpose between board and executive lays the foundation for agreement between the internal system and its supporting external system.

RECOGNIZING PERSONAL DISPOSITIONS

The personal dimension of the model also has implications for board-executive relationships. When board members and executives can recognize that each person in the partnership has his own need-dispositions, the basis for better understanding will have been established. Acceptance of the point that organization spokesmen, such as board members and executives, sometimes give idiosyncratic expression to problems gives the board as a total body an opportunity to understand their personal dispositions and to assess and, if necessary, reduce their impact upon action taken by the board.

This very circumstance confirms the wisdom of using controlling boards to run institutions and of the commonly accepted principle in board operation that the board as a whole, not individual members, has the authority to act for the organization. The need to mediate a position taken by a single member of the board does not need to be a cause for loss of face by the individual or for rancor in the group. Actually, it is inevitable that each man, in addition to filling his official role, will on occasion behave idiosyncratically.

A school board president in a small city school district, a dentist by profession, fraternized freely with his fellow citizens along Main Street and frequently discussed school affairs with them. Often the discussions led the president to give some assurance that the school board would take a particular kind of action, and at the next board meeting he would push for that action. At times the proposal was premature and facts had to be gathered before it could be considered. At other times the proposal was counter to board policy. In either case the remaining board members had to restrain the president's enthusiasms and unpremeditated commitments. The superintendent was grateful that the board as a whole imposed such restraints, and even the president, we suspect, found the board useful for extricating him from his own gregarious dispositions.

Consideration of idiosyncratic dispositions extends to the chief executve as well. If the superintendent, for instance, is a man of great warmth for members of his faculty, he will establish close personal relationships with faculty members, will become acquainted with their families, and will be solicitous for the welfare of each individual. Under these circumstances certain task requirements imposed upon the chief executive will be difficult to fulfill: dismissal of a teacher, selection of one teacher over another for promotion, advancement of one teacher over another on the salary schedule, and willingness to look outside the system for a school principal, for example. That is, decisions that need to be made on the basis of universalistic criteria will tend to be made on the basis of particularistic criteria. This is not to say, of course, that *some* decisions are not better made on the basis of particularistic criteria. If board and executive recognize the superintendent's nurturant dispositions, at least some mediation can be effected, and the superintendent, like the board president mentioned earlier, will find the board a welcome refuge.

CLARIFYING ROLES

Despite the partnership of board and executive, every organization must clarify the role of each. We have already noted that ascribing to the board the making of policy and to the executive the implementation of policy is not an adequate distinction. Cunningham[17] found that one board of education in a period of eight months made 187 decisions, which he classified as follows: administrative, 110; procedural, 61; and policy, 16. Administrative decisions made by boards include such actions as approval of the employment of staff members, approval of expenditures incurred by the school district, and approval of textbooks to be used in the schools. Thus, the board acts as an administrative body, as by law it is required to do.

Moreover, the superintendent can seldom remain out of the policy decisions made by the board. In many cases he supplies information and sometimes he actually recommends what the policy should be. Bowman,[18] as noted, found that the executive participates in school board decision-making by determining (deciding for the board), by supplying information, and by recommending. Indeed, Allison[19] found, as likewise noted, that most board members expect such participation by the superintendent. Bowman also discovered that in larger school districts board members and superintendents were inclined to agree about the role of the superintendent in school board decision making. Even more significant, for our purpose here, board members and superintendents in larger districts tended to agree with professors of educational administration concerning the role of the superintendent in school board decision making. This seems to suggest that a professional view concerning the roles of both boards and executives based on some conceptual rather than *ad hoc* considerations is beginning to emerge. Nevertheless, obviously the conceptualizations themselves must always be open to inquiry and modification in particular cases.

---

[17] Luvern L. Cunningham, "Decision Making Behavior of School Boards," *American School Board Journal*, 145 (February, 1962), pp. 13-16.
[18] Bowman, *op. cit.*
[19] Allison, *op. cit.*

The emergence of a professional view does *not* preclude flexibility in the roles of board and executive to accommodate differences found in the role incumbents and differences in the organization in which they function. A great elaboration of these roles does not seem appropriate here. It has already been mentioned that the board serves as an articulating link between the organization and the larger society. This means that the board has a crucial function in determining the mission or purpose of the organization. Moreover, it has a control function in seeking legitimation for the organization in the larger society. The actual management of the organization toward its purpose is clearly the duty of the chief executive. But, as we have said before, the attempt to divide the functions of the board and superintendent into minute and inflexible tasks is bound to be fruitless.

Rather, our main point is that the board and executive of each organization clarify their respective roles. This endeavor will reveal some activities appropriate only to board members, some activities appropriate only to the executive, and a number of activities in between in which board members and executive deliberate as partners. Even in a partnership, however, different members may perform different roles. Thus, a board member who is also an investment banker may give useful insights regarding the bond market. On the other hand, he does not take over the sale of the bonds, for that function has been delegated to the superintendent and may actually be performed by the business manager who is on the superintendent's staff.

Clarification of board-executive roles requires frequent communication between the partners conducted in a spirit of goodwill and mutual respect. Ordinarily, some of the understandings arrived at will be written down. We know of a school board and a superintendent who have recently spent more than a year revising the handbook on policies and procedures for the school district. More important than a new document is the understanding that has developed in the discussions incident to the revision of the statement.

REDUCING PERCEPTUAL DIFFERENCES

We have spoken about the nature of perceptual differences. The work relationship between board and executive would be facilitated if such differences were reduced. An interesting statement of a board member was found in the minutes of a large city school district. Five years earlier he had been elected to the board as a representative of labor. At that time he was convinced that the board was favoring business over labor, that instructional materials used in the schools tended to magnify the importance of business and to ignore the importance of labor, and that the board was unduly influenced by business groups in the community. But over the years he had discovered that these convictions were unfounded. Actually, he was glad to report that the board did its best to be fair to all segments of the community and to provide the students with materials on all sides of controversial questions.

Clearly, this board member had experienced some change in perception. How did it happen? We are not sure, but we suspect that in the five years of board membership a new perceptual mass had been built into him and it was shared to a great degree by other board members. In other words, they looked at problems within a similar framework, they considered common information about those problems, and differences were brought into the open. To return to the research cited in Chapter 10, there developed a greater overlap in the privately held selective perceptions among the individuals in the role-set in relation to the existential objects, values, and goals.

Bringing matters into the open appears to be the most important way to reduce perceptual conflict. To implement such an objective, board members and the executive must have some opportunity to talk freely with each other. Unfortunately, the legal requirement in many states that *all* board meetings be public and thus open to representatives of the mass media may actually mitigate against the free communication so necessary in assessing perceptual differences. The practice followed by many boards of having study sessions between official board meetings is one way to facilitate free exchange among board members and executive without making every remark a matter of public record. This is not to say, of course, that the discussion of policy and the determination of action not be held in public meetings.

We have held that a board and its chief executive constitute a crucial partnership in the operation of an organization. The work relationships between them can be improved if continuous attempts are made to find agreement on the purpose or mission of the organization, if each partner can recognize and deal sympathetically with the idiosyncratic dispositions of the other, if care is taken to differentiate between the roles of board and executive in spite of the apparent partnership of the two, and if free interaction and communication are assured so that perceptual differences can be reduced.

Negotiating with teachers' organizations

Many school boards have found, rather suddenly, that they must negotiate more or less formally[20] with organizations of teachers—affiliates of the National Education Association (NEA), locals of the American Federation of Teachers (AFT), or independent groups. The emergence of organizational strength on the part of teachers has school board members, school administrators, and many citizens puzzled about how to cope with the new demands. We would like to deal briefly with certain social conditions related to the widespread demands for recognition of teachers' organizations and to suggest how the model may clarify some organizational characteristics pertinent in negotiating with teachers.

SOCIAL CONDITIONS

At least two social conditions appear to be related to the increased requirement that school districts bargain with teachers. One is the growth of an urban, industrialized society in which the relationships between employer and employee are quite different from what they were in a rural, agricultural society. This change has resulted in big business, as typified by the corporation, from which, in turn, has stemmed big labor, as typified by the development of national and international unions. The new relationship between employer and employee was epitomized by passage of the Wagner Act in the 1930s.

More recently, the collective bargaining components established in the Wagner Act and in subsequent legislation for private employment have been transferred in part to public employment. This shift was given additional impetus by President Kennedy's Executive Order 10988 under date of January 17, 1962. Teachers, as the largest group of public employees in the nation, have been influenced by some of the concepts and practices involved in col-

---

[20] Kenton E. Stephens, "Collective Relationships Between Teachers' Organizations and Boards of Education," Doctoral dissertation, University of Chicago, 1964.

lective bargaining, particularly as they are applied to the public sector. Eve[21] found in 1964 that 34 teacher-board disputes in seven different states had gone to state labor relations boards for mediation. Seven additional cases were handled by legally constituted panels in Minnesota. The majority of these arbitrations have been requested by locals of the AFT, which maintain a labor affiliation, but locals of the NEA have also requested arbitration by state labor agencies. In many ways professional associations have found it necessary to emulate the unions.

A second basic condition affecting collective action on the part of teachers is the increasing expertise or professionalism of teachers, measured rather crudely by the extension of the time required for the training of teachers. Within a few decades teacher education curricula, particularly for elementary teachers, have been extended from one or two years to four and five years in length.

Another indication of growing professionalism is the increased specialization in the teaching field. Not many decades ago the main differentiation was grade and high school teaching. Many finer distinctions are now made in terms of subject specialization and in terms of the functions school personnel are to perform. Thus, in addition to content, specialization in the areas of guidance, school psychology, testing, and remedial reading is rather common, and the move to place people with social work orientations in schools, particularly in slum areas, is growing.

Professionals and nonprofessionals, as Blau and Scott[22] have noted, see superordinate-subordinate relationships in an organization quite differently. Professionals know more about their respective specialties than do their administrators, and the administrators need to make use of the knowledge possessed by the professionals in arriving at organizational decisions. Redressing the balance between hierarchical and professional control in school organizations will be one of the pressing problems in the years ahead.

ORGANIZATIONAL CHARACTERISTICS

The model we are applying provides several concepts that help to clarify the emerging demands of teacher groups. Many school

---

[21] Arthur W. Eve, "The Use of State Labor Relations Agencies in Education," Doctoral dissertation, University of Chicago, 1964.
[22] Peter M. Blau and W. Richard Scott, *Formal Organizations*, San Francisco, Chandler, 1962, pp. 60–74.

organizations are characterized by one or more of the following: (1) emphasis upon the normative to the exclusion of the personal dimension in the organization; (2) emphasis upon the vested to the exclusion of the entrusted aspect of authority; (3) acceptance of normative or personal leadership styles, with little recognition of the transactional style of leadership; (4) emphasis upon diffuse rather than specific interpersonal relationships in terms of scope; and (5) failure to recognize and to cope with the selective perception of staff members.

Each of these concepts gives us a way of approaching the demands of teacher groups. Although organizational shortcomings may be no more relevant than personal animosities between representatives of the two sides in understanding some bargaining controversies, in most school crises certain organizational practices have contributed to the impasse. In a strike by New York teachers the normative, impersonal nature of the school system and the meager opportunity of teachers as individuals or through their organizations to share in decision-making became apparent. In a Utah boycott the governor appeared to be limited by his complete acceptance of vested authority and by his refusal to recognize the professional aspirations of teachers or, for that matter, the more expert knowledge of his own study committee.

But we are not interested only in understanding crises between school systems and teachers' organizations. We are concerned with concepts that may help us understand enough about school organizations so as to have rational bases for taking steps to prevent crises, to elicit staff cooperation, and to insure better teaching, and increased pupil learning.

The model can help us see why the teacher is pushing for more recognition and participation. It suggests, moreover, certain organizational adaptations necessary to better teaching and learning. Some organizations are too exclusively concerned with *effectiveness* and have given scant attention to *efficiency*, or they misunderstand the nature of efficiency. For an organization to stress effectiveness, goals, norms, and productivity without regard to the dispositions, strengths, and desires of its members is quite short-sighted. But effectiveness and efficiency are not unrelated. Most people in an organization wish to fulfill the expectations of their roles and thus contribute to the organization's purposes. They also want, however, to contribute in terms of their own needs, dispositions, and particular competences.

A second concern in negotiation between school officials and teachers' organizations is the nature of administrative authority. Without question some authority is vested. School districts and boards of education are legally constituted. Superintendents and principals have been given authority by the legally constituted boards. But an organization with many professionals or semi-professionals must have entrusted, as well as vested, authority. Unless the staff accepts the administrator and even the method by which he is selected, his decisions will make little difference to many operational procedures. In several schools and school systems more attention needs to be paid, formally and informally, to assessing the acceptability of principals and superintendents to the teaching staff.

Closely related to the requirement for both effectiveness and efficiency, and for both vested and entrusted authority, is the need for transactional leadership on the part of the administrator. As noted in Chapter 5, this type of leadership impels the administrator to clarify and reinforce the role expectations of the system on the one hand and to understand and empathize with the individual role incumbents on the other. He acts neither as martinet nor as "good guy" but varies his approach as the occasion demands.

In dealing with teachers individually, as well as in organized groups, board members and administrative personnel might recognize more frequently than they now do that the scope of the relationship between teacher and school system should be specific, not diffuse. Thus, a principal might appropriately expect a teacher to accept some direction with respect to his teaching assignment in the school, but for a principal to attempt to circumscribe the teacher's political activities would ordinarily be inappropriate.

Morale, as noted in Chapter 5, is defined as the product of identification, belongingness, and rationality. These concepts suggest that conditions be such that the teacher can accept the goals of the system as his own and can communicate easily with his fellow teachers. Channels for teacher interaction and participation in policy matters need to be established and teachers must be given a voice not only in implementing policy but in setting policy. Rationality, the other component of morale, suggests that the appropriateness of expectations for carrying out a decision, as well as the reasons for the decision, be made explicit. Thus, if a segment of the program is to be expanded—vocational education, let us say—the reasoning behind the expansion and the steps by which the expansion will be achieved should be made known. Even decisions and procedures apparently adverse to teachers are more palatable if they have evolved from a logical process in which the teachers themselves participated.

Discussions of these organizational characteristics will not provide a board of education or a superintendent of schools with a recipe for dealing with the demands of teacher organizations. However, it is to be hoped that those who must negotiate will be led to seek basic causes of teacher dissatisfaction. Many of those causes may reside in organizational practices which can be ameliorated.

ROLE OF THE ADMINISTRATOR

An obvious question has to do with the role of the chief executive in board-faculty relationships. Is the administrator the board spokesman? Or is he the faculty spokesman? As the available research shows (see Chapter 7), the teachers may hold to one point of view, the school board to another. The AFT takes the position that the superintendent is inevitably the board spokesman and thus is not eligible for membership in the teachers' organization. The NEA, perhaps somewhat wistfully, says that the superintendent and the teachers are on the same side of the table and that both are interested in the advancement of the educational program. There is an element of truth in both views. We think, however, that the model proposed in this book provides a better answer than either of the positions enumerated here.

In short, we suggest that the administrator has a transactional role to perform in the organization. At one point he emphasizes the normative expectations of the organization. At another point he pays attention to the personal needs of people in the organization. It is this capacity to mediate between organization givens and individual dispositions that characterizes the skillful administrator, in our view. To be more specific, the gifted administrator would help board and faculty be their best selves, help each understand the other, facilitate communication between the two groups, refuse to identify completely with either group, and persist in exercising his transactional role.

In a sense, this kind of administration is dangerous. But it is the only kind which permits the administrator an integrity of his own. He is thoroughly aware of the normative and personal dimensions in the organization. He knows that the board will be chiefly concerned with organizational expectations. He knows just as well that the staff will be very sensitive to individual dispositions. He is convinced that the organization can function effectively and individuals can perform efficiently only if the incipient conflict between these two orientations is kept within tolerable limits. To achieve and maintain those limits is his own unique role in the organization.

Summary

This chapter has dealt largely with board-executive relationships. School board members were shown to be community representatives. Even so, as soon as the board member takes his seat he finds himself a member of a body that is interstitial between the organization and the community. The school board is fertile ground for conflict between organizational expectations and community values. Members of boards of education will probably experience both role and self-role conflicts. These conflicts emerge at the time the board selects its executive and in the working relationships between board and executive. Nor is the executive immune to similar conflicts. Brief treatment was also given to negotiations with teachers and the role of the executive as mediator between board and staff and representative of neither.

13

Community relationships

The social system approach to administration was shown to have relevance to staff relationships and board relationships. The framework can also be suggestive in the area of community relationships, although the concepts here are less fully developed and the research is more fragmentary. Every educational institution—public or private, school or college—may be thought of as a social system existing in and related to a larger social system. The relationships growing out of this conceptualization, particularly as they have relevance to the administration of the school or college, are the concern of this chapter.

The organization and the community

As already noted, Parsons ascribes three levels or subsystems to a formal organization: the "technical," "managerial," and "institutional." The institutional, in our terms, refers to the fact that the organization as a system is embedded in a regnant social environment to which it must somehow be integrally related, and which has some "say" in what the organization may or may not do. In education the technical functions belong chiefly to the teachers and the managerial functions largely to administrators. To some extent the controlling boards of organizations perform the institutional functions, but in another sense society itself is the superior agency into which organizations must articulate. To continue in Parsons' words:

> A formal organization in the present sense is a mechanism by which goals somehow important to the society, or to various subsystems of it, are implemented and to some degree defined. But not only does such an organization have to operate in a social environment which imposes the conditions governing the processes of disposal and procurement, it is also part of a wider social system which is the source of the "meaning," legitimation, or higher-level support which makes the implementation of the organization's goals possible. Essentially, this means that just as a technical organization (at a sufficiently high level of the division of labor) is controlled and

"serviced" by a managerial organization, so, in turn, is the managerial organization controlled by the "institutional" structure and agencies of the community.[1]

SOURCES OF COMMUNITY CONTROL

As the model suggests, the organization is part of the culture and thus cannot be independent. Its goals or purposes, the resources it can command, and the treatment it exercises over its customers (in education, its students) are subject to higher-level controls. These controls are of three kinds: the generalized norms and cultural values of the larger society, the formal structure which is intermediary between the managerial and societal levels, and the political arrangements whereby the organization is brought into direct relationship with the larger society.

Schools and colleges are bound by these types of legitimation. Society insists quite directly that schools observe its general norms or cultural values. Court decisions, for example, have long upheld the right of the teacher to serve *in loco parentis* in dealing with school pupils. But if the teacher is unreasonable or neglectful in dealing with pupils, the courts may find him personally liable. What is unreasonable and what is neglectful clearly depend on the cultural values and norms which are given expression through the courts.

The board of control, whether organized for a school or a college, is an interstitial arrangement between the organization and the culture and reflects the higher-level control of the latter. Its relationship to the community and to the executive officer of the school or college was examined in the preceding chapter.

The third control exercised by the larger society over public schools is found in the need most school districts have for seeking financial support from their respective communities. In many states, school districts must submit operating tax levies to the electorate, and in almost all states a referendum is required for bond issues. Public colleges must make similar representations to their state legislatures. Private schools and colleges also are often dependent upon their constituent bodies for financial support.

---

[1] Talcott Parsons, "Some Ingredients of a General Theory of Formal Organization," in Andrew W. Halpin, ed., *Administrative Theory in Education*, Chicago, Midwest Administration Center, University of Chicago, 1958, p. 44.

THE COMMUNITY AS A PLURALISTIC CULTURE

The model suggests that differences may exist between the values of the larger society and the expectations of the organization. Before turning to the implications of these differences, we would do well to note that our society is a pluralistic one. There are regional differences, rural-urban differences, and differences among social classes. Moreover, as noted in Chapter 6, the expectations people hold for the task of the school were found to vary according to occupation and level of schooling. Region and religion also affect the way people perceive the task of the school though not quite as sharply. The school has not one but many reference groups, then, each expecting it to undertake certain tasks. These tasks, and consequently the school expectations, appear to be a function, at least in part, of the values held by the respective reference groups.

Perhaps the most important implication to be drawn from the values-expectations relationship suggested by the model is the clear recognition that differential expectations for the school are not random, obdurate expressions of behavior but genuine expressions of people's values. Any school administrator who learns to think of his community in terms of its various reference groups or subpublics and who understands something about their interrelations and value positions will have a more realistic notion of what is possible in his community and where work must begin if school programs are to receive community support.

This is not to say that values and expectations are identical or that they can be perfectly related. A school program may be compatible with more than one value position. Moreover, values can change. In fact, with more schooling and higher occupational status, many lower-class people become middle-class people and tend to accept middle-class values. The administrator, then, needs to recognize that value orientations constitute one of the dynamics present in an open society. Whether he wishes to maintain or to alter the goals and operation of his school, he must begin by taking into account the relation between the structure of expectations of the school and the structure of values in the community.

EXTENSION OF THE SCHOOL COMMUNITY

When we think of community in terms of a social system, we realize that it is not restricted to a geographic area. The attendance area of a single school is a school community. A school district, often with many attendance areas, is a school community. For many purposes, however, it is clear that an entire state is the school community; and for some purposes, at least, the nation itself becomes the educational community. All of this suggests the overlapping or the ever extending nature of the school community.

Let us illustrate the point by what is often referred to as local school control. There is little question that school districts and their boards of education in the United States exercise more local control over education than is the case in most other nations. At the same time, considerable folklore surrounds the question of local control.[2] School districts always have operated within the limits of the powers delegated to them by their respective state legislatures, and federal influences of some kind always have been present.

This interdependence of school communities was actually built into the governmental structure of our country. Our plan of federalism is sometimes thought to be a device for dividing decisions and functions of government. But as Grodzins[3] has noted, few, if any, functions of government are not shared by local, state, and national governments. The responsibility for public education is not an exception. Even private education has some relationship to all three levels of government, as is illustrated by the enforcement of health and safety standards at the local level, the requirement that private school programs be equivalent to those of public schools often imposed at the state level, and the availability of governmental loans to purchase equipment for science, mathematics, and foreign language instruction at the federal level.

In higher education the terms "public" and "private" and "local" and "national" become even more confusing. Many private institutions are now largely financed by public money. Little[4] reported that public and private institutions participated almost equally in federal programs in higher education. The 100 chief

---

[2] Roald F. Campbell, "The Folklore of Local School Control," *The School Review*, 67 (Spring, 1959), 1–16.
[3] Morton Grodzins, "The Federal Systems," in The Report of the President's Commission on National Goals, *Goals for Americans*, Englewood Cliffs, N.J.: Prentice-Hall, 1960, pp. 265–282.
[4] J. Kenneth Little, *A Survey of Federal Programs in Higher Education*, OE-50044, Bulletin 1963, No. 5, Washington, D.C., U.S. Government Printing Office, 1962.

participants, as measured by total federal income in 1960, included 54 public and 46 private institutions. A number of comprehensive universities, private and public, now receive a major part of their operating funds from the federal government in the form of research and training grants.

Another force emphasizing the overlapping of local, state, and national interests is the interlocking structure of special interest groups in our society. Whether one looks at business, labor, agriculture, or education itself, the same characteristics are present. The U.S. Chamber of Commerce, for instance, has some 4,000 state and local affiliates and direct access to over 30,000 business organizations that make up its membership. With its affiliates it maintains a network for developing policy positions, for promoting their acceptance internally by state and local affiliates and business concerns, and for exerting influence externally on the Congress and other governmental agencies.[5]

To take another example, the NEA is an organization composed of 6 commissions and 33 departments and has a membership of over 900,000. Affiliated with the NEA are about 60 state and over 8,000 local associations. The parent organization and its affiliates have a total membership of about 1,600,000—a decided majority of the teachers in the public schools of the nation.[6] Through its departments, commissions, and delegate assembly the NEA can formulate policy, and through its state and local affiliates that policy can be readily promoted internally. Local, state, and national units of the NEA can then extend pressure on Congress, much as can the U.S. Chamber of Commerce and its affiliates.

Without multiplying examples, it seems clear that special interest groups of all kinds have interlocking networks which connect local, state, and national expressions of the organization and provide it with cohesion and unity. Under these circumstances, there are few, if any, questions that are of concern only to the local community. Racial integration, educational testing, improved programs for the academically talented, and the like, are not left to local school districts or even to states but inevitably provoke national debate and national action.

---

[5] Richard Jamgochian, "The United States Chamber of Commerce and National Educational Policy," Doctoral dissertation, University of Chicago, 1964.

[6] *NEA Handbook*, Washington, D.C., National Education Association, 1965.

The interdependence of local, state, and national interests in education could be further elaborated. The influence of such cultural characteristics as the increasing mobility of population, the growth of urban complexes, and the impact of the mass media could be explored. Our purpose, however, has probably been served. Every school and college has relationships with a particular community, but that community is not only local; it is part of the extended community, and both are part of the larger society.

Community issues and cultural values

The cultural values of the larger society given expression at both local and national levels are inextricably involved in the major issues with which schools, and to a certain extent colleges, are now confronted. Some of those issues and their value connotations will now be examined.

QUALITY EDUCATION

The dominant middle-class culture of America is convinced that quality education is necessary for work, for college, and even for national survival. This conviction has been influenced by such factors as a growing technology, our experience in World War II, and international competition in developing atomic devices. Few school boards and few school administrators have not felt the impatience of lay citizens, government, and private organizations with educational programs as they now exist. The demand that such programs be improved is strong. Some think of improvement in quantitative terms—more requirements, new courses, more homework, a longer school day, and an extended school year. Others think of improvement in qualitative terms—chiefly, more rigor in what is being done or the development of new programs in mathematics, science, social studies, and other fields.

The demand for improved curricula is exemplified in the national curriculum programs,[7] with financial support from

---

[7] This movement is summarized by John I. Goodlad, "The Curriculum," in *The Changing American School*, Part II, Sixty-fifth Yearbook of the National Society for the Study of Education, Chicago, University of Chicago Press, 1966, chap. 2.

the National Science Foundation, the U.S. Office of Education, and private foundations. University scholars in physics, biology, chemistry, mathematics, and more recently English and the social sciences have led in developing new courses of study for schools and guides for the teachers who are to use them. Funds from similar sources have been used to provide institutes for the inservice education of teachers to help them deal more effectively with the new materials. These new programs have been widely incorporated into the secondary schools of the nation, particularly those in suburban school districts.[8]

Implicitly in some cases, explicitly in others, the school "establishment" has been repudiated by the stepped-up demands for quality education. The repudiation may have been symbolized by the White House Conference on Education convened by President Johnson in July, 1965. Although a wide range of problems was on the agenda of that Conference, many notable figures in public schools were not invited to the meeting. Instead, there was generous representation from government, from business, from the foundations, from higher education, and from the communications media. It was clear that education was no longer considered chiefly the business of school men or of professors of education.

When government, business, and other elements in our society call into question the efforts of teachers, school administrators, boards of education, and others who may be included in the establishment, some examination of the phenomenon is required. It may be true that over the past several decades the attempt to provide all pupils the opportunity to complete high school has emphasized quantity more than quality. Moreover, with the decay of the central city—increase of lower-class population, decrease of middle-class population, increase in crime and welfare loads, increase in ghetto housing, and relative loss in tax base—the problems of providing quality education to city children and youth have become almost insurmountable. Couple with these new demands on education the relative inflexibility of bureaucratic structures in education, welfare, urban renewal, and city government, and the present crisis in education can be understood, at least in part. This general condition should in no wise obscure the fact that in some cities or parts of cities and

---

[8] Roald F. Campbell and Robert A. Bunnell, "Differential Impact of National Programs on Secondary Schools," *School Review,* 71 (Winter, 1963), 464–477.

in many suburban districts the schools have made significant attempts to cope with the demands.

At the same time, education has become more relevant to the national well-being than ever before. Hence, it is little wonder that those who sense a relationship between education and such matters as occupational competence, reduction of crime, and economic growth should ask more and more of the schools. Indeed, it is relatively easy to use the school as a scapegoat for what is a failure of the larger society. For instance, although city schools have long been starved financially, only recently have we found a way of channeling large amounts of federal aid to them.

The increased importance of education to the national well-being, a willingness on the part of the larger society to provide more money for educational programs, and some feeling, perhaps more pronounced at the national level, that schools and colleges are loath to accept change and undertake new responsibilities are leading to a rapid expansion of private enterprise in the educational world. *Time* and General Electric have formed an educational firm and induced former U.S. Commissioner of Education, Francis Keppel, to head it. Educational Services Incorporated, a corporation set up under the leadership of Jerrold Zacharias, is a prototype that may have influenced many of the provisions of the Elementary and Secondary Education Act of 1965. Already, tests and other educational materials are being produced by large firms such as International Business Machines and its subsidiary, Science Research Associates, and Xerox with its many component companies. As part of this climate there is also a demand to make even greater use of technology in education, and business firms which make and promote machines and other devices are alert to every possible expansion. The major development in education during this decade may well be the entry of private business into what has been up to now largely a public enterprise.

Although we do not think improvement of schools is as simple as do some of the private or public spokesmen for education, we are inclined to agree that the recent expressions grow out of the values of the culture in which the school is embedded. Articulate spokesmen of that culture in the foundations, in the universities, on the floor of Congress, in our hundreds of school boards, and in other places have insisted that learning be more rigorous, that school subjects be upgraded, that students work harder, and that education become an instrument for social improvement at home and for national survival abroad. In some ways these demands for schools and school pupils seem inconsistent with the values adults hold for themselves. For instance, the youth in school are expected to have traditional values (that is, to work hard so that they will have future gratification) whereas youth and adults out of school are expressing emergent values (that is, experiencing immediate gratification). Be that as it may, the insistence of the larger society on quality education is unmistakable.

CULTURAL DEPRIVATION

The demand for improved school performance led to the shocking discovery that many children from lower-class homes are not ready for school at ages 5 or 6 and for the most part they never do achieve well in school. These youngsters are referred to as the culturally deprived, the educationally disadvantaged, or the difficult 30 percent. Generally, they come from homes in the Negro ghetto, but they also come from the homes of Puerto Ricans, Spanish Americans, American Indians, and Appalachian Mountain whites. Although most of these children and their families are found in city slums, some of them live in rural areas.

The inability of the school to serve lower-class pupils might have been blamed on the pupils rather than the school had it not been for the civil rights revolution. Leaders[9] of that movement have insisted that teachers in many slum schools do not believe it possible to teach lower-class children, and as a consequence much of what they do is merely custodial in nature. Even though we do not believe, as some[10] apparently do, that the school can make *all* the difference regardless of home and neighborhood influences, we do think that it can and must do more than it has done for the disadvantaged child.

Getzels has noted that the culturally disadvantaged child experiences a discontinuity between his early experiences in family and neighborhood and the expectations the school holds for him.[11] This discontinuity applies to both his "language code" and his "value code." His language code is restricted and heavily

---

[9] See, for example, Kenneth B. Clark, *Dark Ghetto*, New York, Harper & Row, 1965.
[10] *Ibid.*, pp. 132–133.
[11] This point is explicated in J. W. Getzels, "Pre-School Education," in *White House Conference on Education*, Washington, D.C., U.S. Government Printing Office, 1965, pp. 116–125.

dependent upon extraverbal channels of communication. Upon entering school he encounters a complex language code and strong reliance on verbal communication. With respect to the value code, the school requires an achievement ethic, but the lower-class child has learned from his early environment a survival or subsistence ethic. In terms of middle-class language and values the child is obviously deprived. This is a clear example of the conflict between the expectations of the school on the one hand and the condition and values of one of our subcultures on the other.

The critical nature of the early years in the child's development has been noted by Bloom.[12] Using age 20 as a base, he concludes that a child at age 5 or 6 has attained 50 percent of his development in certain critical areas, including intelligence and selected personal characteristics. Even his school achievement may reach the 50 percent point by age 9. Conclusions such as these make it clear that the most significant attack on cultural deprivation will require early intervention. This is the rationale for the Head Start Program and other governmental and private efforts to improve preschool and early childhood education.

But school experience and research studies, important as they are, have not been the chief impetus behind the drive to improve the lot of the culturally deprived. The question is one of morals, of values. How can a society which accepts the value of equal opportunity for all permit some of its citizens to remain in a condition in which they cannot make use of the schooling available to them? The argument continues: lack of schooling leads to lack of skill, lack of skill leads to unemployment, and unemployment means welfare assistance and cheap or slum housing. Without substantial intervention the cycle of poverty, deprivation, frustration, and crime continues. We suspect that school intervention alone will not break this cycle. However, the school is a place to begin, and the larger society is insisting that intervention begin there.

SCHOOL INTEGRATION

Closely akin to the issue of cultural deprivation is the movement for school integration. Although the U.S. Supreme Court in the Brown case,[13] and in subsequent decisions, has ruled chiefly

---

[12] Benjamin S. Bloom, *Stability and Change in Human Characteristics*, New York, Wiley, 1964.
[13] *Brown v. Board of Education*, 347 U.S. 483 (1954).

against segregated schools and deliberate steps taken to keep them segregated, the net result is a social demand to eliminate, as far as possible, not only *de jure* but also *de facto* segregation. Segregated schools are thought to be *by* court dicta, *by* civil rights groups, and perhaps *by* most Americans inherently inferior. Historically, the evidence is clear; most all-Negro schools have been inferior.

The cultural demand for integration is much clearer than are the steps to be taken to achieve it. Many solutions, such as those involving the transportation of pupils and the pairing of schools, require the consent and good will of parents in receiving areas as well as sending areas, and thus far consent has been hard to secure. Other plans, such as change in attendance area boundaries and location of new buildings, are met with the rapid mobility of population—the integrated school of today may be an all-Negro school tomorrow. The idea of an educational park where many pupils from diverse neighborhoods are brought together and combined into appropriate groups for educational purposes holds considerable promise. However, this arrangement necessitates the construction of new buildings and the extensive transportation of pupils, both of which create new demands on already inadequate budgets. Even if budgetary limitations could be surmounted, the sheer number of pupils to be assembled in an educational park makes one wonder whether a good educational environment is possible. We suspect that no single device for integrating the schools will be appropriate for all places or all times.

Perhaps the most difficult obstacle to school integration is the heavy concentration of Negroes in an entire city or in major segments of the city. How can Washington, D.C., now 85 percent Negro, and Harlem and South Chicago be integrated in the near future? It would appear that in some places, for the time being at least, quality education for all will have to supersede integrated education as the immediate goal. It also becomes increasingly clear that school integration is dependent upon housing patterns and job opportunity as truly as upon any action that can be taken by school authorities. Again, however, schools are the vehicle through which the values of the larger society are being dramatized.[14]

---

[14] *Daedalus*, (Fall, 1965, and Winter, 1966) has provided an extensive analysis of the Negro American.

RELIGION AND THE SCHOOL

Titles I, II, and III of the Elementary and Secondary Education Act of 1965 require a new accommodation between religion and public schools. Title I funds are being expended for improved school programs in culturally deprived areas in both public and nonpublic schools. Title II funds are being expended for additional library materials and, although title to these materials is to remain with the public agency, they are to be made available to pupils in public and nonpublic schools. Title III may prove to be an even more ingenious compromise in church-state relations. Funds from this act are being used to establish, under the jurisdiction of public agencies, supplementary educational centers in which pupils from both public and nonpublic schools may be served. Although the centers are administered by public institutions, other community organizations, one of which may be nonpublic schools, must participate in their establishment and operation.

An early question about the relationship between religion and the schools involved the right of churches and other private groups to organize and conduct schools. In the Oregon case, in 1925, the right of such groups to operate schools was upheld by the U.S. Supreme Court.[15] A second question, having to do with public support for private schools, has not been disposed of in such unequivocal fashion. To be sure, many state constitutions stipulate that public funds shall not be expended for the support of parochial or nonpublic schools. Also, in the Cochran[16] and Everson[17] cases the U.S. Supreme Court enunciated the "child benefit" theory and declared that public money spent for books and for transportation of pupils in nonpublic schools, as practiced in Louisiana and Pennsylvania respectively, did not violate the federal Constitution. These expenditures were judged to be benefiting the child and were not seen as an aid to religion.

Although the issue of public support of nonpublic schools is not yet settled, the problems surrounding the teaching of religion in public schools have probably aroused even more controversy. In 1962 the U.S. Supreme Court struck down a state-sponsored

---

[15] *Pierce v. Society of Sisters*, 268 U.S. 510 (1925).
[16] *Cochran et al. v. Louisiana State Board of Education et al.*, 281 U.S. 370 (1930).
[17] *Everson v. Board of Education*, 330 U.S. 1 (1947).

optional program of nondenominational prayer in the public schools of New York.[18] This decision brought the accusation of "Godless" schools from many church groups. In 1963 the same court held that reading sections of the Bible without comment in the public schools of Pennsylvania and Maryland violated the establishment clause of the First Amendment.[19] In this decision the doctrine of neutrality was set forth more explicitly than heretofore. The neutrality concept forbids government from either inhibiting or promoting religious beliefs and practices.

If the public school can neither promote nor practice religious beliefs, even on a nonsectarian basis, many people feel there is but one alternative left—the establishment of nonpublic schools. Obviously, this whole matter hinges on the values of various groups in the larger society. Some people believe that moral instruction is rooted in religion, and with religious instruction eliminated there can be no moral instruction. Others believe that moral instruction is independent of religious instruction; they are thus quite comfortable with the neutrality doctrine.

Despite court action on this question, there is still much uncertainty in the minds of school boards and school administrators as they attempt to operate schools within the neutrality concept. Can a prayer be offered on a formal occasion? Is a baccalaureate service permissible? Can public and nonpublic schools agree on a shared-time arrangement? Or, if religion cannot be taught, can one teach *about* religion? Although these are not new questions, present conditions give them a new urgency. The recurring questions and recent legislative compromises referred to here place the public school and its curriculum in the maelstrom of value conflict within the culture in which the school is embedded.

FINANCIAL SUPPORT

Still another issue with which schools are confronted has to do with financial support. If school programs are to be improved, if cultural deprivation is to be reduced, if school integration is to be fostered, if some aid is to be given religious schools, additional money will be required. In a sense, the call for more money is a test of the commitment the larger society has to the values represented by these proposals.

Resources in any society are less than the demands of the members of the society. Thus, more money for education may

---
[18] *Engle* v. *Vitale*, 370 U.S. 421 (1962).
[19] *Abington Township* v. *Schempp*, 374 U.S. 203 (1963).

mean less for private expenditures. Or more for education may mean less for other public services such as roads, welfare, health, and police and fire protection. In any case, when the citizen is asked to vote on a school operating levy or a bond issue, he is faced with a choice, a value choice. And as James and his colleagues[20] have shown, the decision is often based not merely on whether the community can afford the money but on whether the school is seen as fulfilling community values. When members of state legislatures and the Congress are asked to vote on educational appropriations, they too are faced with a choice—to some extent, at least, a value choice.

But values in school financing are reflected not just in the amount of money required to support education. They are also reflected in the question of whether or not money should be provided or accepted from federal sources. A sudden start or a sudden cutoff of a federal program is seen by those who value local initiative as an irresponsible act on the part of a dominating central government. Also, there may have been some demagoguery in the long history of federal aid.[21] For years the issues of racial segregation, nonpublic schools, and federal control were used as effective deterrents to federal aid. To some, these issues posed genuine threats; others, we suspect, used them to hold down spending. But opportunists could not have been successful had not the specter of federal control and related problems seemed very real to many people.

Few traditions in our culture are stronger than that of localism. Even though the centralists won in the establishment of our Constitution,[22] the argument between state and central control has not been quelled to this day. To be sure, localism tends to emerge as a sacred rather than a secular value; it is the subject of oratory. But when the chips are down most people want federal aid for roads, for welfare, for urban renewal, and even for education. At the same time, most people do not want federal domination. It is not uncommon for the Congress to try to reduce the

---

[20] H. Thomas James, J. Alan Thomas, and Harold J. Dyck, "Wealth, Expenditure, and Decision-Making for Education," Cooperative Research Project No. 1241, Washington, D.C., U.S. Office of Education, June 30, 1963.

[21] See Frank J. Munger and Richard F. Fenno, Jr., *National Politics and Federal Aid to Education*, Syracuse, N.Y., Syracuse University Press, 1962.

[22] See Roald F. Campbell and Gerald R. Sroufe, "Towards a Rationale for Federal-State-Local Relations in Education," *Phi Delta Kappan*, 47 (September, 1965), 2–7.

power of the federal bureaucracy and enhance the opportunity for local discretion.

Cultural values and institutional expectations

We have set forth here a number of issues which appear to be related to cultural values and which seem to represent pressing problems to schools and colleges. We shall now deal more explicitly with the relationship between cultural values and expectations held by educational institutions.

Each of the issues—quality programs, cultural deprivation, school integration, religious expression, and financial support—affects the expectations held for the schools by school people. Many believe, for instance, that the demand for quality education is directed too exclusively to the intellectual aspects of human development and ignores almost completely the attitudinal aspects. With respect to the culturally deprived, the school is dominated by middle-class assumptions about language and values, whereas, as already noted, lower-class children are not prepared to cope with such an environment. The demand for school integration seems a threat to the neighborhood school, long established by policy in school systems. The neutrality doctrine, now the announced position of the state regarding religion, requires schools to give up prayer, chapel, and other religious observance even though such practices have been observed for centuries. Even increased financial support, presumably the objective of every school man, presents a new dimension; more and more people are insisting upon differential expenditures, as contrasted to general increase of expenditures, and their evaluation in terms of outcomes or pupil achievement.

We shall examine one of these issues more fully. There is great pressure on the part of the culture to eliminate *de facto* segregation in Northern cities. The U.S. Supreme Court has ruled on the question, the Congress has passed substantive legislation, scholars have analyzed the problem, White House conferences on education and civil rights have dealt with it, and many liberal and civil rights groups have exerted substantial pressure for action. But there has been little actual change in *de facto* segregation. Why this lack of movement?

No simple answer can be given. In some cases there are not enough whites to bring about racial balance. In other cases countervailing forces for segregation are as strong as those against it. In this complex situation a significant impasse between social demands and institutional purpose may be observed. Civil rights groups and others have rallied to the concept that the school must serve as an instrument of social policy, in this instance the reduction of segregation. Many citizens and school people, on the other hand, take the position that schools have an "educational" and not a "social" purpose. The problems of ghetto housing and lack of job opportunity are seen as beyond amelioration by the school. Continued conflict between these two groups tends to make each position more exclusive and its adherents more adamant. Many large city school boards are currently caught squarely between these two positions and are literally immobilized.

The conflict between cultural values and institutional expectations highlights two other phenomena. On the one hand, technology and related factors demand changes in our ways of thinking and in our institutional arrangements. On the other hand, organizational patterns become established and norms grow up around each role in the organization. These norms may even be related to the training programs for the role incumbents and in turn become a part of the "professional" orientation of the neophyte practitioner. Thus, for decades most training programs for school superintendents have emphasized autonomy of school districts, avoidance of political ties with city government, equal opportunity for all children (not compensatory opportunity), the instructional leadership of the administrator, hierarchical relationships with principals and teachers, and the "professional" role of the superintendent in his contacts with the board of education. We shall not discuss the merits of each of these tenets, but be it noted that a superintendent thoroughly imbued with such doctrine probably lacks the flexibility even to assess the new requirements which the culture is placing on its schools.

Superintendents are not the only role incumbents who assume the expectations traditionally associated with their roles. Teachers, counselors, principals, and school board members do the same thing. In each case, the role incumbent develops some inflexibility; he contributes to the stability of the organization. Under such circumstances new conditions or a new recognition of conditions demands institutional changes, and those who represent the institution find themselves unable to accept the need for change or are unprepared to modify their role in the organization.

The problem is made more difficult by the fact that the culture is not monolithic. Values espoused by the various subcultures are not uniformly held. Even in the same school community, particularly a large city, cultural values differ between some whites and Negroes, between religious believers and nonbelievers, between professionals and blue-collar workers, between old-timers and newcomers, between young and old, and in other ways.

To the demands of which of these subcultures should the school respond? As already noted, to respond to some Negroes on integration will incur the displeasure of some whites. To listen to some church members on religious observances in the school will call forth disfavor if not court action from some non-church members. To stress college preparatory courses, as advocated by the professionals, often means slighting courses designed to provide social and vocational skills, both valued by blue-collar workers.

The dilemma of the school confronted by many subgroups, each with a somewhat different value orientation, is compounded by the nature of the community itself. There is no such thing as a local community. People in any geographic area are intimately related to the extended community at state, regional, and national levels. The civil rights groups may have local chapters, but these chapters are tied into national networks. Local churchmen may remonstrate with a local school system about changes in religious practices in the schools, but a much stronger force is found in the national organizations of church leaders, both clerical and lay. Local professionals may insist on more academic rigor in the high schools of a particular city, but their position is strengthened when it is reflected in national curriculum movements which have the support and resources of university scholars and federal agencies. Even spokesmen for local and state governments in education have found it necessary to join in a national movement in "The Compact for Education."[23] In a very real sense each school is confronted with the values not only of its own constituents but of subgroups within the nation. Thus the social system model dealt with in this book is not limited in its application to the local school community but is germane to the larger community as well.

[23] Donald H. Layton, "The Compact for Education," *Administrator's Notebook*, *14*, no. 8, (April, 1966).

Implications for the administrator

Implications of the preceding discussion may be illustrated at two levels. The first has to do with expectations different communities have for the school as an institution, the second with the role perceptions held for the school administrator in different communities.

With respect to institutional expectations, we know an upper-middle-class suburb in which most of the parents are professional and managerial people, a majority of the adults are college graduates, and family incomes are clearly above the average. The high school is expected to give great emphasis to the academic aspects of the program. Almost all high school graduates enter college, and the parents of many of the graduates are most anxious to get them into prestigious institutions. In this situation any school program not perceived by parents as enhancing college entrance is looked upon with suspicion. Thus, programs in industrial arts and home economics incur the displeasure of school patrons and are branded as "life adjustment" offerings.

On the other hand, we know a rural community in which most school patrons are farmers and small-town merchants, there are few college graduates, and incomes are modest. Here the high school is seen in a different light. Academic offerings are less extensive. Almost no foreign languages are available, and courses in science and mathematics are limited. Programs in vocational agriculture and home economics are generously financed and enjoy community support. During the winter months the high school basketball games are a major attraction to youngsters and adults alike. Despite the obvious academic limitations of this school, anyone who suggests that it be closed and pupils transported by bus to the adjoining town so they can enjoy a more comprehensive program arouses the ire of the entire community. Such a plan strikes at the very identity of the community.

Just as cultural values affect expectations held for institutions, they also affect the community's role expectations for teachers and administrators in the school. Again, two actual communities help us make the point. The first is a bedroom suburb near a large city. It is populated with upper-middle-class and upper-class people, prominent professionals and high-level executives whose yearly incomes are many times the national average. A place on the board of education is considered an honor, and by means of a community caucus able people are induced to stand for election to the board.

The superintendent of schools has a Ph.D. degree from a prestige university. At one time he was headmaster of a private school, and he was prominent in one of the early studies made of the advanced placement of high school students. His major intellectual interests include the classics. The superintendent is provided with a number of assistants so that he is not tied to the day-by-day operation of the school. Both in appearance and speech he is an impressive man, much in demand as a speaker at the national and even the international level. The board of education and the community expect him to take time to indulge his own intellectual interests and to share his thoughts with other people in and beyond his school district. His activities give high visibility and prestige to the community. To oversimplify the case, the superintendent is expected to be a "symbol of the community."

Our second community is a rapidly growing industrial city. Since World War II it has been one of the chief manufacturing centers for airplanes and other equipment for the government. Since the city was initially a major agricultural and distribution center, many of its older leaders resent the continuing migration of people, both white and Negro, into the area. Actually, the old leadership is now challenged. Newcomers are finding their way into civic organizations and have recently won places on the city council and on the board of education. Election to the board of education in this city is no genteel process. One must secure nomination through a legally prescribed petition and then campaign vigorously not only with the PTA membership but in every tavern in town.

The superintendent of schools has a Master's degree from a Midwestern state university. He held two small-city superintendencies in a neighboring state before taking his present position. He is not a man of great culture, but he does want to operate a good school program for the children and youth of his school district. He has found it necessary to fight all kinds of minority groups in order to achieve that purpose. At one time the chamber of commerce opposed him, at another the John Birch Society, at another the National Association for the Advancement of Colored People. In each case he marshaled his forces, waged war, and won. His victories were never overwhelming, but perhaps they were as decisive as can be expected in a very diverse community. Apparently his board of education expects him to command personally whatever campaign is necessary. Again to oversimplify, this superintendent is expected to be a "challenger to the community."

Obviously, the role expectations held for the superintendent of schools in these two communities are widely divergent. We are convinced that each community has found the man to meet the expectations it holds for the position. If either departed very far from its expectations, we suspect that the search for a new superintendent would be on. In passing, we suggest that the styles of these two superintendents are so different that each would probably fail miserably were they to change places.

Summary

Despite the contrasts drawn here in the value orientations of different communities and how these orientations have import for both the school and the role of the administrator in the school, we assert once again that no school community is untouched by the larger culture of state, region, or nation. Some school communities, particularly those embracing a single suburban settlement, are more homogeneous than others, but as school districts continue to increase in size, as seems highly probable,[24] even this homogeneity will decrease. At any point in time the perspicacious administrator will be able to make some assessment of cultural values at both local and extended levels.

We are not suggesting that administrators merely accept the value orientations of their communities. Just as the administrator is required to exercise transactional leadership in his organization, he may have to exercise a similar kind of leadership in his community if he is to bring cultural values and school expectations into some measure of defensible congruence. Most administrators must also perform their roles in a manner reasonably compatible with their own value orientations. If an administrator fails to achieve a degree of compatibility between his own values and those of his community, we think he should resign from his position.

---

[24] For an interesting prediction on this matter see Charles S. Benson, *The Cheerful Prospect*, Boston, Houghton Mifflin, 1965.

The last three chapters have indicated that looking at administration as a social process can be helpful in the practice of administration. Such a view, of course, does not permit us to prescribe administrative action. We have no recipes for motivating students, raising the morale of teachers, or insuring the success of school bond elections. We have proposed some social-psychological concepts which may be useful to an administrator as he thinks about his problems and the setting in which they must be solved. In this kind of illumination theory contributes to the practice of administration. It is our hope that preparation programs for administrators at both preservice and inservice levels will provide them with an opportunity to examine theoretical concepts, to assess research growing out of those concepts, and to become skilled in applying such knowledge to the decision-making roles they occupy.

14

Some retrospective and prospective considerations

The crucial characteristic of administration is its complexity, and any exposition, whether systematic or discursive, is bound to oversimplify by abstraction. The choice of whether to attend to this or to that, or at least *more* to this than to that, must be made. Everything cannot be looked at equally, and this is as true of phenomenological as of experimental inquiry. What one can do is be aware of the choices he has made explicitly and realize that some choices have probably also been made implicitly. If one has looked at something more from *this* point of view than from that, it is possible for someone else to right the balance by looking at it more from *that* point of view than from this. But neither should consider what *he* has looked at as everything there is to be seen.

This inquiry began with a fundamental choice from among possible approaches to administration: traits, techniques, theories. We chose theories. But the choice could not be preclusive. We dealt also with the traits of administrators and the techniques of administering. There was also the choice of the phenomena which were central to understanding administrative behavior: sociological, historical, biological, cultural, economic, political, psychological, and so on. We took the sociological, psychological, and cutural as central. But again the choice was not preclusive. We were constrained to consider, however briefly, other aspects as well, notably the economic and political. There were choices also of *which* theory in sociology and *which* theory in psychology would prove most useful and, within the theory, which concepts were likely to be most fruitful in helping to observe, order, and understand the phenomena in which we were interested. There are a *dozen* alternative conceptions of role and a *score* alternative conceptions of personality.

In a sense, the problem is one of wishing to examine and understand as fully as possible a particular piece of terrain and wondering where to stand and which guide to use: a road map, a contour map, a vegetation map, a weather map, a geologic map, a population map, or some other kind. Of course an attempt can be made to superimpose all possible maps in all possible combinations. But it is then not unlikely that the result will be only a blur, and in trying to see everything one will see nothing—or at least nothing very accurately.

The proper purpose of systematic inquiry is not only to obtain the "facts" regarding the substantive problems with which one began but to allow for "second thoughts" regarding the conceptual and methodological choices that have been applied. The desired outcome of scientific study is not merely the accretion of data but the formulation of ideas. The optimum result is not only a conclusion (the finding of worthwhile solutions to a problem) but a commencement (the discovery of fruitful problems for solution).

It is in these terms that we should like to consider now the following issues: (1) organizational statics and dynamics, (2) administrative behavior and individuality, (3) strategies of inquiry, and (4) applicability of the model to administrative dilemmas.

Organizational statics and dynamics

From one point of view, the salient feature of a successful organization is its *stability*. We expect it to be there, and to be pretty much the same way today as it was yesterday. From another point of view, the salient feature of a successful organization is its *mutability*. It seems to undergo change in both its internal and its external relations; it "keeps up with the times" and sometimes even "gets ahead of the times." The same organization can be seen as static and dynamic. It is always necessary to deal with these dual aspects of social systems.

But a characteristic of current social theory making this task, already difficult in any case, especially intractable is the tendency for concepts and methods to be founded almost exclusively on *equilibrium* models along the lines of classical mechanics. This is a typical statement: "The most general and fundamental property of a system is the interdependence of parts or variables. . . . [There] is order in the relationship among the components which enter into a system. This order must have a tendency to self-maintenance, which is very generally expressed in the concept of equilibrium."[1] Parsons derives the following laws on the equilibrium of social systems:

---

[1] Talcott Parsons and Edward A. Shils, eds., *Toward a General Theory of Action*, Cambridge, Mass., Harvard University Press, 1951, p. 107.

1. *The Principle of Inertia:* A given process of action will continue unchanged in rate and direction unless impeded or deflected by opposing motivational forces.
2. *The Principle of Action and Reaction:* If, in a system of action, there is a change in the *direction* of a process, it will tend to be balanced by a *complementary change which is equal in motivational force and opposite in direction.*
3. *The Principle of Effort:* Any change in the rate of an action process is directly proportional to the *magnitude* of the motivational force applied or withdrawn.
4. *The Principle of System-Integration:* Any *pattern* element (mode of *organization* of components) within a system of action will tend to be confirmed in its place within the system or to be eliminated from the system (extinguished) as a function of its contribution to the integrative balance of the system.[2]

There is undoubtedly interdependence among the parts or variables in a social system; it is this interdependence that makes it a *system*. But a danger deriving from an unexamined view of this type of equilibrium formulation is the belief that all relations and interdependencies in the system are balanced, symmetrical, and linear. That is, as suggested in the principles of "action and reaction" and of "effort," if there is a change in one direction of a process, it will be balanced by a complementary and equal change in another direction. If, for example, much conflict or tension in an organization makes for ineffective performance, then less conflict will make for less ineffectiveness, and no conflict will make for effective performance. As has been demonstrated, crucial relations in a social system may not be linear but curvilinear.[3] Too much tension—frustration—is debilitating. But too little tension—boredom—may be equally debilitating. Too much dissatisfaction may inhibit effort. But too much satisfaction can have the same effect. In short, there may be a level of conflict, or tension, or dissatisfaction between "much" and "none" which is optimum for organizational effectiveness. The important relations in a social system are perhaps not symmetrical or linear, as is so often assumed, but asymmetrical and curvilinear.

Another danger in the equilibrium formulation is that the predominant concepts comprising social theory tend to become *structural* rather than *procedural* and speak more to the *statics* than to the *dynamics* of a social system. One of the most impor-

---

[2] Talcott Parsons, R. F. Bales, and E. A. Shils, *Working Papers in the Theory of Action*, New York, Free Press, 1953, pp. 102–103.
[3] See Chapter 9 of the present book.

tant developments in social science during the last generation is role theory. Yet it remains essentially a structural mode of analysis. We know more about the structure of a given role or the structural balances in a role-set than about how roles change or how relationships in a role-set are altered. As Black[4] points out, what is called the *statics* of ordinary material bodies (the theory of bodies in equilibrium) has to be supplemented by independent mechanical principles before we are in a position to say anything about the *motions* of material bodies. Statics may be regarded as a particular case of dynamics, but not vice versa. We may with some confidence infer the structure of an organization by studying its dynamics, but we cannot so confidently infer the dynamics of a social system by describing its structure.

For this reason the present inquiry has emphasized the importance of understanding the behavior of the *person* as well as the structure of his *role*, the idiosyncratic perceptual *process* as well as the normative institutional *prescription*, the *curvilinear* relationships among variables as well as the *linear* relationships, the *imbalances* in organizations as well as the *balances*, and the forces impinging on the institution from *without* as well as from *within*.

Administrative behavior and individuality

It is not only institutional role theory that has been influenced by the mechanistic equilibrium model, but individual personality theory as well. A basic assumption underlying the predominant personality theories, from behaviorism to psychoanalysis, is that individual activity can best be accounted for in terms of a combination of the homeostatic model of self-maintenance and the drive-reduction theory of behavior.[5] Stated most simply, according to this conception, the organism's optimum state is one of rest and equilibrium, and the organism acts in such way as always to return to the optimum state of rest

---

[4] Max Black, "Some Questions About Parsons' Theories," in Max Black, ed., *The Social Theories of Talcott Parsons*, Englewood Cliffs, N.J., Prentice-Hall, 1961, pp. 275–276.
[5] Portions of this section are based on J. W. Getzels, "Creative Thinking, Problem-solving, and Instruction," in E. R. Hilgard, ed., *Theories of Learning and Instruction*, Sixty-third Yearbook of the National Society for the Study of Education, Chicago, University of Chicago Press, 1964, especially pp. 254–257.

and equilibrium. Hunger drives the organism to seek food, and it ceases to seek food when it has eaten; fear drives it to seek cover, and it ceases to seek cover when the danger is over; a problem stimulates it to "think," and it ceases to think when the problem is lessened; and so on. Behavior always involves the abatement of a drive, the diminution of a problem, the reduction of a stimulus.

This conception of personality leads to the belief that the individual is essentially *passive* or at most merely *reactive*. He behaves only in response to a felt drive, an encountered problem, a presented stimulus, and then primarily to return to the former state of rest and equilibrium. He will not seek out stimuli or discover problems for solution himself.

So ingrained is this view of personality that much social theory deals only with the faceless abstraction "actor," neglecting the differentiated person as the source of behavior; much administrative theory draws analogies between the machine—nowadays, the information-processing machine—and the worker; and recent management theory calls attention to the "organization man" as typical of the human being in social systems. In each case the conception of personality is impoverished: The actor is only the image of his role; the machine operates only as it is programmed from the outside; the organization man has no cause or character. In none of these conceptions is provision made for the human disposition to seek out problems for mastery, self-actualization, or the expression of singularity.

But as casual observation and our own studies indicate, and as some personality theorists have increasingly been insisting,[6] there are numerous human activities (from reading mystery stories and working puzzles to exploring caves, climbing dangerous mountains, and undertaking to solve difficulties in organizations even when it is really none of the person's business) which seem to give pleasure through encountering problems, raising the level of stimulation, and asserting individuality. As Berlyne[7] points out, higher animals spend a substantial portion of their time and energy on activities to which only terms such as "exploration" and "curiosity" seem applicable. A conspicuous

---

[6] See, for example, D. O. Hebb, *The Organization of Behavior*, New York, Wiley, 1949; R. W. White, "Motivation Reconsidered: The Concept of Competence," *Psychology Review*, 66 (1959), 297-333; J. McV. Hunt, "Experience and the Development of Motivation: Some Reinterpretations," *Child Development*, 31 (1960), 489-504.

[7] D. E. Berlyne, "Curiosity and Exploration," *Science*, 153 (1966), 25-33.

part of human behavior, moreover, is classifiable as "art" or "science"—activities dealing with biologically *neutral* stimuli, that is, with objects and events that do not seem inherently beneficial or noxious. By no stretch of the imagination can these activities be said to contribute to bodily maintenance through the reduction of so-called primary drives. Rather, problems seem to be sought out because the person needs to deal with what is novel, to exercise initiative, or to express his own character. He strives to *find* stimulation as well as to *avoid* stimulation. The optimum state of the human being may not be *passivity* but *activity*; the human being is not only a *stimulus-reducing* but also a *stimulus-seeking* organism.

There is evidence that when a human being is provided with everything he needs—food, water, shelter, bodily comfort, and so on—but is deprived of varied stimulation and the opportunity to be active, he will in two or three days develop feelings of severe distress. Bexton, Heron, and Scott,[8] for example, paid subjects more than they could otherwise earn, just to do nothing. The subjects were well fed and comfortably housed—all they had to do was remain in bed under conditions which minimized stimulation and activity. Within a short time the experience became so unpleasant that, despite the high pay for presumably doing nothing, it was difficult to keep the subjects in the experiment for more than two or three days, and some subjects left even sooner. Their thinking and problem-solving abilities deteriorated so that they could not answer questions they had had no trouble answering before the experiment began, and upon leaving, they reported feelings of confusion, headaches, and fatigue. In short, man has not only the familiar viscerogenic drives or needs, such as hunger or thirst to be satisfied by *satiation*, but also neurogenic or psychogenic dispositions to be gratified by *stimulation*—dispositions, as we said, for novelty, for dealing with the problematic, for expressing individuality.[9]

From this point of view, the human being is not, as present analogies would have it, like a calculating or information-processing machine that may lie idle indefinitely and responds only when action is triggered by some drive or stimulus. He is a living organism perpetually and uniquely in action—in dreams

---

[8] W. H. Bexton, W. Heron, and J. H. Scott, "Effects of Decreased Variation in Sensory Environment," *Canadian Journal of Psychology*, 8 (1954), 70–76.

[9] Cf. White, *op. cit.*, and Hunt, *op. cit.*

and aspirations as well as in manifest behavior. He must be permitted to act continually and distinctively—there must be opportunity for self-actualization—in order to function efficiently and remain in an optimum physical and psychological state.

The conception of personality as *active* rather than *passive* or *reactive* has at least three important implications for the administrator.[10] First, although people do conform to the expectations of significant others, if an administrator believes that individuals are essentially passive, will not take initiative, and act only in response to the "stick or the carrot," he creates the occasion for a self-fulfilling prophecy: They will indeed do no more than live up to his assumptions. The formulation of personality in active rather than in passive terms mitigates against this type of self-fulfilling prophecy. Second, it changes the basic problem for the administrator from how he can instill interest in problems and initiative for action in people to why *this* person is passive, not interested, or lacking in initiative. It invites the administrator to look at the *individual* rather than at people or actors in the mass. It invites him to think of ways of preventing the *loss* of interest and initiative rather than to deal with their apparent lack as if the lack were the natural state of human personality. Third, and perhaps most important, it enriches the administrator's view of the human being by calling attention to the dynamic stimulus-seeking as well as the homeostatic stimulus-reducing aspects of behavior. The latter are easily recognized and have always been stressed; the former seem ephemeral and are often overlooked. Yet it is the stimulus-seeking aspects of personality that may ultimately be of greater significance, for they provide the potentiality and substratum on which innovation and change are based.

Strategies of inquiry

A portion of this volume has been devoted to reporting research on problems drawn from the model or related to it. The studies represent a wide variety of procedures of inquiry in the social sciences. Thus, the task of public education studies sought data

---

[10] Cf. J. W. Getzels, "The Problem of Interests: a Reconsideration," in H. A. Robinson, ed., "Reading: Seventy-five Years of Progress," Proceedings of the Annual Reading Conference Held at the University of Chicago, 1966, *Supplementary Educational Monographs*, Chicago, University of Chicago Press, 1966, vol. XXVIII, pp. 97–106.

through the *opinion polling* of large samples of the population. McCarty used *clinical interviews* with small samples of school board members. Malo used *personality assessment* methods and Campbell *role-definition* methods with selected subjects. Lipham used *phenomenological observation* of "actual behavior." Brown performed a "laboratory-type" *experiment* to test a series of hypotheses.

Although studies of administration (those reported here as elsewhere) seem to cover the spectrum of available specific procedures, they have, by and large, two general research strategies or underlying characteristics in common. One characteristic is that almost without exception the studies are *cross sectional*. They take an aspect or slice of an administrative phenomenon and examine it at a single point in time. If, for example, the question is whether values have changed, individuals of different ages are studied at the same time rather than the same individuals over a period of time. We learn that young teachers hold different values from older teachers. But we learn little about how the values themselves undergo alteration. Similarly, we learn about the differences among various subgroups in expectations for the school, but little about how the expectations develop. We learn about the role relations in given types of school boards, but little about how the relations are transformed with experience. In short, studies in administration have been devoted largely to the structures rather than the dynamics of organizational life.

The second characteristic is that the studies, again almost without exception, represent a *closed-end* strategy of inquiry. The findings remain with the researcher and are not communicated ("fed back") to the school system where the work was done or applied to similar situations. Or if they *are* communicated, the effect (or lack of effect) of the acquired knowledge on behavior is not examined. There is no thought of intervention on the basis of the results. The researcher goes his way with his conclusions —even when the conclusions show that certain changes in the school ought at least be considered—and the school goes its way, having done its duty by providing the locus of study.

We are not of course derogating cross-sectional and closed-end strategies as such or the contributions of the studies done in these terms. For certain purposes they are exactly the right strategies, and they are probably necessary first steps before other methods are attempted. But two other strategies which have hitherto been largely neglected need to be added. These are the *longitudinal* and the *open-end* strategies—that is, studies that deal with administrative phenomena over time and studies that do not stop with conclusions but go on to examine the effect of applying the conclusions.

We have already mentioned both strategies in discussing specific studies in preceding chapters, but we wish by way of summary here to generalize the points. Cross-sectional and status studies do not provide the continuous observations needed for tracing the effects of administrative behavior on the dynamics of organizations. What, for example, is the consequence of introducing a new superintendent? What is the consequence of recruiting new role incumbents of a particular character? What is the consequence of external events on the functioning of the internal system? The immediate effects may be observed in "single-shot" studies. But the long-term effects—and the *process* of the effects—must be observed sequentially, that is, longitudinally.

Although it is not our intent to prescribe specific research problems or to advocate specific research procedures here, it should not be impossible, for example, to take a new school as the locus for research and study it longitudinally in the systematic terms of the model: the relation of the school expectations to the values of the community, the definition of roles, the recruitment and matching of personalities to the roles, the effect of different personalities on the same roles, the establishment of the formal role-sets and the development of the informal personal relationships, the influence of community events and shifts in values on school expectations, and so on. To be sure, this is not as easy as the cross-sectional strategy. But the payoff would, we believe, more than compensate for the difficulties.

The question of longitudinal as against cross-sectional studies seems straightforward. The question of a closed-end strategy (stopping with the conclusions) as against an open-end strategy (applying the research to manifest problems, attempting to affect practice, and observing the effects of intervention) is rather more complex and often controversial. It raises the issue of "pure" *versus* "practical," "basic" *versus* "applied," and "utilitarian" *versus* "theoretical" inquiry. This is a peculiarly troubled issue in education, although why it should be more vexing for education than for medicine, say, is not clear. Consider the following: A half-century ago, an investigator published a paper on the inheritance of eye color in the Drosophila, a small fly frequently seen near ripe or decaying fruit. The fly itself is of no economic or other importance. On the face of it, a less likely subject for immediate or for that matter potential practical application than the way it inherits the color of its eyes could hardly be imagined. This would seem pure research with a vengeance. Yet this investigation, with others of a similar nature, started a line of inquiry in genetics and biology that has provided incalculable benefits in practical medical therapeutics. Indeed, the investigator was awarded the Nobel prize in *medicine*.[11]

When someone says, "What do I care about the relation between values, roles, personalities, selective perception, and other such notions? What I want to know is about my relation to real teachers—why I don't get along with Jones no matter what I do," what he is saying in effect is, "What do I care about the inheritance of eye color or genes and things like that? All I want to know is how to cure disease." He does not realize that one often depends on the other, and he may be foreclosing a line of inquiry that would give him a clue not only to his specific difficulty with Jones but to the more general problem of interpersonal relations in social systems. The application of basic research to specific problems may come immediately or several years hence, or may not come directly at all, but perhaps some other researcher who is working on a related practical problem will be helped. To return to our medical analogy: On the one hand, those concerned with the practical medical problem were sensitive to the possible contribution of the pure findings with Drosophila; on the other, those working with the pure findings with Drosophila were not unaware of the practical medical problems. In this sense, the strategies of inquiry were open-ended.

The pure and the applied, the basic and the practical, the utilitarian and the theoretical are not so easily separable as some would make them and when expressed as opposites lead to questions which are false and futile. The insistence by many in education that research deal only with immediate specific problems that need solution rather than with significant abstract issues that need understanding is shortsighted. The insistence by others that the only "real" research is pure, basic, or theoretical is also shortsighted, for it keeps the work tied to *closed-end* strategies

---

[11] See A. H. Sturtevant, "Thomas Hunt Morgan," in National Academy of Sciences, *Biographical Memoirs*, vol. 33, New York, Columbia University Press, 1959, pp. 283–325. Also, letter by P. B. Armstrong, M.D., *The New York Times*, August 7, 1966, p. E9.

Applicability of the model to administrative dilemmas

We have dealt with the model not only as a tool for generating inquiry but as a framework for examining practice. Thus, we considered such issues as staff relations, board relations, and community relations. Although models cannot indicate what needs to be done—these must come from the administrator's judgment and resources applied to his understanding—they can contribute to understanding. If we may return to the map analogy, a map cannot tell one the goals or the vehicle, but it can clarify the nature of the terrain to be covered and the problems involved so that a more informed decision about goals and vehicles can be made. From this point of view, the model can be applied to immediate and concrete problems facing the administrator—such as those involving the so-called culturally deprived (or disadvantaged, different) child. In what way are children differentially related to school so that one is culturally deprived (or disadvantaged, or different) and another not? What is meant by "compensatory education"? Compensatory for what? And toward what? What are the dilemmas facing the administrator?

We may recapitulate the primary variables of the model for convenient reference:

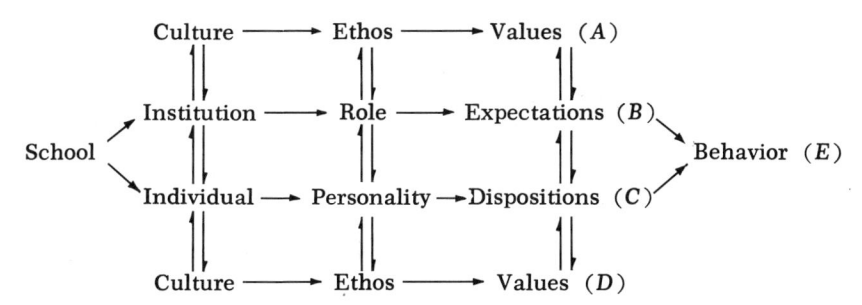

```
                Culture ──→ Ethos ──→ Values  (A)
                   ⇅          ⇅         ⇅
              Institution ──→ Role ──→ Expectations (B)
            ↗      ⇅          ⇅         ⇅              ↘
     School                                              Behavior (E)
            ↘      ⇅          ⇅         ⇅              ↗
              Individual ──→ Personality ──→ Dispositions (C)
                   ⇅          ⇅         ⇅
                Culture ──→ Ethos ──→ Values  (D)
```

If, as we have argued, behavior in school is a function of the cultural values, institutional expectations, and individual dispositions, then in the terms of *this* model, this is the situation for the majority middle-class or nonculturally deprived child in the typical school:[12]

$D \cong A$, that is, the culture in which the child is socialized and the culture which is the context for the school tend to be congruent.

$C \cong D$, that is, the dispositions of the child acquired through socialization and the values of the culture in which he was socialized tend to be congruent.

$B \cong A$, that is, the expectations of the school and the values of the culture which is the context for the school tend to be congruent.

$C \cong B$, that is, the dispositions of the child and the expectations of the school tend to be congruent.

In effect, the cultural values are internalized by the children through the process of socialization and become dispositions for behavior. The expectations of the school are defined in relation to the same values, so that what is required for school performance is congruent with the values of the culture and the dispositions of the children, since the dispositions are also aspects of the values. This situation leads to functional behavior—functional in the sense that what the culture requires, the school expectations include and the dispositions make attractive in the form of personalistically preferred behavior, or at least the expectations of the school are reinforced by the values the child experiences at home.

Now suppose the values and experiences available during socialization are *not* the same as those which serve as the context for the institutional expectations. This is the situation of the lower-class or culturally deprived child with respect to the typical school.

$D \not\cong A$, that is, the culture within which the child is socialized and the culture which is the context for the school tend to be incongruent.

$C \cong D$, that is, the dispositions of the child acquired through socialization and the values of the culture in which he was socialized tend to be congruent (the culture here is the "minority" culture).

$B \cong A$, that is, the expectations of the school and the values of the culture which is the context for the school tend to be congruent (the culture here is the "dominant" culture).

$C \not\cong B$, that is, the dispositions of the child and the expectations of the school tend to be incongruent.

---

[12] Portions of this section are drawn from J. W. Getzels, "A Social Psychology of Education," in Gardner Lindzey and Eliot Aronson, eds., *Handbook of Social Psychology*, Rev. ed., Reading, Mass., Addison-Wesley, in press.

The situation here leads to dysfunctional behavior—dysfunctional for the culture, the institution, and the individual—that is, from the point of view of the cultural values and expectations represented by the school. What then is meant by culturally deprived (or culturally disadvantaged or culturally different)? It means that certain children are deprived of experience with a particular culture—A in our model—not *all* culture. The middle class may also be culturally deprived in relation to the values of *another* culture. Value or culture deprivation is a relational, not a quantitative, term. The lower-class child can have as many values as the middle-class child, or as few. In the current case, it means deprived of the values and experiences needed to get along in a particular segment of the social complex: the *school*.

The term "culture" is sometimes used only in the sense of intellectual or artistic content. A person is "cultured" when he is intellectually and artistically cultivated. He is "not cultured" or "culturally deprived" when he is not intellectually or artistically cultivated. But even so, the term "culturally deprived" does not mean deprived of all intellectual or artistic content. For example, was the early illiterate jazz musician or folk singer less creative than today's sophisticated performers of his music? It means deprived of a *particular* intellectual and artistic content, a content which may again be described as normative or dominant in relation to other contents. It is in this sense once more that we speak of certain of our children as culturally deprived or different, that is, as not having had the same advantages in certain intellectual and artistic experiences at the time they came to school as other children have had.

Whether one view or the other is accepted, the analysis shows these to be the relative positions of the middle-class and the culturally deprived child to the school:

Middle-class or "nonculturally deprived" child	Lower-class or "culturally deprived" child
$D \cong A$	$D \not\cong A$
$C \cong D$	$C \cong D$
$B \cong A$	$B \cong A$
$C \cong B$	$C \not\cong B$

More than this, it suggests to the administrator points at which influence can be exerted to change the dysfunctional aspects of the current situation. One may, for example, undertake to bring the dispositions of the children before entering school, C, into greater congruence with the expectations they will face upon entering school, B. This is essentially what is attempted through "compensatory preschool education" programs like Head Start. It must be noted, however, that this alternative leaves the expectations of the school, B, as they are and, in fact, makes them the criteria for the socialization of the child. Whether such faith in the current expectations of the school is justified is another matter, and one which may well be questioned.

Or one may undertake to alter the subculture making for the deprivation, D, so that it is more congruent with the culture serving as the context for the school, A. This is essentially what is being attempted through open occupancy laws, birth control clinics, nondiscriminatory hiring practices, and school integration. Or one may change the school expectations, B, to take into account the dispositions of the children, C, and the characteristics of the subculture, D. This is essentially what is being done in "special classes," "special schools," and in such projects as the Job Corps. Or one may, perhaps, attempt to effect some change in the dominant culture itself, A, so that there are not such egregious distinctions among subgroups. Exactly which alternative or combination of alternatives will be favored will depend on the specific community, the available resources, the judgment of the administrator, and numerous other factors. But the model brings to a level of awareness the conditions that are present in the system, the resulting stresses and strains on the children, and the possible fulcra for transformation.

Summary

In the preceding chapters of this volume we (1) took as a point of departure Dewey's dictum that "theory is the most practical of all things" and argued for the usefulness of conceptual frameworks in the study of administrative behavior; (2) presented a brief account of the development of theories, concepts, and frames of reference in administration beginning with Taylorism at the turn of the century to the recent contributions from the social sciences; (3) described in some detail one theoretical framework (or conceptual model) that seems to us especially relevant to school administration—with the understanding of course that there are other points of view as well; (4) reported a number of research studies undertaken in the terms of the framework; and (5) examined the implications of the framework for selected aspects of administrative practice. In this final chapter we reconsidered a number of the formulations, especially the concepts of equilibrium in social theory and of homeostasis in personality theory. We suggested the addition of certain strategies of inquiry, now largely neglected in the study of administration. We illustrated the applicability of the model to a current problem facing the school administrator—the education of the so-called culturally deprived child.

We conclude by recalling what we said in the introductory chapter. In presuming to put forward one framework, we have not suggested that it is the only possible framework, or that it is in some ultimate sense the best one. It has, however, proved useful in stimulating and guiding several lines of inquiry into the structure and process of administration and in making clear certain significant issues and decisions faced by administrators in their day-to-day practice. A fruitful conceptualization has in it the seeds of its own elaboration and revision. In fact, we have already made certain alterations and additions since the framework was first set forth. We hope that on the basis of critical examination by students of administration, as well as on the basis of further experience with it in research, teaching, and practice, the present formulation will continue to be elaborated and revised so that higher levels of understanding may be reached. Not only our research and practice but also our conceptualizations and conclusions must be open-ended.

Index

Abbott, Max G., 292
Accentuation as perception mechanism, 314-315
Action, general theory of, 47-49
  See also Social systems
Adaptation, to roles, 119-122
  in social systems, 119-126
Administration, definitions of, 52-53
  study and practice of, 1-9
Administrative Behavior (Simon), 43
Administrative personality, need for research across fields, 245
Affectivity variable, 49, 138-141
Age and educational expectations, 170
Allen, Dwight W., 153-155
Allport, Gordon W., 19, 66-70, 94, 313 n.
Andrews, John H. M., 251-257, 335
Arendt, Hannah, 143
Argyris, Chris, 42, 45, 46, 47, 90, 91, 127, 219
Ascription, 49
Assignment of teachers, 321-325
Assimilation as perception mechanism, 314
Attitude, definition of, 71-72
Authoritarian personality and role conflict, 263-264
Authority, nature of, 133-150
  and theory, 17
  variable, 134-136
Autocratic (or Authoritarian) leadership, 36-39, 145

Bakke, E. Wight, 42, 45, 46, 47, 90, 91, 123, 127, 245
Barnard, Chester I., 40-43, 48, 127, 128, 155, 219
Behavior, administrative, 53-55, 77-78, 105-107
  biological dimension of, 89-90, 90-92

cultural dimension of, 89-90, 92-102, 103-105
individual dimension of, 103-105
and individuality, 400-403
normative dimension of, 56-65, 79-89
organizational, criteria of, 126-133
personal dimension of, 65-77, 79-89
and role expectations, 213
Beliefs, in role expectations, 213
  See also Values
Belongingness, 131-132
Biological dimension of behavior, 89-90, 90-92
Boards, school, 370-374
  and chief executive, relationship of, 359-370
  community-oriented, 188-190
  election of, 352-355
  and faculty relationships, 374-375
  motivations of members, 184-195, 356-359
  nature of, 348-352
  perceptual differences, 363-364, 368-370
  position of, 348-349
  and role clarification, 367-368
  role conflict, 184-195, 349-352
  role confusion, 360-361
  role usurpation, 361-363
  selection of, 352-356
  and self-role conflict, 356-359
  socioeconomic status of, 355-356
Bobbitt, F., 27-29, 39, 321
Bowman, Thomas R., 350, 351, 362, 367
Brown, Alan F., 270-282
Bruner, Jerome S., 286, 311, 336

Campbell, Merton V., 112, 237-243, 247, 307, 309, 310

413

Campbell, Roald F., 15, 16, 355 n., 379, 382, 389 n.
Career-bound superintendent, 152
Carr, L. J., 54, 55, 58
Change, in organizations, 398-400
  in social systems, 150-155
Charismatic authority, 134-136
Charters, W. W., Jr., 15, 16, 213, 214
Child-centered learning, 11-12
Citizen-superintendent relations, 294-297
Coalitions of power, 85
Coladarci, A. P., 8, 16 n., 17, 19, 21
Collective orientation, 49
Community, 376-396
  and administration, 376-381
  control, sources of, 377
  cultural values, 381-393
  expectations, 393
  issues, 381-390
  as pluralistic culture, 378
  role perception, 393-395
  role in society, 378-381
Community-oriented board members, 188-190
Compensatory education, 407-410
Composite educational expectations, 159-161
Conflict, 108-119
  cultural-institutional, 110-112
  perceptual, 116-118
  personality, 115-116, 263-264
  role, 113-115, 202-210
  role-personality, 112-113
    See also Boards; Perception; Personality; Role; Superintendent; Teacher; Values
Connectionism, 10-11
Consideration, 128
Consultant relations, 118, 303-306
  types of, 304
Coordination, 32-33
Creative Experience (Follett), 31
Criteria of organizational behavior, 126-132
  effectiveness and efficiency, 127-129
  satisfaction and morale, 129-132
Cultural deprivation, 384-385, 407-410
Cultural differences, 157-181
Cultural dimension of behavior, 89-90, 92-102, 103-105
Cultural values, 93-107, 110-112, 381-393
  See also Values

Decision making, relation between board and executive, 349-352
Democratic leadership, 36-39, 145
Dewey, John, 9, 14, 15, 22
Dickson, William J., 33, 34, 35, 139
Differential values, 92-102
  See also Values
Diffuseness, 49, 136-138
Dilemmas of choice in action systems, 49
Dilemmas of value, 100-101
Dismissal, 337-344
Dispositions, *see* Need-dispositions
Downey, Lawrence W., 157, 158, 168, 174, 179, 355
Drive, definition of, 71-72

Educational level and educational expectations, 162-163
Educator and noneducator expectations for schools, 172-177
Effectiveness, meaning of, 127-129
  of principals, 228-236
  in teaching, 336-337, 372-373
Efficiency, meaning of, 127-129
Emergent values, 99-101, 287-297
  See also Values
Employment of teachers, 321-325
Entrusted authority, 135-136
Equilibrium, concept of, in human personality, 400-403
  limitations of, 399, 401-403
  in social systems, 398-400
Ethnocentrism and role conflict, 264
Evaluation of staff performance, 332-337
Expectations, educational, 157-181
  See also Role, expectations
Experimental studies, need for, 215-216
Extrinsic sanctions, 142-144

Factualism and theory, 17
Fayol, Henri, 25, 26, 27, 42
Ferneau, E., 118, 303, 304, 306
Financial support of education, 388-390
Follett, Mary Parker, 31-33, 40, 42
Formal organization, 41-42
Frustration, reaction to, and conflict, 264-265

Index

Functions of the Executive, The (Barnard), 40, 43, 48, 127
Future-time orientation as a value, 98

General and Industrial Management (Fayol), 25
Geographic region and educational expectations, 168–170
Getzels, J. W., 8, 10 n., 16 n., 17, 19, 21, 52 n., 53, 66, 71 n., 80, 82, 86, 90, 92, 96, 102, 103, 106, 109, 110 n., 112 n., 116, 126 n., 131, 133 n., 145 n., 146, 198, 199, 200, 201, 202, 225 n., 259, 261, 262, 264, 265, 266, 268, 310 n., 320, 384 n., 400 n., 403 n., 408 n.
Goldman, Samuel, 173, 175, 176, 177
Gragg, William L., 15, 16
Gross, Neal C., 42, 48, 109, 114, 190, 191, 195, 196, 197, 198, 213, 351
Group-centered learning, 12–13
Group conformity as a value, 100
Grouping, types of, 281–282
  and differential supervision, 282
Guba, E. G., 8 n., 53, 80, 82, 110 n., 116, 126 n., 131, 145 n., 146, 198, 199, 200, 201, 202, 236, 259, 261, 262, 264, 265, 266, 268, 320, 328 n.
Gulick, Luther, 26, 27, 42

Hagen, E. E., 150
Halpin, Andrew W., 42, 128, 233, 303
Hencley, S. P., 117, 203–207, 298, 300–302
Hills, R. J., 164, 165, 166
Human relations movement, and study of administration, 30–39

Identification, emotional, and theory, 18–19
  as socialization mechanism, 104–105
  variable, 131, 133
Idiographic dimension, 65–77
  See also Individual dimension of behavior; Leadership-followership styles; Need-dispositions; Personal, dimension of behavior; Personality
Independence (or autonomous self) as a value, 98
Individual dimension of behavior, 103–105
  in the social system, 65–66
  See also Need-dispositions; Personal; Personality
Informal organization, 41–42
Initiating structure, 128
Inner-directed values, 99
Inquiry, strategies of, 403–407
  See also Research
Institutional values, 99
Institutions, 157–249
  definitions of, 56–57
  properties of, 57–59
  sanctions, 59
  See also Normative, dimension of behavior; Role expectations
Instrumental values, 99
Integration, and education, 385–386
  in Follett, 31–33
  mechanisms of, 119–126
  school, 385–387
  in social systems, 48
Intellectual dimension, task of education, 158
Interest, definition of, 71–72
Interpersonal perception, 86–89
  theory of learning, 12–13
Intrinsic sanctions, 142–144

Kluckhohn, E. V., 72, 73, 75, 96

Labor, contrasted with work, 143–144
Laissez-faire leadership, 36–39
Language and theory, 18
Leadership, types of, 36–38
Leadership-followership styles, nature of, 133–150
Learning, child-centered, 11–12
  group-centered, 12–13
  interpersonal theory of, 12–13
  teacher-centered, 10–11
Lewin, K., 36, 42, 81, 155
Linton, Ralph, 54, 61, 218
Lipham, J. M., 145, 229–231, 235, 247, 248 n.
Local control of schools, limitations of, 378–381
  source of, 377–381

Longitudinal studies, need for, 214–215, 315–316
versus cross-sectional studies, 404
See also Research

McCarty, Donald J., 184–195, 211, 212, 356, 358, 359, 404
McEachern, Alexander W., 48, 114, 195 n., 213
McPhee, Roderick F., 292, 294, 296
Malo, Albert H., 221, 222, 223, 225, 227, 228, 229, 247
Management, scientific, and study of administration, 23–30
Management and the Worker (Roethlisberger and Dickson), 33
Mason, Ward S., 48, 114, 195 n., 213
Mayo, Elton, 33, 35, 36, 40, 42
Merton, Robert K., 50, 83, 84, 85, 120, 121, 127
Moral relativism, 100
Morale, meaning of, 129–133, 373–374
Morris, Charles, 94, 102
Moser, Robert P., 208–209
Motives of school board members, 186–188, 356–359
Moyer, Donald C., 209–211
Murray, Henry A., 18, 72, 73, 75, 221, 222, 223

Naegele, Kaspar, 96, 97, 98
Need-dispositions, 79–83, 112–113
and administrator, 346–347
definition of, 70–76
hierarchy of, 75–76
integration with institutional expectations, 119–126
in personality definition, 70–77
of teachers, 330–332
See also Individual dimension of behavior; Personal, dimension of behavior; Personality
Negotiations, professional, 370–375
Nomothetic dimension, 56–65
See also Institutions; Leadership-followership styles; Normative, dimension of behavior; Role
Noneducator expectations for schools, 172–177

Normative, dimension of behavior, 56–65, 79–89
style of leadership, 145–147
See also Institutions; Role expectations
Normative leadership, 145–147

Occupational status and educational expectations, 161–162
Organismic dimension of behavior, 90–92
See also Biological dimension of behavior
Organizations, and administration, 345–346
change, problems of, 150–155
conflict, sources of, 108–119
expectations, 344–345
limits and diversity, 323–325
statics and dynamics, 398–400
Other-directed values, 99

Parsons, Talcott, 47–48, 49, 50, 54, 55, 59, 60, 62, 63, 68, 69, 74, 75, 87, 91, 134 n., 141, 348, 376, 377, 398, 399, 400
Particularism, 49, 139–141
Perception, 286, 297–314
conflict, 116–118, 299–303
differences, in board, 363–364
differences, reduction of, 368–370
errors in, 298–303
issues and mechanisms of, 310–315
of roles, 297–306
selective, in role-personality interaction, 83–84, 86
selective interpersonal, 312–314, 326–327
self-role, 306–310
Perceptual agreement or disagreement effect on interpersonal relations, 303–306
Perceptual error, types of, 298–300
Performance, teacher, evaluation of, 332–337
Personal, dimension of behavior, 65–77, 79–89, 90–92
leadership, 145, 147–148
task of education, 158
See also Individual dimension of behavior; Need-dispositions; Personality
Personality, 79–83, 218, 220, 244–250, 282–285

Personality (*Continued*)
  adjustment and role conflict, 262–263
  assessment method, in study of role-personality relations, 220–236
  authoritarian, and role conflict, 263–264
  compatibility, in teachers, 320
  conflicts, 115–116, 263, 264
  definitions of, 66–72
  dispositions, and role expectations, conflicts in, 112–113
  as individual dimension element, 66–70
  principal, variables of, 230–233
  and role relations, 79–89, 220–244, 263–264
  socialization of, 47, 104, 123–126
  teacher, and administrators, 250–258
  teacher, and role conflict, 258–270
  teacher, and subject taught, 250–258
  teacher, and supervisory stress, 270–282
  See also Individual dimension of behavior; Need-dispositions; Personal dimension of behavior
Personalization of roles, 47, 123–127, 338–340
  need for research, 245–246
Place-bound superintendent, 152
Policy formation and policy execution as source of role confusion and usurpation, 360–362
POSDCoRB, 27
Postinduction socialization, 124–126
Power, coalitions of, 85
  See also Authority
Practice, administrative, 1–9, 16–22
  continuity with theory and research, 9–16
  model and administrative dilemmas, 407–410
Preference, definition of, 71–72
Preinduction socialization, 124–126
Present-time orientation as a value, 99
Prince, Richard, 114, 288, 289, 290, 291, 292, 293

Principal, school, behavioral patterns of, 233–235
  effectiveness of, 228–230
  evaluation of teachers, 243–244, 332–337
  leadership of, 208–209
  personality of, 230–233
  role of expectations for, 209–211
  and self-role conflict, 218
  teacher confidence in, 242–244
  teacher relations with, 237–244, 293–294
  transactional role, 344–347
  values of, 291–292
Principles of Scientific Management (Taylor), 24
Private enterprise and education, 383
Process, administrative, 26–27, 46–47
Productive dimension, task of education, 158
Promotability to administrative roles, 220–228
Public School Administration (Cubberley), 29
Pupil-teacher relations, 292–293
Pupil values, relation to teacher values, 287–289
  and school performance, 289–291
  and types of school, 289
Puritan morality, 98

Racial differences and educational expectations, 171–172
Rational authority, 134–136
Rationality, 44, 131–132
Rationalization as perception mechanism, 314
Reassignment, 337–342
Reference groups and conflict, 113–114, 202–210
Religion, and educational expectations, 171
  and the schools, 387–388
Research, administrative, 1–9, 16–22, 403–407
  continuity with theory and practice, 9–16
  criterion problems, 212
  methodological problems, 212–214, 247–248
  sampling problems, 211–212
  strategies of inquiry, 403–407
  suggestions for further work, 178–

Research (*Continued*)
    180, 211–216, 244–248, 282–284, 315–316
Riesman, David, 99, 100, 101, 110
Roethlisberger, F. J., 33, 34, 35, 139
Role, 79–83, 218–220, 244–249
    adaptation, 119–123
    characteristics of, 61–64
    clarification, in boards, 367–368
    compatibility, in teachers, 318–320
    conflict, 113–115, 319–320
        of board members, 184–195, 356–359
        interreference-group, 202–209
        interrole, 183–202
        intrareference-group, 209–211
        and personality, 258–270
        and superintendency, 195–198
        and teachers, 198–202
    confusion, in school boards, 360–361
    definition of, 59–60
    definition method in study of role-personality relations, 236–244
    diffuseness, 49
    expectations, 61–62, 64, 157–161, 178–181, 182, 211–217
        attribution of, 213
        clarification of, 327–330
        community, 393
        conflicts, 116–119
        delineation, 64–65
        institutional, 110–112
            and cultural values, 390–393
        integration with need-dispositions, 119–126
        organizational, and administration, 344–345
        and personality disposition conflicts, 112–113
        research comparisons of, 214
        research definition problems, 213
    as institution unit, 59–64
    perception, 297–306
        community, 393–396
        errors in, 298–303
        selective, 83–89
    and personality dispositions, 83–89, 112–113
    and personality interaction, 79–89
    and personality relations, in business organizations, 220–228
    in school administration, 228–236
    in teaching, 237–244, 338
    personalization of, 123–126, 338–340
    reassignment, teachers, 340–342
    recognition, by teachers, 334–335
    set, in role-personality interaction, 83–84, 84–86, 120–121
    and value orientations, 292–297
    specificity, 49
    stress, and teacher performance, 270–282
    usurpation, in school boards, 361–363
        See also Institutions; Normative, dimension of behavior

Sacred values, 96–98
Sanctions variable, 59, 141–145
    See also Institution
Sarbin, T. R., 60, 61, 62
Satisfaction, meaning of, 129–133
Scope variable, 136–138
Seager, Roger C., 157, 158, 160, 162, 163, 168
Secular values, 97–102
Segregation, de facto and de jure, 390–391
Selection, of board members, 352–355
    of chief executive, 359–364
Selective perception, 83–84, 86–89, 286, 326–327
    See also Interpersonal perception; Role, perception
Self-actualization, 119–122
Self-orientation, 49
Self-oriented board members, 188–190
Self-role relations, 83–87
    See also Personality, and role relations; Role, and personality relations
Shils, E. A., 47 n., 60, 62, 63, 68, 69, 74, 75, 87, 91, 94, 140, 398, 399
Simon, Herbert A., 42, 43, 44, 45, 59, 219
Simplification as perception mechanism, 314
Slagle, Allen T., 157, 158, 161, 162, 168

Index

Sociability as a value, 99
Social class status and educational expectations, 164–168
Social dimension, task of education, 158
Social science and study of administration, 40–51
Social stimulus value of personality, 67–88
  See also Personality
Social systems, as administration context, 53–55
  analysis of, 56–78
  characteristics of, 54–55
  definition of, 54–55
Socialization, of personality, 47, 104, 123–126
  need for research, 246
Specificity, 49, 136–138
Spindler, G. D., 97 n., 100, 101, 110, 291, 292
Stimulus-seeking aspects of personality, 401–403
  implications for the administrator, 403
Stress, curvilinear relation with performance, 270–273
  and teacher performance, 270–282
Subject matter taught, relation to teacher personality, 250–254
  relation to teacher-administrator interaction, 254–258
Subordinate-superordinate relationships, nature of, 133–150
Superintendent, school, board relationships, 359–370
  career-bound, 152
  characteristics of, 29–30
  citizen relations, 294–297
  consultant relations, 303–306
  expectations for, 202–208, 298–300, 393–395
  and perceptual error, 298–300
  place-bound, 152
  policy-making role, 367–368
  and reference groups, 203–208, 301–303
  role conflict, 114, 195–198
  role in professional negotiations, 370–375
  selection of, 359–364
  transactional role, 344–347
Supervision, of teachers, 325
  reaction to, 270–282
  See also Administration

Supervisory stress, and need for achievement, 277–278
  and neuroticism, 275–276
  and scholastic aptitude, 276–277
  and teaching effectiveness, 275
Sweitzer, Robert E., 302

Task of public education, 157–174
Taylor, Frederick W., 23–26, 29, 39, 40, 42, 321
Teacher, and administration, relationships of, 250–258, 318–347
  assignment, 321–325
  centered learning, 10–11
  confidence in administrator's leadership, 242–243
  dismissal, 342–344
  effectiveness, 241–242, 336–337
  employment, 321–325
  need-dispositions, 330–332
  organizations, negotiations with, 370–375
  performance, 332–337
  personality, 250–285, 320
  principal relations, 293–294
  pupil relations, 292–293
  ratings by principal, 243–244
  reassignment, 337–342
  role compatibility, 318–320
  role conflict, 198–202
  role expectations, 327–330
  role-personality relations, 237–244
  role personalization, 338–340
  role reassignment, 340–342
  role recognition, 334–335
  satisfaction, 239–241
  self-role perceptions, 307–310
  supervision, 325
  working conditions, 325
Teachers organizations, negotiations with, 370–374
Teaching situation, and role conflict, 200–202
  personality and role conflict in, 259–270
Technology, administration as a, 3–5
Thelen, Herbert A., 53, 90, 92, 102, 103, 110 n., 281, 282
Theory, administrative, 1–5
  avoidance of, 16–22
  continuity with research and practice, 9–16
  defense of, 21–22

Theory (*Continued*)
   as focus of administration, 5–9
   functions of, in study and practice, 8–9
   historical development, 8, 23–51
   objections to, 16–22
Traditional authority, 134–136
Traditional values, 92–99, 287–297
   See also Values
Traitist approach to administration, 1–3
Transactional leadership, 146, 148–150, 344–346, 374
Typology of perceptual conflict, 299–303

Universalism, 49, 139–141
Urban problem and education, 382, 407–410
Urwick, L., 27, 42

Values, 286–287
   cultural, 93–107, 381–393
      and community issues, 381–390
      conflicts in, 110–112
      and institutional expectations, 390–393
   emergent, 99–101
   individual, 287–292
   institutional, 99
   instrumental, 99
   other-directed, 99
   principal, 291–292
   pupil, 288–291
   and role-set relations, 292–297
   sacred and secular, 96–102
   teacher, 288–289, 291–292
   traditional, 97–99
Vector relationships in a social system, 153–155
Vested authority, 135–136

Ways to live, values as, 94–96, 102
Western Electric Company, 33
Wheelis, A., 99, 101, 110
Williams, Robin M., Jr., 48, 50, 51
Work contrasted with labor, 143–144
Work-success ethic, 97–98

Yale University, Labor and Management Center, 45